"A marvelous story, marvelously told. Coffin was a major figure for nearly two decades of American history, and a flamboyant, energetic, and inspirational one at that. It's helpful in understanding much of this history to understand Coffin's role in it."—Ronald Story, University of Massachusetts, Amherst

More praise for *William Sloane Coffin Jr.*

"Having traveled, body and soul, with Reverend William Coffin through the years of America's transformation in the period of civil rights and anti-war activism, I find his story to be some of the most profound testimony illuminating the struggles, the triumphs, and the tragedy of contravening forces that left so much of the task to the next generations. Bill's life and advocacy possess an ironically powerful relationship to the world dilemmas in which we find ourselves today. Bill's advocacies and reflections, filled with inspiration and sometimes furiously passionate grace, may well help to inform and guide us in what promises to be as urgent a future struggle as those that are the subject of this book."—Peter Yarrow

"Anyone who heard Coffin preach in his heyday has not forgotten the gravelly charisma of this social-justice prophet. Goldstein brilliantly shows how secular and religious strands of American culture came together in Coffin's biblically based liberalism. *William Sloane Coffin Jr.: A Holy Impatience* is gripping biography."—Richard Wightman Fox, author of *Reinhold Niebuhr: A Biography*

"Goldstein's Coffin is a flawed and courageous man. Paying careful attention to Coffin's theological development as well as to his politics, Goldstein gives us a rich and vivid portrait of a liberal Christian fully engaged with his tumultuous times. Goldstein tracks Coffin's search for a theology of love strong enough to contest the evils of war and nuclear threat. *William Sloane Coffin Jr.* immediately establishes itself as one of the great American religious biographies. The book is beautifully researched, elegantly written, and in the end deeply moving and inspiring."—Robert A. Orsi, Harvard Divinity School

"William Sloane Coffin's contribution to the movement against the war in Vietnam was tremendously important to the movement's sense of legitimacy and its political success, as Warren Goldstein's biography ably demonstrates. An impressive and very needed book."—Maurice Isserman, Hamilton College

"Warren Goldstein presents to us a multifaceted Coffin—priest, peacemaker, prophet, and passionate human being. Thank God his wisdom will be preserved for generations to come. His courageous voice instructs us in the living of our days."—The Rev. Dr. Joan Brown Campbell, Department of Religion, Chautauqua Institute

William Sloane Coffin Jr.

YALE UNIVERSITY PRESS · NEW HAVEN AND LONDON

WARREN GOLDSTEIN

William Sloane Coffin Jr.

A HOLY IMPATIENCE

Set in Adobe Garamond with Monotype Gill Sans by Duke & Company.
Printed in the United States of America by Vail-Ballou Press.

Library of Congress Cataloging-in-Publication Data
Goldstein, Warren.
William Sloane Coffin Jr. : a holy impatience / Warren Goldstein.
p. cm.
Includes bibliographical references and index.
ISBN 0-300-10221-6 (alk. paper)
1. Coffin, William Sloane. 2. Political activists—United States—Biography.
3. Presbyterian Church (U.S.A.)—Clergy—Biography. 4. United Church of
Christ—Clergy—Biography. I. Title. BX9225.C6243G65 2004
285'.1'092—dc22   2003019754

Page iii: Coffin holds a press conference at Riverside Church in January 1980,
after his Christmas visit with American hostages in Iran. © Bettmann/CORBIS

A catalogue record for this book is available from the British
Library.

The paper in this book meets the guidelines for permanence
and durability of the Committee on Production Guidelines for
Book Longevity of the Council on Library Resources.

10 9 8 7 6 5 4 3 2

For my children:

Isaac Eugene Goldstein
Katherine Emma Goldstein
Jacob Frederick Goldstein

May they hold onto their own "holy impatience" with injustice.

CONTENTS

Preface

On Rosh Hashanah in 2000, I attended morning services at a little Reform temple on Marco Island, Florida. Most of the worshippers, as well as the rabbi, had reached their seventies. Because the Jewish New Year fell in the middle of the presidential campaign and a Jew was running for the vice-presidency for the first time on a major party ticket, Rabbi Howard Greenstein took up the subject of religion in politics. In the middle of a thoughtful sermon about what it meant for a Jew in politics to take his religion seriously, Rabbi Greenstein launched into an impassioned declaration of the centrality of religion to all important American social movements, from abolitionism and the labor movement to the civil rights and women's movements. To general nodding in the sanctuary, he recalled the example and words of "rabbis, priests, and ministers like Rabbi Steven Wise or Abba Hillel Silver, Martin Luther King Jr., or William Sloane Coffin Jr." Rabbi Greenstein chose well. Of these men, only Coffin was alive. In fact, he was the only one who had been alive since King's death more than three decades earlier.

Flamboyant civil rights, antiwar, and disarmament preacher, the best-known college chaplain in the country during the 1960s, senior minister of New York City's Riverside Church for a decade, Coffin has been, after Martin Luther King Jr., the most significant liberal religious voice in the United States for the past forty years. After King's assassination in 1968, Coffin became the preeminent exponent of religious liberalism in the country, King's most influential disciple in the white religious world. As American political culture shifted rightward in the 1980s and afterwards, and political and religious liberalism went into decline, Coffin became the outstanding representative of prophetic liberal religious dissent. Now in semi-retirement in Strafford, Vermont, he remains the last of a once flourishing breed in American public life: the liberal Protestant minister preaching to the nation's faith and conscience.

Often misunderstood simply as a political activist, Coffin has in fact been above all a Christian preacher, committed to the prophetic role of naming and condemning sinfulness while calling on Americans to take up the paths of righteousness, justice, and peace. For the past half century, from pulpits throughout the country, with eloquent conviction and witty aphorisms, he has been mixing prophetic denunciation with an invitation to share in the redemptive joy of God's love.

On the two most important public issues of the 1960s—civil rights and the war in Vietnam—Coffin provided key religious leadership, in favor of the first, in opposition to the second. From the heart of the American establishment, Coffin first challenged white complicity in racial segregation and then fought his government's policies in Vietnam, eventually joining those young men who refused cooperation with military conscription. In both cases, in order to dramatize the religious and moral issues at stake, he put himself in harm's way: physically and legally on a dangerous Freedom Ride in 1961, and legally by publicly supporting draft resistance in 1967. From Riverside, the flagship church of American mainline Protestantism, Coffin became the country's most influential religious advocate during the 1970s and 1980s for nuclear disarmament. Persuaded by friends and parishioners to look more deeply into homosexuality, he found himself convinced by the gospel to preach widely—and face arrest —on behalf of rights for homosexuals, in the secular as well as religious worlds.

The subtitle of this biography comes from a prayer Coffin offered on Reformation Sunday, October 26, 1958—his first year as chaplain of Yale University. That morning he prayed for unity instead of "sectarian prejudice," for "minds filled with a vision of cooperative discipleship and . . . hearts alive with the fire of those first disciples." He asked God "to kindle in our hearts a holy impatience with the sinful factions that have rent Thy Church."

Throughout his career Coffin displayed a moral impatience with racial and religious prejudice, with a Christianity more attached to rules and divisions than to unity and love, and with nationalism that exalted making war rather than peace. Sometimes his restlessness led him to impulsive actions and pronouncements; more often, he cultivated the art of the "strategic pause," waiting for events to decide his fate or for the right moment to act. Although Coffin, now nearly eighty years old, has become the elder statesman of American liberal religion, his wife describes him even today as "an old man in a hurry." Continually engaged in what he has called a "lover's quarrel" with his country and his world, Coffin has yet to lose his "holy impatience" with prejudice, injustice, and war.

Acknowledgments

Writing this biography, as my family—and Bill and Randy Coffin—know all too well, has taken longer than I expected. As a result, I have accumulated an intimidating number of debts, and it gives me great pleasure to be able finally to acknowledge them in this space.

On three separate occasions the National Endowment for the Humanities made it possible for me to focus entirely on the research and writing: by means of summer stipends in 1994 and 1999 and a research fellowship in the fall of 2000. In the summer of 1997 I also attended an NEH Summer Seminar for College Teachers, titled "Social Historians Write Biography," at the Newberry Library in Chicago. There I had the good fortune to experience the intellectual leadership of the seminar leaders, Jim Grossman and Elliott Gorn. Among the seminar participants Victoria Bissell Brown of Grinnell College gave me an especially astute reading of my first three chapters.

At the State University of New York's College at Old Westbury, where I began this project, I received two Presidential Faculty Development Grants (in 1993 and 1994) and two grants from the York State/United University Professions Professional Development and Quality of Working Life Committee (in 1994 and 1995). These grants made it possible for me to travel and conduct many of the interviews on which this biography relies. I was able to devote the entire 1995–1996 academic year to this book thanks to a Research and Writing Grant from the John D. and Catherine T. MacArthur Foundation Program on Peace and International Cooperation. Finally, a summer stipend from the Louisville Institute in 1999 helped me give this project the focused writing time it needed.

Librarians at the Burke Library, Union Theological Seminary in the City of New York, were extremely helpful, as were librarians at the Manuscripts and

Archives Division of Yale's Sterling Memorial Library. Jenny Burdis cheerfully transcribed many hours of taped interviews.

To those dozens of people who were willing to sit down with me for several hours and share their memories of Bill Coffin, I am immensely grateful. The Sources list includes only those interviews that I used directly in the book, so I would like to thank the people I interviewed who are not mentioned there: David Dickerman, Peter Edelman, Kai Erikson, Gavin Ferriby, Joan Forsberg, Bricker Gibson, Olivia Hayes, James McDaniel, Arthur Miller, Dory Mitchell, Avery Post, Terry Provence, Sandra Rooney, Anita Shapiro, Samuel Slie, James Smucker, Rochelle Stackhouse, and Richard Warch. To those I should have interviewed and did not, I can only offer my apologies and point out that hundreds of people have known Coffin well, the stories had begun to repeat themselves, and I simply had to stop somewhere.

At Yale University Press, Chuck Grench acquired this book and offered much encouragement in the early going. After he left Yale, Lara Heimert (assisted by Keith Condon) ably shepherded the book to publication, soliciting helpful outside readings and giving me very astute and valuable advice. At Lara's request, Maurice Isserman and Ronald Story gave the manuscript extremely helpful readings. In fact, through a series of unlikely coincidences, Ron Story has ended up a reader on all three of my books—offering a brand of generous criticism that must be unique in academia. Jessie Dolch confirmed my belief that the copyeditor is the author's best friend. In these difficult days of publishing, when even nonprofit presses are cutting back drastically, I am particularly grateful for the exceptional care—and extremely sharp eye—with which she edited my manuscript.

In general, though, writing books is a lonely business, which is why authors need to rely so strongly on friends and colleagues willing to read and mark up our drafts, listen to our laments, and cheer us on when the finish line appears to be receding. Here I want to honor Elliott Gorn of Brown University, Marc Gunther of *Fortune* magazine, George Kannar of the University at Buffalo Law School, Leo Ribuffo of George Washington University, and Steven Rosenthal of the University of Hartford. Each one took precious time away from his own work and read every word of the draft manuscript, highlighting bad prose, flagging weak arguments and sagging narrative, and saving me from many errors. One of the most intense intellectual experiences I have ever had was rewriting the manuscript with their marked-up versions in front of me, engaged in a vigorous, even contentious, "conversation" with five of the smartest writers I know. This is a much better book for their efforts, even though I must, alas, take sole responsibility for all of its remaining weaknesses.

Since they first agreed to cooperate with me on this biography, Bill and

Randy Coffin have been unfailingly generous with their family papers, photos, audiotapes and videotapes, and, most of all, time. They encouraged family and friends to do likewise and never protested when I asked hard, even offensive, questions in front of a tape recorder. They waited patiently as they wondered when this work would finally emerge from my study. And while they both got to read the penultimate draft of the manuscript, they never even attempted to influence anything I've written here. I could not have written this book without their willingness to open their lives to me—an academic historian they barely knew—and trust that I would do justice to them and to Bill Coffin's career. For their hospitality, for their extraordinary generosity, and for their trust, I will always be enormously grateful.

In ways that I did not anticipate—and of which they probably remain unaware—members of my family have given me a terrific education in the relationship between religion and politics in the years I have been working on this book. My parents, David and Inez Goldstein, gave me a properly sympathetic reading of the manuscript, despite their unstated wonder that their Jewish son should be so interested in the career of yet another Christian minister. With joy and gratitude (and some struggle), I have watched my children— Isaac, Katherine, and Jacob Goldstein—become B'nai Mitzvot, attend church, and develop their religious and political approaches to the world as they grew into young adulthood. Raised Jewish and Christian, they experience their religious faith as inseparable from the biblical concern for peace and justice.

The idea for this biography came from my wife, Donna Schaper, a United Church of Christ minister, who introduced me to Bill Coffin. She has doubtless often regretted her brainstorm. Nevertheless, throughout what she called "life with Bill," she has nearly always been willing to hash over ideas, help me think about complicated issues, and serve as a guide through the world of liberal Protestantism. An exceptional preacher and pastor who has always understood the struggle for justice as fundamental to her Christianity, she embodies Bill Coffin's legacy as few others do. For her passion and her joy, her impatience with religious intolerance, and her patience with me, I will always give thanks.

William Sloane Coffin Jr.

The Great War, Greenwich Village, and the Upper East Side

1917: "A Great Game and Never a Dull Moment"

With its slaughter and horror, World War I scarred a continent and a generation. For thousands of Americans, however, particularly those whose service lay outside the trenches, the Great War became a crusade, the crowning experience of the Progressive movement. For the thirty-eight-year-old bachelor William Sloane Coffin, the war provided "a great opportunity for a service that is certainly most appreciated." The Yale-educated Coffin was on a leave from his position as a vice-president of W. & J. Sloane and Company and from his life as a well-known New York City businessman, philanthropist, and real estate developer. Too old for the army, Coffin had signed on with the Foyers du Soldat, a Paris-based morale agency financed by the Young Men's Christian Association (YMCA). In France Coffin helped set up rest centers near the lines that gave soldiers a touch of home: cigarettes, coffee, hot chocolate, letter-writing materials, occasional entertainment, and every now and then, a woman's face.

Coffin's Paris activities often seemed an extension of the patrician social life he had enjoyed in New York. He dined at the Ritz; attended and gave suppers in honor of this friend or that relative; welcomed fellow Yale men, including his older brother Henry; joined an arts and letters discussion club; and advised his father and other partners on his stateside real estate holdings. Aware of the ironies, he occasionally worried that "we are too luxurious over here and too fond of good living."[1]

Coffin displayed a lightheartedness toward physical danger that could have been courage or simple bravado. Having bombers "buzzing over your head like huge mosquitoes, coming nearer and nearer, until you know they are right over you," he wrote his mother, raised the "interesting question as to where the pellets would land. However, we remained quietly in bed and philosophically

discussed the unpleasantness of warfare." Descended from Scottish Presbyterians on his mother's side, New England Yankees on his father's, Coffin had
not been raised to linger among his emotions. "You live and work in a perfectly
normal way," he confided to his father, "although occasionally you hear a shell
explode and know of the murderous battle going on in the distance. Such is
life." Still, Coffin's limited insights and occasional diffidence could not mask
his genuine sense of purpose and involvement.[2]

After a thrilling few days in the spring of 1918 helping soldiers and civilians
close to the German lines, Coffin related the entire experience in great and
telling detail. He and a colleague served hundreds of pounds of bread and
cheese, managing to avoid a German plane bombing and strafing the area; the
following morning, "I wore blisters in my hands cutting bread and turning
that spigot," he effused to his mother, "but it was the greatest joy you can imagine! We also gave the men cigarettes. . . . One officer came up and started to
take some, but I quietly remarked that there would not be enough for all so
he left them and took none." When a desperate woman begged Coffin to sell
her some bread, "I told her it was absolutely against the rules to sell her any,
but it was a perfect joy to give her some, and you have never seen a more astonished or grateful woman in your life!" Here, Coffin displayed nearly all of his
essential qualities: his casual attitude toward danger; his personal generosity;
his pleasure in hard work; his fairness across class lines; his admiration for quiet
courage in the face of disaster; his genteel exercise of authority; his patrician
sense of humor, as he teased the poor woman seeking bread; and his delight
in authentic experience.[3]

Although the Great War produced a fierce cultural reaction in the following
decade, ranging from the literature of disillusion to mass peace movements,
Coffin and many others sought adventure and opportunity, a chance to be
tested in the crucible of real life and to help reshape the world. "If only we had
enough men," he wrote his mother with characteristic optimism, "we could
speed ahead at a great rate. New opportunities arise daily." Anyone could "prove
that war is hell," he acknowledged, "but there is another side, thank God. . . .
Let us forget the horrors and dream of the future as we do here all the time."[4]

He sought out experiences to engage himself more fully with the new
world he saw being born out of the war. Coffin predicted a risen France fore-
going complacency and adopting American-style practicality and educational
values. Through the YMCA, Protestantism was on the march, routing "papal
opposition to education and democracy." He understood that "our country
will have gained the most." He pointed to the "economy and sacrifice we have
learned," the birth of a commercial fleet "which can surpass Germany and
almost challenge England," and the mass education of "illiterates" in the Ameri-

can army. "And most of all," he noted astutely, "we have an acknowledged world leadership in finance and in politics and in ideals."[5]

In his attitude toward World War I Coffin exemplified the Progressive spirit: the overarching commitment to universal "progress," the practical idealism, and above all, the dominance of American economic and political ways. America's new financial and political influence went hand in hand with its moral and religious authority. A registered Republican, Coffin thrilled to Wilsonian idealism and occasionally appeared a heretic to his more traditionally Republican father.[6] Not surprisingly, perhaps (and like many), Coffin extended his time in Europe after the Armistice, not returning to the States until the spring of 1919.

The Making of a Francophile

Catherine Butterfield was born in Kansas City in 1892, the youngest of three children. When her mother died, perhaps of tuberculosis, her traveling salesman father put her and her sister Margaret in an Episcopal convent and boarding school in Kenosha, Wisconsin. Upon graduation, Catherine moved east to Boston and Simmons College. A year later she left Simmons and joined the Butterfield clan—her father, John, her brother, Jack, and her sister, Margaret —in New York's Greenwich Village.[7]

In the Village of John Reed and Louise Bryant, Dorothy Day and Mabel Dodge, Elizabeth Gurley Flynn and Randolph Bourne, Catherine breathed the heady air of prewar American cultural and political radicalism. "There were Art Exhibitions galore," she wrote later, as well as anarchists and revolutionaries who "overthrew the government loudly and daily in Union Square on 14th street." Catherine worked in a bookstore and volunteered at a settlement house. She recalled "the thrill of passing sandwiches at occasional parish house meetings to invited Socialists, aloof but eloquent." Like many young women of her class and time, Catherine Butterfield yearned for more than her society offered. "I liked to think of myself as a radical," she wrote, "but the only contributions to reform I can remember were marching with the Suffragettes, and working in some now forgotten way" for prison reform. She recalled "plenty of beaux who took me to dine and dance" but joined much of her generation in thinking, "sometimes rather wistfully, that I had been born too late for 'History.'"[8]

With the outbreak of war in 1914, "History" stormed into the lives of Greenwich Village radicals and reformers, artists and poets—all eager to observe the grand conflict. Future "lost generation" writers Ernest Hemingway, John Dos Passos, and e. e. cummings packed off to drive ambulances in Europe, along with Jack Butterfield. Although History was proving itself active and lethal,

Catherine found herself relegated to the sidelines, to "benefits and knitting—knitting miles of lumpy wool scarves and socks for men in the trenches." Particularly after the United States declared war in April 1917, she "longed to do something for those heroic French *poilus* [soldiers]," even though she "hadn't the remotest idea" how or where. The war itself, and its inexhaustible demands, came to her rescue. "One wildly exciting day" she learned that she "had been accepted for service in France" with the YMCA. In June 1918 she boarded a merry ship to France.[9]

In Paris Catherine met her future sooner than she had imagined. Attending a Foyers du Soldat recruitment talk by William Sloane Coffin—"A heaven-sent answer to my longings!" she put it many years later—she signed up. Here was the action Catherine had craved, even though, as she admitted to her grandchildren, "What did we know about Army Life? or Soldier Morale? or anything?" In the little town of Betz-sur-l'Oise, not far from Paris, Catherine and a friend wore gray, nunlike veils and ministered to the soldiers: putting on shows and dinners, making cigarette runs to Paris, writing to the wives and families of the dead and injured.[10]

The young women learned quickly, soon attaining proficiency in "Système D," the underground bartering system that all armies evolve to get around sluggish bureaucracy. "The only indispensable is tobacco," she confided to her diary, "which so far we have managed to keep in stock thanks to the Système D. That, we have learned to practice with fewer and fewer scruples and scandalous success. Youth and sex have such an unfair advantage!" Soldiers and officers, wounded and healthy, all seem to have benefited from the hint of home, and a bit of feminine influence. During the crucial battles of June and July, Catherine's diary recorded the excitement, passion, energy, and exhaustion of a young woman making her way skillfully in a world haunted daily by danger and filth, injury and death.

> July 16 . . . tried to comfort an old peasant from Armentières whose son had just died . . . I wish I were old and wise.
>
> July 19 Horrible sounds of guns and air raids all night . . . the constant, agonizing crisis of cigarettes, the basic component of army morale.
>
> July 20–August 2 Ten days of breathless and exhausting events . . . Army movies including *Charlot* arrived unexpectedly. Succès fou. Tobacco famine. Tragedy . . . A passing officer announced that Jack was wounded at Soissons . . . I managed a cross-country dash by troop train and truck to Chantilly, where I found him in an American Field Hospital, gassed, and both legs full of shrapnel. Otherwise, intact, thank God. Our hospital here overflowing . . . Ambulance drivers indefatigable, M.D.'s magnificent

. . . All of us dead but somehow exaltés. Everyone senses the military tide is turning.[11]

The diary displayed her self-possession, her boldness, and her ability both to feel the romance of being around men at war and to keep the distance necessary to do her job. She spent her first night in the field in the unoccupied room of a villager's son, "who would be startled to find me among the postcards and Vie Parisienne ladies papering his walls." The bedbugs bothered her, not the pinups. Several days later, Catherine noted with amusement the "adorable concern" of the French colonel who "warned me that for a thousand years Frenchmen had been making love as well as war."[12]

Catherine brimmed over with romantic swings of emotion, from "le cafard" (the blues) to exaltation, to the sweet sadness common to wartime comings, goings, and ironies. One day's entry concluded, "Romantic and melancholy by candle light!"; another, five days later, ended, "Sad, wonderful evening."[13] Catherine might have found some of the same delights and sadnesses working in a settlement house, but she might not have felt the same connection to such a grand human struggle, one of the deepest appeals of any war.

How fitting, then, that she met her future husband in France in the midst of the most intense experiences of her life. The surviving record is far from generous on what passed between William Sloane Coffin and Catherine Butterfield. In her seventies Catherine burned nearly all her husband's letters to her, but she did save some of her own entries and letters and reminisced about him at length in her later life. Just before the Armistice, for example, Catherine bumped into Will Coffin at the Foyers headquarters in Paris and "spent a gay and wholly unexpected day" with him. Lunch at the gourmet restaurant Lapérouse merged into an evening at the Opéra Comique. Catherine enthused about renovated old houses, describing her favorite block of houses on Charlton Street in New York—which turned out to belong to Will. She thought him "oldish" at thirty-nine but "interesting in the way young men aren't—no concern with ego since he obviously has accomplished a great deal in New York."[14]

It seemed a natural match. Catherine was young, beautiful, and Protestant; filled with feeling for the American doughboys and French *poilus;* cultured and quick enough to hold her own with generals and diplomats; by then a thoroughgoing Francophile; and, like Will Coffin, caught up in "service" to the grand cause. She even felt passionate about his principal hobby of real estate renovation and development. What she lacked in family pedigree she made up for with manners and self-possession. When Will returned home, Catherine stayed in Europe, and they began corresponding.

After a couple of summer months running a Foyer in Germany by herself,

Catherine hatched the idea of building her own refugee center "in some desolate corner of the ruins until the French Government comes to the peasants' rescue." She kept Will abreast of her plan, and when she returned to the States in the fall of 1919 for "a frantic month of money-begging," he provided emotional and material support. She returned in October or November to open a canteen and refugee relief center in the "totally devastated" town of Vimy in the mining region of northeast France, "a vast plain of mud." Catherine stayed in close touch with her benefactor, who offered to handle Christmas gifts for the children. His generosity served her charges well: the children "begin to look pinker and fatter and their shoes come within three sizes of fitting," she wrote. Their collaboration drew them closer together; he came to visit the following spring.[15]

Nearly two years riding the emotional roller coaster of war and its aftermath had worn Catherine out; she made plans to come home in July of 1920. "You saw the dramatic and picturesque side of the ruins," she wrote her beau soon after his visit, "but I don't know if you guessed the effect of months of dead trees and wreckage on a weak creature like me. . . . I had reached the point where I hadn't a sensation left except sympathy." His cheerful reminder of an outside world, particularly "memories of New York and our former existence," served as a tonic to her spirit, saving her, perhaps, "from a fatal cafard." The elegant Will Coffin, representing a comfortable but still committed life, had made quite an impression. She had worried, though, about what lay ahead: "I must confess that the transition from the Vimy Route de la Gare to Fifth Avenue had been rather frightening me." Now, after seeing him, she felt more at ease. "You at least have helped bridge" the gap, she wrote confidently, "and will be there with a steadying hand."[16]

Coffin met her on the dock in New York, and after a brief, almost anticlimactic courtship, they were soon married on Cape Cod, where Catherine's sister, Margaret, had settled.

Coffins and Sloanes: The Upper East Side

While Catherine may have aspired to the life led by William Sloane Coffin (known to his friends as Will, and whom she called Billy), joining it required what she later called a shift in her angle of vision, "from the relative informality of Greenwich Village to the structured pattern of the Upper East Side Establishment." It also required a shift from the bittersweet, day-to-day struggle against dirt and death that she had been waging for the past two years to a world in which servants did the cleaning and knew to keep a safe distance. If the Coffins did not live at the summit of New York society, they resided very close to it indeed. The fortunes of the Coffins, who were neither nouveau riche nor heirs to old money, had risen substantially in the late nineteenth century, when Will's father, Edmund Coffin, born in 1844, became the first of the family to attend Yale College (graduating in 1866) and then created a powerful family alliance by marrying Euphemia Douglass Sloane.[17]

When Euphemia Sloane and Edmund Coffin married, they merged families and fortunes. The next generation of Coffin boys carried Sloane in their names, and Euphemia's family's business, W. & J. Sloane (which became one of the premier furnishings establishments in New York City) provided employment and income for the men of the family. But if much of the family's earnings came from Sloane's, its status owed more to the Coffins and their connection to Yale. Not that the Coffins were middling folk. Edmund's father, also named Edmund, at one time owned a farm along the Hudson River on land that has become Sixty-ninth Street, as well as riverfront property in Irvington. The younger Edmund shared his father's interest in real estate but also did quite well as a lawyer, numbering among his clients the mining firm Phelps, Dodge Corporation.

Edmund and Euphemia Coffin had two children, Henry Sloane and William Sloane, to whose "moral development" (in Catherine's words) both parents paid close attention. Even sympathetic accounts of Edmund Coffin make it clear that he belonged to the "old school": stern, rigid, Republican, and undemonstrative, indulging his "deeply affectionate side" only as a grandfather. But there was more to him than this picture suggests. Coffin attended church regularly and served as a trustee of the Brick Presbyterian Church. Through his associations with some Phelps, Dodge partners, Coffin got involved with the New York City efforts of the well-known evangelist Dwight L. Moody and became the pro bono attorney for Union Theological Seminary.[18]

Edmund Coffin brought his family into the world of the church (particularly the Presbyterian Church) and the world of Yale University; his family's history continued to wind through that of both institutions for more than a century. Yale was an institution of far greater political and cultural importance than most American colleges and universities of the time. In the late nineteenth century, Yale served the American elite by educating and preparing its sons for leadership of the American economic and political system. Drawing students from across the country, Yale sought geographical diversity in order to assemble, socialize, mold, and train the national leaders of the next generation. Unlike Harvard, which focused far more on the New England elite and the cultivation of the manly individual, Yale concentrated on the collective. "The spirit of Yale," claimed the future president of Stanford University, Daniel Coit Gilman, "a mysterious and subtle influence, is the spirit of the hive,—intelligence, industry, order, obedience, community, living for others, not for one's self, the greatest happiness in the utmost service."[19]

Even though the winds of secular Darwinism were whistling through the American academy, Yale remained, as one historian put it, "the flagship school" of interdenominational Protestantism. At the same time, during the late nineteenth and early twentieth century the "manly" spirit took hold of college life, enshrining student-organized "extra-curricular" activities, particularly group athletics—and, above all, football—at the pinnacle of social success. Built by the visionary organizer Walter Camp, Yale's football program had become all but unbeatable by the 1880s and regularly thrashed rival Harvard. Owen Johnson, author of the popular novel of 1890s student life *Stover at Yale* (1912), compared Yale football to the beef trust, which also had "every by-product organized, down to the last possibility."[20]

The popularity of college sports helped marry Christianity to an ethic of vigorous, masculine service and create the movement (already popular in England) that became known as "muscular Christianity." While Yale still required daily chapel, the locus of campus religious activity had shifted to the student-run Yale Christian Association, the YMCA organization on campus, known for the building it occupied—Dwight Hall. Henry Sloane Coffin served as Dwight Hall president in his senior year; his younger brother Will succeeded him in turn. Religion for Will Coffin—and this may have been his father's most important legacy to him—was, above all, public, expressed in church attendance, hymn singing, social life, activism on behalf of the less fortunate, and intellectual work. He wrote his senior thesis on Saint Paul and even won a debate prize for a speech on "Saint Paul and American Democracy."[21]

Finally, this school for the sons of the elite had even more elite circles within it, known as secret societies. Among these, the most legendary remains Skull and Bones. Edmund Coffin had been a member; his sons—Henry '97 and Will '00—followed. Will's fellow initiates, known to his wife and children as the "Bonesmen," and often as "Uncles," stayed close family friends for many years.

The Protestantism of this world was neither accidental nor incidental. For even while American society was in the midst of an enormous demographic transformation brought on by waves of Catholic and Jewish immigrants from southern and eastern Europe, the men who ran America's largest and most influential economic and cultural institutions—industrial corporations, law firms, banks, hospitals, universities, museums, libraries, professional societies, and schools of medicine, law, and divinity—remained overwhelmingly Protestant. Protestants had made up the bulk of the population of the colonies and then of the United States. Even African-American slaves became Protestants, if of their own kind. Nearly all of the extraordinary religious schisms and debates in American religious history until the middle of the nineteenth century —when for the first time large numbers of Irish and German Catholics arrived on American shores—took place between and among Protestants.

While Catholics and Jews had varying levels of influence in municipal and state politics, and in the House of Representatives, they were by and large excluded from national-level politics, presidential cabinets (and candidacies), and the federal judiciary. In the 1890s, moreover, a particularly vicious epidemic of anti-Semitism broke out among the Protestant upper classes, who, in their metropolitan clubs, college fraternities, boarding schools, and summer resorts, appeared to be circling the wagons against the onslaught of successful Jewish businessmen and bankers, as well as the "unwashed hordes" of new immigrants. Because of his general liberality of spirit, Will Coffin would have resisted the nastier versions of this outbreak of prejudice; but for a member of New York City's business, charitable, social, and religious elite like Coffin, his Protestant identity—and that of his associates—was as natural and as fundamental as dressing for dinner.[22]

Even as a young man, Coffin deepened the family tradition of service. The social and religious energy of his college years carried over into numerous endeavors in New York City after his graduation. Coffin began working at W. & J. Sloane's, but there, too, he pursued unconventional initiatives. As a way both of educating the employees and of gaining prestige for the company, Coffin launched a lecture series on the history of design.

His first business love was real estate, which he bought, sold, and managed under the rubric of the "Henry William Company" (named for himself and his older brother). Coffin especially loved to renovate run-down properties and make them affordable for those of modest means; he seems to have had real talent for doing well while doing good—as long as housing prices and the economy boomed through the twenties. Not surprisingly, those he approached for investment capital were often fellow Yale alumni, such as his former roommate Edward Harkness and Bonesman Percy Rockefeller. Coffin also served on the New York City Housing Corporation, showing a keen interest in clearing slums to be replaced by decent housing.[23]

Coffin shouldered an extraordinary range of philanthropic responsibilities his entire adult life, beginning long before his marriage. In New York he taught Sunday School at Christ Church, one of the "mission churches" (in Hell's Kitchen) affiliated with his home church, Brick Presbyterian. With other Brick churchers, Coffin organized gym classes, boys' clubs, literary clubs, mothers' sewing circles, and the like. He soon established the custom of an annual party at his parents' home for all these workers. He joined the New York City Mission

Society in 1901, and on his return from Europe in 1919 became its president (a post he held until his death). In 1908 he joined his cousin William Sloane on the board of the Presbyterian Hospital. "His mother worried at his lack of interest in girls and in social events," Catherine wrote of this period. "As it was, he preferred bringing home some friend, or an associate in his social work, to spend a quiet evening in talk." These philanthropic efforts placed substantial demands on his family life. "For twenty-five years," according to Catherine, "first to his mother's dismay, later to his wife's . . . he gulped down Sunday roast beef and Yorkshire pudding to dash down to Christ Church for the three o'clock Sunday School."[24]

Catherine adored and admired her Billy and loved the culture and comfort of her life with him, despite her youth (she was thirteen years his junior) and unfamiliarity with the customs of the very wealthy. She and her husband appear to have been genuine companions. They frequently took up the same projects and constantly discussed each other's business, worldly and charitable. Her memoirs display an intimate knowledge of his real estate, museum, and business affairs. In a world that put much value on the independent activities of husbands and wives, and little on the modern sense of "togetherness," Will and Catherine swam against the tide. Catherine may also have felt comforted and fathered by the older Coffin, by his brother and father, by the Bonesmen, and by the older men whose favor she curried in her charitable work.[25]

For the first years of their marriage Catherine and her husband lived with the recently widowed Edmund in his large house on East Seventy-first Street. There life followed rigid patterns. For dinner at seven adults changed into evening clothes that had been laid out by the butler, who presided over the household. When Catherine gave birth to their first child (named for Edmund, and called Ned) in 1921, Will gave her an eighty-acre estate on Long Island, near Oyster Bay, on which the couple built a huge Georgian house and to which they repaired during summers and occasional winter weekends. The family spent at least one summer month in Europe, traveling in the grand style on Cunard Lines, visiting Brittany or Versailles and, once, a Swiss chalet.

This was a heady life for a midwestern girl who had spent her school years in a Kenosha boarding school. Catherine's memories of high society in the 1920s recall Edith Wharton's descriptions of an older Old New York but also suggest an outsider's unease among the fabulously and famously wealthy. For example, at a fundraising dinner for one of Will's causes, the repair of bombed-out French Protestant churches, she recalled sitting between "Cornelius Vanderbilt and John D. Rockefeller, Jr., trying not to calculate (grossly) which church could be restored for the cost of the dinner alone, with its gold plates and masses of orchids from the owner's greenhouses." Amid the continual fundraising, memorial dinners, and committee meetings and the full round of social obligations, her husband seems to have had a gift for "raising the temperature of even the dreariest meetings."[26]

Into this world—wealthy, liberally Protestant, Republican in politics, structured, public and philanthropic, energetic, driven by a sense of noblesse oblige, and suffused with the optimism of the postwar boom economy— William Sloane Coffin Jr. was born on June 1, 1924.

Early Years

On Top of the World

The arrival of grandchildren—first Ned in 1921 and then Bill three years later—so complicated the routines of the Coffin household and its staff that during Catherine's pregnancy the following year with Bill's sister, Margot, the younger Coffins decided to move into their own place. They bought a two-story penthouse apartment in a building then going up at 333 East Sixty-eighth Street. Fifteen floors above the street, designed with the aid of a Skull and Bones architect classmate of Will, the residence boasted spectacular views of Manhattan and the East River. Young Bill watched as the Empire State Building rose above the skyline; a photograph taken from the penthouse in the thirties provides a spectacular panorama of the city lights.[1]

In New York Bill Coffin lived a full boy's life: he played at home, attended the Buckley School for Boys by day, and spent summers exploring the estate on Long Island. His "most intimate relations," he recalled later, were with servants who functioned as surrogate parents: the Swiss governess, Mademoiselle Lovey, and the chauffeur, Bach. The governess clearly adored the children, or at least the boys, who remembered her with tremendous affection. The chauffeur taught Bill to box, a school activity encouraged by the combative lyrics of the school song: "Face your foes and fight them, / Up, my lads, and smite them. / Better to die than to retreat." With Bach in attendance one Father's Day, Bill won Buckley's featherweight boxing title.[2]

When not at school, Bill, Ned, and Margot lived and played in the nursery, where Catherine came to read to her children around suppertime. "I always pretty much thought of [her] as with Dad rather than with us," Bill Coffin recalled. "Mother was certainly a presence, but not in the same way that the governess was." Coffin *père* greeted his children in the nursery as well, to much clamor and chaos, but generally dined at home with his wife, or out, without children. "It was always a great surprise when Daddy came," Ned Coffin recalled, "exciting, but very fleeting." His father figured even less in Bill's early memories. At Catherine's instigation the children were expected to play instruments and perform for family events. Sunday evenings the family gathered for hymn sings and the "Kinder [Children's] Symphony," later succeeded by a recorder quintet.[3]

Bill thrived at Buckley, where weekly report cards signed by parents gave numerical marks in all subjects, a class average as well as class rank, a graph charting academic progress, and comments from the division head. The elder Coffin added occasional praise ("splendid start," "better yet"), as did Catherine. William Sr. had his parents' penchant for moral instruction, to which he added the importance of physical toughening. He wrote the seven-year-old Bill from shipboard in 1930 to tell him about an English boy who "throws the big medicine ball with the men in the morning. Whenever the big ball hits him on the chest, it knocks him flat on his back. Each time he gets up smiling and says, 'very sorry sir, my fault.' The men like to play with this brave, English boy."[4]

Bill frequently led his classes or was in the top two or three of the dozen pupils. One report card provided some early evidence of the way others perceived him:

> Has no close friends but is generally well liked; the boys sometimes think he is unfair; is not always a good sport; is too independent to be very responsible to authority . . . but likes public approval; is more matter-of-fact and logical than imaginative . . . dislikes all criticism but acts on it; courteous; ready to fight at the drop of a hat; . . . is ambitious and spurred by competition; has a cheerful disposition but is high-strung.
>
> Outstanding in athletics; could do more in team play if he co-operated better.

This report describes a boy not quite ten, yet already formed in important ways: independent, aggressive, disliking authority, athletically competitive and ambitious, enjoying public approval.[5]

Catherine doted on her children. Her letters to them (when she and Will took a brief hiking trip into New Hampshire) spilled over with imagination and charm, wit and care for their feelings. The children felt loved by their governesses; adults attended them; they lacked for nothing materially; and they never doubted that their parents loved them. Between the governesses and travel, the Coffin children grew up bilingual, heirs to their mother's love of all things French. All of the Coffins considered themselves citizens of a larger community and deemed it normal to take part in international affairs. Excellent examples of how the American elite brought up its children, Ned, Bill, and Margot grew up feeling responsibility for the world and considering public responsibilities quite natural.

Catherine Butterfield and William Sloane Coffin represented their class admirably. Their definition of public service had a limited reach. They preferred a certain distance from the poor people who were the "objects" of much public service—though they sought more of this contact than did most of their friends and family. And they quite naturally passed on the casual racial and ethnic prejudices and snobbery of their set. Still, they gave their children a sense of adventure, an inclination toward service, and, most important of all, the self-confidence that comes with privilege.[6]

The Crash

Until she died, Catherine recalled this period as a golden, slightly unreal past, in the way fairy tales record the time of the happy realm ruled by the wise and good king. For underneath the apparent stability and charmed prosperity, darker forces were gathering. While the stock market crash in 1929 did not wipe out the Coffin fortune, the Great Depression that followed put enormous pressure both on the dividend-paying stock of W. & J. Sloane and Company and on the Coffins' many tenants. Not the kind of landlords who quickly turned people out of their buildings, the Coffins still had to pay the mortgages.

Will had assumed full management of the Henry William Company when his father died in 1928; it was a thankless position after 1929. Coffin had put a good bit of his money into his low-income housing projects during previous decades, buying up blocks of tenements and renovating them. But real estate ventures that had made money and sense in the twenties collapsed in the early thirties.

Even wealthy New Yorkers faced growing economic pressure in the early years of the Depression. During the family's European vacation in 1930, Catherine showed a concern for economies absent since her earlier days in France. She wrote her husband, who was sailing back to New York, about a club that was "cheaper and twice as interesting as most restaurants." In Switzerland she reported on the prices of rooms and offered him sympathy and comfort as he returned to the "prevailing gloom. . . . I know how much your morale and courageous point of view will mean to everyone so I try not to begrudge you to them." Making the most of his skill, and doubtless trading on his substantial reputation, Coffin managed to keep the family finances afloat, apparently without cruelty. "One of his biggest civic services," according to Catherine, "was the carrying of numbers of families during those dreadful years from 1931 to 1933." Still, unavoidable realities prompted painful choices.[7]

The family's major income during what Catherine called "that rather desperate year of 1933" came from selling their exquisite property in Oyster Bay. And three decades later, Catherine confided to a young friend that in order to pay a long overdue bill she had had to part with her favorite fur coat. The Depression intruded on an otherwise celebratory occasion that year, as Will celebrated his fifty-fourth birthday at a dinner party at home in April. The children read him a poem (composed by Catherine, who loved doggerel), with recorder accompaniment:

> For when the Depression hit us flat
> Art took no notice at all of that;
> And every March one groans to pay
> When tax collectors come 'round our way—
> A difficult situation for
> A gentleman going on fifty-four.[8]

The levity could not mask the increasingly difficult reality. Not only a well-known businessman, by the early 1930s Coffin had become one of the most important philanthropists in the city. He contributed large sums himself and raised hundreds of thousands of dollars for a variety of causes. Despite her pride in her husband's achievements and growing reputation, Catherine began to worry about his "over-crowded, complicated existence." As the Depression deepened, she became anxious about the "endless problems and pressures from people and organizations . . . that came to Dad day after day for solutions. He had been begged to slow down, but that was not his way."[9]

The storm hit with full force on the afternoon of Saturday, December 16, 1933. Ned was celebrating his twelfth birthday; Bill was nine, Margot eight. Old family friends were being married that afternoon, and Henry Sloane Coffin, by then pastor of the Madison Avenue Presbyterian Church, was officiating. Will Coffin had gone to his office in the morning and then to the Metropolitan Museum of Art for lunch. On his way home he fell, appearing to slip on the museum steps. Helped up, he drove himself home, strode into his apartment and past the open nursery door where the boys were playing marbles, ignored their welcome, and walked straight to his dressing room. He lay down on his bed. When Catherine came in a short time later, she saw him motionless, "hands clasped on his breast"—dead. "Mercifully," she recalled many years later, "he had gone as he would have wished, in full stride, with flags flying. I remember realizing that, and feeling confusedly grateful for him, that those constant problems, of which he never complained, had fallen from his shoulders."

William Sloane Coffin Sr., as he appeared on the front page of major New York newspapers in December 1933 following his death at age fifty-four of an apparent heart attack. Courtesy of Randy Wilson Coffin.

Henry was performing the wedding, so she reached one of the Bonesmen. Soon the apartment filled, and the governess took the children first to a movie, then to their Uncle Henry's for the rest of the weekend.[10]

Front-page news in the *New York Times,* Coffin's death received heavy coverage in all the newspapers. Editorials in the *Times* and the *Herald* pointed to his remarkable breadth of public service, to the way he married his appreciation of fine things to his belief that those less fortunate than he had a right to them. As president of the Metropolitan Museum of Art, the *Times* observed, "he strove to popularize the institution." The large funeral drew the social, religious, business, educational, and social welfare leadership of New York, including such pillars of the American elite as J. P. Morgan, Elihu Root, Nelson Rockefeller, Marshall Field, and Steven C. Clark.[11]

Catherine Coffin experienced the triple loss of a husband she adored, the principal source of her income, and the key to her position in New York society. Had the country not been in the midst of the Depression, or had so much of her husband's investments not been tied up in real estate, she could have weathered the gale, absorbed the loss, and carried herself as a dignified widow in the city.

Newspapers reported an estate worth at least $400,000: $50,000 trust funds for each of the children, and $250,000 in cash for Catherine herself. In fact, however, the real estate holdings were mortgaged to the hilt; the real estate business languished in the deepest doldrums; and tenants were not paying rent. The estate consequently was producing little income, while it had large debts and little liquidity. W. & J. Sloane stock—"once the Goose, which for decades had laid such golden eggs for the family stockholders"—was paying no dividends, and Catherine had no independent source of income. All three Coffin children attended private schools; the family relied on a substantial domestic staff; and they lived in a very expensive residence.[12]

Catherine fled to her sister's for the holidays and then returned to New York for the spring while the children finished the school year. With the help of Will's friends and associates, she sorted through her affairs and decided on a course of action. "My first urgent job," she recalled, "was to find other places for the maids." Then there was the sumptuous apartment: "Who could buy in those impoverished days a seventeen-room, hundred thousand dollar penthouse with a large annual maintenance charge? Finally, the other apartment owners (Dad had been President of the corporation) agreed to accept it without payment." Of the other properties, some Catherine sold, some she paid lenders to take off her hands, a few she continued to hold. Henry had taken charge of the Henry William Company (which produced very little income) and looked out for what could benefit Catherine and the children.[13]

But the main issue for Catherine was that "it was not feasible for us to remain in New York." Catherine was too proud to clutch at the edges of the society in which she had once circulated so confidently. She settled on Carmel, California: "The reputation of California schools, the climate, the low cost of living, the music festivals and experimental theater, the beauty of Carmel and its marvelous beach, also the proximity of San Francisco and of Cousin Natalie, whom I liked and who was concerned for us, finally tipped the scales." Whatever instinct led her far away, that of psychological self-preservation played a role. Far from New York she would not be reminded of losses at every turn.[14]

However much she put a good face on the move, both for her own pride and for her children's morale, she was heading into exile. Even so, in the summer of 1934, these exiles sailed by way of the Panama Canal, where an admiral entertained them. For the millions of less fortunate Americans wandering toward California in search of work, these were years of searing poverty. Catherine's far different voyage to California landed her where her income from property and investments would still support her in comfort without her needing to work for wages. Still, the relocation meant a kind of hardship for her, if not for her children.

Exile

Met in San Francisco by their cousins the Greenes, the Coffins soon made their way to Carmel, where they rented a four-bedroom bungalow, and Catherine became "a very, very strong presence in our lives." In fact, recalled Bill Coffin, "the first very vivid memory I have [of her] is the day Dad died. I can still see her face—lots of tears, but very much holding it together and just telling us that Dad had died and that everything was going to be all right."[15]

With no nursery in the one-story house, she became her children's primary caretaker. While Catherine did hire a maid, no phalanx of servants separated the adult and child worlds. Without fully realizing it, the Coffin family had joined the middle class, a fact made plain when, wearing the short pants of private education in the East, the boys were escorted by their mother to their first day of public school. When Catherine saw how out of place Ned looked, she immediately bought him a pair of jeans. Evidently concluding that the younger Bill would fit in more easily, she inadvertently contributed to his rough-and-tumble initiation. Bill quickly responded to the ridicule of his new classmates with credential-establishing fistfights.[16]

The children found it odd to have Catherine intimately involved with the details of their daily lives. She read to them every morning. "It's hard being read to in eighth grade," Ned recalled. To keep them from fidgeting, she taught them to knit. By contrast, during a month of vacation at New Hampshire's Squam Lake just two years earlier, Catherine, overcome with exhaustion from "committee work," had been at a sanitarium where she had gone to rest for several months. Though Will Coffin had come up from New York on weekends, servants and a tutor did most of the child care. The only contact between Catherine and the children took place through the mails.

Bill remembered her, ambivalently, as "very loving, very caring" in Carmel but also as a "driving presence." Margot felt she was "unrelenting, absolutely unrelenting." She demanded much from her family, who, unshielded by a governess, now felt the full power of this remarkable woman's personality. Though living in exile, Catherine refused to let them forget their origins or their obligations to their name and class. Relying on the familial feelings—and financial generosity—of her in-laws and the Bonesmen, she knew that her family's interest lay in their not becoming an object of pity.

"She said you can't let your minds rusticate," Bill recalled, so they produced a magazine called the *Carmel Sunrise* and sold subscriptions to aunts, uncles, and friends. The resulting correspondence kept her connected to her former life, but Catherine also wanted to make sure that her children remained a presence to their family and potential benefactors. Similarly, she organized the children to stage holiday presentations for their better-off cousins, whom they visited in San Francisco at Christmas.[17]

At this crucial moment in the Coffin family history, Catherine was watching what was left of her fortune slowly evaporate. The New York real estate was neither selling nor producing income. Because of other investments she would never be penniless, but she had considered the possibility of having to go back to work. There in Carmel, three thousand miles from the New York society that had governed her life since 1920, Catherine Coffin emerged from the shadow of her marriage to an accomplished older man. At once

Catherine Butterfield Coffin in 1935 at age forty-three, in Carmel, California, where she presided over her family after the death of her husband. Courtesy of William Sloane Coffin Jr.

liberated and newly burdened by her husband's death, she took charge of her family.

Her resources included her late husband's name and her own intelligence, beauty, iron will, fierce protectiveness toward her family, and attachment to the good life of the wealthy. Ned, her oldest, was solid and responsible. Margot was still very young, and Catherine preferred boys in any event. In Bill she had what she needed. First, he was aggressive. On that first day of school, Bill felt the insults, determined on combat, staked out territory, and chose his opponents carefully. Second, he quickly became an athlete, playing basketball and baseball on local championship teams. Third, music took hold of him, in many different ways and, perhaps most importantly, with Catherine's powerful encouragement.

Music had already figured in all the Coffin children's lives, but it became more of a force in Bill's. In contrast to the evident joy that he took in performance, Margot remembered being "dragged kicking and screaming" to the children's holiday performances for the Greenes, and Ned was glad that "Bill loved these things" because that "took a big load off me." In California, Bill played guitar and sang evangelical hymns with the housemaid at her fundamentalist church. He also played the clarinet, piano in the school orchestra, and guitar in a student trio. As Bill started to play the piano "with some seriousness," his teacher told him that with hard work he might have a "future as a concert pianist." With ambitions of becoming a conductor, he listened faithfully to weekend classical radio broadcasts. Catherine made sure he practiced, and she worried that he might break a finger playing baseball and have to give up the piano.[18]

When Catherine took stock of her family, then, she saw Bill's aggressiveness, his physical talent, his musical ability, and his spirit: his extroverted charm, his interest in being at the center of things, his ambition. He quickly became her favorite and what a friend described as her "life's work." As Ned went off to boarding school for ninth grade, timing favored Bill as well, even though he naturally protected himself from this knowledge: "I didn't sense that I was her favorite, at that time," he reflected, "and if I had, I probably would have denied it."[19]

Bill went off to camp for part of the summer of 1935, and Catherine reported gaily to him on the annual Bach festival. When her attention turned to Bill, however, she zeroed in on his self-control and his manners. "Are you getting fat?" she inquired. "Don't forget the cash prize I offered for every pound!" He was to give her regards to the camp director and counselor: "N'oublie pas ta politesse, n'est-ce pas?" (Don't forget your manners, okay?) Catherine also gave emotional lessons. "You were a grand sport not to complain of home-

Young Bill Coffin at the piano. During his years in Carmel, when he was in sixth through eighth grades, Coffin began to dream of a career as a musician. Courtesy of Randy Wilson Coffin.

sickness those first few days," she congratulated her eleven-year-old. "Almost everyone who cares deeply for his family goes through those feelings sooner or later," she instructed, "and the sooner you do it, the sooner you learn that 'joy and woe are woven fine,' and they go together to make up life."[20]

Catherine herself gave only the slightest hint of the worries that beset her during the difficult years after her husband's death. She had never really had the time to grieve deeply, she explained to her children forty years after the blow, "because of the sudden uncertainties, and the difficult decisions which had to be made immediately. . . . After that, my days were filled, mercifully, but time-consumingly—with your greater demands." The children had adapted so well that she "hesitated to inject any sorrow of the past into your brave new world." Most importantly, however, she recalled being "haunted by the child-hood memory of seeing my father cry, probably after my mother's death which I do not recall. But he had always represented security, and my foundations were shaken for years. Obviously, I couldn't risk that for you."[21]

The strain of running her own household evidently became overwhelming at times. No record survives of what prompted Catherine to go away in June 1936, but she missed the assembly at which Bill received an athletic letter and had not returned by the time Ned arrived home from boarding school. Her sister Margaret came to visit in April and may have taken the children while Catherine got away for a bit. She may also have been taking a "rest cure," as suggested by a letter from Bill, who hoped she was "feeling much better." He reported cheerfully on the end of school and told Catherine about his date for a picnic—"Alice was my girl as you can well imagine."[22]

Though the Coffin family stayed in Carmel only a few years, they were critical in Bill's life. In public school for the first and only time, he began to demonstrate impressive talent in three areas: in music, in athletics, and—elected eighth-grade president—in attracting the admiration of his peers. He wrote later that his Carmel years were the "least complicated" and "most joyful" time of his life.[23]

This time ended as Bill approached his thirteenth birthday in the spring of 1937, in the form of an invitation from the East that again uprooted their lives. Uncle Henry Sloane Coffin, by then president of Union Theological Seminary in New York, proposed sending Ned and Bill to Deerfield Academy in Massachusetts, where the boys could receive a proper eastern boarding school education. Though Ned agreed immediately, Bill objected—on behalf of Carmel, which he knew and liked, and on behalf of his awakened desire to study music seriously.

Catherine knew better. Not only was Uncle Henry planning for his nephews' future—he was offering all of them a return from exile. Not about to look this gift horse in the mouth, but thoroughly captivated by what Bill's talent could offer both of them, she produced a compromise: if Bill did well at Deerfield the next year, she promised her son, the following year she would take him to Paris to study music. Now Bill accepted eagerly. Catherine apparently mentioned her plan to Henry, but met opposition. Thereafter, it seems that mother and children kept their plans secret.[24]

At Deerfield Bill worked hard at schoolwork and at football. If Catherine had worried about his self-discipline and self-control, she would have been overjoyed at his letters. "I'm afraid I'm a little late writing this letter but as soon as I explain you'll excuse me," he began one. "Work is getting heavy," so much so that he wanted to give up music temporarily: "To give you an idea of work, we have had four tests in Latin this week, I have to debate this Saturday and I must prepare a 6 page composition and talk on Buddhism! I think now you can see why I need every minute I get. So I work now for work (of a better sort) next year."[25]

Bill talked music at length with his friend Jimmy Thomas, who invited him to the opera in New York near Christmas. Bill also came into his own as a football player, setting a scoring record for his division. In one game, he reported, the coach had no sooner told the second string quarterback to run the ball when the "first thing he did was to throw a pass to me for about 35 yds." When a run failed, he "threw another pass from about their 35 yd line and by some miracle I got a hold of it and managed to make a touchdown." According to Thomas, this was no miracle: "If you threw the ball up in the air and Coffin was anywhere near it, you knew who was going to catch it. . . . He had tremendous drive."

Bill's self-confidence and leadership skills shone as well. In football games, according to Thomas, "if he thought that the play was wrong and it should be done another way, he would speak up and say so, and he would say so also to the coach." To Thomas (a national youth equestrian champion), Coffin appeared multitalented even as a ninth-grader. "I could do most things well or very well," he reflected, "but he did everything well."[26]

But Bill's achievements complicated matters, as he wrote Catherine after Uncle Henry had preached at a Sunday service: "Uncle Henry said that of course you weren't going to keep me abroad after the good start I had gotten here. He was very emphatic! Then he asked Ned what the plans were. Oh what a tense moment. I was about to say the plans for the future were very uncertain when Ned (bless his dear little heart), said they were very uncertain. Gee, if he had spilled the beans! I foresee an argument which will take more than your little smile to smother your opponent."[27]

Bill was onto something. Catherine's willingness to risk opposing Henry on such an important matter displayed the depth of her feeling for Bill and his potential, as well as her own hunger to return to France. She could have been jeopardizing much. The acknowledged leader of the Coffin clan, Henry held the purse strings. No fuzzy thinker on financial matters, he was an involved, hardheaded, occasionally nit-picking manager of his own holdings as well as Catherine's. That Henry weathered the Depression better than other family members he owed to Will (who had insisted that Henry inherit their mother's blue chip securities) and to his more conservative financial strategies. Widely loved as a pastor and seminary president, Henry had a generous heart and genuine concern for his brother's family, as well as some hard-up cousins. He paid Bill's and Ned's tuition at Deerfield, and much more later. If Catherine was playing with fire, she seems to have known how to do so without serious consequence.[28]

Catherine made good on her promise. Shortly after Bill's fourteenth birthday, in the summer of 1938, the little family sailed for Europe. The shadows of war were everywhere, but Catherine and her charges remained undaunted. Catherine was going home. And she was taking along her husband's namesake, recipient of her most profound emotions.

Europe: Music and War

Paris and Harmony

In 1938 the world watched with alarm as German and Italian fascism crested. That summer, as refugees streamed out of Europe, Catherine Coffin took her family across the Atlantic to a different kind of refuge.

On her first trip to France since her husband's death, Catherine began in Fontainebleu, where the family had vacationed in 1930. Here, the renowned Nadia Boulanger—pianist, conductor, and professor of harmony—presided over the American Summer Conservatory. Just fourteen and filled with enthusiasm, Bill Coffin studied with Boulanger, pouring himself into what he hoped would be his life's work. "He did interminable exercises," Ned recalled. Catherine had no intention of returning to the States at the end of the summer, even though Uncle Henry still wanted Bill back at Deerfield. Securing Boulanger's positive assessment of Bill's progress, she announced her intention to stay. Ned returned to Deerfield for his senior year while Catherine put Margot in a Swiss boarding school. Alone, Bill and Catherine headed for Paris.[1]

Bill studied harmony with Boulanger and took piano lessons from Jacques Février, a former student of the eminent pianist Marguerite Long. Catherine rented two small rooms on the rue de Rennes from a poor widow who kept the place "so cold," according to Coffin, "I had to have a bucket of hot water to put my hands in before I practiced."[2] He eagerly played five hours a day—mornings through early afternoon—all year long, a discipline that was essential, his teachers said, if he was to have any chance of attaining the highest level. The muscles in his hands were already hardening in ways that would prevent his growth as a pianist.

Afternoons Bill roamed the city, soaking up Parisian culture. With no friends, which seems to have bothered neither him nor his mother, he became, in his own words, "an aesthetic little snob." Sporting a beret and affecting a Charles Boyer accent, Bill gave informal tours to the tourists he despised and bought concert tickets with his tips.[3]

Bill and Catherine immersed themselves in music: concerts, opera, theater, ballet. They saw almost no one save some old friends. Nevertheless, mother and son thrived, delighting in the city, in his work at the piano, and in Paris's musical cornucopia. They heard, among others, such outstanding pianists as Arthur Rubinstein, Vladimir Horowitz, Boulanger, and the composer Francis Poulenc. Catherine studied at the Louvre.[4]

She took heart from her son's personal and musical progress. In the summer of 1939, however, she faced a difficult decision, one complicated by Bill's desire to stay in Paris, Uncle Henry's insistence on their agreement that Bill return to Deerfield, and the growing likelihood of war in Europe. As she wrote her brother-in-law, the issue was not whether Bill would prepare for college, but how he could do so without forsaking the possibility of a musical career. Her letter—a triumph of logical reasoning suffused with maternal passion— cited several of Bill's piano teachers, all of whom concurred that he possessed exceptional talent and admirable dedication; the celebrated pianist Alfred Cortot, for example, had told her that "Bill is obviously behind in his technique but his playing shows that 'il est fait pour la musique' [he is made for music]; and that no one should accept the responsibility of cutting off such ambition and promise."[5] Catherine then invoked the spirit of her late husband, who "never deprived anyone of his chance, no matter how much he disagreed, and . . . believed in things of the mind more than in material success."

At the same time Catherine had to allay Henry's fears of his late brother's "artistic" side, as well as of the ne'er-do-well side of her own family. They both knew that Will's not-for-profit interests had left his family's finances a shambles and that if he had spent more time on business he might have lived longer and more prosperously, in which case Catherine might not be appealing to Henry at all. They also knew that Catherine's brother Jack, who possessed "the same artist's response to life as Bill," had become an amiable drunk. If Jack "had had a definite talent to develop," she argued, "it probably would have given him much greater steadiness." As for Bill, she assured Henry that he had "shown more self-direction and responsibility this winter than I would have believed possible a year ago."

What remained was Henry's offer to educate his brother's children, no inconsequential matter. Here, Catherine displayed a shrewd sense of when (either for her own integrity or for the sake of the negotiation) to offer to go it alone. "We both think it not unreasonable that you should think us unappreciative of the sacrifice you had so unselfishly planned," she told him. "For this reason as well as for any other which may arise, you must feel completely free to withdraw the offer."

Despite the vigor of her argument, Catherine claimed to be emotionally uninvolved in Bill's musical development. She clearly felt the need to be cautious, analytical, and objective rather than "supportive." "It might reassure you on my count," she confided to Henry, "if I told you—although it hurts my maternal feelings both to think of it and tell it!—that when I told him, after his first appearance in a large students' recital, that I thought he did well, he remarked, 'I'm so glad, for that is the first approving thing you have said of my music.' I hadn't realized how scrupulously—and apparently heartlessly—I had held to my resolve to do and say nothing which might encourage or influence him."

Catherine appealed both to her own emotional reserve and to Henry's in pointing out Bill's rational approach to the problem: "There hasn't been a shade of emotionalism in any of his conversation, and his whole attitude towards himself and his work seems to me very healthy and objective." Whether a fourteen-year-old with an artistic temperament could in fact bring such objectivity to bear on himself may be open to question. But Catherine had no doubt that this skill was an essential part of growing up, one Bill had to master along with his fingering technique. Henry's response has not survived, but Catherine had clearly persuaded herself to stay another year.

Bill Coffin seems to have skipped the adolescent rebellion of many teenage boys. During the very years that most boys begin to break away from their parents, to explore different paths, Bill lived alone with his mother in a small apartment and saw very few people. He had almost no contact with adult males besides his teacher and the musicians he admired at a distance. He and his mother devoted their lives to his music. Much later, Margot suggested that mother and son had been unusually close during this period. Catherine's watchfulness could have been very enjoyable for the boy. Between his mother and the piano, he may have felt little need to create an emotional life of his own. His recollections of this period, unlike those of seventh grade, mention not a single romantic interest. He seems to have channeled all of his adolescent sexual energy into the piano. In any event, whatever thoughts Bill may have had about girls had to compete with the overpowering presence of his mother.

Outside of their self-contained world, however, war approached. After Germany invaded Czechoslovakia in the spring of 1939, the family held its summer reunion near the Swiss border, at Lake Annecy. Gathered for a radio concert on September 1, they were stunned by a news bulletin of the German invasion of Poland. While the older French guests wept, remembering the last war, Bill, now fifteen, felt a surge of excitement (earlier that year he had attended a thrilling Bastille Day parade showcasing Franco-British friendship and military prowess). Catherine cried with the others.[6]

As the Roosevelt administration declared neutrality and instructed American citizens to flee the war zone, Catherine and her brood again scattered. Due at Yale for the fall term, Ned took off for Le Havre so he "could be near a boat when one became available." Once assured of Ned's escape, Catherine and Bill took Margot to her boarding school and then circled back to Geneva, where Bill enrolled at the École Internationale de Genève and began studying piano, harmony, and counterpoint. Here, Bill's music became social. He played in the school orchestra, and Catherine became thoroughly wrapped up in her son's musical life. She reported regularly on Bill's rapid progress: his new pieces, his first conducting effort (for which Catherine even copied scores), and the fact that he was playing for his former teacher Marguerite Long.[7]

Bill experienced the war cheerfully. He played in a school benefit for Finland (then facing Russian invasion) and likened the resisting Finns to the American revolutionaries at Lexington and Concord. When Germany invaded Denmark and Norway, then Holland and Belgium, the thoughts of this nearly sixteen-year-old turned naturally to the French Foreign Legion.

During the spring of 1940 Catherine worked hard to figure out the future of her family. Ned was ensconced at Yale, but where to live? What about Bill and Margot, whose original tickets had them sailing out of Rotterdam? Were they in danger? In long letters to her sister Catherine sought to settle these questions. She had finally concluded that Bill had a chance to make the first rank of pianists—"*if* he is given the chance."[8] But the war was putting Europe off-limits, so she planned music school for Bill during the summer and his return to Deerfield in the fall.

For Bill the year in Geneva had confirmed both his musical talents and his ongoing need for the intensive practice that could shape him into a professional. He played for audiences for the first time, not only in the school orchestra, but also in chamber groups around Geneva. At the same time his life became more "normal." He mingled again with boys and girls his own age and played goalie on the school's unbeaten soccer team.[9]

Bill Coffin's first conscious experiences of Europe mingled music and Paris, the French language and the threat of war. He felt—personally—the German militarist threat to people and things he cared about. Moved by a visit to Ignace Paderewski, the exiled pianist and former Polish prime minister, whose country Adolf Hitler and Josef Stalin had just divided, Bill found the defense of culture inextricably linked with the fight against tyranny.

Germany's invasion of the Low Countries in early May sped the Coffins' departure. Bill remembered hasty farewells, fetching Margot from her school, and boarding a train for Genoa at the end of May, trying to get out before Italy's borders closed. They bought tickets for a ship waiting at dockside but needed exit visas to board. Bill spent his sixteenth birthday, June 1, 1940, in line for seven hours to get his family's passports stamped. At the very end of that long day, he saw a huge Irish athlete use bluster and physical intimidation to get his passport stamped, overcoming the resistance of an Italian bureaucrat. He never forgot how sheer physical presence triumphed over the functionary.[10]

Packed with European refugees sympathetic to the Allies, the ship home also carried a small band of Nazis on their way to the German embassy in the States. Delighted at the German advances, "They strutted the deck like supermen," Coffin recalled. "It was all I could do not to pick a fight." When Germany captured Paris, most of the passengers mourned as the Germans popped champagne.[11]

Back Home

The Coffins all ended up in the Northeast: Ned back to Yale, Margot to Miss Hall's School in Pittsfield, Massachusetts, and Bill to Phillips Academy in Andover (just north of Boston), which offered more music than Deerfield. Despite his at least occasional frustration with his sister-in-law, Uncle Henry paid Bill's tuition (as well as Ned's at Yale). Catherine's Paris gamble had paid off: Bill's piano reached heights neither of them had anticipated; her family's western exile had ended for good; and they had managed not to alienate the head of the family.

According to Andover headmaster Claude Fuess, Bill's schoolwork quickly earned honors in history and English. "His record has been so uniformly fine," Fuess told Catherine, "that I have given him certain privileges, and he has justified my confidence." He wrote Henry Sloane Coffin that Bill's "general scholastic aptitude is probably as high as anybody's in our very large school." Fuess may have exaggerated, since teachers' comments on Bill's papers showed less enthusiasm: "thin," "this has no life" were typical examples; grades on the surviving material ranged through the eighties.

Where Bill Coffin truly excelled was at the piano, in performance and as a singer. "Of his music activities," Fuess wrote more accurately, "you have probably heard much, and his ability has not been exaggerated." His music brought him campus acclaim: he played piano with the school orchestra, sang in the glee club, led the "8 in 1" octet, and played one of the comic male leads (Sir Joseph Porter) in Gilbert and Sullivan's *H.M.S. Pinafore*. He was elected to a fraternity and also found time to run varsity track.[12]

Bill had become a recognizable type: the charming, magnetic Big Man on

Campus who attracted male and female admirers, whose company was sought by far more people than he could—or wanted to—satisfy. As Glee Club president, Bill helped arrange the dances that followed the club's concerts with neighboring girls' schools. A social leader in these affairs, he once set up a kissing booth to "benefit the war effort." He kept up a lively correspondence with girls, many of whom were drawn to his vitality and charm; they pleaded with him for more letters, more contact.[13]

The adult Coffin persona emerged during these years: aggressive charm, physical energy, verbal facility. Its elements were held together not by religion or politics but by music. Bill's musical gifts gave him power over his fellows, over women, and over his teachers. Music was not only the core of his life— it was a kind of generative glue that held things together while nurturing and driving his remarkable personality.

Bill experienced everything through music, even politics, as in his visit to Paderewski and the benefit concert for Finland. He wrote an "open letter" to the composer and pianist Percy Grainger, who had apparently proposed that music of enemy composers ought not to be played during wartime. "Shocked and disappointed" by Grainger, Bill laid out his position rather awkwardly in a mixture of earnest argument and flip debating points. "Music, to me," he wrote, was a "universal language" that transcended "geographical frontiers and economic interest," for which "society has felt almost as great a psychological need . . . as it has for religion." He combined this point of view with a pretentious condescension—"I feel sincerely sorry for the mind that sees Schubert or Mozart mixed in with National Socialism"—and an appeal to our better natures, hoping "we could go through with this war without adopting some of the baser and extraordinarily naive practices of our enemies." Catherine could have been proud of her son's heartfelt internationalism, which she had done her best to encourage. Young Bill Coffin, fluent in French, studying German, argued as best he could against the divisions of belligerent nationalism, against demonizing the enemy.[14]

Yet Bill also recognized the power and appeal of forcefulness, and sheer force. In a paper he wrote as a junior or senior, he displayed his fascination with the power of the individual, especially in relation to the mass of humanity, while retelling the story of the 1939 Bastille Day parade on the Champs-Elysées. Bill may have thrilled to the tanks and planes at the time, but in "The Parade," he wrote about different groups of people, especially the police.[15]

The police, in this account, began by strolling and "swinging their clubs loosely and casually." More spectators arrived, the crowd grew, and more people closed in on the narrator. The crowd had become a mob. Bill focused on the policeman: "Watch the cop," he instructed. "His face is no longer limp nor does his club hang idly in his hand. The lines of his face are set and he clenches the club in his fist. His whole being expresses purpose and determination. He looks sharply, acts quickly."

People pushed out of the Métro station. There was "pressure, pressure on all sides. Faces turn paler, eyes are wider, everything is tense." The exit was blocked; "something must be done." The cop "has seen the situation, has appraised it, has determined the only course of action. The people . . . hesitate and are lost. The cop knows what he is about. He knows that hesitation is no match for his asserted purpose and authority. Besides, doesn't he have the club?"

This hymn of praise to the man of action, to the aroused force of decision and authority—a face no longer "limp," a club no longer hanging "idly"— drew on the boy's experience on the Genoa dock on his sixteenth birthday. There, too, the crowd had pushed and pulsed with fear and panic. Bill's sympathies, however, lay with the intimidating Irishman, with the cops who could manage the "mob," and perhaps with another group he sketched, "those who watch a parade from the window." These analysts saw beneath the surface from "their superior position" and could direct events "as one would guide with a radio beam."

At one time or another in this paper, the young Coffin identified with each of the three groups: the crowd, the cops, and the window watchers. He had been, after all, among the crowd himself that Bastille Day. As part of the mass, even as an "aesthetic little snob" in Paris, he had been confident that France would hold out against German force. He had been proved wrong, however, and so now paid more attention to the "window-watchers," who could see more deeply and clearly. Separated from the lively feel of things, they saw and understood what forces were gathering long before those at street level had an inkling of what lay ahead.

But the most fascinating characters were clearly the police, those exemplars of decisive action, physical determination, and authoritative power. They could move hundreds of people, and they acted rather than watched. They got involved in defending the common good rather than holding back and analyzing coolly, academically, from a distance. They wielded a potent masculinity (instead of radio beams) and deployed the threat of violence. When Bill wrote this paper, he was far removed from his days as a young boxer at Buckley and the fistfights of Carmel. A musician enrolled in one of the country's elite prep schools, Bill was playing no contact sports and even took one less course so he could practice the piano four hours a day. In "The Parade," Bill let different kinds of fantasies take flight, those of physically powerful and coolly controlling men more suited to a world at war.

During Bill's years at Andover, from 1940 to 1942, Catherine lived in nearby

Cambridge, where she had decided to resume her college education at Radcliffe. She and Bill corresponded regularly and visited back and forth. She kept a very close—and often critical—eye on his development, fretting about the details of his personal hygiene ("don't forget to change your socks daily") even as she praised him for his maturity and self-control.[16]

For Catherine, maturity and self-control were all but indistinguishable— and especially important in the wake of the Japanese attack on Pearl Harbor. "Like the rest of us you must have been living in turmoil these past two days," she wrote Bill on December 9, "for no matter how much one's mind seems to be prepared, the emotions are never fully armor-plated, are they?" She worried, not at all unreasonably, that under the pressure of events, her sons might decide to do something rash—like enlist—and that she wanted desperately to avoid. "It will be long and hard and we shall probably all be needed in one capacity or another," she wrote. "But until then, as I have just written him [Ned], the best preparation it seems to me, is to keep at our jobs, learning to think things through. For in the post war world—if not sooner—the men who can get at the bottom of the problem will be needed for the reconstruction. . . . Temperamentally you are certainly far better equipped than most for leadership. . . . But I agree with Ned that the thing to do is to wait until one is needed before leaving the job in hand, and to try to complete that as well as possible."[17]

She and Ned made sense, even though this argument conveniently required no departure from the comfortable environs of Yale University and Phillips Academy. While "rumors have been thick and fast in regard to bombers over NY—then Boston, etc.," she noted pointedly, "everyone is commendably calm."[18]

Catherine had good reasons for this tempered and logical response to the bombing of Pearl Harbor and the U.S. entry into World War II. War had come for the second time in her lifetime, and death could be stalking her sons. She had seen boys their age die in makeshift hospitals, had sought—helplessly— to comfort their parents. From her own experience she knew the romantic power of a wartime crusade, and she knew the susceptibility of young men. Her dashing brother Jack (to whom she frequently compared Bill) had been wounded in France, and if the war had not turned him into an alcoholic, it had certainly contributed. Her husband, too, had been taken from her before his time, a fact with which she lived every day. Catherine relied a great deal on the men in her life, and war put them at risk.

But the last war had also meant opportunity for her, for her husband, for her nation. For the first time, she addressed Bill as an "artist," the most revered term in her vocabulary, and used it to temper his passions. Those who found satisfaction in "cheap patriotism" would leap first into the unknown. Surely an artist with leadership potential ought not to go off half-cocked. Surely Coffins, educated and bred for leadership, ought to take their place at the head of the column—not at the front of the enlistment line. Her arguments may not have been needed, but neither Ned nor Bill enlisted.[19]

The piano kept Bill close to home physically as well as spiritually. It clearly mattered more to him than anything else at school. He played once with the Quincy Orchestra, won the school piano prize, and finished his senior year on the "credit list"—something like a third honor roll. After graduating he entered the Yale Music School in the fall of 1942.

Catherine moved to New Haven that summer to make a home for her boys, their first together since they had left Carmel for Deerfield five years earlier and where she lived until her death in 1982. After graduating in December, Ned was going to the Naval Language School in Colorado to study Japanese. Once he left, Bill's own "eagerness to get into the war" grew stronger. He first tried the romantic route and applied to the French Foreign Legion. When his draft board vetoed the idea, Coffin then wrote to the new Office of Strategic Services (OSS). Rejected, his interviewer told him, for his lack of "Gallic features," Coffin "resigned" himself to waiting for his draft notice, which finally arrived in April 1943.

Bill had poured himself into the piano that year, "haunted," he wrote later, by the prospect of being "too old to gain adequate technical proficiency" at the end of the war. Although he practiced furiously for his last two weeks as a civilian, the truth is that he was more than ready for a different life. "When I put on my uniform in Fort Dix, New Jersey," he recalled, "I felt a serenity of spirit that I had rarely known before." With both sons gone in uniform, and the end of the war nowhere in sight, Catherine Coffin needed all of her self-control. Bill sent his first letter from Camp Wheeler, Georgia, wishing her a Happy Mother's Day.[20]

From Bach to Bayonets: Coffin at War

"I love the sweat and grind and man to man fighting," Bill Coffin wrote his mother after four months in the army, "where the individual has his chance."[21] Pianist and aesthete, the nineteen-year-old Coffin had already been changed by military life. No longer a mere admirer of the men of action, he had become one—and liked the life so much that he spent four years in uniform, from 1943 to 1947, twice extending his tour of duty after the war was over.

Coffin took to the physical life—the structure, the strenuousness, the intensity—to the "man's life," as though it were Beethoven. His experience, shared by many thousands of other citizen-soldiers, taught him a distaste for bureaucracy and hunger for physical action that characterized the rest of his life. "I really owe the army a lot," acknowledged Coffin fully five decades after basic training.[22]

Catherine wrote Bill several times a week, recounting her musical and social doings, news of Ned and Margot, books she was reading, and her ideas about politics and the war effort. Though she usually wrote in a cheery and encouraging tone, she occasionally showed that she was still scrutinizing Bill with a tough-minded, future-oriented vigor as well. Less frequently, he reported on his military training, his delight at promotions and other achievements, his observations of his fellow soldiers, and his experiences with religion.

Catherine may have been startled by the way her young artist took to army life in the Georgia countryside. Made "company runner" on his first overnight bivouac, Private Coffin reported that "this was rather pleasant, clicking heels, saluting snappily and other such forms of that necessary Army exhibitionism." Army life quickly became even more compelling. He described the "excellent preliminary dry shooting training" in great detail. When his company was selected as "the best marching outfit" in a regimental parade, he hoped the honor would "put some spirit into some of these morons . . . I got a real charge out of the whole affair."[23]

Soon Coffin had stopped criticizing his compatriots. "We are getting conditioned and really quite proficient," he wrote home. "We of the 'bloody second' are fast becoming the most spirited and belligerent platoon of the company." By early August his bonding was complete; he now complained about the officers instead of the men: "the dumbest lieutenants I have ever met . . . sloppy marchers, always making little slips. . . . Fortunately our sergeant is back training us." At last in the world of men, Bill felt at home.[24]

He delighted in the sheer physicality of the army. As he wrote later, "All the physical energy bottled up during four years of four hours a day at the piano now came pouring out." A half-century after the fact, he grinned with unfashionable pleasure while recalling how much he enjoyed the bayonet drill. Contemporary letters painted a vivid picture. "You'd be very much amused and probably horrified by our dirty fighting course," the nineteen-year-old wrote his mother. "It consists principally of two main objects: To be able to apply a strangle hold and to be able to quickly and effectively kick or reach for the most vulnerable parts, usually referred to as the 'family jewels.' . . . Oh it's great stuff—almost as good as the bayonet which is still my favorite exercise. There's much satisfaction in a vicious thrust, jab, slash, smash, vertical, horizontal or overhead butt stroke. It couldn't be more uncivilized, but oh how I love it. Ain't it awful."[25]

Drafted in 1943 just before his nineteenth birthday, Coffin immersed himself in the physical
intensity and "man's life" of the U.S. Army.
Courtesy of Randy Wilson Coffin.

Coffin's frankness and crudity suggest a little boy playing army for the first
time, or the overcivilized young man out to shock his refined mother. Catherine did not shock easily. "You know how proud I am of your bayonet thrust-
ing, mortar base-ing, machine gunning, prowess," she replied.

Coffin's most powerful emotional relationship remained that with his
mother. He seems to have sublimated most of his sexual energy into soldiering, into the chaste pursuit of "nice girls" (he did not patronize prostitutes),
and, curiously, into his letters home. He concluded one letter to his mother
with a promise to "simulate kissing you and reloading and beginning again in
slow or rapid fire as you wish. Here's hoping for the bull[s-eye]. I love you
darling."[26]

Catherine encouraged his romantic efforts. Bill referred to "the usual female
correspondence" at mail call, and they often discussed Bill's love life. In September he wrote excitedly about an upcoming weekend in Atlanta during which
he hoped that his "noble restraining nature is at last to get a little reward" from
his hosts' attractive daughter. Catherine wished him luck with "fingers crossed,"
for "certainly you deserve Reward!" She took pride in his accomplishments,
whether military or romantic. "Your card announcing the success of Atlanta
has just filled me with delight," she wrote. "I look forward to the details when
you emerge from the 'woods' where I gather you are mortar bombing and machine gunning, or going through some other vicious little practices."[27]

Catherine's mothering, which included providing synopses of great men's
lives, recalled her husband's emphasis on the importance of moral instruction.
Of the painter Claude Monet, she observed pointedly, "You would have liked
him—big and good-natured, the hardest kind of worker, never satisfied, generous to others, and a loyal friend." She quoted Baudelaire on the strength of

conviction needed by great men, and recommended a biography of Benjamin Disraeli.[28]

By the time he left Camp Wheeler, Coffin had acquired new respect for Americans he had barely known existed before he entered the army. As a cosmopolitan northeasterner and a well-educated, upper-class Presbyterian, Coffin had started off contemptuous of the local culture and especially of the poorly educated, working-class Southern Baptists. In condescending letters home, he poked fun at their lack of musical taste and complained that the Baptists had a "tedious" morality and were "too damn preoccupied with being saved."[29]

By the end of basic training, however, Coffin had mellowed considerably toward his fellow soldiers, toward the South, and even toward the Baptists. To his mother he sang the praises of the "nice Baptist family" that kept inviting him to Sunday dinner, where it was "marvelous to get into a homey atmosphere, real southern cooking and congenial people." He and a buddy sang at a large revival meeting one evening, and Coffin changed his tune. "I must say the friendliness, the sincerity and particularly the bible learning of these southern baptists is really impressive," he wrote home. "Their enthusiasm puts many of our more intellectual services to absolute shame, and this spirit is very deep-rooted and reflects in everything they do." His comrades in arms, too, had been growing on him. Even though they had little in common with Coffin's Andover chums, "they certainly are a grand bunch, each with a real personality, generous instincts, and a fine spirit which I really think only Americans possess." By August he had begun to move into a leadership role; he was made a squad leader—and loved it.[30]

Coffin saw and noticed segregation for the first time at Camp Wheeler, in the form of signs in town for "Colored" and "Whites," the total absence of blacks in the camp, and the common talk of "niggers." He remembered being "stunned" at the prejudices of a certain training sergeant, "how much I thought he was a decent fellow and what an incredible bigot he was—the way he talked about niggers."[31]

After the most socially democratic months of his life, Coffin unexpectedly received orders in September transferring him to the Military Intelligence Training Center at Camp Ritchie, Maryland, probably because of his fluency in French. He regretted leaving his "grand bunch of real American boys." Basic training had worked its democratic magic, just as it had for young American men since the Revolution. But Coffin had not completely abandoned his upbringing. His account of an incident a week before his departure showed that he had retained some immunity from the cruder passions of war. His battalion assembled "to be whipped into a spirit of hatred for the slimy Jap and Nazi. It was stupid, barbaric, and useless. . . . To make us aware of the enemy's cunning and treachery is fine but to try and instill a *permanent* hatred and desire to inflict upon him more terrible and horrible torture is just plain s--t."[32]

Over the next several years the contours of Coffin's soldiering personality began to harden. He combined mild interest in his religious surroundings with admiration of and appreciation for military tactics and the American fighting man, self-pitying or rakish reports on female companionship, a dislike for bureaucracy, disdain for loafers, and indignation at perceived moral wrongs. He threw himself into the army, especially when it required intensive study or vigorous activity.

Camp Ritchie rarely demanded either, so the restless and energetic Coffin was often bored. Fortunately, he ran into friends from Andover, David Chavchavadze and Chingis Guirey. As they hitchhiked to New York and New Haven on a weekend pass, Guirey taught Coffin Russian folk songs. In New Haven Coffin partied with his music school chums, visited his mother's friends, and made family calls.[33]

When the opportunity arose to attend Officer Candidate School (OCS), Catherine urged him to do so; like most mothers, she wanted to keep both her sons out of the low-level combat positions where the chances of injury or death were greatest. (She may not have known the mortality rates among second lieutenants.) She also had grand hopes for Bill in the postwar world. "It will take the young and ardent," she rhapsodized, "the Bill Coffins—to persuade the skeptical and indifferent, and to carry on the belief even if the majority turn to science or some other false god." When Coffin and Guirey both won admission to OCS, Coffin joyfully headed back to Georgia at the end of February 1944, this time to Fort Benning.[34]

Fascinated by the gadgetry of the machine gun and M-1 rifle, map-reading and maneuvers, tactics and physical exertion, Coffin was captivated by the intensity of officers' training. His pride in his physical accomplishments was tested and confirmed. He boasted, for instance, that he had received the "highest rating of the platoon—a 98%" on a strenuous fitness test. A few days later he accompanied several friends out to the obstacle courses and looked them over "with a scientific eye for speedier methods."[35]

Coffin took exceptionally comprehensive notes—preserved in his papers—on everything from motor pool setup to night patrols. "Life continues to be exceedingly interesting," he told his family, offering as evidence the "demonstrations of gun drill," which were "performed by special squads with such speed and precision it is marvelous. It is one of the most beautiful things I've seen in the army; just like the execution of a difficult scale passage, great, great dexterity, perfectly time[d]."[36]

In OCS training at Fort Benning Coffin met African Americans for the first time. Like most of his fellow trainees, they were college educated (from black institutions such as Fisk, Howard, and Tuskegee), but they were segregated in a different barracks and all belonged to a single platoon. He saw that they all but memorized the army manuals and answered officers' questions almost by rote. "And I said to them," he recalled, "'Why are you studying these manuals so much?' They said, 'They cannot throw us out if we know the manuals.'" Coffin got to know these men both out of curiosity and because he had been shocked by the overt racism he had seen the previous summer at Camp Wheeler. Seeing how well the black trainees handled their turn at leading the entire company was the "final proof of black-white equality." Even southern whites ended up impressed by the technical skills and leadership qualities of the black officers. These were valuable lessons for a young man who had never known any African Americans at all and had grown up with the ingrained, if generally passive and casual, racism of his milieu.[37]

Half of Coffin's entering class at OCS flunked out of the demanding course, and he may have come close, for he could not grasp the fundamentals of garrison life: equipment cleaning, bed-making, and the like. The company commander called him in for a "heart to heart chat," having "decided I had more drive, guts, and delinquencies than anyone else in the company—'a mighty poor combination,'" and upbraided him for a "'Joe College' carelessness" about such matters. Pleased with his new democratic sensibilities, and sensitive to the judgment of a male authority figure, Coffin was stung, and determined to do better.[38] In June 1944 he graduated and returned to Camp Ritchie as a second lieutenant.

Coffin felt ambivalent about what he once referred to as his "uselessly prolonged chastity." He appears to have had plenty of opportunities to lose his virginity. Elaine Manson, an attractive, intelligent former secretary at the Yale Music School (who had joined the Marines), displayed a cultured ardor toward him that Bill kept at arm's length. She acknowledged her lack of discretion and how often she reread his letters; they spent several weekends together in Washington, on which Coffin reported to his mother. "It seems to me," she mused upon Bill's return to Georgia, "that for an infantryman you have the girl in every port tradition pretty well established." He assured her that she retained a special place in his heart. One of his letters concluded, "Je t'aime, je t'aime, je t'aime and so on for 1,143 times as some French painter wrote his mistress. Some jerk." The last two words could not entirely blunt Coffin's imitation of that French painter writing his mistress—though Coffin, of course, was writing his mother. For her part, Catherine acknowledged her birthday present that year (perfume, "one of my greatest weaknesses") in a similarly florid manner: from "another of my greatest weaknesses, M. le Caporal." For thanks, she suggested that Bill "please ask the likeliest WAC" for "the fondest thank-you 'smooch' she can manage." Still, while reporting proudly on his many dates and soirées, Bill wanted Catherine to understand that he remained a virgin. He signed off one letter with "mounting excitement at the thought of seeing you again my dear, . . . Bill alias The Chaste."[39]

In early October of 1944, at long last, Coffin sailed for Europe with a large group of specialists in German and French. Unfortunately, he complained that he ended up "somewhere in England. This is commonly known as being shafted."[40] While he hoped to move on soon, he had much else to think about. On his very first night on English soil, he met a young woman at a pub with whom, in a hayloft later that evening, he lost his virginity.

Coffin described this encounter in his memoir with a sweet nostalgic tenderness. "I seemed to be in the grip of some lovely if scary destiny," he recalled. His "upbringing" and "deepest feelings" were that "people were to be loved" rather than used. As a result, he "had lived an unsophisticated life—by army standards extraordinarily so." He had been both resisting "considerable temptation" and having "the usual boyish doubts about my manhood," to the point that he wondered "if I wasn't really being more cowardly than moral." He had decided, finally, to "let nature take its course" once he got to Europe.[41]

Coffin's contemporary account was more immediate and more revealing.[42] "The nights have hardly been unpleasant," he reported to Catherine with forced casualness, "with the first night off ending up with a beautiful blonde—quite unexpectedly and much to everyone's envy. However it threatened to become involving and a little strenuous—I had to walk 14 miles in the early morning hours to get back to camp—so it rather broke off. British beer 8 1/2 d. is excellent though not quite up to Schlitz. A thousand kisses." Ready for manhood, perhaps, the twenty-year-old Coffin was less prepared for women. Involvement was the problem, not the fourteen miles. He tried to mask his discomfort and retreat with a passive British turn of phrase—"it rather broke off"—while he quickly changed the subject. Reenacting the experience of soldiers (and camp followers) for thousands of years, Coffin explained a week or two later that his "relations with this very good looking but that's about all blonde were calculated for an early departure. Now she asks everyone why I don't come to see her any more."

For despite his written ribaldry, the sexually inexperienced Coffin was shocked by wartime life in England. He affected a coolness and distance belied by his obvious excitement. "The girl situation is something," he marveled. "La vie libre flourishes to an unbelievable extent and quite openly. If it's like this in England I can imagine what it will be like on the continent. It's an interesting development and certainly a natural one to a certain degree—though I never suspected it would be pushed so far over here."[43]

Coffin's attempt at detached analysis failed: "interesting" conveyed none of what he saw. Wide-eyed, the young soldier resembled a small-town midwestern boy encountering the arcades of New York's Forty-second Street, or the beaches of the Riviera, for the first time. Even his report on the famous buildings of central London pointed out that the "night life around here continues ever the same with fast times being the order of the day." New to a country at war, new to women's sexual desire, Coffin was emotionally unprepared for those fast and intense times. Not that he was uninterested. But given the intimacy and depth of his relationship with Catherine, he preferred less charged, less demanding relationships.

At the same time, he thrilled—without reservation—to the intense emotional engagement of what he called repeatedly the "man's life," a life apart from the refined and proper existence of drawing rooms, cultured conversation, and Schubert *lieder*. Bayonets, equipment assembly and disassembly, marching and calisthenics, obstacle courses, night marches, and tactics—this was the right stuff. "You know," he reflected toward the end of his officer training (echoing late-nineteenth- and early-twentieth-century muscular Christians), "for every civilized male I think it's a good thing to live for a short time strictly a man's life in a basic sense. A rough physical life, suffering and strain, when you have a lot of things demanding immediate attention and there's no hemming and hawing about getting them done."[44]

The problem was that he was stuck in England for a month and a half with the Sixteenth Replacement Depot, impatiently waiting for orders. Not until November did he and his unit from Ritchie get to Le Vésinet, outside of Paris, where Coffin was assigned as an interpreter at army headquarters in Paris. He was torn, rejoicing in his return to the city of his boyhood, but wanting to be more active in the war effort. Soon his request for a transfer to the infantry was granted. On December 16, Ned's birthday, twenty-year-old Bill announced to his mother (with unconscious cruelty, for he was evidently unaware of the eleventh anniversary of his father's death) that he was at last headed into combat: "tomorrow I quit MIS [Military Intelligence Service] for good. . . . You've no idea how happy I am. After all a man must serve his soul no matter what."[45]

Coffin joined a small group of replacement lieutenants on the edge of the Compiègne forest several days before Christmas, only a few dozen kilometers from where his mother had spent the waning months of the First World War. Lonely, very likely scared of what was to come, he wrote to Catherine on

Christmas eve with a young G.I.'s bravado: "The thing that seems to be do-ing most of the stirring at the moment is a bottle of gin—its last mad rush before its life blood is eagerly drained off."[46]

Because Coffin arrived last of the little group, no orders awaited him. The captain in charge offered him the choice of going immediately to the front or staying in the camp "for not more than two weeks training troops." Coffin easily accepted this offer to train troops, which seemed all the more attractive coming from what he remembered as the captain's "fatherly face." He promptly threw himself into the training program with his captain, which turned out to be so successful that the camp commandant kept the two officers on. "Don't argue," Coffin remembered him saying. "This work is as important as any you'd do at the front."

As two weeks turned into months, an embarrassed Coffin complained to Ned, "I also resolved to forget about having any direct part in it [the war] my-self. I've seen more men shanghaied into foxholes but I'm G-Damned if I can volunteer myself into one." This line of reasoning may have salved his con-science, since there is simply no evidence that he kept trying to get into that foxhole. And the experience of many other young officers in World War II (in-cluding Coffin's Andover classmate George H. W. Bush) suggests that if Coffin had wanted above all else to get into combat, he could have done so. In his memoir Coffin recalled being struck, along with his OCS comrades, by the D day reports "that the highest casualty rates were among second lieutenants leading infantry platoons." His initial fear, loneliness, and confusion responded to the captain's fatherly presence and later to the colonel in charge of the camp, a "man's man" whom Coffin admired. The early death of Coffin's father gave older men enormous influence over him, and they may also have responded to his sonlike devotion. At crucial points in his life, Coffin allowed such men to make choices for him.[47]

Whatever his expressed misgivings, Coffin loved running the training and took pride in the work. "The men are coming around all right," he wrote in early January, "and there's a lot of satisfaction in seeing them get hardened and disciplined and I help their enthusiasm no end." Like so many prominent men of his era—including John F. Kennedy, George H. W. Bush, Gerald Ford, George McGovern, and Norman Mailer, for example—Coffin was matured and educated and came to young manhood in uniform and in war, almost en-tirely among other men.[48]

By age twenty-one Bill Coffin had been transformed by his two years in the army. Until entering boot camp he had lived most of his life among the wealthy and cultured. He had gone to public school for a total of three years (all in Carmel). The rest of his education had taken place in the most elite private schools America had to offer—Buckley, Deerfield, Andover, Yale. In Paris and Geneva he and his mother had enjoyed a cultured gentility despite modest circumstances. He had learned to charm men and women, but rarely anyone outside the privileged or artistic circles of his mother's world. He had absorbed the commonplace racism and anti-Semitism of his class and felt little compunction about expressing it in letters. Andover and the Yale Music School did little to challenge his development. Instead, they strengthened the likelihood that he would spend the rest of his life in such rarefied circumstances.

World War II and the U.S. Army intervened powerfully in the lives of the Coffin family. No matter how cultivated, no matter how elevated, no matter how insulated from the brutal circumstances of most of humanity, the Coffins, too, were swept along by the grand movements of this war, as they had been by the Depression and, a generation earlier, by the Great War. But they also had the resources to find opportunity where others met with loss. Catherine Coffin took courses at the Louvre during the Depression while her gifted son studied with some of the finest musicians in France. After her marriage in 1920, she never took in washing or boarders and never worked for money.

Young Bill Coffin, inspired by the crusade to save European civilization, opened his heart to the army, and to American masculine democratic culture. He was invigorated by the rough physicality, by the immersion in masculinity, by a cause and a task large enough to challenge his intellect and his physical capacity. The young man gushed over the American G.I., the "man's life" he was living, the beauty of weaponry and tactics. The army even challenged his racism and gave him crucial lessons in black-white equality. Despite his father's death, despite the Depression, despite the war, Coffin's life was governed by a sunny optimism altogether appropriate for a youth, even one at war. But there was a new world being born out of the cataclysm of World War II, one that would temper and test this idealism.

THREE

Russians White and Red

"My Russian Soul"

Bill Coffin had a hunter's instinct for sensing opportunities. If there were a time to wait for people and forces to gather and rearrange themselves, he seems to have known when it was, and how to do so. With the war in Europe all but over in the spring of 1945, his training work in Compiègne had evaporated. Bored and restless, Coffin put in for a transfer to the South Pacific, where the war still raged. His friend Chingis Guirey had other ideas.

Guirey, the irrepressibly flamboyant, soulful son of a famous anti-Soviet Circassian military commander, had met Coffin at Yale. The young men became good friends during the war, first at Camp Ritchie and then at Fort Benning, where they underwent officers' training together. Now based in military intelligence at Le Vésinet, Guirey had been serving as a Russian interpreter for the American forces when they first met the Russian army in April. Fond of Coffin and wise in the ways of bureaucracy, Guirey schemed to enroll his buddy in an intensive Russian language course offered by the newly established Russian Liaison School (at Le Vésinet), which trained officers to negotiate with the Russian army in Europe. He arranged for Coffin to be called in for an interview in early May 1945.

Guirey managed an elaborate ruse to persuade the commandant that Coffin ought to be admitted into the school. He had Coffin sit at the piano and sing the two folk songs he had taught him several years earlier while hitchhiking. Though Coffin had no idea what he was singing, his superb musical ear had caught the words and accent perfectly; the interview turned into a bout of singing and dancing, lubricated by vodka, at the conclusion of which the school commandant agreed to take Coffin on.

Initially, as Coffin recounted in his memoir, he had no intention of entering the school and informed Guirey "that my heart was still set on the front. I couldn't bear the idea of a soft job while others were fighting."[1] Accompanied by the disappointed Guirey, Coffin walked slowly to the station, and missed his train back to Compiègne. Guirey seized on the omen and spent the next two hours in a passionate monologue, fighting for Coffin's soul and future.

Convinced that too many Americans had naive illusions about their wartime allies, Guirey wanted worldly and sophisticated men who could grasp diplomatic nuance and bargain hard with the Soviets. Upper-class Russians like Guirey and their mutual friend David Chavchavadze (educated, like Coffin, at Andover and Yale) could "naturally handle situations with tact and finesse," but there were so few of them that "to date we have been at a disadvantage."[2] Guirey himself had been deeply involved in the painful business of repatriation and was trying to get Americans to understand why so many displaced Soviet citizens did not want to return home. Guirey's words "affected me so deeply," Coffin recalled much later, "that I began to vacillate between going to the Pacific and coming to Paris. I must have been on dead center when the next train arrived, because as I boarded it, I heard myself say, 'Okay, whatever orders arrive first will decide the issue.'"

But in reality Coffin was already sold. His commitment to the front never had the strength he thought it did. "As I might have expected," Coffin wrote, "Guirey persuaded Shouvaloff [the commandant] on Monday to send a messenger in a jeep to hand-deliver the orders and to bring me back personally to Le Vésinet." Coffin gave a slightly different rendering to his mother, but the essentials remained. "My lot was cast a couple of weeks ago," he wrote in mid-May, "but as it wasn't definite I haven't mentioned it before. I was called back to the [sic] Intelligence for an interview on Guirey's instigation. It seems that there is a great need for Russian speaking personnel and the need was not anticipated in time—awful hard to anticipate such a thing you know." The passive voice ("My lot was cast," not "I cast my lot") and spirit dominated both accounts. Embarrassed at having avoided combat again, yet fascinated by the prospect of the high-level work he could do with Russians, he masked his ambition by disclaiming all responsibility for his choice.

Coffin had made his first important career decision without consulting his mother. During this period, starting just before his twenty-first birthday, Coffin made a number of these decisions; explanations always came later. "In many ways it seems all wrong to return to the same place I left five months ago with every intention of getting to [the] front as infantry," he continued. "I sure never got there though the amount of work we did training troops settles my conscience. But it wasn't a fighting job and I was all set for the Pacific. It wasn't guaranteed I'd get there though and work at the 16th was getting very difficult."

Backing and filling—"though," "but," and "though" again—Coffin had both to "settle his conscience" and to satisfy Catherine—no mean feat. Given "present circumstances and of course the long run," he concluded, "it seemed awful foolish not to seize the chance. In the post war world, knowledge of Russian will be invaluable." The contemporary version left out the elaborate deception; the singing, dancing, and drinking; the schemers' concealment of the fact that Coffin knew no Russian at all. A week later Coffin wrote briefly, noting that he was "learning Russian—damn good deal all Guirey's idea."[3]

In both versions Coffin allowed Guirey to pose and to resolve his dilemma. Why did he walk so slowly to his train that he missed it—by his own admission, something he had never done before? Neither version even mentioned what could easily have been uppermost in his mind: the appeal of returning to Paris, where seven years earlier he had plunged into the discipline of the piano and the emotional world of music. Unconsciously, perhaps, but shrewdly nonetheless, he had hesitated at just the right moment and "allowed" others to make this life-and-death decision. Strategic waiting, refusing to resolve a dilemma prematurely, turned out to be an excellent policy. The price, a guilty conscience, Coffin usually found bearable.

Coffin plunged himself into Russian. Even without an uneasy conscience, he needed exacting work that demanded full use of his mental or physical capacities. Music had filled this role in the past; boot camp and OCS had served in the States, as had the round-the-clock training regimen at Compiègne. Coffin attended three classes daily while cramming his reading, vocabulary study, and conversation with his tutor into the remaining hours. Even if Catherine disapproved, she had succeeded in building her son's personality far better than she realized.

On a Wednesday night in May a week into his new studies, less than two weeks shy of turning twenty-one, the young lieutenant talked his way into a performance at the Russian Theater in Paris. "Naturally I didn't understand much," he reported, but "a charming little wench gave a very spirited peasant dance with all the usual twirls and flourishes of arms and especially feet. I decided that was the stuff for me so tomorrow night I shall head for Paris and try and locate this girl and try and persuade her to give me a few lessons . . . obviously the only solution to learning to speak. Just someone to go and talk to, you know. . . . Will write you results Friday."[4]

The "results" were the stuff of romance. First Coffin tracked down the dancer's street in the Fifteenth Arrondissement. Then, Thursday evening he took the half-hour train in from Le Vésinet and began a house-by-house search down the longish rue des Cevennes.[5]

At least one night, probably two, he rode home empty-handed. But Saturday evening, on the verge of giving up, Coffin located his quarry. He asked the concièrge for Mademoiselle Piskounoff, and she answered, "Which one?" Nonplussed, he replied, "The one who does theater." The concièrge was not so easily won over, answering, "They both do." As it was already late, Coffin resolved to return the next day.

Sunday afternoon Manya Piskounoff was on her way to a party with a friend. But the telephone rang in the corridor, and the concièrge told Manya that an American was asking for her. Certain that he really wanted her sister Marfa, Manya tried to put Coffin off, but he raced up the stairs and "stopped right in front of me, and I was looking very annoyed, and he had a bouquet of flowers behind him. I said nothing. He began, 'Bonjour, I am—' I was just waiting for him to say it was my sister he wanted, then I'd say, 'enough, already.' He said 'no, no, not at all, you're mistaken, I saw you at the theater last week,' and he takes out the program." Impressed by Coffin's accent in the little Russian he knew, she and her friend decided to take him along to the party, where "he charmed everyone; . . . he sang, he was gay, people were very happy to see someone who already spoke real Russian. . . . And I thought it would end like that."

Coffin, too, was captivated, perhaps not least by his starring role. As he wrote Catherine, the piano "helped my status no end. . . . Soon everybody was singing, dancing, toasting, smoking, talking, and everything else all at once. I showed them the Virginia reel which as you can imagine they performed with great gusto. They seemed to think that I had a great talent for Russian dancing —and I did too, at the time."[6] Over the next few weeks Coffin threw himself into this whirl, drawn by music, by Manya's beauty and spirit, and by his own drive to learn Russian. His pursuit of Manya, like his studying, was systematic and practical. "He began to phone me at my office," Manya recalled, "saying, 'Look, the weekend,' . . . he thought one would be free for him, always . . . he came every weekend. And during the week . . . [h]e made very rapid progress."

While exploring what he began to call his "Russian soul," Coffin never forgot his studies. Once he covertly introduced Manya to one of his teachers "to see if I spoke well," she remembered. After a full day's work Coffin was ready for play, and his energies meshed perfectly with those of the émigré community. Marfa and Manya took Coffin "everywhere in the most natural way. I've met loads of Russians."

Twenty-four years old (three years older than Coffin), Manya Piskounoff worked as a secretary by day and an actress evenings and weekends. She was petite, at the very least pretty—considered beautiful by some—and shrewd in her choice of escorts.

The daughter of a well-known Cossack horseman who had fought the

Bolsheviks until his defeat and exile in the 1920s, Manya emigrated with her family when she was three and lost her mother soon after. Her father, Kuzma Pavlovich Piskounoff, had, along with his comrades, toured Europe and the United States during the twenties as stunt riders. Now they worked in factories in the grim Parisian suburbs (where most of the workers were French Communists) and nursed their memories with vodka.

The French Resistance had shaved Manya's head because, according to Coffin's friend George Bailey, "she was supposed to have been a collaborator with the Germans." Bailey easily forgave her wartime indiscretion: "And as an actress, of course she would come to the attention of German officers who went to the theater, and she gained the attention of the American officer who went to the theater." Coffin remembered that Manya was wearing a bandanna when he met her; "But I didn't press it. Who needs unpleasantries?"[7]

After the war, Soviet repatriation officers operated with near impunity in France. Manya had in fact first suspected Coffin of being a Communist French policeman in disguise, possibly come to investigate her practice of hiding refugees. In his memoir Coffin described a visit to Drancy when Soviet repatriation officials came to take a refugee away. "In the presence of an American officer in uniform," he wrote, "they were embarrassed to use force and finally left."[8]

It could only have helped Manya's reputation to be so closely identified with a vigorous, charming, and politically naive American officer. For his part, Coffin had discovered a great well of enchanting, dramatic emotional life. The first time he met Manya's father and his cronies, they prevailed on her to recite some Pushkin. As "tears rolled down the cheeks" of the old Cossacks, Coffin, "who couldn't understand a great deal, was deeply moved." Another time "I heard her reduce an entire class to sniffles in a 20 minute Dostoyevsky soliloquy," he wrote. "Even I, who of course missed most of it, sort of felt a lump. But then I just have a Russian soul. You know it's nice being strictly anglo saxon [*sic*] in all this. *It keeps you independent at the same time that you don't miss out on anything*" (emphasis added). Coffin's comment, at once inelegant and astute, displayed the inner reserve that kept him from fully embracing the sentimental and nostalgic, often drunken and occasionally violent, exile culture. He fell in love with Manya—though he never wrote that to his mother. Instead, he waxed on about "the latest, quickest, most enjoyable way of learning languages." He attempted to reassure Catherine that he and Manya were not lovers.[9]

Soon Coffin's three-month Russian course had finished and he went to work in the field, first to headquarters of the American XXII Corps in Pilsen, Czechoslovakia, where he assumed command of a small liaison team. His relationship with Manya changed as well. He visited her now and then, rarely for more than a weekend, and frequently without advance warning. She became a way station in his peripatetic life as he hunted for adventure on assignments all over Europe.

The half-dozen letters from Manya that survive from this period give a picture of a warm, heartfelt, intimate relationship. Writing in an educated, classical style that could express friendship as well as romantic love, she talked frequently of how much "we"—meaning she, her sister, and her father—missed Coffin and gave news of the family, the weather, and the plays she acted in. She referred often to the difficulties of communication, and the epistolary relationship was suffused with uncertainty and regret.

Manya herself was an irregular correspondent. "You're perhaps mad at us that we haven't written to you for so long," she wrote between Christmas and the New Year, 1946. She had received his "lovely letters," as well as his Christmas present: fur coats for her and Marfa. "You know that despite the fact that we did not write to you, we still love you. . . . Forgive me, my dear Vasya. Don't get mad at us." Still, they had been hoping to be "surprised" by him during the holidays, so Manya had put off writing until she knew he was not coming. Calmly, she informed him that she had turned twenty-five, an event he missed.[10]

By spring she found it more difficult to accept his distance. When Coffin eventually wrote, she appeared happy but concluded with a flash of anger: "Write to us. And, better yet, visit. Prove that you are capable of at least something." Fortunately, Coffin and his sergeant soon got permission for a longer leave, and they did visit Paris.[11]

In Pilsen Coffin's life bore little resemblance to that of most soldiers. As a translator and an operative, he helped solve problems that arose between the Russian and American armies. These ranged from releasing a trainload of coal held up at a Russian checkpoint to investigating a report that American citizens were being held in a German POW camp under Russian control in Czechoslovakia. Coffin learned what many Americans dealing with the Russians learned: that the Red Army put a premium on following orders, not individual initiative in the field. But he also learned more important lessons: that the heavy drinking of Soviet officers grew partly out of anxiety, even depression, over the prospect of returning "home"; that conscripted Soviet soldiers were willing to risk desertion and its stark penalties. Coffin received a fast education. The first captured deserter he returned to the Soviets "was taken by a drunken captain into a field to one side of the guard house and shot. Thereafter I dismissed the MPs and drove the deserter by myself into a forest where I would slow down until he understood that he was to jump out."[12]

Liaison work took place in an overwhelmingly male, heavy drinking environment filled with foolishness, tall tales, and chicanery. Ground-level negotiation with the Soviets—often called "vodka diplomacy"—required being able to hold one's liquor while thinking on one's feet; to fight or sing at a moment's notice; to make toasts, crack jokes, and improvise. Coffin loved it.

On his very first assignment his drunken Russian counterpart proposed a friendly fight—in the middle of the night—to pass the time until his superiors woke up. By the time Coffin returned from one negotiation involving "a few road block disputes," he had "dined on borscht and fruit, and wined on German cognac, and also got the business done. They were very genial hosts."[13]

This world put a premium on strength, daring, and a willingness to fight. Coffin had all three. It is worth wondering whether he would have felt the need to engage in such constant physical testing if had seen combat. For Coffin still nursed ideas of himself as a boxer. George Bailey, who met Coffin at the Liaison School, was appalled to find him challenging superior officers to arm-wrestling contests, and not caring that he beat them. When Coffin discovered that Bailey had boxed professionally, he could not resist challenging the bigger man, who reluctantly but decisively disabused Coffin of his pretensions. Coffin continued to carry a good deal of pride in his judo abilities, which he had used to advantage in that first nighttime "negotiation."[14]

Coffin liked the Soviet officers immensely, perhaps especially because they were political opponents and military allies and he could talk with them. But he also enjoyed their sentimentality and openness and their broad gestures, the very emotional expressiveness suppressed in his upbringing. Over the next few months he made friends with a number of Soviet officers, and even wrote his mother, "I hope one day to be looking their addresses up in Moscow, Kiev, Gorki and elsewhere."[15]

As American and Russian troops prepared to leave Czechoslovakia in November 1945, Coffin was trying to get a transfer to Vienna, though he must have begun to think more seriously about life after the army, for around this time Catherine responded to his inquiry regarding veterans' benefits. Europe offered rare pleasures, however, as Coffin made clear in his report on his escort of Andrei Vishinsky (Russia's chief prosecutor for the 1930s show trials and the Nuremberg trials) and his entourage through Czechoslovakia to Nuremberg. Characteristically, Coffin tried to insinuate himself with the fearsome Vishinsky, inquiring when "he thought he'd get around to hanging Goering. He grinned and said, 'Well, we'll have to take a look'—'to see how short you can make the rope,' I suggested, at which he laughed and peered at me through his bifocals." Still, the prosecutor thanked the cheeky young translator with two bottles of "real Russian cognac which ranges from 60–70% alcohol."[16]

Coffin's efforts to get transferred to Vienna went for naught. In late November he was assigned to the Third Army headquarters at Bad Tolz, a resort near Munich and the Bavarian Alps, as personal interpreter for General Lucian Truscott. Since there was virtually no work for him, and he never laid eyes on General Truscott, he used his time learning to ski.

Coffin's skiing lessons resembled nearly every project in his life: masculine, intense, challenging (in this case physically), laced with drinking and music, and offering material for boasting. In this case Coffin had happened on Sepp Kessler, a former Wehrmacht paratrooper and mountain guide and an escapee from a French POW camp, who offered to teach him to ski in exchange for food and drink. Stocking up from the local commissary, Coffin took two weeks of furlough over Christmas and New Year's Day and headed into the mountains. "What he managed to teach me in two weeks," Coffin crowed to his mother, "fooled even himself and certainly all the other Bavarians up for the holidays." They skied all day and talked politics, drank whiskey, played guitar, and taught each other songs at night. It was, Coffin wrote home, "a perfect two weeks." Coffin retold the story with relish in his memoir, emphasizing the contest— and the bond—between the expert "Kraut" fighting "the war all over again" as he drove the "Ami" (German slang for an American) unmercifully. Coffin's memories evoked a romantic glow: "Several times we returned to the hut by moon or star light. Warmed by the fire and the whisky, Sepp would reminisce bitterly about the war and the Nazis, whom he hated. Then reaching for his guitar he'd say, 'Ach, it's all over. Let's forget it. I'll teach you a song and you teach me one.'"[17]

This little story continued to have such resonance for Coffin because he experienced his emotional life more intensely with men than with women. He described those two weeks as "perfect," not as "perfect but for the lack of Manya." It was during those precise two weeks, his first Christmas after meeting Manya, that she and her family had hoped for a "surprise" visit from their dear Vasya. Although Coffin attracted women easily—his charm, vivacity, and looks were "catnip to the ladies," in Bailey's phrase—he was far more engaged by the world of men. Coffin concluded the chapter in his memoir about learning Russian by mentioning his visits to Drancy, "where instead of giving me his bone-crushing handshake, Kuzma Pavlovich came to embrace me as a son." Twenty-one years old, fatherless for a dozen years, Coffin responded viscerally to such "manly men."[18]

Work in Bad Tolz, on the other hand, reminded Coffin of Camp Ritchie and the least masculine side of the army. He complained about intellectuals and bureaucrats; by mid-December, he wrote his mother, he was again "stewing in the messed up juice of Military Intelligence." Proud of how he had trained hundreds of soldiers in Compiègne, Coffin complained that a certain captain's "handling of the enlisted men around here is disgraceful." He slid easily into a rant against paper pushers, "perfectly content to sit behind desks," who enjoy "their barricade against the difficult realistic world."[19]

In January, however, Coffin was transferred to Hof, Germany, very close to the borders of both Czechoslovakia and the Soviet Zone in Germany (soon to be East Germany). Contrary to his expectations, the "limited work consists almost entirely of repatriation." On the other hand, the liaison team was commanded by his friend George Bailey, who apparently spent most of his time reading. Life had an indolent, even luxurious rhythm. The Americans lived in sumptuous surroundings, waited on by German housekeepers who, in at least one case, provided sexual services as well.[20]

Even so, Coffin's performance came to the notice of superiors. He received a commendation letter after less than a month in Hof, from a lieutenant colonel Joseph Dasher, who had observed him in Pilsen in November and then again in Hof in January. "On both occasions," Dasher wrote, Coffin "demonstrated a high degree of efficiency, devotion to duty, and an absorbing interest in his duties," as well as "courtesy, spirit of cooperation, and initiative." The young lieutenant "appears to possess exceptional qualities of leadership and commands the respect and admiration of his subordinates."[21]

Within weeks, Coffin's life changed, and he was plunged into an intense month-long project in the "difficult realistic world"—the emotional and political maelstrom of forcible repatriation.

Plattling

When the massive upheavals of World War II subsided, as many as 30 million people had been displaced from their native countries. Of these, more than 5 million were Soviet citizens, by far the largest group from a single country. A Soviet-American repatriation agreement, signed in February 1945 at the Yalta Conference, committed the United States to repatriate—to return to the Soviet Union, forcibly if necessary—all Soviet citizens held in Allied-controlled territory.

To the USSR's great embarrassment, perhaps a million Soviet soldiers had fought for Germany in varying capacities during the war. While the Soviet Union wanted all of its citizens back, the Kremlin showed special interest in the tens of thousands captured in German uniform. Whatever their reasons for being behind German lines—and there were many, ranging from German capture to outright desertion—few of these wanted to return to the Soviet Union for fear of being branded "traitors" or "deserters" by their government, which insisted that there were no Soviet prisoners of war, only turncoats.

The best known of these prisoners were followers of the infamous General Andrei Andreevich Vlasov. Vlasov, a Soviet military hero decorated for his role in defending Moscow in 1941, had been captured by the Germans in July 1942, along with nine divisions and seven brigades. The Germans used him as an anti-Soviet, collaborationist figurehead without giving him much of a military role. In fact, at the end of the war Vlasov's Russian Liberation Army helped liberate Prague from the Nazis and then surrendered to the Americans.

After the war, the Soviet Union mounted an intense campaign for the return of its citizens, and with (at first) little reluctance, the United States cooperated. In the five months between May and September 1945, Supreme Headquarters, Allied Expeditionary Forces (SHAEF), conveyed roughly 2 million Soviet displaced persons (DPs) to their homeland—including, in mid-May, the great majority of Vlasov's army, some thirty-three thousand men in Czechoslovakia, Bavaria, and Austria, including the general himself.[22]

Smaller groups proved more difficult, and a series of painful and violent incidents over the next year tested the resolve and the consciences of American soldiers, officers, and policymakers. For there were still thousands of Soviet POWs, mostly but not all Vlasovites, who had been captured in German uniform, now scattered all over the European theater, and even in the United States.[23]

Signing the Yalta repatriation agreement had not stopped internal American disagreement over implementing it. As a result, the fate of a group of Russian POWs held on American soil swung back and forth during 1945. By mid-June, after having been transferred from Europe to camps throughout the United States, 154 POWs finally ended up in Fort Dix, New Jersey. There they waited, tense and anxious, while the U.S. government debated the issue and then resolved to repatriate them.

On the morning of June 29, the prisoners saw that they were being transferred and—accurately fearing the worst—rioted. When hysterical captives failed to provoke their captors into shooting them, they shut themselves in their barracks and tried to torch the building. After heavy use of tear gas brought an end to the uprising, American soldiers found three nooses holding dead men by their necks, apparent suicides. Their rebellion led to a War Department investigation, more transfers, an apparent last-minute reprieve, and rescreenings, which pulled several out of the group. Just over two months later, as Coffin was finishing his three months at the Russian Liaison School, U.S. officials handed over the remaining 146 Vlasovites to Soviet repatriation officials in Hof, Germany. After several months of renewed internal debate, U.S. officials issued a modification of American policy: while Soviet civilians would no longer be forcibly repatriated, military collaborators and ex-POWs could be sent back against their will.[24]

While the new policy may have eased the consciences of American officials, the great majority of Soviet civilian nationals had already been returned. Most of the remaining Soviet DPs were prisoners of war, as had been the unfortunates at Fort Dix and most of the others at Camp Kempten. Sorting among them remained an extremely difficult task and would eventually require the use of force.

Less than a month after the new ruling took effect, American soldiers again found themselves in the midst of translating an apparently reasonable policy into a lethal reality. In January 1946 American and Polish guards holding nearly four hundred Soviet collaborators at Dachau tried to put them on a train for the Soviet Zone. POWs barricaded themselves inside one of their barracks, tried unsuccessfully to burn the building, and then set about killing themselves. When authorities eventually retook the building, the "scene inside was one of human carnage," according to historian Mark Elliott. "Guards cut down some trying to hang themselves from the rafters; two others disemboweled themselves; another man forced his head through a window and ran his throat over the glass fragments; others begged to be shot." Thirty-one had tried to commit suicide, and eleven had succeeded. Most were loaded onto trains and sent to the Soviet Zone. When the wounded could travel, Americans took them to a camp in Plattling, Bavaria, where the Americans were assembling the remaining Vlasovites.[25]

On February 5, 1946, Coffin arrived at the Plattling DP camp, chief army interpreter (assisted by his friend Sergeant Alexander Rusanowsky, also from Hof) for a team of screening officers—three boards of three full colonels each —charged with determining which of 3,300 Soviet POWs who had been captured in German uniform were going to be repatriated to the Soviet Union. Coffin and Rusanowsky thought that the true purpose of the operation was a genuine secret outside of the American personnel, whose cover story was that they were only "gathering information about the men's reasons for leaving the Soviet Union." But the inmates must have heard the stories of the Dachau survivors.[26]

Coffin's excitement at being on the inside mingled with pride in his new expertise. "I've just been brought into the most interesting and certainly the most important work I've ever had in the Army," he wrote home. "Unfortunately I can't say much about it but it consists of really throwing an international ball around and my job is to advise colonels and generals." When it was all over, he predicted, "I'll probably have more fascinating dope than I've had in a long time. Are you mystified? Well it's really good." This was heady stuff for a first lieutenant. A week later he remained absorbed by his "big job," looking forward to the time when he would be "very much the wiser for this little business."

The next week Coffin allowed that the "business" had its "rather unpleasant aspects. The world is certainly made up of individuals and peoples and of the two groups the individuals certainly get it in the neck." Fortunately, what he had learned was so "fascinating" that it made up for the downside.

Coffin and Rusanowsky apparently began to have misgivings. "I felt we were doing what was agreed to by Roosevelt, Stalin, and Churchill at Yalta," Rusanowsky recalled, even though he and Coffin both felt "strange" about it. Still, they went along: "of course loyalty to our mission and job and the U.S. Army and at that time, you have to remember, he [Coffin] was a charging first lieutenant in the infantry." The night before the transfer, he remembered, was filled with poignancy: "I was upset and we didn't have too much to say about it." The camp inmates had organized a variety show—singing, dancing, poetry, skits—in honor of the nine colonels, all of whom had chosen to stay in their hotel drinking away their guilt. They sent Coffin and Rusanowsky in their place.

The next morning, February 24, as Coffin wrote home ten days later, the "actual repatriation [was] carried out by a 'dawn attack' in terrific force—a most unusual operation—incidentally extremely successful. 1500 out of 3300 were sent back." According to Rusanowsky, "it was a swoop, six o'clock in the morning, some of them still in their underwear in bed, and going to bathrooms."

Accounts of this operation differ markedly. Elliott claims that, as at Fort Dix and Dachau, barricades were erected, men "hung themselves and were cut down . . . heads smashed windows and necks voluntarily met glass fragments still fixed in their frames. . . . It was a wonder only five died." Coffin wrote in his memoir that he "saw several men commit suicide. Two rammed their heads through windows sawing their necks on the broken glass until they cut their jugular veins. Another took his leather bootstraps, tied a loop to the top of his triple-decker bunk, put his head through the noose and did a backflip over the edge which broke his neck."[27]

The record, however, does not fully support this grisly account. Elliott relied on Coffin and others whose sources are not clear. Coffin's published version —thirty years later—conflicted with his contemporary report in a number of particulars. His lengthy recap to his mother, for example, mentioned the danger of suicides, while observing, "It was something a little short of a miracle when only two managed to hospitalize themselves. But then, you've never seen such precautions as were taken." Prisoners did hurt themselves, and some would have committed suicide had they been able. An Army Signal Corps film of the operation showed a prisoner baring his torso to expose the presumably self-inflicted cuts across his chest and belly.

Coffin's storytelling technique, which frequently relied on absorbing other people's ideas, stories, lines, and sometimes even their experiences, appears in this case to have incorporated details from the repatriation at Dachau. ("You may have read of the attempted and partially successful mass suicides carried out by some of these characters in an earlier repatriation movement," he wrote home.) An extant photograph of a noose attached to a top bunk in a Dachau barrack may have made its way into Coffin's memory. Rusanowsky recalled that Coffin did witness a suicide attempt but that no one died.

A little over a week afterwards, Coffin described and defended the operation—which he called "far too interesting and important not to do it well" —at some length to his mother. "The only hitch was" that these "poor guys," many of whom were "terrifically smart," also had "the flaw of the fanatic in their reasoning." Coffin liked many of them but felt they had been "compromised by their ties with the Germans—far more than the NKVD [Soviet secret police] compromised Stalin's constitution." He then mused on the "potential menace of these Russians, Poles, Yugoslavs, Balts and others who refuse to go home. They are going to be a terrible nuisance, poor people." Coffin was writing in full emotional retreat from what he had just witnessed. Even if he had seen no suicides, no desperate men pleading for an early end to their lives, he knew that he had helped send men to prison and worse.

Two months later he expressed occasional pointed sarcasm about the episode, as when he wrote to his mother about "these super army jobs which by now are quite repulsive (lying your head off so you can ship people back to Russia without giving them a chance to slit their throats)." Rusanowsky explained Coffin's shallow analysis of the Plattling operation as "trying to justify that we were doing the right thing."[28]

Coffin's superiors, on the other hand, put him up for the Army Commendation Ribbon. According to the official recommendation, Coffin displayed "tact and keen intelligence in a delicate situation" and was able "to thoroughly instruct the necessary personnel in all phases of the confused background" of the POWs at Plattling. Apparently, Coffin supervised the "anti-communist displaced person interpreters" as well, doing "a superb job in preventing them from influencing the judgment proceedings adversely to the USSR." No wonder Coffin and Rusanowsky felt uneasy about the medals. "Lt. Coffin," Colonel Edward Fickett concluded, "was in large measure responsible for the good relations which prevailed between Red Army and US Army personnel throughout the entire repatriation proceedings."[29]

Like so many young men faced with wartime ironies, Coffin did his best to ignore them. In early March he wrote home telling the funny story of a Russian lieutenant colonel who, staying overnight in Coffin's quarters, managed to pull "a fast one" and bed down with his secretary, a fact announced by the "rather violent shaking of the house" at about 1:00 A.M. Then he mentioned fifty-five Russians who "dropped in" and with whom he "spent a good evening" singing Russian songs. "Tomorrow," he noted blithely, "we'll hand them over. It takes about a month from here to Moscow by normal repatriation channels." Coffin did not appear to be stewing over the fates of repatriated POWs. He had responded to his first experience of life-and-death moral complexity with bravado, self-justification, pragmatism, and sarcasm.

Thirty years later, excerpting his memoir in a cover story for the liberal magazine *Christianity and Crisis* under the title "Learning about Loyalty from Stalin and Hitler," Coffin assigned the Plattling incident a crucial role in his moral development. There, he focused on his failure to warn the camp inmates of their approaching fate and his own moral equivocation in the face of evil orders. It produced a memory "so painful that it's almost impossible for me to write about."[30]

Although he had begun the operation skeptical of any Russian who could have fought for Hitler, as Coffin heard story after story of life under Stalin— "not only of the cruelties of collectivization in the thirties, but of the arrests, shootings, and wholesale deportations of families"—his judgment softened. For these Russians, after all, where lay the profound moral distinction between Hitler and Stalin? As his qualms grew, he "tried to talk to some of the American colonels," he wrote, "who I could see were finding the operation more and more distasteful. But . . . they had their orders and they were going to obey them."

Coffin grew furious with himself for his part in the charade. He recalled spending the entire evening of the variety show in tight-lipped agony: "I too had my orders. It was one thing to let individual deserters escape in the woods. It was something else again to blow a Top Secret operation ordered by Washington itself with the Soviet government ready to make a terrible row if it failed."

On the day of the operation he noticed two Soviet soldiers "looting the men's belongings. Beside myself with frustration, I jumped in and knocked them both out. But it was a futile, stupid act." Having failed the moral and political test, and frustrated by an extremely complex situation over which one individual could have had very little influence, Coffin intervened in the only way he knew how—physically.

The affair left him "a burden of guilt I am sure to carry the rest of my life." But he had also drawn important lessons from the experience, writing that "it made it easier for me in 1967 to commit civil disobedience in opposition to the war in Vietnam. The forced repatriation of those two thousand Russians showed me that in matters of life and death the responsibility of those who take orders is as great as those who give them. And finally what I did, or rather didn't do, at Plattling has made me sympathize with the Americans I consider war criminals in the Vietnam conflict. Some of them at least must now be experiencing the same bad moments I have had so often thinking of the lives I might have saved."

That his twenty-one-year-old self was less profoundly pained than the older man underscored his moral growth in the meantime. When it came time to write about his role at Plattling, Coffin shaped the incident—and a good many details—into the moral tale it had become for him, acknowledging his complicity with evil and his inability to disobey unjust orders. Clearly, the "burden of guilt" had become heavier with time.

He had been a young man in over his head, at first excited by a secret, top-level operation, then toughing out a morally difficult assignment. Later, both Rusanowsky and Coffin regretted their roles and felt they ought to have blown the whistle to their charges. But in Rusanowsky's words, "as distasteful as it was, we just did our job. And, back then—my wife is reminding me—back then I didn't question it. Of course I didn't."[31]

Coffin could not fully escape the dilemmas of his life. For there was still Manya, who would have been horrified to learn of his role repatriating anti-Soviet Russians. Coffin wrote her nothing about Plattling. Her early April letter appears more poignant in retrospect. She had just heard from Coffin "and was very glad to know that you're okay, that you're alive and healthy and even happy despite lots of work. You like your work. . . . I didn't write because I was waiting for the response to my last letter to you. But because you didn't reply for so long, I thought that you perhaps went home to America."[32]

The Family Claim

With little to do in Hof, Coffin returned to studying Russian and skiing whenever he could. His life seems to have consisted of a combination of hijinks (romantic and otherwise) and occasional liaison and repatriation work. Once he ended up "playing father or probably mother I'm not quite sure which" to a young American corporal whom he was trying to separate from his pregnant German girlfriend—that is, if she would not have an abortion.[33]

Without a grand project, however, Coffin had started thinking about returning home, to Catherine and to Yale to resume academic studies. Ecstatic at the prospect, his mother investigated possibilities in the Russian department. Coffin stoked her enthusiasm, which only intensified with Ned's return in late April: "If I don't get out this summer I'll never forgive myself. . . . À bientôt j'éspère." In mid-May, still giddy with the prospect of having both her boys safely home from the war, Catherine sent birthday greetings. But Bill's letter crossed hers, carrying a cruel disappointment, perhaps even more painful for its casual tone: "Concerning yours truly the Army pulled a fast one. Any officer employed in a linguistic capacity will not be released until he has 42 months of service—recent memorandum. That's that—six more months . . . no use crying about it."[34]

Coffin was hunting for a Russian tutor "who, for good food and a little pay will be willing to work with me day and night for 6 months." Catherine had bowed to the "fast one" but had already been having misgivings about her son's immersion in things Russian, so when he announced that he had turned down an offer to be General Mark Clark's French interpreter for the Allied Council meetings in Vienna—"an interesting experience and 'contacts'"—in favor of an "unusual opportunity for real study," she attacked. Coffin must have expected something of the sort. "I was in a quandary," he admitted, "but I just so wanted to study again and . . . the results of it seemed to almost balance the experience and 'contacts' that I turned the offer down. . . . I hope you agree—but I don't blame you if you don't."[35]

She did not. In a long, closely reasoned letter she sympathized with his "urge to settle down and work" but argued, "One doesn't throw over jobs just to indulge an urge, even a commendable one." So, she reasoned on, he must have "something definite" in mind after Yale. Worried that he was after an "OSS job in which you might wish to act inside of Russia," she pled for him to "reconsider" a career that would be so "unsatisfactory" and inevitably "short term." Then she got to the heart of the matter: "Frankly," she confessed, "I fear that expansive sentimental strain in your nature which your friends may applaud as 'the Russian soul.' . . . One needs the self discipline and the analytical sense which comes with hard, critical work." Catherine Coffin was battling for her life's work.

Her son fought back, though he felt obliged to mollify his closest friend and severest critic. He wanted to become expert in things Russian, a "wide open" field "which would probably best exploit whatever fortunately inherited gifts I have." He had no interest in the OSS, but "the story and question of Russia, Russians, and how and why they do as they do, has gotten a very firm hold on me—this includes the language, which, for me anyhow, is a beautiful and fascinating one."

He admitted that the translating job would improve his French and be good for his résumé, but "where would my Russian be?" Similarly, "As for 'connections' (horrible word isn't it)," he admitted, "there's no diminishing their importance," but he thought he was already good at making "connections" when necessary.[36]

At twenty-two Coffin was having his first real disagreement with his mother.

He knew what she wanted for him and sensed, if dimly, that it resembled the path she and his father had taken thirty years earlier. Catherine, who had married into her husband's privileged world, who had lost that husband and an immense fortune, held onto her connections gracefully, but tenaciously. Bill, who knew nothing about looking after money or a family, but who carried his father's name and inherited the confidence of the youthful rich, had no sense of the fragility of fortunes.

The very fact that Bill could feel so secure about the future offered tribute to Catherine's recovery from that disastrous day in December 1933. Her success (in managing her family, her money, her connections) had given her son the economic and psychological freedom to choose a different path: one less rational, more sentimental and "expansive" (certainly boozier)—and his own. The interpreter's job was a position in which he would speak only another man's words; it was worth taking only for the connections. So of course he turned it down. William Sloane Coffin Jr. wanted to make a name for himself, and so he considered a field that no one in his family knew anything about. His choice led to a greater emotional separation from Catherine than the war had.

Coffin gained confidence in his new manhood. He may also have been trying to shock his mother with his tales of ribaldry and roughhousing, drinking, and masculine camaraderie. But Catherine was not so easily put off. In the two letters per week that have survived, she freely offered advice on matters about which she knew little. She cautioned him to be careful of arguing too forcefully with his Russian counterparts, who might put "black marks" in their dossier on him, which would "in turn make your appointment to any Russian job 'unacceptable' to the USSR gov't in the future."[37]

Despite Catherine's worries, Coffin had begun to think about his future role through his study of Russian history and literature under his tutor. He did not like Tolstoy's disturbing insistence on the power of impersonal laws and the force of the "hive." Coffin worried that "if in the world today, one or a few individuals couldn't change the course of events when it's obvious the people as a whole can't, then we are certainly in a very bad way." He preferred Dostoyevsky, where individuals did significant battle. Whichever career path Coffin chose, and he was leaning toward diplomacy, it would have to emphasize the abilities, talents, and impact of the individual rather than the group.[38]

Still expecting Bill for the 1947 spring term at Yale, she forced the issue in October: "When do you foresee prospects of return to these U.S.? Certain plans still unformulated for disposal of rooms here, need your reply soon." Coffin put off a decision, counseled patience, and offered his own, well-tested observation that "most good things seem to have to wait."[39]

Catherine had talked to professors, to the admissions office, and to her friends and was taken aback: "I had thought of the present 'hitch' (if that is the army term) as a necessary evil to be foreclosed as soon as possible." He could finish a degree in perhaps three years, she reported. Russian appeared to be in demand, but she could not predict what would be happening in the State Department some years hence. Bill's course of study "should be advantageous in competition for jobs," she allowed, "although I imagine that experience and the right sponsor's endorsement would be more valuable. As the cynics or realists put it, 'Not what you know, but who you know.'"

Along the same lines, he ought to be attentive to the secret societies at Yale, which, despite the derision of outsiders, and the occasional "loathsome" focus on them as a personal goal, offered "the chances to be of service, as well as to form the deepest of attachments." With her late husband's Bonesmen in mind, she reminded his namesake that "by his ties with all kinds of men in all kinds of places, Dad was in a position to accomplish things in the line of public service that he might never have done otherwise."[40]

Her son had been strategizing more than he admitted, however, and re-upped until June 1947. He blamed the mails and the army, again displaying a disingenuous passivity. At once apologetic and blustery, he initiated one of the more important conversations of his life. When the army "forced the issue" by "demanding an immediate answer," he had "tried to stall," but unsuccessfully: "Naturally I feel badly at having put the whole matter off for so long though I never expected the cards to be forced so early." He tried to reassure her that the "next six months will certainly not be wasted."[41]

Catherine's response indicates what Coffin was up against as he sought to differentiate himself from his formidable mother. She knew that he had procrastinated in order to avoid her upset and her criticism, but her love was "always equal to disappointments." She was not going to let him off the hook, however: "The truth is that you are oversensitive both in receiving criticism and in inflicting hurt. 'Life is not designed to administer to man's comfort,' as Stevenson once remarked."

Still, he had, in his own way, succeeded. By the end of the letter she granted that "in this case you have every right to your own decision." But she could not escape her conflicting emotions as she struggled to let him grow up. She wielded powerful emotional weapons, including what Jane Addams half a century earlier had called "the family claim": "I suggest that you write *at once* to Uncle Henry, giving him your reasons—briefly and without apologies—for the decision. He would appreciate that confidence even if he disagrees with the reasoning."[42]

Coffin was also charting a way out of his family's genteel Republicanism. They first got embroiled in an argument about American Communism, the significance of which lay only in Bill's assertion of political independence. Then, when Catherine complained about labor leaders, he wondered whether "management could only assume a more positive role" in labor disputes: "It's only that people in Europe are not agreed with many American Republicans (including you I believe) that these individual freedoms can exist only in a capitalistic state."[43]

Reflecting much later on this dispute, Coffin had no doubts about the wisdom of his choice. Learning Russian was "a damn good thing for a guy who thought he might be a diplomat. What the hell, you know? To have two languages you speak fluently, French and Russian, and then after a while German? I was twenty-two years old, hadn't been to college yet—I was doing just fine. I was right to stay there."[44]

He was also having a very good time. He and his merry band of interpreters enjoyed an unusual, barely regimented life with much room for jollity, sexual adventures, and drinking bouts, all the while feeling connected to great world events and the authentic lives of desperate people. At least three times in 1946—in June and October and November—still based in Hof, Coffin visited Manya in Paris. He and Rusanowsky sneaked George Bailey in and out of Czechoslovakia at Christmas time. For a week Coffin accompanied a group of Russians, who sorted through artifacts Germans had stolen "by day" and engaged in "considerable festivity by night." All the while he kept studying with his tutor, a Lithuanian refugee from a local DP camp whom Coffin intended sponsoring for emigration to the United States.[45]

But time was running out on Coffin's European life. A few months after his "victory" with Catherine, he yielded to the family pressure regarding Yale, including that of his older brother, by now returned from the navy. He wrote in mid-December that he had cabled and written the dean of admissions (as suggested by Catherine). Catherine soon wrote that she had received a copy of his letter of admission. He was on his way home.[46]

In his memoir Coffin wrote at length about Manya Piskounoff, especially about his decision to leave Europe without her. He theorized that Manya and matters Russian represented the "more romantic, passionate part of myself which I have always had trouble integrating into an Anglo-Saxon nature and duty-oriented upbringing." He also "just couldn't picture" his mother with Manya.[47]

Manya's letters suggested a relationship of some intensity. He had become a great friend to the entire family and she missed him terribly, even before he had plans to return to the States. "Yesterday you left," she wrote Coffin soon after he had re-upped for six months, and "it was so hard in my soul that I cried for half of the day." Coffin had given her some money, which both touched and unnerved her. She told him not to forget a story in which a man gave a woman a hundred rubles "because he did not have intentions to see her again and was leaving forever. I, however, hope that you want to see me again." But, she also fretted, perhaps "it would be better if you do not come and be with us ever again. We are very attached to you, Vasya. And then when you leave forever, it will be very hard. What do you think?"

However painful the knowledge, they both knew Coffin was eventually going back to the States and that Coffin was not making a commitment to her. Because he knew this reality was harder on her, he apparently tried to prepare her for the inevitable. Two weeks later she heard from him that he had arrived safely at Hof, and wrote immediately. Admitting that she had been "a little bit sentimental" in her last letter, she resolved that "following your advice, I will think of you less and less. Remember, you told me that it's not good to be dependent."[48]

Coffin had been hearing marriage talk at home, and it made him uneasy. Before visiting Manya in June, he wondered why "everybody harps on matrimony all the time? Every letter I receive baldly expounds it or subtly plays coy with it. There's no time like the future in this respect." A few months later he boasted that despite his time in the army he had "no charming wife and hasn't been accused of any offspring." And right around the same time George Bailey reported on his visit to the States, announcing that he had "become an enthusiastic devotee of your mother—an extraordinary woman" and further opining, presciently, that Coffin "should—as Shaw says—have a helluva time wifing yourself with one who can match the standard she has set." But Coffin had no intentions at all in this area.[49]

In October 1946, with a week-long pass to Paris, he painted the town with Manya, Marfa, and Kuzma Pavlovich and the crowd around the Russian Theater. He also visited his old piano teacher, Février, and family friends. At the end of November Coffin took Rusanowsky with him to Paris again where, in a few intense days, he accomplished "what normally should take a[t] least a month." He again saw old Parisian friends, as well as his new Russian ones, and even made "contacts," as he was careful to tell his mother.[50]

Although neither Bill nor Manya knew it, this was their last time together before his departure. While Manya pined for him at the holidays, he and Rusanowsky entertained Bailey at Hof. In late January 1947 she was still "counting days" that remained until his next visit, "I'm hoping not the last one." But if

Coffin had planned a final visit, he never made it. His last letter from Europe, a few months shy of his twenty-fifth birthday, revealed much about who he had become. He had gone to say good-bye to Kessler, but

> fell once again completely under the spell of the mountains—result instead of going to Paris I spent the last 10 days skiing in the Bavarian Alps.
>
> It was a rough decision but after seven months of no exercise and heavy studying the mountains proved too tempting. . . . I did some marvelous skiing, saw many old friends from last year and met a lot of new ones, at night played the guitar, gazed at the boundless range of mountains under the starlight and got completely reoriented again. It's an indescribable feeling. . . .
>
> Going home is terrifically exciting, even more so than I expected. The only sad part is leaving all these people who have really showed me so much: the little dignified Russian Jewish professor who spent 3 years at Dachau while his family was bayoneted by the SS while trying to hide in holes in the woods; the 40 year old Latvian girl who lost all her family during the Russian revolution, everything she ever owned 8 times during bombardments in Berlin, had a chance to go to America but wouldn't leave her old uncle; the Russian engineer and his oculist wife who was banned from the university because her instruction (purely medical) wasn't in keeping with Marxist principles—just to mention a few of the more interesting. Knowing these people so clearly indicates our obligations.[51]

Coffin preferred emotional intensity with groups, with nature, or in performance, both athletic and musical. His appreciation for moral depth came through anonymous people he knew through his work. Through them he had experienced the great issues of the day and began to feel large-scale obligations. Manya and her community had vanished in this report, except as a "rough decision." In his memoir he recalled writing to her and feeling "disgusted and tormented by my indecision." Manya remembered no such letter.[52]

She wrote him in mid-May—at the Coffin house on St. Ronan Street in New Haven—and tried to put the best face on the situation. She alternated talk of friends and newsy chat about plays, concerts, family, the cat, and the weather, with stark notes of abandonment. She thanked him for a package, but also asked, "Why is it so fast that you have forgotten your friends?" "I don't want to believe that you have forgotten me," she hoped. "I am waiting for your immediate letter. Otherwise I will cross you out of my memory forever and off the list of my friends." Coffin had written that "the love affair is maybe over . . . but the friendship is continuing." Less convinced, she was "waiting for the proof, that is, for your letter." Fifty years later, Manya objected to describing Coffin as having fallen in love (tombé amoreux) with her. He had, she offered, "des sentiments de beaucoup d'amitié, plus tendre qu'une simple amitié, voilà" (feelings of great friendship, more tender than simple friendship).[53]

But Coffin loved Manya in the only way that he could: in the moment, in her presence, with drama and action. Bailey thought, accurately, that he "wasn't ready to give as much of himself as he would have to have done." He knew she wanted more, but a long-term relationship—marriage—faced powerful obstacles. He displayed no genuine indecision. First, like most army officers in their early twenties, Coffin was enjoying his independence and had no desire to get married. Next, Manya herself would have faced a real dilemma regarding her father and sister, whom she adored and for whom she felt responsible. Third, Coffin had the feeling that he was cut out for big things. "He regarded it as his heritage, his legacy, to make a career," Bailey recalled, "a very considerable career." A Russian émigré actress and dancer—who had been accused of collaboration—could hardly have helped that career.[54]

The final obstacle was Catherine Coffin, who represented not only the United States, Yale, and the Coffin family heritage, but also the most powerful female presence in Coffin's life. Although Coffin could not see it at the time, Catherine remained the unconscious standard by which all other women would be judged—and found wanting. For despite the ribaldry and romantic conspiracy, his relationship with Catherine was intense, idealized, and chaste. In what could have been a bloody emotional battle, she did not even need to write a letter. The war over, her favorite child was coming home safely. It may have been Catherine's greatest victory.

The Education of a Warrior-Priest

The Halls of Academe

By the time he returned to his mother and to Yale, Coffin had spent nearly four years in uniform. He had lost his virginity and fallen in love. In the service of his country he had trained thousands of soldiers for combat while never facing enemy fire, and had risen from private to first lieutenant. He had learned to speak Russian fluently enough to translate for generals. He had followed orders to deceive thousands of Russian refugees before helping to send fifteen hundred to prison or death in the Soviet Union, and for that he had received the Army Commendation Ribbon and a promotion. He had learned to conduct "vodka diplomacy" with Russians, chew over the war with Germans, negotiate with prostitutes, ski the Alps, and navigate Europe on a motorcycle. Coffin had become physically powerful and supremely self-confident, even overconfident. He had given up serious study of the piano, while continuing to play to charm or move audiences. He had carved out a measure of independence from his formidable mother, all the while fulfilling her deepest wishes. He had forsaken a love affair and returned to the United States to take up what his family, friends, and colleagues assumed would be a brilliant career.

This new life began, as it had for the men in his family since before the Civil War, at Yale. But for Coffin, like other World War II veterans, college had a different flavor than it possessed for previous generations. Uninterested in an extended adolescence or country club experience, veterans tended to be more instrumental about their education, more in a hurry to get on with their lives. Coffin bypassed the admissions office and applied for advanced standing directly to the college dean. Between the influence of his mother's friend, Professor of French Henri Peyre, the fact that Uncle Henry sat on the Yale Corporation, and Coffin's Russian studies, he went to summer school and entered as a junior in the fall of 1947.

He lived in his mother's house and concentrated mostly on schoolwork. Outside the classroom he headed the Yale chapter of the liberal American Veterans Committee and sang in the Yale Glee Club (serving as president his senior year). Following his grandfather, father, and uncle he received the coveted call from Skull and Bones in the spring of 1948. He also sang in the choir at Yale's Battell Chapel, for which he received a small stipend.

As preparation for a diplomatic career, Coffin majored in political science, taking courses in economics, comparative government, political theory, classical civilization, collective bargaining, and Russian history. His papers and exams, which usually earned grades in the eighties and nineties, demonstrated both a fluent style and a mature grasp of course material.

Coffin used a study technique that he had developed in the army: a well-organized, double-column style of note-taking that enabled him to distinguish large points from supporting evidence, and in which he recorded numerous quotations. His exceptional aural memory allowed him to compile a repertoire of hundreds of quotations.

Less practically, but more passionately, Coffin also began to grapple with his wartime experiences. He had seen "too much evil" for his "boyhood idealism," he wrote later, and needed stronger fare. So while dutifully pursuing his major, he also dove into French literature and American Protestant theology. He read the atheist existentialists Albert Camus, Jean-Paul Sartre, and André Malraux, along with the theologians Reinhold and H. Richard Niebuhr and Paul Tillich. Convinced that Sartre and Camus, particularly, "were asking all the right questions," Coffin could not shake the sense that "these atheists were a little romantic in their stoicism: 'We suffer more than others because we don't have the comfort of a loving God.'" By contrast, the theologians "seemed to be in touch with a deeper reality . . . a heaven which made more sense out of everything." Or, as he put it later, "My head was with the atheists; my heart was with the religious people."[1]

In a series of papers for the agnostic Peyre, Coffin pushed himself to develop his ideas. Exploring love, morality, and faith, he wrote about Marcel Proust, Malraux, Jean Giraudoux, Paul Claudel, Henrik Ibsen, and André Gide (among others). He vigorously engaged religious topics for the first time, arguing in one paper that "religion appeals to all the faculties of man: his intelligence, his will, his courage, and his sensibility for struggle against the low demands—if I may say so—of the less elevated side of our nature." He defended Claudel's religious stance against that of the agnostic (or atheist) existentialists. "One could argue that it is possible to have moral conflicts divorced from all religious thought," he allowed, but "a moral conflict that at the same time has a religious character produces a psychological effect much greater to the extent that it excites the more spiritual and therefore stronger emotions." Coffin may have been struggling to make sense of the Plattling events, or of the Holocaust, for even if his family background had prepared him for religious sentiments in a general way, he had never spent much energy on them before. Now, however, he "kept thinking more and more that the religious people have got something which I would love to find, but I hadn't found it."[2]

He sang in the choir at Battell on Sundays for "five dollars a week or some fine sum" and paid attention to the preachers and the prayers, and "every now and then I'd just be suddenly taken with what was said and then I'd forget about everything else."[3] For instance, he remembered an "Episcopal colloquy, so called, that says 'Almighty God unto whom all hearts are opened, all desires known, and from whom no secrets are hid, cleanse the thoughts of our hearts by the inspiration of thy holy spirit, that we may perfectly love thee and worthily magnify thy holy name' . . . [and] I suddenly thought, 'Holy smoke, no wonder people don't believe in God.' And I remembered Nietzsche said, 'God had to die, he sees too much or knows too much.' Why would one ever want to believe in a God who knew you that well? And then the next line, 'cleanse the thoughts of our hearts,' and I thought, 'No, it should be cleanse the thoughts of our *minds,* so why does the prayer say "cleanse the thoughts of our hearts"?' And then I'd just meditate, going from the heart to the mind. . . . If your heart's like a stone, you're not going to have decent thoughts, but if your heart's full of love, that'll have a kind of limbering effect on the mind. Things like that."

The "great religious music"—"all those big religious oratorios and requiems" —also influenced him. "So unconsciously," he recalled, "I was being prepared."

He still did not cleave to other Christians, particularly the campus fundamentalists, who "sensed that I was fair game" and pursued him. Their answers to his questions, however, "were much too easy," and he felt they barely concealed their hostility toward the unredeemed under a veneer of "sweetness."

Coffin's spiritual quest received a powerful boost during his senior year in the midst of a funeral for a friend who had died in an automobile accident. "I was really sad and angry, too. It should never have happened," Coffin recalled. At the service, Coffin sat at the end of a pew in the cold stone chapel, "And suddenly I hear from the back of the church this man . . . intoning pompously the great words of Job: 'The Lord gave and the Lord hath taken away' . . . and hearing those words being spoken in that voice just set me off. . . . Who the hell is this?" The Episcopal priest strode down the aisle, reading from the prayer book, and Coffin suddenly thought to himself, "I'm going to stick my foot out. I'm going to set him flat on his kiester on this stone floor. Anyone who has the nerve to come down here as if it wasn't something tragic, as if it wasn't the worst thing possible. And just as I was about to stick my leg out, a small voice, as it were, asked me, 'What are you objecting to, Coffin? The first or the second part of the phrase?' Well, I thought it was the second part. And suddenly it hit me—No, I'm really objecting to 'the Lord gave.'"

As he wrote in his memoir, "Suddenly, I caught the full impart of 'the Lord *gave*': the world very simply is not ours, at best we're guests." At the service, he remembered, "I kept my leg in and just began to think about that." He didn't remember anything else that happened during the rest of the service.

Though this "mini-religious experience" did not lay all Coffin's doubts to rest, he did begin to see his new insight as "the understanding against which all the spears of human pride had to be hurled and shattered." For like most talented young men, Coffin had preferred to think of the world as fundamentally man-made. Influenced by reading Reinhold Niebuhr, who ridiculed this stance, Coffin began to see his earlier perspective as representing the sin of pride: putting humans at the center of the universe instead of God.

Coffin used Peyre's course to explore a range of ideas regarding morality and politics. Writing about Ibsen, for example, he made a case for the "écrivain engagé," or "committed writer," against those critics "who wish to conserve for the literary domain the character of the ivory tower." Coffin himself was taking up "la vie engagée," and he wanted intellectual company. Then, just after Harry Truman's surprise election victory over Thomas Dewey in November 1948, Coffin explored his own "social philosophy." Occasioned by Peyre's surprise at Coffin's "great elation" over the election (he knew Catherine's allegiance to the Republican Party), the paper offered the most explicit statement of Coffin's political views to date.[4]

Coffin's essay, organized around the French Revolution's three principles of liberté, égalité, and fraternité, demonstrated a left-liberal, social democratic internationalism. He called his liberalism "almost a fetishism," one founded on the "discovery of the individual," to his mind "the greatest discovery of the world" but for "the discovery of one Almighty God." Fearing that American political liberty could survive only "as long as people enjoy a minimum of security," Coffin took the relatively conventional liberal position that America needed an economy more subject to democratic control: "Planning from the top must therefore be blended with participation from below. Only under these conditions is man free to be his best self," the real meaning of "liberté." Though ambivalent about unions (he supported their protection of workers but criticized their undemocratic ways), he felt that their "representatives must participate in management decisions."

Under "égalité" Coffin sought the equality of opportunity rather than equality of result. While he blasted the "heavy tribute" exacted by "inherited wealth," he also argued, against Marx, that the "reward of success must always reflect the measure of merit." For "fraternité," he imagined a sense of social solidarity to keep society from being "like a can of peas—a mere collection of independent closed systems." Acknowledging the power of American individualism, he joined many thinkers of the thirties in hoping, vaguely, that "modern machinery" and the "many collective forms of modern industrial society" would stimulate "social integration." And again, like many in the immediate postwar years, he made a brief appeal on behalf of "the inevitability of a federal world government."[5]

Coffin remembered himself, accurately, as "a good deal left of center" but lacking "ideological rigidity." Still, like many liberals, he drew the line at working with Communists. Henry Wallace's Progressive Party presidential bid in 1948, which attracted much Communist support, split the American Veterans Committee, and Coffin helped expel its Communist members. Similarly, as much as Coffin admired Paul Robeson's voice, it "grieved" him that Robeson sang "I Dreamed I Saw Joe Hill Last Night" for the Wallace campaign. His political values had come from his liberal Republican family, not from the culture of labor or left-wing movements.[6]

Larger intellectual and political currents also influenced Coffin. While conservative anti-Communism had been a staple of American politics for decades, it was *liberal* anti-Communism that swept over the political landscape in the late forties and early fifties, making possible the witch-hunts now known as McCarthyism. Presidents Harry Truman and Dwight Eisenhower, who wielded far more political and cultural power than Senator Joseph McCarthy ever did, bore far more responsibility for the national mood.[7]

Unlike most Americans, Coffin did not fear Communism. He had known —and fought and drank and debated and negotiated with—real Soviet Communists and had the soldier's grudging respect for his opponents. Rarely at home in a crowd, literally or figuratively, Coffin had to make his own anti-Communism wittier and more sophisticated than that of the multitude. In this way he resembled other members of what was becoming the postwar foreign policy establishment: young, liberal, often Ivy League–educated men who had seen the war and the postwar struggle between Communists and their opponents in Europe and were drawn to intelligence work in order to defend social democracy against the USSR.[8]

So when he received an invitation to speak at the Yale alumni luncheon in February of his senior year, Coffin sought to reassure his elders that "the Yale blue is not turning pink." He drew explicitly on his experience in Europe, where he had had to defend the American record on poverty and racism too many times to Russians who seemed very well informed on U.S. shortcomings, to argue against eliminating "a few Communists and a good many who aren't from university faculties. [Vito] Marcantonio [the left-wing U.S. representative from East Harlem], I venture to say, will end his career in Congress the day a few more people take note of the conditions in his East Side New York District." Deftly, Coffin pooh-poohed the worries of Old Blues. Since "the average Yale graduate, with the passing years, gently displaces to the right," he joked, true danger lay in the "campus right-wing Republican who will have displaced right off the political horizon before his fifth reunion rolls around!"[9]

This skillful little talk showed Coffin coming into his own as a speaker: a veteran and a Yale man who could speak with authority drawn from both. He put his learning—or note-taking—on display, with no less than six quotations from poets and philosophers. He also demonstrated how religious thinking was beginning to play a larger part in his life. "Profound experiences of life and death have given many of us a lively sense of God," he explained to the alumni. Neither science nor the "intellectual merry-go-round" of "so many philosophies" was much help in explaining "pain and suffering or the basic value of life." But religion provided neither simple answers nor psychological comfort. "We don't consider religion a nice warm bath in which to sit after a rugged day and forget the cares of the world," he claimed, setting himself against the increasingly dominant ethos of American religious life. Instead, he argued for an engaged, vigorous faith that provided the strength to "make us face the world over and over again." In religious terms, therefore, Coffin could continue a version of the strenuous, engaged masculine life he had lived in the army. Even without firm vocational plans, Coffin was gradually integrating religious modes of thought into his overall approach to the world.

His religious perspective derived mostly from America's preeminent Protestant theologian, Reinhold Niebuhr. Then at the pinnacle of his secular and religious influence (he had been featured on the cover of *Time*'s twenty-fifth-anniversary issue in March 1948), Niebuhr was also one of the country's best-known liberals, holder of an endowed professorship at Union Theological Seminary, an editor of *Christianity and Crisis,* and a founder of the liberal, anti-Communist Americans for Democratic Action. Just as important for Coffin, Niebuhr combined indefatigable speaking, writing, and political activism with a deep sense of tragedy. As Niebuhr's biographer Richard Wightman Fox put it, "The culture craved a spokesman for the tragic sense of life; Niebuhr had the intellectual skill, religious credentials, and personal charisma to step forward and seize the day." The concluding sentences of Coffin's paper on social philosophy (which he recycled into his alumni luncheon speech several months later) fit perfectly into what Fox called Niebuhr's "Sisyphean perspective." Humankind hung by its fingernails from dangerous cliffs, Coffin warned. "We know that we can either climb painfully up to the sunlight, or drop off into dark oblivion. Under these conditions we cannot fail to realize that the ascent is worth every last ounce of our effort." The joy, the obligation, and the passion all flowed from the effort—the physical, psychological, and spiritual engagement with peril. That was the struggle Niebuhr offered to Americans, and while some took it in a more "world weary" direction, others, particularly young men, heard its call to worthy battle.[10]

Coffin quickly came to the attention of his elders. During his junior year he worked for Yale Law School Professor Eugene V. Rostow in a campaign on behalf of the Stratton Bill, an ultimately—though very modestly—successful proposal to allow greater numbers of European DPs, especially Jews, to enter the United States. Rostow, who had been Connecticut chairman of the effort, wrote a letter introducing Coffin to such foreign policy mandarins as Dean Acheson and Chester Bowles and describing him as "a very unusual person who came back with a brilliant Army record to work magnificently" for the Stratton Bill. "He is, besides, a very gay and promising lad, who can sing dirty songs in five languages, including Russian and Ukrainian. He is the nephew of Dr. Henry Sloane Coffin." Since Coffin was considering the Foreign Service, "he's well worth investing some advice on." If Catherine had known of this letter, she would have seen her advice about connections affirmed.[11]

It is difficult to see how Coffin could ever have been happy in the diplomatic corps. He loved solo performances of all kinds, chafed against niceties, and did not much like following instructions. Operating on his own, he could use his entire personal repertoire, as he did during a summer job in 1948, traveling through France for Operation Democracy. This effort, the creation of former Arizona Congresswoman Isabella Greenway King (the mother of Coffin's Yale friend John Greenway), got American towns to "adopt" and assist French towns that had been damaged during the war. Coffin represented the United States with bravado and schmaltz, even singing "Auld Lang Syne" at one town's D day pageant.

When not carrying out his formal responsibilities, Coffin made the trip into a social and sightseeing whirl, visiting his sister, Margot, then working in Paris. He "indoctrinated" her into the "milieu russe à Paris," she reported home, "a steady round of singing, dancing, and vodka" that lasted all night and included Manya, her sister Marfa, and George Bailey. He took off solo on a motorcycle and saw his old ski instructor Sepp Kessler and a flautist (and former flame) named Geneviève Noufflard, then living in Copenhagen.[12]

Still just twenty-five, Coffin had developed a persona as a swashbuckler and raconteur, songster and romancer of women. Strong, handsome, six feet tall and about 170 pounds, physically and mentally agile, Coffin had become a man's man, at home in refined musical culture and Yale clubs, who charmed mothers and grandmothers as well as contemporaries and older men. In two short but full years, he had strengthened his intellectual capacities, begun to think about politics, started to articulate spiritual positions, and become a well-regarded, well-connected leader of his fellows. No wonder he came to the attention of the Central Intelligence Agency (doubtless through CIA representatives at Yale) and received an invitation to interview in Washington during February of his senior year.

It did not hurt Coffin's standing that Margot's new husband had joined the agency and that Coffin's interviews took place in their Georgetown townhouse. Nor did it hurt the recruiters' chances with Coffin that they were liberal Ivy-League types, opposed to Stalinism and eager to help social democrats in Western Europe against the Moscow-supported Communist parties. Coffin was on the verge of joining a legion of young, Ivy League–educated liberals who went into the CIA during the early Cold War period. Attracted to working on the same side as anti-Soviet Russians (as opposed to deceiving them into repatriation), Coffin relished the idea of "fighting fire with fire." Within weeks of agreeing to two years of cloak-and-dagger work, however, he found himself drawn to another kind of combat.

The long arm of Henry Sloane Coffin, just retired from the presidency of Union, reached out with an invitation that same spring (from his successor) to attend a conference for college seniors who might be interested in the ministry. Though he did not advertise the gathering as recruitment, the director, George W. "Bill" Webber, relied on religion professors and college chaplains to recommend candidates and invited about 125 young men each year to come to Union and hear "the elite of the academic world" in the field of religion.[13]

Coffin attended "out of deference to Uncle Henry," because he did not have a date, and because Niebuhr, whom Coffin later wrote about as being "as eloquent a man as I had ever heard," was on the program. He had not gone expecting a career challenge, but Niebuhr, who led off Saturday morning, "was fantastic. By the time he was finished, everybody was saying, 'Rheinie, here am I.'" Coffin, in other words, suddenly started thinking seriously about the ministry. "My main objection was overcome that weekend," he recalled, "my main objection being [that] the church is really irrelevant: soft face over the hard collar." Instead, "those objections were swept aside by the people speaking and by the places we went to see." Throughout the weekend, ministry began to appear to him as a vigorous and exciting profession.[14]

Union Theological Seminary in those years provided not only an education in theology, it promoted ethical involvement in the world and encouraged students to attack hard social problems. Union-trained ministers were not being encouraged to settle for well-heeled pulpits where they could preach elegant sermons. They worked against middle-class complacency and upper-class condescension. Niebuhr, James Muilenberg, John Bennett, and Webber himself showed ministry as a calling, one engaged in a crusade against the evils of racism and poverty, shallowness and injustice. For a generation of young men who had faced evil in the form of Nazis and a world war, this kind of ministry seemed a chance to continue the struggle against all the forms the devil could take.

Webber took his recruits to the East Harlem Protestant Parish where he and some other young clergy—and their wives—had organized a cooperative ministry to tackle urban problems through storefront churches. Enthralled by the fierce mixture of politics and religion, toughness and relevance, Coffin spent several hours talking to Webber, also a veteran. Finally, Webber hit on the magic words, arguing that ministers "had greater freedom to say and do what they wanted than good people in any other vocation." Coffin had a visceral dislike for bureaucracy and an eagerness for engagement, for in the army he had missed the "action"—direct confrontation with the enemy. And he loved operating on his own. Union offered such a compelling cause that Coffin promptly withdrew from the CIA and sent an application to Union on Monday. "Not because I had worked out the neat theology," he reflected later. "I hadn't. I had more sentiment than I had conviction. But I feel that once you feel a kind of rush of energy, you feel something significant happened. You've been claimed in some way and you've got to act on it. And there's no use wasting any time. If you don't, you've probably lost an opportunity."[15]

Coffin's choice of the ministry surprised his European friends, who remembered his at best irreverent and at worst hostile attitude toward organized religion. And he clearly lacked the gentle manner generally associated with a successful minister. But Coffin had been looking for something along these lines at Yale. His papers displayed a seeker's interest in answers, not merely a clever undergraduate's pleasure in batting ideas about. Theologians spoke to him in a way that political scientists did not. More practically, the large presence of Henry Sloane Coffin—the most eminent, respected, and well-off Coffin of his generation, the paterfamilias—made ministry seem an important profession. Catherine, too, had occasionally talked about the importance of the church in remaking the postwar world and appears to have quickly accepted her son's new vocation.

Given Coffin's enormous energy, he needed a vocation larger than himself. In the past that role had been played by sports, by the piano, by wartime infantry training, by Russian, and by his college studies. Ministry—especially the crusading, tough-minded, independent kind espoused by Reinhold Niebuhr and Bill Webber at the seminary where Uncle Henry had presided for decades, in the city where Coffin had spent his earliest years—offered an ideal combination. He would be able to make use of his pedigree, education, and family connections at the same time as he could act independently, get good answers to his big questions, and use his wit and intelligence, energy and charm, musical skill and knowledge—all in the service of a battle against evil.

Coffin began to direct his intellectual life toward his new vocation. His senior thesis, "Notes Towards a History of Bolshevik Trade Unionism," remained just that: a lifeless sixty-page compilation of quotations from official documents regarding the proper relationship between the party, the state, and the trade unions. On the other hand, in "A Sermon on Prayer," written during his last month in college, Coffin referred to himself as a religious man for the first time and appeared to be exploring entirely new personal facets.[16]

Observing that prayer began "with a sense of need," he quoted King Solomon and Abraham Lincoln to suggest that "the strongest and wisest men are apt to be those who feel this need most." "Prayer then is first of all humility," he argued, adding, "it is easier to be humble in some quiet corner. . . . most of us need to be alone in order to climb down off the pedestal on which we so automatically pose in public. Solitude breeds sincerity." For Coffin, these were new thoughts. Rarely humble or interested in solitude, he preferred noisy public settings. Alone in the Bavarian mountains a few years earlier, he had befriended complete strangers and sung with them into the night. He might even have given up serious piano so easily because so much of a musician's life was so solitary. Building on his concern for "fraternité," Coffin also hoped that praying for others could "develop in us a sense of responsibility for the needs of the world, and real love for our fellowmen." Since it forced him into such unfamiliar psychological territory, prayer in this argument was a spiritual and social discipline, beginning in solitude, countering people's natural selfishness, and ending up binding human beings to each other and to God.

In the fall of 1949 Coffin entered Union Theological Seminary, the 113-year-old institution in Morningside Heights, on Manhattan's Upper West Side, on the edges of Harlem, and across from Riverside Church. The single greatest intellectual powerhouse in liberal Protestantism and the largest northern seminary, whose neo-Gothic architecture resembled that of Yale, Union drew students from a wide variety of denominations, as well as from all over the country.

Although first-year students were not allowed to study with the most eminent members of the faculty—Niebuhr, Tillich, Bennett—Coffin enjoyed himself immensely as he gradually changed "from the seeker who looks hoping something's there, to the kind who knows something's there, if only he can find it." He studied Old and New Testament and worked in East Harlem during the summer of 1950. His only surviving paper, which his professor thought excellent, showed Coffin absorbing the historical-critical method (the literary and historical analysis of the creation of the Bible) with care and verve.[17]

By October 1949, Coffin had already debuted on the speaking circuit, addressing a Wisconsin gathering of Student Christian Associations. Examining "the Christian enterprise in a civilization that has lost its way," Coffin demonstrated remarkable confidence in his new Christian calling.[18] The task, put simply, was to "show how Christianity is the life worth living." He pleaded for Christians to become at least as articulate as "some parlor Marxist with his slick little formulas," for theologians had too often committed "the unforgivable sin of making Christianity sound dull." Coffin sought to put the "fire" back into theology: "We must look for fresh, first-hand, personal material if we are to present Christianity as the most exciting proposition that ever confronted man." Following in his uncle's footsteps, Coffin ridiculed sectarianism, the needless expense of energy on "internal church differences with no relevance to any major problems in the world today."

His conclusion seemed particularly well-suited to his personality. "When a non-believer pictures a Christian," Coffin observed, "he is apt to think not only of a tender-hearted fellow, but a tender-minded one as well. Modern Christianity is in particular need of tough intellectual fibre." That "toughness" could not be confined to the classroom or lecture hall: "Ivory towers are not for us," he announced, while hailing from one of the greatest such towers in America. Christianity lived in the trenches, in "the mud and scum of things" (quoting Ralph Waldo Emerson). And above all Christianity was love, not a "tiresome, uncreative piety frowning on occasional excesses, but an endless fight against all forms of injustice."

This wide-ranging speech laid out the themes of Coffin's ministry for many years: religious ecumenism and the inadequacy of secularism; the offenses committed by the ivory tower, by boring theology, and by pious lip-pursing; his admiration for the tough-minded; his respect for the authenticity of experience; and his abiding faith in the power of love. By adopting these themes as his own, Coffin did not break new theological ground: many of them had been staples of the Social Gospel movement at the turn of the century and lived on for several generations.

In his internship with the East Harlem Protestant Parish Coffin came into

When Coffin entered Union Theological Seminary in New York in 1949, he approached his studies with the same intensity he had given to physical endeavors in the army. Courtesy of William Sloane Coffin Jr.

his first real contact with the American poor, about whom, he averred, he had "always had a bad conscience." Buzzing around the neighborhood on his motorcycle, Coffin organized singing, played the piano, leafleted street corners, sat for some of the ministers' children, and called on residents in their homes. He "got over some of the sentimentalization of the poor" so common among those who work far from poverty but still saw "the wisdom of the uneducated." He also had to face the scrutiny of supervisors on the lookout for class condescension. By and large, though, the experience was an important and positive one, and Coffin, again like his Social Gospel forbears, envisioned his ministerial future in just such a parish.[19]

Another crusade intervened, however, as the Korean War broke out in late June of 1950. Coffin gave no thought to whether—only how—he was going to serve his country. Atoning for his "terrible failure" at Plattling played a role in his decision, Coffin recalled, but, more important, he had "this real old-fashioned belief that when your country goes to war, you serve your country." He either "had to go back in a uniform and go over there and fight or go into the CIA." Since he was uninterested in combat and maintained his passion for "things Russian," the CIA made the most sense. After three years of studying, he was also ready for a change of pace, and some of his closest friends still lived in Europe. "It's not as schizophrenic as it might superficially appear," he reasoned years later, "because the difference between [the] CIA and seminary to me in those days was not great. It's pursuing the same kind of goal of righteousness as I saw it." The CIA still wanted him, so Coffin decided to leave seminary for a couple of years. When his security clearance came through in October, he moved to Washington and began training in earnest as a cold warrior.[20]

By 1950, the Cold War had turned hot. Americans generally attributed the Chinese Communist victory in 1949 to Soviet expansionism. The Soviet Union itself had exploded a nuclear bomb in August of that year, prompting President Harry Truman to speed up development of an American "super," the hydrogen bomb. At the same time, Truman ordered the defense policy review that became National Security Council Paper Number 68, which envisioned a global struggle between Communist efforts at world domination and a fully armed "free world" ready to do battle—covertly and overtly—with the Soviet empire and its minions.

The CIA had been established in 1947 as the successor to the wartime Office of Strategic Services, and its early intelligence-gathering abilities bore little resemblance to the modern era of satellite surveillance, electronic eavesdropping, and high-altitude aerial photography. Instead, in order to obtain information about life or developments inside the USSR, the agency relied on informants, people who could be flown into the country under radar, collect information, and either return with it or radio it back. Coffin was posted as a case officer to one such effort, based in Munich, in January 1951. For the next two years he recruited, prepared, trained, and inspired Soviet émigrés to reenter the USSR as American spies.[21]

This was a complicated business, and not only because of the technical difficulties; there were contradictory views at the heart of the enterprise within the CIA itself. One school of thought held that the Soviet Union could be toppled and therefore that agents placed in the country should be organizing cells and other activities designed to encourage the fall of the regime. The competing view, to which operations director David Murphy subscribed, was more skeptical of the possibility of overthrowing the Soviet government. For émigré groups, the former belief was an article of faith, providing much of the motivation for agent volunteers. While Murphy had no hopes that these agents could organize a successful underground movement, he cooperated with their fantasy as long as it might help them provide the intelligence he was under pressure to collect. Coffin served as the perfect intermediary between the émigrés and the CIA brass. Trainees ended up "devoted" to him, according to Coffin's colleague Serge Karpovich, a thirty-year agency veteran who worked alongside him for two years.

The mission combined Coffin's love of swashbuckling, his ability to operate in different environments with a wide variety of people, and his need for high purpose and total absorption. "He was a romantic," recalled Karpovich. "He wanted the excitement." In Europe Coffin took the name of the Wild

West lawman (and partner of Wyatt Earp) Doc Holliday and became Captain Holliday.

He and an émigré co-worker recruited potential agents—young men—out of refugee camps. Once screened by the agency, the recruits undertook a long, extraordinarily intensive training program, from lectures in economics to espionage techniques, map reading, Morse code, and short-wave radio operation. Simultaneously, they underwent strenuous physical conditioning, including parachute jumping instruction. Then they had to memorize their missions, their cover stories, and how to respond to interrogators if they were caught. Finally, they were "dropped": parachuted in at night from low-flying planes based in U.S. airfields hours from the Soviet border, planes that frequently returned full of bullet holes.

Because the training was so long and arduous (Coffin trained only three teams in two years) and the missions so dangerous, the would-be agents' morale counted enormously. The case officer not only had to be an effective teacher; he also had to be a friend and leader, capable of inspiring his men. Coffin performed this task superbly. "We were infinitely more successful than anybody else in terms of . . . getting guys all the way through," reported Karpovich. "They'd lose most of them in training." Much of the credit went to Coffin, "one of the most charismatic" people he'd ever known. Murphy concurred; Coffin was "outstanding—he was the tops." He could "radiate this sense of conviction and this sense of strength, a real preacher in many respects." The whole Coffin persona came into play. As Murphy recalled, "I mean, Bill's singing was incredible. His ability to get them to sing when they were down. All of this was fantastic." For his part, Coffin loved the "physically demanding" nature of the work, but it was also "fun because it was . . . a very tight knit group. And the morale was always very high. That was part of my function, to make sure it stayed that way."

Neither the camaraderie nor the sense of mission, however, could hide what slowly became clear: that the operation was in most respects failing. Coffin's first agent sent back one "all's well" signal the night he parachuted into the Soviet Union—and then no more. Coffin thought the second training cycle had also been a complete failure; his CIA colleagues hinted otherwise. About the third group, the largest he trained, there was no doubt. Soviet authorities captured the men, and *Pravda* ran a front-page story with their real names, the location of the CIA safe house, and the cover names of the CIA training team. Coffin's unit barely had time to flee the house before reporters arrived. They assumed, quite reasonably, that most of those captured were executed.[22]

Coffin concluded, probably correctly (given the history of Cold War intelligence), that there had been a leak in the organization. But even failure meant

"Captain Holliday" in 1951. From 1950 to 1953, during the height of the early Cold War, Coffin worked for the CIA in Germany recruiting and training Russian émigrés to infiltrate the Soviet Union. He could "radiate this sense of conviction and this sense of strength," according to his boss, that made him an outstanding leader. "Captain Holliday," his secret name, was based on that of Doc Holliday, Wyatt Earp's Wild West partner. Courtesy of Randy Wilson Coffin.

something different to a career intelligence officer than it did to a layperson. Reflecting on the operation decades later, Murphy argued "that it proved to us that the idea of dispatching to the Soviet Union by illegal means . . . and expecting these people to be able to use the documentation we gave them, the cover stories we gave them, to integrate successfully into Soviet life and to serve as long term agents was simply not feasible." Nonetheless, officers involved in the operation gained valuable language and cultural expertise and "served as a major component of Soviet operations throughout the world because of what they'd learned there."

Feeling a need to distance himself from the CIA experience, Coffin wrote in his memoir that these years contributed little to his personal growth. But while he recalled "never" reading a book during that period, in reality he read widely, struggling to apply what he had learned at Yale and Union to the "real world." He tried, with mixed results, to interpret his experience, but he constantly tested his skills: at leadership, at writing, at analysis, at storytelling, even at romance. The books and plays he mentioned in correspondence to his mother included novels by F. Scott Fitzgerald, William Faulkner, Norman Mailer, Theodore Dreiser, Henry James, E. M. Forster, and Fyodor Dostoyevsky. In nonfiction, he read Niebuhr's *The Irony of American History,* some of Dumas Malone's *Jefferson and His Time,* and James Burnham's *The Coming Defeat of Communism.*[23]

After taking trainees on two-mile runs at 6:30 A.M., Coffin wrote stories and addressed religious and intellectual issues in his correspondence. Rather than simply catalogue his reading, he reacted vigorously to the authors and tried to identify the nub of their styles and modes of thought. After seeing Jean-Paul Sartre's "magnificently acted" *Le Diable et le Bon Dieu* in Paris, for example, he penned a diatribe about "the irrelevance of mind left strictly to its own devises [*sic*]." Coffin was developing a critique of "mind *tout pur* in the service of nothing but itself." It was "high time," he concluded, that "Sartre got his duff off his high seat of learning and started to renew contact with life in its rawer forms," which was precisely what Coffin thought he was doing. He then quoted Henri Peyre's frequent comment, "Essayez de profondir votre pensée" (try to deepen your thinking).[24]

Engaged in work he felt to be of great consequence, Coffin easily angered at frivolous or shallow characters, such as those in *The Great Gatsby*. Coffin believed that Fitzgerald showed too much "solicitude" for his "young clerks in the dusk, wasting the most poignant moments of night and life." It was one thing, he jabbed, "to throw a wistful glance over the shoulder, another thing to make a determined about face and march backward." Earnestly (if at times pompously), Coffin was carving out the intellectual, moral, and religious territory of his own career.[25]

Coffin became serious about coining epigrams during this period, rationalizing, "To crusade is fine, but the choice of banner slogans and weapons is so important." In one letter he wondered, "How to become civilized without becoming sterilized?" following up with the question, "How to keep natural tastes fresh against stale wisdom?" In a meditation on modern-day Germany, Coffin suggested, "A system is only an abstract morality unable to absorb an active personal guilt." He even fashioned a variation on Reinhold Niebuhr's "Serenity Prayer"—"Acceptance and purposefulness: the first for things that can't be changed, the second for those that can"—with a caveat: "The rub—the difference between categories is never clear."[26]

Coffin's central theme during these years was the question of human purpose: the overriding sense of direction that could give meaning to people's lives. Though he had asked for George Kennan's *American Diplomacy, 1900–1950* as a Christmas present in 1951, Coffin doubted whether Kennan's idea of national interest could serve as a "guiding motive" when it only appeared "safe." He preferred "strong medicine"—something to which people could truly dedicate themselves—to such paltry ends as national interest or E. M. Forster's tolerance. On the front lines of the Cold War, Coffin objected to small ends because he hungered for spiritual battle, not the diplomatic pursuit of rational interests.[27]

Though his colleagues rarely saw his religious side—and indeed expressed surprise at his eventual career choice—Coffin carried on his religious education during these years. In the midst of the East-West struggle, he was developing his theological approach to the world. Coffin saw the Cold War as a battle between God and Man and considered it crucial to mount a movement on behalf of God, lest "we shall all be pushed into the Man corner." In "granting free will, God created a Father-son, rather than master-slave relationship between himself and man." Once free will had been granted, sin—man's love for himself rather than God—became "inevitable." God could interfere in human beings' actions (keeping them from sinning, say) only at the cost of the father-child relationship, and of human freedom. "God doesn't *make* us suffer," Coffin insisted. "He watches us suffer and how much greater than ours must his suffering be." These were powerful ideas for a young man lacking a father, who had been seeking surrogate fathers for some time. This conceptualization of the relationship between God and human beings maximized the possibility of human freedom. Loyalty to God did not demand restriction of human activity. This theology seemed tailor-made for Coffin's rather unconventional service to God in the CIA.[28]

Coffin's exposure to Niebuhr, combined with his momentous, secret employment, led him into thoughts about pride, which he understood as sinful but, like many gifted young leaders, was not entirely ready to jettison. "Maybe we are not pretentious," he hoped vainly, "in counting ourselves among the ten who may some day cause the city to be spared." Coffin wrote admiringly of his trainee agents, who could call on such "selfless" personal reserves as "political idealism, religion, courage, humor," but also "the big selfish one—pride." For when pride left a man, the "sight is pathetic—there is absolutely nothing left." On the other hand, Coffin's critiques of pride could sound completely Niebuhrian, as when he noted that belief short of total acceptance "is a victory of pride or selfishness."[29]

Coffin later gave the impression that he "didn't have much of a life outside" the work and that his only involvements with women were with "secretaries, and that's about it." In fact, during this time he carried on lively, substantial relationships with at least three different women, at varying degrees of intensity, complexity, and romantic fervor: his old flames Manya Piskounoff and Geneviève Noufflard (with whom, he wrote not entirely accurately, he had become "viels amis" [old friends]), and a CIA officer in Germany named Betty Swantek, with whom Coffin became so involved that she apparently—and forlornly—expected Coffin to marry her. As he related the stories of his romantic encounters, of which he was sometimes the hero, and sometimes the goat, he was developing a real flair for narrative, for the humorous anecdote, the bittersweet encounter.[30]

Coffin had visited Manya almost as soon as he arrived in Europe in 1950 and soon ran into his competition, whom he derided as "good old Iura," a "good but dull habit waiting patiently to be accepted by the wisdom of middle age." Iura Stromberg loved Manya, however, and appeared prepared to wait her—and Coffin—out. "Needless to say I often wonder why I butt into his life intermittently and particularly into hers," Coffin reflected. "Maybe because, as the Russian proverb says, in the fall of one's life the memories of spring are so important. And spring should be spring, damn it . . . (n.b. Don't take any of this stuff more seriously than I do!)" By turns exercised and dismissive, Coffin's rhetoric indicated confusion, and his unwillingness to acknowledge the obvious: that he wanted to be with Manya only "intermittently"—and on his terms. Soon they were having their "final supper" before their "inevitable parting." He had "begun to recognize the familiar physical symptoms: contractions of the stomach to be followed on the train by the very real physical sensation of an aching heart. 'You and I are always parting, Vasya.' She says such things so simply. There is no resistance to tragedy. She licks it by turning the other cheek. But without being morbid or masochistic. She just accepts—pure and simple. C'est beau."[31]

By his own account, Coffin began refashioning his mood that very night. In his train compartment, he found "himself automatically looking around" and saw a young woman, perhaps twenty-one, with "large brown understanding eyes" and a "spiritual nature, simple and intelligent." To get her attention Coffin pulled the leg of another passenger—a stolid, bourgeois, easily teased professorial type—until he got a conversation going. When he left, she announced, "You know, you radiate confidence in an extraordinary manner." "That's funny," he replied, "I don't feel much confidence this evening." She took the bait. They talked all night, he of Paris, she of religion and her fiancé. He bought her flowers in Frankfurt, where they looked at each other "for a long moment." They kissed on both cheeks, and she melted into the crowd. "It is a nice story, isn't it?" he asked. "A little romantic, but then . . . ! Marie was a beautiful girl." Coffin loved collecting romantic stories, so he constantly put himself in their way.[32]

Manya's letters displayed a persistent melancholy, laced with longing and reproof. Several months after his January visit, Coffin returned, this time in response to her request for help with her father, who had been injured on the job. Coffin offered to take the old man to his training site in Germany, which he did shortly, an act of kindness Manya recalled fondly more than four decades later. Still, "I was so upset when you left," she began the letter containing her father's travel arrangements, "that at the last minute I forgot everything I wanted to tell you," which had included "many tender words." She accused him of writing her father and sister without sending "me even a hello." Was Coffin "mad at me?" "I think about you all the time," she confessed, "and these thoughts bother me like a toothache." She pined for another visit. Her message "could have been romantic, but it's a sign of the present time that I am writing using a pen and not a goose feather . . . I am kissing you as I am loving you." Coffin's presence lifted Manya out of the sadness of sad émigré life. Iura proved a poor substitute; hence the palpable longing in her letters.[33]

Catherine Coffin had never been happy about Bill's choice of the CIA. She wanted him in a public career. After his first year abroad she asked him to consult with her before making additional commitments, a request Coffin granted. By fall 1952, however, he had decided on at least another year. Displeased, Catherine accepted his decision, and Coffin gushed gratitude: "I was so thankful to you for the greatness of your forgiveness to me."[34]

Her strategy worked. Over the next few months he began to write more about what he was missing in Europe: he did not have enough reading and writing time; he needed "recueillement" [meditation] and "approfondissement" [deepening]: "The seminary—and you—may well be the answer." He also may have been ready to start exercising his talents on a larger, more public stage. In early 1953 he gave her what she really wanted: "I have just told the boss that I shall be resigning as of next fall to go back to the Seminary." And by the end of February he did even better, announcing "a complete OK from Uncle Henry on a decision to enroll next fall at Yale [Divinity School] instead of Union." Since moving to New Haven in 1942, Catherine had established herself as a well-known cultural hostess. Her "salon" included the playwright Thornton Wilder, as well as a wide range of Yale-connected writers, critics, and professors. She had a basement apartment in her house near the Divinity School, which she offered Bill. She had also been having eye trouble, which helped convince him to transfer to Yale rather than return to Union.[35]

Even so, Catherine seemed unhappy about something and appears to have raised questions about her son's commitment to the ministry. Having "observed myself in a variety of circumstances," he replied, "I realize that my chances now for real spiritual growth—fair at best!—depend on the external discipline of a seminary and the constant pressure of a minister's obligations to those he would help and lead." Coffin knew his own self-indulgent streak and wanted to counteract it, to channel his energies into usefulness. "I feel I have neither the inclination nor the mind to become a first-rate scholar," he reasoned accurately. "However to be a first-rate minister it is enough to be a good scholar and have a deep understanding of other people's needs. This is a little more my line. And then, how frustrating to be talking most of the time about Mother Russia when you could be talking most of the time about (or listening, or studying!) about God! Finally I wouldn't feel justified in giving up my present line of work for anything but the ministry."

Coffin knew that uncontrollable events could intervene in the best-laid plans, as they had done three times before in his lifetime: his father's death and the outbreaks, respectively, of World War II and the Korean War. So he threw in a caveat—"Of course with the world as it is I'll be lucky to become a minister but the two years of seminary will serve in any capacity"—but in his own mind he had resolved the question of his career for good.[36]

Given how strongly and clearly Coffin made these arguments, the surprising thing is how little he had talked about them with his colleagues and friends. Manya Piskounoff, for example, recalled "not one word" about religion during the entire time she knew him in France, "ni pour, ni contre" (neither for nor against). Coffin had learned to compartmentalize different parts of his life. Neither Karpovich nor Murphy was entirely surprised that Coffin decided to leave the CIA. Karpovich observed that the failure of the final mission could have confirmed Coffin in his decision to head home. Murphy pointed out that Stalin's death in 1953 was going to make great changes in their work and that Coffin had a finite attention span. Still, as much as Murphy had valued Coffin as a case officer, and tried to talk him into staying, he knew Coffin would have been ill suited to agency work in the long term: "It would have been a life that was much too confining. . . . You know, Bill Coffin doesn't melt into the woodwork!"[37]

Coffin wrote home that while the "'emergency' of course endures," the "dearth of good ideas and men has improved." Convinced that his colleagues had "found the right direction and in it have taken a few rather firm steps," he predicted blandly that with a "hard core of intelligent, energetic, and committed men, I think progress will be made." He needed to justify his desire to return. Equally significant were the terms in which he had made his decision. He praised scholarship but not a life devoted to it. He preferred to understand people and their needs in order to "help and lead" them. He had no interest in being a spectator, analyzing from the sidelines.[38]

Coffin had proved exceptionally talented as a trainer and inspirer of men. Soviet émigrés devoted themselves to him even though he was not one of them and spoke their language as a foreigner—a talented foreigner but a foreigner nevertheless. He was also capable of inspiring devotion from intelligent and talented women—and enjoyed their devotion until their expectations, which he did little to reduce, burst. He was capable both of extraordinary commitment to a cause and of extraordinary inattention to individuals.

In a conversation one spring afternoon in 1952 or 1953, Karpovich recalled, just after he and Coffin had sent off a group of agents, four men—Coffin, Karpovich, Bailey, and the host, an English teacher named Boris—were chewing over E. M. Forster's recently published collection of essays *Two Cheers for*

Democracy, the centerpiece of which was titled "What I Believe." In that essay Forster wrote, "I hate the idea of causes. And if I had to choose between betraying my country and betraying my friend, I hope I should have the guts to betray my country." The men ended up in a "tremendous debate" in which Bailey and Karpovich sided with Forster—preferring to betray one's country —and Boris and Coffin against—preferring to betray a friend. Karpovich was surprised to find Coffin on the other side, while others may wonder how a career CIA officer could admire the choice to betray country over a friend.

Bailey argued forty-five years later that Coffin was "an idealist—an ideologue" who did not believe in making exceptions to rules. But in a contemporary letter home Coffin approvingly quoted one of his Munich trainees to the effect that "patriotism is in essence the love of one's neighbor which should always hold precedence over a less concrete love of humanity. To keep patriotism from turning into chauvinism one had constantly to apply the measure of Christianity." This explained why "so many ardent communists I have met outside of the USSR are in the impossible position of serving Humanity while despising their neighbor." Coffin stayed friends with Karpovich, Bailey, Murphy, and Chavchavadze (off and on) for the next fifty years.[39]

But Karpovich also pointed out that "he's betrayed friends, . . . not meaning to, of course." He "overpowers them, right, and then he abandons them," he explained. "I know one case where it's caused a lot of pain." He was referring to Coffin's relationship with his fellow trainer "Andrei," whom Coffin wrote admiringly about in his memoir and who had named Coffin godfather to his son. When Andrei died of a heart attack several years later, according to Karpovich, Coffin never called or contacted his family.[40]

When Coffin finally left Germany in June 1953, he, Karpovich, and Bailey and his wife, Beatta, drove south through Italy, then north through France up to Paris. "And here in Paris," marveled Karpovich, "Bill visited all his former girlfriends at once! But not together. In series." Only none of them thought they were "former." Geneviève Noufflard "shocked" Bailey by asking, " 'How do I get Bill Coffin?' " Coffin visited Betty Swantek in her hotel, where he had reportedly planned to finally break off their relationship.

Coffin had heard a rumor that Manya had gotten married to "good old Iura," so he first went to see Marfa. Only when she reassured him did Coffin seek out Manya at her office, where he told her he was going home to seminary. Soon there was a big party out at Drancy, where they had little time in private. Coffin's departure brought her a certain relief, she recalled, though it may have taken her some time to feel it: "I was very tormented by things." Coffin never asked her to accompany him to the States. Had he, she would have been at least tempted to abandon her family, her responsibilities as the oldest child, and her community. Since Coffin left instead, she more easily married Iura the following March. "He waited," she explained simply.[41]

As he prepared to reenter seminary in the United States, the twenty-nine-year-old Coffin had developed an intriguing bundle of contradictory qualities: a thoroughgoing hedonism and an athlete's physical and mental self-discipline; an increasingly well-read and agile intellect mixed with contempt for professional intellectuals; belief in a tough-minded, anti-Soviet crusade and a sentimental gushiness about Russians and Russian culture; an opportunistic libido (Coffin "has to have a woman," insisted Bailey, "that's all there is to it") and a tendency toward bittersweet romanticism; a belief in comradeship and an athletic competitiveness so fierce that he could accuse a close friend of cheating in a shipboard Ping-Pong tournament when there were no stakes at all.[42]

In the secret war Coffin had become a leader of men and undergone an intensive course in human nature and the demands of idealism. He had learned to expect what he called the "torment of decision," even if, as concerned women, he generally chose to look away rather than face it squarely. He made lifelong friends, and abandoned others. Trying to deepen his thought, he seemed ready to undertake a new mission: the spiritual challenge of Christian ministry.

FIVE

From Education to Vocation

Yale Divinity School

"My wife would say," confessed John Maguire, Coffin's Yale Divinity School classmate (and later president of Claremont University), that Bill Coffin was "the single most dashing guy that she'd ever met. I mean, more panache, more blarney, more *bullshit*. I mean, here's a guy who one minute would jump down and sing some Schubert *lieder* and all the women would swoon; and then would be 'coaxed' into telling about parachuting behind the lines somewhere to save somebody; then break into Russian songs . . . songster, charmer, *bon vivant*, great raconteur, . . . a risk-taker . . . just living life up."[1]

"Oh, there was no one like him," recalled Browne Barr, Coffin's preaching professor and friend, mixing pride and frustration. "You couldn't really teach Coffin." A magnetic figure on campus, Coffin had a reputation for whizzing about New Haven on his powerful BMW motorcycle and cajoling friends—including Barr and Maguire—onto the back seat, only to terrify them with stunts. Older and more experienced than other students, carrying a well-known name, Coffin had cachet that attracted faculty members as well. "Before he was through, he had a category all his own," Barr recalled: "the most distinguished student."[2]

If not teachable in a traditional sense, Coffin nevertheless plunged into study, enjoying the swing of the pendulum back from the more physical experience of the CIA. He had picked a good moment. Yale's faculty included H. Richard Niebuhr, Reinhold's more meditative younger brother, who taught theology and ethics; Robert L. Calhoun in systematic (or historical) theology; Julian Hartt in religion and philosophy; and Roland Bainton, the eminent church historian known for his superb storytelling. Despite the lack of activists like Reinhold Niebuhr and Bill Webber at Union, Coffin and Maguire both recalled Yale as intellectually exciting.

In a class by himself at Yale Divinity School from 1953 to 1956, Coffin made the most of his persona as secret warrior, daredevil, linguist, musician, and charmer. Courtesy of Randy Wilson Coffin.

For Coffin, Richard Niebuhr's presence dominated the Divinity School. (Then overshadowed by his celebrity brother, Richard is now also recognized as one of the most important American theologians of the past century.) At Yale Coffin elaborated the theology that governed his interpretation of Christianity for the rest of his life. From Calhoun, for example, he learned the difference between "conventional Christianity," meaning that articulated by most believers and practiced in most churches, and "orthodox Christianity": the "thought and action of saints and scholars throughout the ages."[3]

Coffin liked this insider's view of "real Christianity," as opposed to the "conventional," dumbed-down stuff peddled to the folks in the pews. His intellectual elitism merged with his recent experience in intelligence (where he worked with utterly committed men and women); as a result he preferred the thought of those most engaged with their faith: the orthodox. He enjoyed discovering that the "best Christian thinkers" had always been tougher on Christians than any secular critics had been. For Coffin loved the back and forth of vigorous argument and delighted in learning that he was not giving himself over to a soft, intellectually sheltered or sheltering discipline.

Although Coffin called his Christianity "orthodox," it was really "neo-orthodox," heavily influenced by Reinhold Niebuhr, particularly as articulated by Niebuhr in *The Nature and Destiny of Man*. Given his appetites and athleticism, Coffin had long felt uneasy about the "body-spirit dualism" of conventional Christianity and its focus on "sins of the flesh" as the locus of evil. From Calhoun, he learned to attribute evil not to the base desires of the body, but to "the corruption of freedom, the perversion of that which is most godlike in us." This understanding had much in common with that of Niebuhr, who placed evil "at the very centre of human personality: in the will." Man's "sin is the wrong use of his freedom and its consequent destruction." Coffin's course work on Augustine for Calhoun, which resurfaced in his early sermons, showed

Coffin absorbing the neo-orthodoxy of his day and making it his own. For the neo-orthodox, pride—not what Augustine called *concupiscienta*—was the most fundamental human sin. As Coffin wrote in his Statement of Faith (1956), "Self glorification—pride—be it individual or collective, is I believe the root of all human evil. . . . [it] is a state of being in which we are alienated from God. This state of being I understand as sin."[4]

For the vodka diplomat who danced and partied with Russians until the early morning hours, who "could stay up all night, drink all night, smoke cigars and carry on" (according to Maguire), a theology focused on bodily guilt would have felt stifling. Now he was discovering a faith that, if not exactly endorsing worldly sensuality, refused to locate sin in the belly, the muscles, or the groin. "I could see," Coffin wrote, "that while conventional Christianity seemed all too often a religion of creeds and laws, which were frequently repressive, orthodox Christianity was liberating." Like Niebuhr in *Nature and Destiny,* Coffin drew on St. Paul as the key interpreter of Christianity, and on the "Hebraic-prophetic" roots of Christianity, in opposition to what had become known as the more rational "Hellenistic" tradition. Buttressed by Niebuhr, Coffin extended his critique of intellectual pride (of "mind *tout pur*" as he had put it criticizing Sartre), of the search for knowledge for its own sake, of the world-view defined by Descartes' *cogito ergo sum.* Here he had the benefit of his experience of music, the deeper truths of which, he often argued, were sensed rather than understood. Coffin's revelatory experience during the funeral of his friend back in his senior year had been helped along by the organist's rendition of a Bach choral prelude. Coffin understood things intuitively, and then used reason, as he put it later, to "work things out."[5]

Coffin's adoption of neo-orthodox "Hebraism" had unforeseen consequences: an emphasis on "prophetic Christianity" (which he knew little about because he never studied the prophets in seminary) and his openness to ecumenism, particularly as regarded Jews. For the whole notion of a "Judeo-Christian" heritage and creed, according to the historian Mark Silk, was literally created and publicized in the face and wake of fascist anti-Semitism by Christian and Jewish neo-orthodox theologians ranging from Niebuhr and his Union colleague Paul Tillich to Jewish Theological Seminary's Abraham Joshua Heschel and the more popular Will Herberg.[6]

The combination of Coffin's willingness to study, the excellence of his teachers, his social leadership, and the comfort of the Yale milieu worked a kind of magic on him. From that point forward, while he easily read secular thinkers, novelists, and poets, he reacted to them in almost exclusively Christian terms. In 1956, for example, he wrote a paper on psychotherapy that earned a seventy-five from a frankly annoyed professor who wondered why Coffin had ignored most of the (secular) material in the course. He later wrote that his best guide to "human depravity" and "the Christian understanding of redemption" was Dostoyevsky's *Crime and Punishment,* which he had begun reading after college and now read in both Russian and English.[7]

His second and third years, Coffin began to learn chaplaincy, serving as a pastor to Presbyterian students and as an assistant to Yale's Chaplain A. Sidney Lovett. He conducted the smaller chapel services, preached short sermons, organized programs, and counseled students. As a result, it took him four rather than the usual three years to get his divinity degree.

Yale Divinity School was the perfect place for Coffin. In addition to studying intensely, he kept up extremely active social and intellectual lives. Maguire described a general excitement at once philosophical, literary, artistic, and sexual—a "wonderfully larkish and freeing" atmosphere. "Existentialism" was the "catch-all" term for the feeling that "allowed those of us who were reared in very strict backgrounds to break out in the name of living in the now." He described evenings reading poetry and putting on musical revues that parodied contemporary philosophy: "There's no being, like non-being, like non-being I know" (spoofing Sartre's *Being and Nothingness* to the tune of "There's No Business Like Show Business"). The sexual dimension to this Bohemian zeitgeist—well in advance of the "revolution" of the following decade—may have been mostly an undercurrent; participants nevertheless felt it intensely. Coffin, Maguire recalled, pretended to a good deal of experience in this regard: "Nine years older, he claims to have learned his Russian in a whorehouse in Paris where the Russian girls who were in the house taught it to him and he just lived in there. That was so exciting. The thought of Coffin living in the whorehouse."[8]

Courtship and Marriage

Bill Coffin met Eva Rubinstein on a blind date in the Christmas season of 1953. The oldest child of the world-renowned pianist Arthur Rubinstein, the twenty-year-old actress and ballet dancer was living away from home for the first time. The home she had moved out of revolved around her father: his concerts, his friends, his fame, and his imperious, incessant, even petulant demands for adoration. Rubinstein *père* had wanted a daughter, according to his biographer, so that he could "possess her love entirely," and his daughter Eva had lived with those expectations her entire life. At the same time, she had to live with terrible secrets: her father told her about some of his affairs that he was hiding from his wife, Eva's mother, in effect making his own daughter an accomplice to his philandering. He could alternate his enormous charm with vicious abuse. "If you disagreed about a book or a film," according to Eva, "all of a sudden you were an idiot, having fifteen minutes before been the best, the most loved, the most intelligent." Neither emotionally nor financially independent enough to "handle" living on her own very well, she recalled, she felt the oddness of living without her father's forceful presence.[9]

She was strikingly beautiful to contemporaries, though not to herself; sexually inexperienced; and haunted by the feeling that her life was frivolous, uninvolved with the things that really mattered. "My goodness!" she recalled her first reaction to Coffin. "He speaks German and French! And he sings and he's musical and he wanted to be a pianist and isn't it amazing!" Her landlady (an older friend whom she trusted) had no doubts at all: "Well! How can one resist *that*?" As a result, Eva remembered thinking, "Oh dear, I should take this very seriously."[10]

Coffin provided a connection to authentic experience as well as to a kinder masculinity than she saw at home. Eager to escape the "mythology, theater, unreality" of her parents' home, she felt that Coffin offered "the first touch of reality in my life." Bill Coffin would "be such a good *man* because he's going to be a minister," she thought, "and he won't do all the terrible things that men do," by which she meant being unfaithful. Coffin talked to her about Dostoyevsky and asked her opinion about things, about ideas, and she felt elevated. He wrote that they "danced the New Year in," and that afterwards he "was nervous if she was more than ten feet away."

They saw each other some the next spring when she was dancing in her first Broadway show and the production came to New Haven before opening in New York. Coffin recalled being miffed because between rehearsals and shows Rubinstein had little time for him. She recalled a week of brutal rehearsals on a tiny stage and his and Catherine Coffin's insistence on throwing a late supper for the cast of dancers, despite Rubinstein's protest—and prediction —that the exhausted cast simply would not come.

There probably could not have been a truly auspicious time for Eva Rubinstein to meet Catherine Coffin. Entering a house that the hostess had prepared for thirty guests, knowing that she would be the only one, made things worse. "I knew instantly," she recalled vividly, "that I was not good enough for her boy." Even if he had agreed with his mother, Coffin wrote later that his "pride was wounded" by Rubinstein's preoccupation with her show, "so much so that by the end of the week I decided our relationship had little future. That summer I didn't see her at all."

Coffin soon became involved with a married friend of his sister, Margot, Harriet Gibney (now Harriet Harvey), who lived in New York with her journalist husband Frank. They met on a weekend sail from Newport to Martha's Vineyard organized by Margot and her husband. Coffin, according to Harriet, "was in a playful mood and I was in a playful mood. . . . it was almost a brotherly, sisterly relationship, but very exciting for both of us." One evening they took a very long walk, and "there was a little sexual play but not much," she remembered. That summer she stayed in Salisbury, Connecticut, and she and Coffin saw each other weekdays while Frank Gibney worked in New York City.[11]

Coffin and Harriet continued this relationship—and she would later play a much larger role in his life—but he eventually turned his thoughts back to Eva Rubinstein. He had not forgotten her, though she had thought to let the relationship "peter out." At some point during the following year, she recalled, he tracked her down in Paris where she was acting and dancing in a series of plays and sent her a letter in which "he said things that meant a lot to him, and I somehow didn't take it as profoundly. . . . And I just didn't answer it." Coffin understood that he had been rejected. Eva was busy and had at least two beaux during this period, one of whom wanted to marry her. She fell for an older actor—and discovered sex: "it was just fun, it was marvelous."

In the fall of 1955 she was playing Broadway again. Coffin was beginning his last year at Yale Divinity School and had decided to seek an urban store-front church similar to the East Harlem Protestant Parish. In Coffin's memory Eva "called again from New York" out of the blue. She recalled, more probably, that he did the calling, "turned up suddenly," and asked to see her.

Coffin had turned thirty-one that June, and Maguire remembered him announcing that he had to get married that year. Male clergy already belonged to a sexually suspect profession. If they did not want questions raised about their masculinity, they needed wives. Eva had glamour, beauty, and a name. With exotic looks by American standards, at home in European culture and languages, she might have reminded Coffin of Manya. "I was also an actress and genealogically offbeat," she mused many years later, "so maybe it was like a pale shadow of the real one."

Soon Coffin began to focus his intentions entirely on Eva. They began to see each other regularly. "And we would be reading Dostoyevsky," Eva said. "And he would be taking me to church and we were having all sorts of very long talks. And the next thing you know, we're getting very serious about all this." Coffin went to New York frequently; occasionally she came up to New Haven after her Saturday evening performance and stayed over to attend classes with him on Monday. To outsiders, it appeared that Coffin wooed Eva with energy and verve.[12]

That fall, while Catherine vacationed in Europe, they began sleeping together, and in mid-November Coffin wrote his mother of "a new and wonderful relationship." Knowing she would be surprised, he continued, "It is with Eva, yes with Eva! Hold on while I try to make the unbelievable believable. As you know for almost two years I have been careful not to see too much of Eva feeling the risk of an emotional involvement on my part too great and the chances of a long term arrangement too small. Shortly after you left I found out not only that Eva has had a great affection for me for some time, but also that she has also considered the possibility of becoming a minister's wife."

Fully a man of his time, Coffin presented Eva proudly as talented but willing to quit the stage as soon as she married. "She is convinced she could never be a good actress and wife," he wrote, "and really cares only about being the latter." Even so, "Her mind is much better than I ever suspected. It is not overly stocked but it is very responsible and after all she is only just 22." Fortunately, she also had experience running a "household with enormous efficiency and charm. Presently she is supervising a cook, governess and maid, and her little brother and sister." Eva Rubinstein had met the key conditions, Coffin thought: she would be an eager and intelligent wife, and an effective domestic manager.[13]

He avoided mention of her father, except to point out his likely opposition to the marriage on the grounds of Coffin's future profession. In reality, though he disliked organized religion, the emotionally childish Rubinstein cared less about a potential son-in-law's career than the very fact of a rival for his daughter's affections. Late in his life, Rubinstein stopped one of his friends who had been trying to talk to him about the gospel. "Don't worry about me," he said. "When I get to heaven I have no problem. I am Jewish, and if Moses is there at the gate, he will let me in. . . . my wife is Catholic—maybe it is St. Peter who is at the gate . . . so *he* will let me in. And I have a son-in-law who is an Episcopalian [sic] minister—so how can I lose!" As his biographer concluded, "he did not take the issue very seriously."[14]

According to a story Coffin told many times before putting it in his memoir, and which remains the single most widely known of all Coffin stories, the maestro once declared to his daughter that he did not want a Billy Graham for a son-in-law. "You can tell him," Coffin claims to have retorted—also to Eva—"that I don't want a Liberace as a father-in-law." But Coffin wisely avoided saying this to his face, and Eva Rubinstein would never have dared such insolence to her father. Male clergy delighted in this parable, a tale of the minister's witty, manly comeback and put-down of the powerful, womanizing maestro as the gay, sequined showman.[15]

Religion itself played little—if any—role in the marriage decision or deliberations. The nonobservant Arthur Rubinstein felt pride in his Jewishness as a matter of ethnicity, not of religious belief. Born Catholic, his wife, Aniela, had converted to Lutheranism to divorce her first husband. The parents gave their children no religious education and celebrated Christmas when their Catholic grandmother lived with them.[16]

For her part, Eva felt scandalized, fascinated, and relieved by Coffin's lack of deference toward her father, his willingness to declare opinions, his readiness to do battle in the world. "So I figured he was my knight in shining armor," she recalled. "Yes, it was sort of a great relief to find somebody who was going to now take the burden. I would not have to make decisions, I would not have to think."

As he sought to persuade Catherine, Coffin appeared to be working on his own ambivalence as well. "I think I must be very much in love with her," he wrote. "If this sounds doubtful it is only because I am trying to be honest and because love is such a big word in my vocabulary. I have never used it with any girl before." He acknowledged differences in their capacities. "I don't suppose I could ever love as unconditionally as she does," he confided. "I would remain a bachelor rather than leave the ministry—of this I am sure. Eva, however, would leave everything for the man she loves—and for her children. Her mother confirmed this impression."[17]

Neither Coffin nor Mme. Rubinstein saw Eva very clearly, as she was not quite as taken with the idea of marriage as they thought. She was not, she recalled, having very much fun. Their sexual relationship disappointed her, and she found herself heading for marriage without quite deciding for it. "It was interesting," she said of the time they spent together, "it was profound; it was meaningful. It was important. But it . . . never made me feel good."

Coffin thought her devoted though not "overly possessive" and soon told Catherine that he felt "beyond the questioning stage." He thanked his mother profusely for her apparent support but encouraged her not to return early from Europe on his account. He knew he could plead his case more effectively at long distance, assuring Catherine that "Eva is *very fond* of you if a little awestruck." He had chosen well to resume the courtship—and to announce his feelings—while his mother traveled abroad. Coffin had never courted a girl or woman with his mother nearby, and since he then lived in a basement apartment in her house, Catherine's physical proximity posed obvious problems. He repeatedly suggested that she prolong her travels, even that she first visit Ned in Toledo before returning East, hoping to carry his suit to its conclusion before his mother could intervene.[18]

The main issue remained the maestro, whose opposition, instead of "crushing" Eva's love, Coffin noted, had "the tendency to drive her into my arms." As Coffin admitted much later to Eva, he had enjoyed the challenge. For her part, Eva told her father's biographer years afterward, she had married partly as "revenge" against her father's self-centered and domineering ways; Coffin was "the first man who had ever talked back to my father, who didn't kowtow."[19]

They became engaged in late fall or winter of 1955, in a moment Rubinstein described decades later with chill dreariness. They were driving through rain to spend a weekend together with friends "and he asked me in the car and I remember the windshield wipers going back and forth, and I was saying to myself, yes, no, yes, no, yes, no, yes, no, and I said yes. Isn't that awful? It's true. . . . It's an awful thing to admit, but that's how it happened."

Some months later, however, she broke off their engagement late one night after one of her father's concerts in New York. Coffin, distraught, went to tell his mother, who had come for the occasion. The next day Catherine requested that Eva call on her, whereupon she pleaded Bill's case to the overwhelmed young woman.

Eva Rubinstein wondered why Catherine would take up a cause she did not believe in, concluding that Catherine, who must have been touched by her son's distress, must also have been offended: "One doesn't reject Bill Coffin!" But Catherine had more complicated motives. First, she wanted Bill's primary loyalties for herself. She had spent too many years too deeply involved in his development to feel anything else. And no young woman was going to measure up to her standards. Still, she also knew that Bill had to marry eventually, so she would have to face this great disappointment sooner or later, and probably sooner. By the time she returned from Europe, Catherine had likely made her peace with the inevitable. For in the terms she cared about, Bill could have done much worse.

Unfailingly shrewd regarding Bill's career, Catherine would have noted Eva's social connections, her family's wealth, the panache she would bring to a minister's household. She could have guessed at the effect a rich, artistic, delicately beautiful young woman would have on her son's plans to take an urban storefront church. Eva would be a valuable ally in protecting Bill from his occasional tendency to ignore connections, to undervalue the world represented by Yale. She was, moreover, in her son's words, "sufficiently snobbish to be quite taken with" the idea.[20]

Whether due to Catherine's intervention, Coffin's persuasiveness, or the power of the social forces around her, Eva soon relented. Browne Barr, however, who had befriended her (and provided some informal premarital counseling for the couple), shared her doubts. Undergoing psychoanalysis himself, Barr urged his prize student to see a psychiatrist. "He didn't really understand his feelings at a good many levels," Barr said of Coffin. "Why was he so aggressive, what was he getting out of it for himself? Why did he have to be the center of attention at every party?" Coffin went for several sessions but "couldn't take it," Barr recalled. "I think he was scared shitless about [these questions]. What was he going to find in a psychiatrist that was going to frighten him so that he didn't want to look any further? Maybe . . . the lack of his ability to love."[21]

Eva felt something missing, but if Coffin had had similar fears, he would have had trouble acting on them. By the spring of 1956 the engagement had become public, and Coffin's long anticipated career was finally falling into place. Marrying Eva even helped him make the career decision he really wanted. For he had already twice turned down an invitation to fill in for Andover's chaplain, who was taking a sabbatical the following year. Now, rightly convinced that Eva (and her family) would object to taking up residence in an urban slum, Coffin called the headmaster back "sheepishly," inquiring if the offer were still open; it was, and this time he accepted. Coffin had decided—in a momentous, if foreordained, choice—to work for the kind of people he knew best: upper-class, white Protestant northeasterners.[22]

While Coffin was analyzing his feelings toward Eva Rubinstein, and explaining them to his mother, he was also developing his understanding of Christian love in his academic work. Love had become, as he wrote to his mother, "a big word" in his vocabulary. Coffin did not concentrate on love to the exclusion of other subjects, although it was the subject of one of his first guest preaching appearances, at the Millbrook School in January 1954, which he reused later that year at Tarrytown and Shipley schools.[23]

In the fall of 1955, Coffin wrote a paper about love for a preaching course. He then rewrote the paper for delivery as a Christmas sermon, taking out the bleaker sections and adding, possibly with Eva's help, pages on the "joy of Christmas." Here he engaged the live and current questions of his own life—particularly of love and family—churning and working them into a public performance, in the process articulating emotions he found difficult to acknowledge privately. In the new material Coffin emphasized and reemphasized the faithfulness and love of God the father and filled the sermon with images of fatherly love, exuding tenderness rather than grandeur. "The father cannot come to his child in a blaze of glory," he wrote. "The child would be overawed. . . . He would fear judgment, and fearing judgment, secretly hate the judge." This was the precise problem with Arthur Rubinstein, whose "overawing presence" was causing such a storm over his marriage, and whom Coffin badly wanted to win over. A true father, Coffin wrote of God, "is love itself, and love seeks in return not hate, only love." Fatherless for twenty-two years, Coffin yearned for the father-God he described.[24]

Although Catherine Coffin had tried to be both mother and father, combining love and discipline, support and criticism, Bill Coffin had been seeking father substitutes for years. The fatherly face of the captain near the front at Compiègne had kept him safe that night just before Christmas in 1944, and possibly for the rest of his life. Coffin never tired of recalling the bear hugs he received from Manya's father, known to Coffin and his CIA colleagues as Pop.

William Sloane Coffin Sr. had not been the bear-hugging—or even the hugging
—type. Nor had Uncle Henry, a reserved, physically undemonstrative gentle-
man of the "old school." Though afraid of him when he was a child, Coffin
had come to love Henry Sloane Coffin, who had influenced generations of
Presbyterians as pastor of the Madison Avenue Presbyterian Church, president
of Union, and moderator of the Presbyterian Church. Though they rarely
talked of Bill's studies or vocation, Uncle Henry was the single family member
in whose footsteps Coffin was following most closely. He had died a year earlier
at Thanksgiving, leaving Coffin even more alone.[25]

Preaching about God choosing to come to Earth as a child, Coffin gave
voice to his own struggles to love and feel loved by God as well as by Eva Rubinstein. Coffin drew parallels between the prodigal son's return to his father and
Christians' return to God the father: "As the dry stone in the wilderness awaited
the rod of Moses to bring forth life-giving water, so we, dry stones in our waste-
land, await the touch of a deliverer." Was Eva his deliverer, or was it his faith,
stimulated by the coming marriage?

In words, the sermon resolved a number of problems for Coffin: how to
meet Eva in love, how to handle the lack of fatherly love in his own life, how
to account for the power of God's love. In this performance, he accounted for
himself as well, a prodigal son returning to the fold just as he was about to assume the adult role of husband and, presumably, father. In this mood ("Bethlehem is in the heart of every man. Christmas is any time") and in very similar
terms, he wrote to Catherine days before Christmas that "My own heart is just
spilling over! I am certain Eva is right for me and cannot get over the miracle
that it should be so."[26] The following December they were married in the
chapel at Union Theological Seminary.

Ordination and Chaplaincy: "The Temperature of the Tiles"

Founded in 1778, Phillips Academy, also known simply as Andover, has
been one of the nation's premier elite secondary boarding schools for more
than two centuries. Its alumni include two presidents (both Bushes), Supreme
Court justices, senators, governors, representatives, eminent businessmen, educators, publishers, journalists, artists, academics, writers, and activists. In New
England elegance, size, and beauty, the campus has few rivals among educational institutions at any level. Like most prep schools, Andover has been profoundly conservative for most of its history, providing a liberal arts education
for the children of America's oldest monied families. Through much of the
nineteenth and twentieth centuries, Andover graduates—even those of mediocre
achievement—could count on admission to elite colleges and universities as

well. If ideas could often be exciting inside its classrooms, the overall atmosphere remained clubby and "natural" for those who belonged, stuffy and cruel for those who did not. Like the WASP elite it served, the school remained, well into the twentieth century, exclusive, overwhelmingly Protestant, and discriminatory in racial, religious, and ethnic matters.

Coffin began working at Andover after graduating from divinity school in 1956, teaching summer school and giving short sermons for a daily chapel service. The service ordaining Coffin to the Presbyterian ministry took place in the chapel on August 12. Gray Baldwin, who had been Coffin's chaplain in the forties, came back from his sabbatical to participate; Barr preached the sermon; and the president of Union, Henry Pitney Van Dusen, gave the "charge" to the ordinand. Coffin's name and reputation—he may have been the best-known mainline Protestant divinity student in the country in 1956—could draw such worthies even at the very outset of what all expected to be an auspicious career.

Coffin took up his position at Andover in the middle of a decade of religious revival, in which "under God" was added to the Pledge of Allegiance and "In God We Trust" to American currency. Billy Graham became a national figure, an advisor to President Eisenhower. When Graham brought his revival to New York City in 1957, his popularity pushed the mainline religious press, faculty at Union (including Niebuhr), and even the National Council of Churches to take him seriously, and in some cases to look for common ground.[27]

Fueled by the population surge of the baby boom, Catholic and nearly all Protestant denominations, liberals as well as conservatives, experienced explosive growth during the 1950s. Churches flourished by following the postwar white migration to the suburbs; Americans spent more than a billion dollars building new churches in 1960. At the same time, much mainline Protestant religious practice had devolved into bland and conformist affirmation of the status quo, while ministers and church activities focused on pastoral counseling and the trials of private life. Within certain divinity schools, and within the ministry itself, discontent with this "suburban captivity" was growing; Coffin played a part in the nascent insurgency.[28]

At Andover he made fast friends, quick enemies, and a splash. The director of the summer session noted the "extraordinarily high morale," partly due to the unusually "vital role" played by the chaplain. Joshua Miner, then a physics teacher and later one of the principals in American Outward Bound, found himself at once drawn to the new man on campus and appalled by his apparent casualness about his work: "I'd say, 'What are you going to do today?' 'I don't know, I haven't decided yet.' And that used to make me mad." Coffin was tweaking Miner; he was often carrying typed, nine-hundred- to one-thousand-word sermons.[29]

Miner and the brash young chaplain became close friends. They played squash and joked and drank, and Coffin christened the Miners' new son Daniel. When Coffin first heard that the parents wanted to have the christening at the shore rather than in the chapel, he got miffed: "'Well,'" Miner recalled him saying, "'let me tell you something, Miner. If the House of the Lord isn't good enough for you, I'm not going to christen Daniel.'" But the next day Coffin backtracked, promising to christen the boy. He was objecting to the country club atmosphere, with "everybody in their short britches and drinking gin-and-tonics and I know what's up—anything but religion and a religious environment." Coffin stood for orthodoxy—with a twist. He wore shorts himself, scandalizing the child's grandmother, and, Miner reported, gave "one of the greatest talks I've ever heard in my life," alternating irreverence with the utmost seriousness about "welcoming Daniel into the Christian fraternity."

The incident demonstrated Coffin's growing skill at bringing Christianity to people's lives, where they lived them. He wanted this crowd in the church, but to hook them he had to meet them in their world, one Coffin knew how to play like a keyboard, down to his own shocking short britches. His confidence came partly from his personality and partly from the brand of Christianity he preached. For Coffin, and for a generation of urban and social justice warriors, neo-orthodoxy had a tough-guy swagger to it—"let me tell you something Miner"—that dismissed any hint of ineffectuality.

In the chapel, too, Coffin shook up his parishioners. "Coffin came storming in after witnessing an incident at breakfast that upset him," recalled a former student more than fifty years later. A student had carried his breakfast tray to a table, whereupon the five students already sitting there got up and moved away. Coffin was incensed and "blasted us for conformity and nastiness" for the entire chapel period. "What was remarkable for me was Coffin's fury," he remembered. "I was amazed that an adult could care so much what we did to each other. I could not imagine that the world could be organized differently. Coffin's tirade was the first hint that it might be possible."[30]

"Provocative" from the moment he arrived on campus, according to Miner and his wife, Phoebe, "he'd give a sermon and describe a rape on a cold tile floor of a New York drugstore and you can almost feel the temperature of the tiles as he describes this in every detail. Faculty would get up and walk out." Bad music bothered Coffin as much as bad religion. "He would say, 'Stop the organ, Mrs. Banta! Stop the organ! Stop the organ!' And he'd fly down off the pulpit with his robes out behind him. 'Do you call that singing? I tell you what we're gonna do.'" He organized worshippers on different sides of the aisle to compete in alternating verses, "And if we can't get those slates up there to rattle on the roof, let's go! All right, Mrs. Banta, crank it up again!" Some took offense, and left. "And the kids, of course, would just love it." Coffin made enemies this way, but he also stirred up the campus with the spirit he brought to the chapel.

Eva Coffin added to her husband's impact when she took up residence after the wedding in December. The only "celebrity wife" on campus, she brought "glamour," according to Phoebe Miner. First playing Cordelia in the student production of *King Lear,* Eva joined Coffin in a music and dance routine for the winter program of the Ladies' Benevolent Society that the Miners remembered vividly after four decades. While she danced, he played the piano, then lifted her, and then did the squatting and kicking Russian dances. "They were both very dramatic people and obviously not cut in the academic mold," Phoebe Miner recalled. "They were sort of larger than life. It was jarring to the community."

Coffin's year taught him some important lessons, and revealed new aspects of his professional life and character. First, he learned—anew, perhaps—that he could have an important effect on a community through his words and personality. Second, he learned that being provocative alone had limitations. As the headmaster warned, "Look, you're doing a terrific job in stirring the students up, but you better have someplace for them to put their energies. Otherwise it's irresponsible." Many years later, Coffin still approved of the criticism.[31]

Finally, Coffin found his real vocation in chaplaincy, perhaps the ideal perch from which to afflict the comfortable, if not to comfort the afflicted. Coffin held forth a good deal at Andover, and even stray letters show the issues he was engaging at the time. In an informal report to Gray Baldwin he mentioned a teacher's objections to the "respectful distance I would like to have the mind keep behind the heart." At the same time, Coffin listened carefully to the "incredibly bright and likable" students who, despite a tendency to play "intellectual volleyball," seemed open to finding "answers" to the bigger questions about values and life. "You can always hear a pin drop whenever you start talking about anxiety," he told Baldwin. "Anxiety would seem to me to be the existential entry to Christianity for this age."[32]

Coffin's analysis belied the later popular image of the fifties as the bland, serenely prosperous time celebrated by *Life* magazine. In fact, given the amount of international and domestic conflict during these years, as well as the sheer dread that pervaded popular culture—expressed as fear of juvenile delinquency, alien monsters, and nuclear war—the wonder is that the decade ever acquired its Happy Days reputation. Certainly the major thinkers of the time, such as C. Wright Mills, Herbert Marcuse, Erik Erikson, Hannah Arendt, the Niebuhr brothers, Abraham Joshua Heschel, and Erich Fromm, gave an edgier picture of the Eisenhower years.

Personal counseling, a large part of any chaplain's job, showed Coffin the depth of some students' cynicism and the extent to which their personal problems seemed to be rooted in the values of their wealthy parents. Coffin liked the students but wanted to provide them "more concrete value-forming experiences outside the classroom, such as living more simply, or living for some time in the slums." He began to see that even though Andover teaching did not explicitly promote the value of wealth, "living in surroundings that only wealth could provide tended inevitably to enhance its value." He thought that the Andover faculty resisted his ideas because they were too invested in their own classroom expertise. But they also had a vested interest in the privilege breathed in the atmosphere and announced by the buildings at Phillips Academy.[33]

So did the Coffins, who liked being around people with money and culture. "I found such satisfaction in the teaching, preaching, and counseling that went into being chaplain," Coffin wrote later, "that I gave up my original plan of working in the urban slums."[34] He may even have sensed the corollary truth: that given his upbringing, education, and personality, he would have been neither happy nor particularly effective working in the slums. Marriage and Andover set him firmly on the course of chaplain to the well-off. For the following year Coffin received invitations to two comparable positions, chaplaincies at Andover's rival Phillips Exeter Academy, and Williams College. Preferring a more adult community, he and Eva chose Williams.

Williams: The Taste of Controversy

Located in the northwestern corner of Massachusetts, surrounded by the Berkshires, Williams College was an "insidiously isolated place," Coffin remembered, at once exquisitely beautiful and suffused with "the air of unreality." The major issues on campus appeared to revolve around social life, principally fraternities. "The bland leading the bland," Coffin called Williams society.[35]

Culturally, Coffin fit perfectly into Williams: a pipe-smoking Yale and Andover man, a member of Skull and Bones, with a beautiful and artistic wife, a first child on the way (Amy Coffin was born in early 1958), and a sophisticated, romantically secret war record he could embellish. "You can throw in something about being a paratrooper for a little excitement," he offered the college newspaper reporter, who dutifully swallowed the bait.[36]

Coffin was bored. He was also offended by the discrimination against Jews that he saw on campus and in the fraternity system. His own casual anti-Semitism had been challenged in Europe, where he had visited Buchenwald after the war. "What the Germans did to the Jews was to me so appalling and so shocking," he recalled, "that we should fight a war condemning the Nazis for the horrors they perpetrated, particularly against the Jews, and then come back and have country clubs that didn't take Jews. It was absolutely outrageous to me."[37]

The southern civil rights movement had burst onto the national scene in December 1955 as the Montgomery bus boycott propelled Martin Luther King Jr. from a comfortable pulpit into his new role as national spokesman for the aspirations of African Americans. King's example must have been of great interest to Coffin. A well-educated, well-spoken middle-class preacher, King used biblical preaching to affirm American ideals while attacking social injustice. The year-long bus boycott combined religion and politics, the spiritual strength of thousands of black Montgomery residents and their clergy leaders' tactical brilliance, all under the threat of lethal violence. Its progress and eventual success gained nationwide press attention and also stirred the interest of the religious press and northern white clergy. This interest increased dramatically during the crisis in Little Rock, Arkansas, in 1957 when President Eisenhower had to send the U.S. Army to protect the court-ordered rights of black children to attend Central High School.

Like many northern clergy, Coffin found the courage of the southern civil rights protesters inspirational and the viciousness of segregationists' response shocking. Soon after arriving at Williams he began to stir up the moral and religious atmosphere with a discussion of the ongoing crisis in Little Rock. By November, he had published "A Christian Interpretation" of the Little Rock events in the alumni magazine. Coffin relied on the Bible, not sociology: "When the Bible says 'love your neighbor' it never assumes the neighbor is loveable; in fact quite the opposite. . . . hence, in the Old Testament the injunction to love the stranger within the gates, and in the New Testament the injunction to love one's enemies."[38]

He made himself well known, according to the campus newspaper, "through dynamic leadership and understanding of students."[39] According to his wife, he had a physical presence as well. "I saw Bill quell a food fight, a really hysterical food fight," she recalled. "He just had it under control in about two seconds, and nobody else could make it stop. . . . He had that thing that communicates to a crowd, finds the right word that changes the atmosphere."

Williams students spent an enormous amount of time talking about their fraternities during the late 1950s, debating fine points of fraternity life and regulations, particularly selection policies. By December, Coffin was beginning to engage the fraternity question publicly, suggesting that students were "vastly different in class or in conversation than they are in the fraternity" and that many students were "more 'fraternal' than their fraternities."[40]

For the first time in his life, Coffin became the focal point for public controversy. In February he spoke out against the low level of conversation at a "career weekend" panel that ignored the genuine "dilemmas" of modern business life—and apparently fired up students and alumni. Then the next month, three students announced their resignations from their fraternities in a special issue of the chapel's newsletter. Campus opinion divided, according to *The Williams Record*, ranging from "complete sympathy to furious indignation." When a prankster posted a false notice that Coffin would speak on "Are Fraternities Christian?" the chaplain decided to attend, along with 150 others. In the "tense atmosphere" of a hearing, he presented the views of the resignees, who were protesting the "institutionalized selectivity" of the rushing process. Coffin attacked the fraternities on a variety of grounds but mainly because they discriminated, either explicitly or implicitly, against Jews and blacks as well as against those outside a "narrow range of associates." As he put it later, "putting a narrow-minded student in a fraternity and expecting him to become more broad-minded was about as realistic as putting a wino in a wine cellar and expecting him to lay off the bottle."[41]

Coffin's role in stimulating debate and controversy moved to a new level one Saturday evening in mid-April. As he and Eva were coming back from seeing the movie *An American in Paris* she asked him, "Why couldn't we go to Paris sometime? Nothing ever happens in Williamstown." When she caught sight of the house, she wondered why the baby-sitter had opened the downstairs window of the study. "And suddenly, I said, 'Wait a minute, this isn't open! This is glass all over the floor!'" The window had been shot out; shotgun pellets and shards of glass lay strewn all over the living room. The baby-sitter and three-month-old Amy Coffin were upstairs and had mistaken the shotgun blast for a backfiring car.[42]

A student reporter asked Coffin whether he thought his stand on fraternities had something to do with the attack. "If so," he retorted, "somebody scares awfully easily." The following Wednesday night, while both Coffins were out of town and another baby-sitter was caring for Amy, someone threw a couple of cherry bombs into their backyard. The shotgun incident had already "scared the hell out of Eva." She was "still visibly shaken" the day after the cherry bomb attack. Amid widespread assumptions that fraternity boys were responsible for the shooting, the local police, college authorities, and newspaper staff cooperated in an investigation that quickly produced confessions from two students (drunken "Dekes," Coffin wrote) who were promptly expelled. As the *Record* put it in a year-end roundup, Coffin was "the most talked-about man of the spring term."[43]

SIX

"Bus-Riding Chaplain"

Call and Response

In late February 1958 Yale President A. Whitney Griswold was heading south for a vacation. The mail had brought bad, if not completely unexpected, news. Truman Douglass, head of the Board of Home Missions of the Congregational and Christian Churches, had become the third nationally prominent minister to turn down Griswold's invitation to replace the retiring A. Sidney Lovett as university chaplain.[1]

In the meantime, men whom the president trusted were lobbying him. Philosopher Paul Weiss, the first tenured Jew on the Yale faculty, whom Griswold had asked to listen for "large rumblings from the faculty," reported that "the most diverse types say that the right man to get as Chaplain is William Coffin. . . . apparently a large number of faculty, religious and non-religious, Christian and otherwise, think that Coffin is the man. I think so too." English professor Richard B. Sewall reported on his recent trip to Williams where he "saw much of Bill Coffin. Can't resist telling you how confirmed I am in my feeling that he is a magnificent candidate for the chaplaincy of Yale. . . . In six months he has transformed the religious climate at Williams." Impressed, Griswold scribbled a note to his secretary: "Pls. ack. by phone & say I'd like to hear more when I get back."[2]

Lovett himself recommended that the search committee "should now drop our sights closer to younger men" and "strongly urge[d] the committee to take another look at Bill Coffin." Something clicked in Griswold. His note at the top of Lovett's letter read, "All outdated by action of comm + invitation to Bill C." Griswold called Coffin in early March, and, Coffin remembered, "I told him yes with indecent haste." In fact, Coffin recalled, "By the time I was at Andover, certainly by the time I was at Williams," the Yale chaplaincy was "the only job I really wanted. . . . I had my heart set on that." Just thirty-three years old, William Sloane Coffin Jr. had become chaplain of the third oldest institution of higher learning in the United States.[3]

The appointment drew a remarkable range of support, suggesting an anointing more than a job offer, as though onlookers had been waiting for years to see just which extraordinary post Bill Coffin would assume. Charles Seymour, former Yale president (and close friend of CIA Director Allen Dulles), wrote Coffin that, "sub os: my advice was not sought but, if it had been you would have been my first choice and I cannot express the depth of my satisfaction. How your Uncle Henry's heart would have been warmed!" Dulles himself wrote, as did former OSS men Norman Holmes Pearson of the English Department (and a feeder for the CIA) and Archie Foord, master of Calhoun College, as well as a Yale graduate who let drop that he was "here in Washington working for your old company." Many declared that Coffin was the "perfect" candidate for the position, including members of the Yale Corporation, some of whom were already on a first name basis with the young minister.[4]

Early on, Coffin got earthy comradeship from Griswold and a blunt warning from the older guard. Worried about being expected to continue Lovett's "avuncular role," Coffin was relieved "when the president called me into his office and the first thing he said to me was, 'Are you going to bless every God-damned sewer in town the way your predecessor did?' A load just dropped off." Provost Norman Buck, on the other hand, warned Coffin to be aware of—and keep —his place as a brash young man.[5]

For decades the position had been dominated by pastoral counseling of students and the university's numerous ceremonial needs. The much-loved A. Sidney Lovett, known as "Uncle Sid" to generations of Yale men, had specialized in these functions. Yale's religious programs consisted of a poorly coordinated hodgepodge: Dwight Hall, individual denominational ministries, the thinly attended daily chapel services, in addition to the University Church and weekly worship at the cathedral-like Battell Chapel.

Coffin knew enough to nose around his new job at first. "I knew it would be a lot of pastoral counseling," Coffin remembered. "I knew it would be preaching. I knew it would be bringing in visiting preachers; but on the programmatic side I didn't arrive with any agenda." He quickly discovered that "not much was going on. This was like Williams. This was the bland leading the bland."[6]

At Williams Coffin had begun to make religious convictions part of public dialogue. Every meeting he attended, everywhere he preached, he struggled to make liberal Protestantism relevant to the modern world. At Yale Coffin led an unabashed effort to put a vigorous, demanding, loving God into public discourse. In his first year, for example, he criticized (in the left-liberal magazine *The Nation*) the value-neutral "pseudo-objectivity" of modern liberal education. God, he argued, had been reduced to a quaint anachronism and an extracurricular activity. Coffin set out to change the way students thought about God and their lives.[7]

Coffin belonged to a wider effort among social critics and religious leaders to jolt students out of middle-class complacency. But he gave unusual energy and imagination to the cause. "There is a big need," he wrote in response to a survey during his first few months on campus, "to present the relevance of Christianity to all major areas of life [and] to the campus as a whole."[8] He proposed reorganizing and dramatically expanding the study programs and interdenominational meetings that could provide a forum for students to engage modern religious issues. He wanted to make Battell Chapel a proud locus for ecumenical worship.

Yale's denominational ministers, he argued, had a "pastoral obligation" to make sure that students had a genuinely cosmopolitan experience of religion, that they did "not go every Sunday to that local church which most nearly resembles their own home town's cozy little church." Coffin wanted the student study program to be "far more ecumenical, far less denominational in its outlook." With less fragmentation, "more boys will be released for real service to the campus and to the community." Ordained Presbyterian, with a Presbyterian pedigree going back at least two generations, Coffin played a vocal role in what one commentator has called "the declining significance of denominationalism" in the postwar era.[9]

He made no effort to hide Christian messages under secular rubrics, to sneak in discussion of "values" or "meaning" without identifying their religious source. A biblically grounded, liberal Protestant minister, Coffin enjoyed the role of evangelist and wanted the entire Yale chaplaincy to reflect that unapologetic thrust and engagement with the world. Elections, plays, even movies all provided occasions for religious discussion. "We must be alert to seize them when they come," he concluded, encapsulating his emotional and philosophical approach to the world.

Coffin wanted interfaith as well as interdenominational religious services, for "Hillel boys can obviously work closely with Christian boys in this area." Not that Coffin was trying to evangelize among the Jewish students. Instead, he wanted a rabbi who would do for Judaism what he was proposing to do for Christianity. "We need to make a big effort to get a first rate rabbi on the campus," he argued, who would be both "an excellent pastor to Jewish students" and "willing to present Judaism vigorously and openly to the campus as a whole." Coffin gave campus Roman Catholicism far less attention. As he pointed out, the priest in charge of the Catholic student ministry received no university support, relying instead on alumni contributions.

Coffin soon got a chance to have a significant effect on the matter of Jewish students at Yale. Yale's new Hillel director, Rabbi Richard Israel, who arrived a year after Coffin, had been trying to find out if a quota limited Jewish admissions to Yale. While the number was not public knowledge, the percentage of Jews had hovered in the range of 10 to 15 percent for quite a long time, while at both Harvard and Cornell Jews made up nearly 25 percent of the undergraduate student body. Prodded by Israel, Coffin went to see Griswold and eventually got the information. He had been convinced that Yale's numbers fell substantially below Princeton's and Williams's, but the facts showed otherwise: Yale's Class of 1963 (which had entered in 1959) had roughly 11.5 percent Jews, about the same as the Class of 1964 at Princeton and a little higher than that at Williams. Coffin retreated temporarily: "So I guess I was wrong. My apologies. I shall continue to approach this question with my usual wisdom and patience as well as energy!"[10]

But neither Coffin nor Israel let the matter drop. Coffin discussed the question of Jewish admissions with a number of administration officials. His notes on meetings with Dean William DeVane and Provost Buck indicated the persistence of stereotypes at the highest levels: "However bright not all Jewish applicants are 'beauties.' 'Twerps,' said Buck. Personalities not always attractive, self-serving, aggressive. Lack of breadth of view."[11]

Still, Coffin and Israel pressed Griswold—successfully—to put his administration on record against discrimination in the admissions process. By March 1962 (for the class of 1966), Griswold had issued a new admissions policy that explicitly committed Yale to "removing economic, social, religious . . . barriers to" equal opportunity. The number of Jewish undergraduates began slowly to rise. In the fall of 1962, more young Jewish men entered Yale University than ever before at one time. While the number of Jewish freshmen did not always increase from year to year, the overall number of Jewish undergraduates climbed steadily, from 481 in 1962, 491 in 1963, 523 in 1964, 616 in 1965, 718 in 1966, 829 in 1967, and 906 in 1968. Thereafter, the number appears to have reached a "natural" level of between a quarter and a third of the student body.[12]

The issues facing Jewish students at Yale went beyond numbers. For years, for example, the senior prom had been held at the New Haven Lawn Club, which admitted Jews only as guests. When Daniel Horowitz (Class of 1960) came to see Coffin about changing the venue, Coffin told him, "You're absolutely right. Go for it." Horowitz then "made a big fuss," as Coffin recalled, and "the telephone rang one afternoon and there was the gentle voice of Dean DeVane," asking, "'Bill, do we have to go through with this?' And I said, in my gentlest voice, 'Dean DeVane, yes.' He said, 'Thank you, that's all I needed to hear from you.'"[13]

Both Coffin and Israel pushed for Jewish students to be able to eat Kosher meals on the Yale meal plan and for alternate exam dates for Jewish students who did not want to "make a choice of pleasing their conscience or the University" on the Jewish Sabbath, as Israel put it in a letter to the university secretary. By April 1962 they had succeeded in changing Yale University policy to allow Jewish students to take make-up exams in the event of such conflicts.[14]

Although Coffin's temperament would never have allowed him to become imprisoned in his office, pastoral counseling, mainly of students, absorbed much of his time: "Every afternoon—and this is true for most of my eighteen years—I would be in the office and just do pastoral counseling." To a skeptical interviewer he explained, "I found that any time anybody wanted to talk on a deeply personal level I was very interested. Only about one student a year struck me as boring." It was, he recalled, "a great privilege to be invited into the sanctuary of somebody's soul, as it were—the secret garden of another person's soul." Coffin's youth made that part of his job easier at first. But even when he got older, and "somewhat impatient with the same old problems," counseling provided "an awful lot of material for sermons."[15]

Much of this counseling dealt with students' feelings about their parents. With a wisdom beyond his years, Coffin consistently counseled reconciliation, forgiveness, and love, even when he did not use these words. Coffin's counsel to love, however, was no simple bit of mushiness. He "used to press very hard in those early days, feeling a lot of drifting and a lot of listlessness with these students. . . . They didn't have much passion. They thought *cogito ergo sum* was what it was all about and Yale was encouraging them to think that, whereas I felt very deeply it's *amo ergo sum*" (I love, therefore I am).[16]

Coffin's insistence on the principle of *amo ergo sum* put him at odds with the dominant ethos of a research university. He simply did not believe in one of the key underpinnings of university life and culture: the possibility of objective, disinterested scholarship. He often said that he was "pro-intellect and anti-intellectual," which meant, in his view, that the intellectual enterprise itself, the pursuit of knowledge for its own sake, had little to recommend it.

From the many pulpits Yale offered, Coffin prayed, preached, and agitated on the themes of love and engagement. Greeting the freshmen in 1959, he prayed for a "concern to share in the action and passion of our time; a like determination to end all that is stale, irrelevant, false in our university, nation, and world." At the end of that year his commencement prayer asked for safety "from all perils—the clamorous desires of self-preservation, the trivial, the superficial, and all the pervasive and powerful perversions of our time that would cheapen the humanity of human beings." The concern for authenticity, for life engaged with the stuff of existence, permeated liberal intellectual and religious culture of the 1950s. Coffin, whose own exuberant thirst for experience had guided him since the onset of World War II, tried to pull students into authentic experience and out of what he felt to be "the superficiality, the triviality of American life." He had an impressive array of tools at his disposal: a quick and incisive wit, utter self-confidence, a native's grasp of elite WASP culture, and confidence in an activist Christianity.[17]

Coffin himself needed "to share in the action and passion" of his time and sought out experiences that could match his flamboyance. So when James Robinson of Operation Crossroads Africa invited him in the summer of 1959 to lead a group of students to Guinea the following summer, Coffin's spirits soared. Crossroads Africa recruited interracial groups of students, as well as work group leaders, to work in newly independent African countries. That year Coffin put a good bit of effort into promoting this combination of goodwill tour and work camp, recruiting students and helping some of them raise money for the airfare. As spring 1960 approached and the reality of leaving his family—his and Eva's third child was born that March—for "two long months" came closer, Coffin appears to have felt some pangs of conscience. But a family summer vacation at Squam Lake could not compete with a distant land that promised adventure, the chance to use French daily, and the opportunity to be an American ambassador in the larger world.[18]

The trip proved invaluable for the Americans, if less obviously beneficial to the Africans. American civil rights issues pervaded their experience, both within the group and between the Americans and the Africans. According to Coffin, "the two Southern whites frequently joined with the three Northern Negroes to do a wonderful educational job on the Northern whites regarding their own unrecognized personal biases." Coffin himself may have been on the receiving end of this education as well, for the entire group was "shocked to find that, after New York and Washington, Little Rock seemed to be the best known town in the United States."[19]

In fact, in every town they visited their hosts organized an "exchange of views," and the very first question the Americans faced concerned "the American racial" situation. Other questions dealt with the Cold War (nonsensical to Guineans), Algeria (America's "exceedingly equivocal" position on colonialism), and U.S. support for South Africa. The group saw America through different eyes and learned new ways of thinking about race and international politics. Perhaps most important, the trip had stimulated a "new interest in the American race situation and in American foreign policy" among the students. Coffin had also reinforced his own convictions that there could be no substitute for authentic experience. Back at Yale, he persuaded Griswold to hire a full-time career counselor to help broker "non–status quo" positions for Yale men.[20]

In the fall of 1960, Coffin reported to some former students, "More people are not only studying things African, but eager to work in Africa, eager particularly to follow in your footsteps on a teaching contract." For years Coffin's correspondence with the Guinea group remained warm, close, and extensive. In 1963, he wrote Robinson, three of them were in Africa; two had joined the Peace Corps; two were doing graduate work on Africa; three were active in the civil rights movement; and one was working as a social worker in New York. All of these pursuits were "to some degree attributable to our summer in Guinea."[21]

Even before his trip to Guinea, Coffin had preached on civil rights. He frequently received invitations to preach at New England prep schools, as well as at other colleges, universities, and churches, and used these occasions to bring up the issue. After hearing Coffin speak at a "Religious Emphasis" program at Virginia Polytechnic Institute in January 1960, the local YMCA director thanked Coffin profusely for "pushing us to the wall on our number one problem." Since his correspondent had been thinking about going abroad during the summer, Coffin predicted that he would soon "realize, as I have been forced to realize after seven years of work abroad, that segregation is really treasonous, in that it undercuts everything United States foreign policy is trying to accomplish the world around."[22]

An elderly member of the First Presbyterian Church of Stamford, Connecticut, complained to Griswold about Coffin's "rudeness" to her pastor, his criticism of Billy Graham and Norman Vincent Peale, and his efforts "to incite some High School teenagers who happened to be there to make placards and go out picketing places to show their support of the negroes." Coffin admitted to Griswold that he might have been a little "over aggressive. You know my weakness." Coffin apologized to the minister "for charging without more sense of direction. . . . I had just heard Thurgood Marshall and was feeling like John Wayne."[23]

In early 1960, the civil rights movement had entered a new phase, as African-American students began "sit-ins" at segregated lunch counters across the South. The new nonviolent "direct action" movement spread quickly, garnering national press as violent segregationists publicly beat nonresisting protesters and the students' northern supporters picketed national chains such as Woolworth's. Inspired by these new tactics, Coffin used his rhetorical gifts to "charge ahead."

After his summer in Guinea, Coffin's guest preaching zeroed in on "the race question" and he became more willing to challenge, even to offend, his audiences. With other chaplains, he had been mulling over the idea of publicly refusing invitations to speak at private schools with no Negro students. He raised this possibility with students at The Masters School, a private girls' school in Westchester County, New York. The furious headmaster, absent during Coffin's talk, accused him of "a use of shock tactics that borders on the irresponsible" and of "placing highly undesirable pressure on a group of serious, thoughtful youngsters, many of whom are going to feel a sense of guilt and frustration about an issue that lies outside of their control."[24]

Coffin's lengthy reply showed how his thinking about moral suasion and political effectiveness was developing. Though he ought to have "reported the discussion" to his hosts, he had not expected their distress: "After all, racial discrimination is not only a religious issue but also the number one social problem of the United States, and it was only natural for the girls to ask 'What can we do, here?'"

"Perhaps you are right that I used shock tactics," he admitted. "But how else do you get at the well-shielded?" The school had yet to admit its first black student, and since "many of the girls did not even know this . . . I cannot help feeling that the shock you refer to was less a matter of tactics than of facts stated." As for the girls' "guilt," Coffin argued that for students "to be concerned with such an obviously moral issue is in itself a good thing, not a hurtful one." And "would not a strong expression of student sentiment serve as an incentive both to the trustees to admit Negroes and to Negro students to apply?"

Shock tactics might not be ideal, "But when for years 'patience' has been used as a rationalization for irresponsibility, when fear continues to win out over moral concern, what other tactics are effective?" Deftly turning the headmaster's concerns upside down, Coffin attacked: "Let those who fear what people will say and do if Negroes be admitted fear also what others will say and do if Negroes be excluded." Finally, Coffin framed the issue in Christian terms: "Frankly this represents a deliberate disturbance of the peace based on the Christian conviction that peace is not the absence of tension but the presence of justice."

While Coffin made aggressive, imaginative use of his position as university chaplain, his impatience with academia appears to have been growing. Perhaps that impatience contributed to the swelling congregations at Battell Chapel. While John F. Kennedy, the new, young, energetic American president, was articulating an ethos of active engagement with the world, Coffin had clearly tapped into the same cultural current. He had created a similar swirl around the Yale chaplain's office, one infused with the language of moral urgency and thoroughgoing commitment, but without clear political direction. On the evidence of his Easter Sunday sermon in 1961, Coffin felt frustrated with how so many people could proceed with life and business as usual while the civil rights movement was transforming the South and independence movements were upending the colonial world. Resurrection had visceral contemporary relevance

Yale chaplain and New Frontiersman. Pictured here in the early 1960s, Coffin projected an image of masculine, can-do confidence perfectly in tune with the spirit of President John F. Kennedy's New Frontier. Courtesy of William Sloane Coffin Jr.

for him: "Not education of the mind but a total transformation of one's whole being is what we need. Enough of these less than halfway measures! There is something pathetic about people running around lighting lights when what we need is to have the whole bloody night come to an end."[25]

The Road Forks: The Freedom Ride

Like most young firebrands, Coffin had given little thought to how the logic of his beliefs and the restless energy of his personality might produce a combustible mixture. Less than a month after this sermon he got a chance to find out, as he propelled himself into the middle of a dangerous civil rights conflict a thousand miles from the comfortable environs of Battell Chapel.

For when Coffin preached on Easter Sunday in 1961, the civil rights movement had been on fire for more than a year. Beginning February 1, 1960, in Greensboro, North Carolina, African-American college students electrified students and older civil rights activists around the country by sitting down at the whites-only sections of downtown lunch counters. Within weeks sit-ins had spread to other cities in North Carolina, to South Carolina, and to Nashville, Tennessee, soon to be the heart of the student civil rights movement.

The willingness of young African Americans and their white supporters to risk brutal beatings, jail time, and fines in order to fight segregation upended the civil rights movement. It put enormous pressure on the existing organizations and leaders, many of whom were unnerved by the less organized, more dangerous, less controllable protests of the young people. But they had hit on a strategy that pushed nonviolent tactics to an entirely new level. Martin Luther King Jr., according to reporter and writer Taylor Branch, "embraced the students for taking the step he had been toying with for the past three years—of *seeking out* a nonviolent confrontation with the segregation laws." Their college presidents, on the other hand, and more established groups like the NAACP, at first advised caution or kept their distance. Within just a few months, however, the early successes of the rapidly growing student movement led to the formation of the Student Nonviolent Coordinating Committee, or SNCC. For the next year, SNCC members and actions provided much of the energy for the newly revitalized movement.[26]

Inspired by the sit-in movement and the embarrassing violence it provoked, civil rights activists searched for new ways to use nonviolence to chip away at the structure of Southern segregation. One avenue involved getting the Justice Department to enforce antidiscrimination provisions of the Interstate Commerce Act, particularly because the Supreme Court had recently held that a restaurant in a Trailways bus terminal could not refuse service to a black customer in the "white" section of the dining room.

Martin Luther King discussed these issues briefly with Attorney General Robert Kennedy in mid-April 1961. But the most explosive initiative was being undertaken by the Congress of Racial Equality (CORE), a civil rights organization founded during World War II by the pacifist and Gandhian Fellowship of Reconciliation (FOR). CORE had sponsored an integrated interstate bus ride through the South in 1947 to highlight a Supreme Court decision banning certain forms of discrimination in interstate travel. Riders had been beaten and received jail terms, but the legal case never went anywhere. Fifteen years later, with the civil rights movement reborn and bursting with new blood and tactical innovation, CORE decided to try again. A group of thirteen Freedom Riders set out on May 4 from Washington, D.C., to travel by bus all the way to New Orleans, along the way challenging, in Director James Farmer's words, "every form of segregation met by the bus passenger."

The group of six whites and seven blacks experienced several minor incidents and one serious beating during the first week, and they were attracting little national publicity. Everything changed on Saturday, May 13, 1961, the day before Mother's Day. Outside of Anniston, Alabama, an armed mob destroyed one of their buses and savagely beat the Freedom Riders. In Birmingham later that day, Police Commissioner Eugene "Bull" Connor's police stepped aside and gave the local Ku Klux Klan fifteen minutes to beat the riders again.

The mob thrashed reporters and smashed their cameras; seven onlookers were hospitalized. Some photos of the melee survived, however, and found their way to the front pages of newspapers worldwide. Overnight the Freedom Ride had become an international cause célèbre.

The publicity forced the Kennedy administration to act. Attorney General Robert Kennedy himself got on the phone with Alabama Governor John Patterson, as well as with bus company officials and Birmingham civil rights activist Fred Shuttlesworth, trying to guarantee the riders' safety. As negotiations faltered, so did the determination of the riders, who decided they had already achieved most of their goal; they would fly the rest of the way. They had, after all, successfully forced the intervention of the federal government to protect their lives. Kennedy had sent John Seigenthaler, his administrative assistant, to Birmingham, where he helped the airport manager outwit an eager mob and accompanied the Freedom Riders on their flight to New Orleans.

But just when the administration thought the crisis was over, it started up again. After two days of intense debate the Nashville student civil rights movement, led by James Bevel and Diane Nash, decided to send a delegation to Birmingham to resume the Freedom Ride. This news angered both Kennedys. The president, already feeling the pressure of his upcoming summit meeting in Vienna with Soviet Premier Nikita Khrushchev, wanted to avoid the embarrassment of an internationally broadcast civil rights debacle. He demanded of Harris Wofford, his special assistant for civil rights, "Can't you get your god-damned friends off those buses? Stop them." Assistant Attorney General Burke Marshall, head of the Justice Department's Civil Rights Division, called Seigenthaler in New Orleans and instructed him to try to "turn them around." Unable to control what seemed on the surface to be simple, straightforward events, Robert Kennedy found himself furious both at Governor Patterson and at civil rights activists for pushing matters to such an explosive point.

On the morning of Saturday, May 20, the Nashville group arrived in Montgomery. There, in a nearly precise parallel to the Birmingham fiasco a week earlier, and despite a series of complex negotiations and repeated assurances of protection by the authorities, police disappeared for ten to fifteen minutes while a mob pounded, stomped, and bloodied the nonviolent young people, as well as reporters, photographers, and Seigenthaler—cold-cocked with a pipe as he tried to rescue two female Freedom Riders.

That same evening John and Billie Maguire drove from Wesleyan to New Haven for an early celebration of Bill Coffin's birthday. Maguire, it turned out, had run into Martin Luther King Jr. (whom he knew fairly well) on a plane the previous month. King had explained the Freedom Ride strategy, adding, "We may need you some time." Maguire had told Coffin about the encounter, "but I don't think either of us had taken it seriously until it really did appear to us that this ride could be terminated by bombs." They had not yet heard of the Montgomery riot and, Maguire recalled, "we were speaking very bravely, that if anything happened to the Freedom Riders, we would go down and keep this thing going, which was, in a way, real bravura because up to that point, no representative white clergy or teachers had gotten into it." Events caught them up quickly.

For while the Maguires and the Coffins were engaged in what Maguire later called a lot of "good stiff talk," John Patterson was refusing to take phone calls from the attorney general of the United States. Enraged, Robert Kennedy sent in federal marshals. Martin Luther King Jr. flew to Montgomery on Sunday, and the marshals escorted him from the airport to the house of Ralph Abernathy, who had founded the Southern Christian Leadership Conference (SCLC) with King in 1957.

Sunday morning Coffin drove to Andover to preach. After seeing the news, he called Maguire, insistent that they get involved. Maguire demurred at first, wanting to finish his first year of teaching, but Coffin was persuasive. He knew little about national civil rights strategy, but he had never "been angrier and certainly never more ashamed of the United States," he wrote later, "than I was looking at the pictures of the beatings." Since Coffin was on his way to Washington, D.C., for a Peace Corps National Advisory Council meeting, he offered to try to drum up support for another Freedom Ride among his new colleagues. He failed to recruit anyone, as most were concerned about the president "going to Vienna in the midst of all this civil unrest."

Coffin and Maguire decided to press on themselves, aware that they would be the first northern whites—the first with "respectable" credentials—to join the Freedom Ride movement. They wanted Martin Luther King's imprimatur, so they called him at Abernathy's home in Montgomery. "Well, I don't want to put any pressure on you," Maguire remembered King saying, "but we need every bit of help we can get." For him, that "clinched it . . . I knew I had to go." Searching for comrades, Coffin and Maguire struck out with all the southern professors they knew, black or white, including one theologian who had written eloquently on the evils of segregation. Closer to home they signed up Yale Divinity School professor Gaylord Noyce. David Swift, Maguire's department chair at Wesleyan, recruited himself when Maguire explained his plans to him. To integrate this all-white group, Coffin called George Smith, a member of his Crossroads Africa group the previous summer, now finishing Yale Law School. Smith agreed, and his dean, Eugene Rostow, agreed to let him make up exams he might miss. The little band made plans to fly to Atlanta on Tuesday afternoon.

Coffin had not even considered that he might be getting in over his head —that is, until he received a phone call Tuesday morning from Burke Marshall, who had heard about Coffin's proposed Freedom Ride, perhaps from fellow Yale alumnus Rostow. Civil rights issues lay in a political minefield. John F. Kennedy's razor-thin election victory had depended on segregationist southern Democratic support, and these "Dixiecrats" wielded enormous power in Congress. Coffin had given no thought to whether his impulsive trip South might disturb delicate understandings between the administration and congressional leaders. Marshall spoke diplomatically, but there was no mistaking his message: the United States government wanted Coffin to cancel. The message could easily have originated with Robert Kennedy, perhaps even from the president. Coffin was shaken.

Torn between King's invitation and his own government's high-level opposition, Coffin felt in a "terrible quandary." Confronted with a far deeper choice than he realized, Coffin had to decide between two very different Americas: the one he knew well, and had served in hot war and cold as an infantry and intelligence officer; and one he barely knew at all, but felt increasingly called to serve. The first America, represented by "mother Yale" and Catherine Coffin's wide circle of elegant and sophisticated friends, inhabited the elegant WASP realms of safety and privilege. For despite his disparagements of fraternity life, campus racism, and anti-Semitism and his critique of superficiality, Coffin remained a charter member of what soon came to be called the Establishment. A handsome, articulate, Ivy League man's man, he was perfectly positioned for a fruitful relationship with the youthfully masculine and energetic administration of John F. Kennedy. Only two months earlier he had accepted an appointment to the national advisory council for the Peace Corps; he could expect more prestigious assignments in the future.

The "other America," represented most visibly by Martin Luther King Jr. but usually by no one at all—the disfranchised, the poor, the colored peoples —occupied the other side of the social and cultural tracks. Propelled by the logic of his preaching, by his temperament, and by the courageous actions of black civil rights activists, Coffin had already begun edging toward the boundaries of his settled loyalties, toward King's America. Now he had to make a choice.

On the New Haven Green, just a block from Coffin's office, Yale students were rallying in support of the Freedom Riders who had been so brutally beaten in Montgomery. Coffin, Maguire, and Noyce all addressed the crowd of five hundred, without mentioning their plans. Coffin sought out Rostow, an older fellow member of the Yale elite, brother of the president's national security advisor and Coffin's "mentor on matters of civil rights." He got the advice he wanted. As so often in his life, it was, Coffin wrote, "a case of the right man saying the right thing at the right time." At the end of the rally the group drove to New York to catch a plane to Atlanta.[27]

Coffin's decision sheds light on the power of a genuine movement. Without the public example and sheer bravery of the (mostly young) southern civil rights workers, white northerners would not have risked bodily harm on behalf of people they did not know and who lived in an utterly different world. For the Freedom Riders had already accomplished the nearly unimaginable: by being prepared to sacrifice their lives openly and nonviolently, a small group of unknown African Americans had forced the most powerful man in the world to act against his own political interests and to deploy—however reluctantly—the resources of the U.S. government to protect them and their allies. It was a measure of the civil rights movement's success in the early 1960s that the dean of the Yale Law School could so easily encourage the Yale University chaplain to undertake civil disobedience in the service of black rights.

At the Atlanta airport SCLC representatives met Coffin's group and took them to a black-owned motel; two black seminarians, Clyde Carter and Charles Jones, joined them. The SCLC held a press conference Wednesday morning at Ebenezer Baptist Church, and the civil rights neophytes (whose first press conference this was) got a dose of reporters' antagonism toward "outside agitators." As they boarded their bus to Montgomery, Maguire recalled, "the hostility was incredible! The people were just glaring at us." Departing shortly after noon, they received a police escort at first, but when they crossed into Alabama the trooper peeled off; inside the bus, apprehensions rose.

As the big Greyhound rumbled through the southern mill towns on the route to Montgomery—Lanett, Cusseta, Roanoke Junction, Opelika—crowds along the way appeared ready for action. The armed mob at Lanett, just over the Alabama line, frightened the driver out of risking the stop. The "toughs in T-shirts were out," Maguire recalled; in "a couple of these towns, they came right to the bus with sticks in hand and beat on the side, 'Come out, you Nigger-lovers.'" Coffin, who had had no training in nonviolence, prowled the aisle restlessly, "thinking of judo more than nonviolence." Coffin "wanted to take these guys on," Maguire remembered, trying to get him to keep his head down where it made a less inviting target. Soon the riders picked up a National Guard escort.

They pulled into the Montgomery bus depot at about five, where, escorted by a paratrooper, the seven riders disembarked and waited uneasily by the side of the bus in the late afternoon heat, sweat soaking their suits. Earlier in the day buses carrying two groups of Freedom Riders (from the Nashville group) had finally departed for Mississippi, and a crowd still surrounded the bus station. Hundreds of National Guardsmen protected the newest arrivals. As

In May 1961, Coffin and his friend John Maguire were the first "respectable" northern whites involved in the civil rights movement's efforts to desegregate interstate transportation through Freedom Rides. His group disembarked in Montgomery, Alabama, where they were surrounded by a large crowd of hostile white residents held back by local police and the National Guard. Coffin learned how to talk to the press by watching the Rev. Ralph Abernathy, who was on his way to pick up the little party. AP Photo/Perry Aycock. Courtesy of AP/Wide World Photos.

Maguire recalled, "We were out there about twenty minutes in this extraordinarily tense situation, with bricks occasionally being lobbed over, sort of trying to smile, and very frightened."[28]

At last two cars, one driven by Ralph Abernathy, made their way through the crowd according to plan. Coffin got a brief lesson in the art of the interview when a reporter ran up to the car and asked Abernathy whether he was "afraid of embarrassing" President Kennedy while he met with Khrushchev in Europe, as Robert Kennedy had warned. "Well," Abernathy parried, "doesn't the attorney general know we've been embarrassed all our lives?"

That evening at Abernathy's house, which was ringed by National Guardsmen, Coffin, Maguire, and the others could see just how close they were to the center of the maelstrom. As they had walked into Abernathy's house, Martin Luther King Jr. lay on a bed deep in a phone conversation with Burke Marshall. Across town, Governor Patterson was again stonewalling Robert Kennedy, refusing to guarantee the safety of the group if they boarded a bus to Jackson, Mississippi. And Robert Kennedy's frustration with the Freedom Riders had finally boiled over. In his first statement on Wednesday he told student leaders that "no Federal marshals would accompany them" on future rides. Later in the day, as he received word of the arrival of Coffin's group, he issued a second press release. "Besides the Freedom Riders," he declared against all known evidence, "there are curiosity seekers, publicity seekers and others who are seeking to serve their own causes," a claim that could only throw suspicion on the genuine Freedom Riders. He called for a "cooling off period," suggesting that travelers "delay their trips until the present state of confusion and danger has passed and an atmosphere of reason and normalcy has been restored." Taylor Branch has suggested that for Kennedy the new group "represented a distressing change in the composition of the protesters." Ivy League professors were less easily dismissed than "Quakers, kooks, students, pacifists, or even Negro Gandhians." But by trying to halt the Freedom Rides, Kennedy had played right into Patterson's hands. "It's the first common sense the federal government has displayed in many days," the governor crowed.

National opinion-makers, led by the administration, were accusing the Freedom Riders of stirring up unnecessary trouble. They felt isolated and caricatured, some of them surely afraid and unsure about continuing. Looking for support, Coffin asked Abernathy how he answered Kennedy's desire for calm. Abernathy's reply again showed Coffin how to think from the perspective of his new commitments: "the Attorney General's statement does not specify the causes of the danger and confusion. A return to what he calls 'normalcy' would mean a return to injustice."

Frustrated, restless, and feeling that he had to do *something* while King negotiated with Kennedy, Coffin, accompanied by Maguire, crossed the street to a phone booth near Abernathy's house and tried to use his Yale connections. When, incredibly, his person-to-person collect call to the White House reached the president's top foreign policy aide, McGeorge Bundy (Yale '40, and a fellow Bonesman), Coffin described the tense scene in Montgomery and pleaded for the president to take the moral high ground on civil rights. Coffin received a quick, unpleasant education. Connections only got Bundy to take the call; he remained cold, distant, and unimpressed. Coffin then called Harris Wofford, who listened "with sympathy" but then accurately predicted Kennedy's cautious course. Wofford had been virtually frozen out of the telephone loop. That very evening Robert Kennedy had called him to complain bitterly about the Freedom Riders and question their patriotism.

Having exhausted his connections, Coffin understood that it would take a different kind of pressure to change the administration's attitude. When he and Maguire returned, King had finished his conversations with Kennedy. The attorney general either would not or could not make a deal with Patterson that would protect the riders if they tried to get to Jackson, Mississippi. Maguire wept as King laid out "the simple issue: do you want to go on?"

Rather than let them answer, King led them in prayer. The black men got down on their knees first, then the whites, one by one. Abernathy, then King, prayed "for patience and for courage." King sent them off to talk and to sleep, instructing them to decide the next day. Thursday morning they reassembled and took a secret ballot. The vote was unanimous—push on.

That morning Coffin and his fellow Freedom Riders became national celebrities. The *New York Times* ran a story on their departure from Atlanta and their arrival in Montgomery, accompanied by an admiring profile of the "Bus-Riding Chaplain." The only person quoted, Coffin had told reporters "that the party had assembled on the spur of a moment, inspired by the news of the experiences of the original Freedom Riders" and that "my president doesn't even know I'm down here." The *Times* pointed out that Coffin's white companions included distinguished scholars and members of Phi Beta Kappa.[29] Robert Kennedy's political nightmare was coming true. Once the Freedom Rides started attracting "respectable" northern whites, other mainstream liberals and religious leaders might join them.

As Coffin and the others made their way to the bus depot, again escorted through a mob by National Guardsmen (and accompanied by Abernathy and black civil rights leaders Fred Shuttlesworth and Wyatt T. Walker, and King aide Bernard Lee), they had little notion of the pivotal role they were playing in a national drama. Once inside the terminal, attended only by reporters and photographers, they bought tickets and waited for their bus over coffee at the terminal lunch counter. Within minutes Sheriff Mac Sim Butler arrested all eleven in the party.

Coffin's first arrest very likely saved him from serious physical harm. Patterson announced, accurately, that his group of Freedom Riders "had come against the urging of the United States Attorney General and in violation of our agreement." After the arrest, National Guard troops who had been guarding bus and railroad stations, as well as the airport, were "quietly withdrawn." Even so, the National Guard commander, State Adjutant General Henry V. Graham, planned to continue martial law over the weekend and until Freedom Riders ended what he called "their stupid, immoral and criminal provocations."

Robert Kennedy made it clear that this group would get no special treatment. He announced the withdrawal of 566 federal marshals from Alabama, leaving just 100 in place. To reporters, he heaped scorn on the Freedom Riders, "the safest people in America," and told the *Washington Post*, "It took a lot of guts for the first group to go, but not much for the others."[30]

The arrest earned a front-page photograph and UPI story in the *New York*

Times (under the one-column headline "Yale's Chaplain Among 11 Seized In Montgomery") and another photo inside (underneath a full-page headline). (The *New York Post* also ran the story and photo on its front page.) The first photo featured the sheriff, the second, Coffin and Maguire. Captions identified Coffin and one or more of the whites, including Sheriff Butler, while referring to nameless "Negro students" and "local Negro integration leaders."[31]

Public criticism grew fiercer. The *Times* weighed in with a front-page story, alongside the story of Coffin's arrest, titled "Dr. King Refuses To End Bus Test." The article, while accurately reporting King's rejection of Kennedy's "cooling off" period, included long quotations from two anonymous "leaders" of the civil rights struggle, one black, one white, questioning the Freedom Riders' tactics. "Non-violence that deliberately provokes violence," the paper editorialized against the Freedom Rides the same day, "is a logical contradiction." In fact, in order to expose the violence at the core of segregation, nonviolent activists often undertook actions that invited a violent response.[32]

Once in jail, the riders' connections again proved useful. When Coffin reached Eva after his bail had been set at a thousand dollars, he learned that the university secretary and several faculty members had already begun raising the bail money for him, Noyce, and Smith. Jail itself was easy for the white riders, who were held separately from the black prisoners. They did calisthenics in their underwear, and Coffin worked on his Sunday sermon. Abernathy and Walker held prayer services for the other inmates in the black section of the jail and led them in singing. By the next day friends, students, and faculty at Yale and Wesleyan had already raised five thousand dollars; the northerners posted bail and were released.

Met by reporters as he left jail, Coffin showed that he had been preparing his response: "You are well aware that we have been detained for more than twenty-eight hours, a procedure which is blatantly illegal and a travesty of justice." He pointedly reminded newsmen of his Peace Corps responsibilities: "every man and woman who will go to Tanganyika, the Philippines and Colombia this fall will bear the burden of Montgomery, Alabama."[33]

When Coffin and Maguire got to Abernathy's house after leaving jail, they ran into a reporter for *Life* magazine wanting a story for the next issue. They had two hours. With Maguire's help, Coffin dictated the piece to the reporter; it ran, along with a full-page photo of Coffin outside of Battell Chapel, as the last two pages of a long "Story of the Week" on the Freedom Rides.[34]

In "Why Yale Chaplain Rode: Christians Can't Be Outside," Coffin crammed a welter of insights and aphorisms into five hundred words and displayed his flair for standing conventional wisdom on its head. Contrary to the southern charge that the group was made up of "outsiders" who wanted to "stir up trouble," he argued, "if you're an American and a Christian, you can't be an outsider on racial discrimination, whether practiced in the North or in the South. . . . On this issue all Americans are insiders." He had hoped that his group might encourage "the sea of silent moderates in the South to raise their voices," since they were allowing the "extremists" all the attention. "As always," he quipped, "it has been the listless, not the lawless, who are the deciding factor."

More substantively, he explained why he opposed the "cooling off period," using what he had learned from Ralph Abernathy: "But why should Negroes always be asked to make the concessions? . . . A cooling off period will be effective only if it is backed by the promise of a fairer future for the Negro." Citing Al Capone's operating slogan for Chicago—"We don't want no trouble"— Coffin demonstrated his knack for one-liners: "This is always the sentiment of those who want peace at any price—as long as they have the peace and someone else pays the price."

Coffin had come to the same Gandhian philosophical position that King later made explicit in his "Letter from Birmingham Jail." "Nonviolent direct action," King wrote in 1963, "seeks to create such a crisis and foster such a tension that a community which has constantly refused to negotiate is forced to confront the issue." In the Freedom Ride, Coffin was able to combine a Christian injunction to act wherever he found injustice and a philosophy of direct action—both of which suited his temperament perfectly. This fertile mixture of faith, strategy, and personality took Coffin a long way.

While Coffin flew home to Yale on Saturday, the civil rights leadership worked out a structure to continue the Freedom Rides, which King had already promised would resume "in full force" the following week. Still, as Taylor Branch points out, the *Times* coverage of Coffin's arrest and Freedom Ride strategy marked the last time the paper put a Freedom Ride story on its front page. Though the rides continued all summer long, law enforcement officials avoided publicity by shuttling Freedom Riders "efficiently, almost protectively," into Mississippi jails.[35]

Most Americans disapproved of the Freedom Riders; Robert Kennedy found them infuriating; and the Kennedy administration began ignoring them. But the moral power of the first few rides had reached deep into the halls of power, changing the White House's political calculus. Robert Kennedy came to work on Monday, May 29, something of a changed man. He told his staff that King's idea about getting the Interstate Commerce Commission to reaffirm its charter might not be such a bad idea. He instructed Justice Department lawyers to press the famously slow-moving commission until it made the appropriate ruling. Three months later, on September 1, Kennedy had a declaration that within thirty days "all seating in buses would be without reference to race, color, creed, and all carriers would have to have that sign in the buses . . . in all the terminals the 'colored' and 'white' signs had to come down at the fountains and at the restrooms."[36]

The "Enfant Terrible"

The Freedom Ride catapulted the thirty-seven-year-old Coffin into the national spotlight. Previously, his access to powerful circles and influential editors had come through his family connections, school ties, and Yale position. Now, however impulsively, even recklessly—but with great personal courage —he had developed a different constituency, a rival source of power: the reporters and media outlets who saw him as good copy. Coffin had become a newsmaker, an arrival on the public scene of American religious politics.

Life magazine had enormous influence in American cultural life, and the article alone would have made him a national celebrity. But many newspapers had picked up the wire stories about Coffin's group, and the Freedom Rides made the news magazines as well. *Time* treated them mainly as a victory for Robert Kennedy and profiled four activists with varying degrees of condescension: Diane Nash and James Lawson of Nashville, James Farmer of CORE, and Coffin, the only white, focusing on his privileged status and his and Eva's pedigrees. *Newsweek* paid him brief, snide attention: "At Montgomery, William S. Coffin, Jr., the chaplain of Yale University, no less, showed up."[37]

Coffin had no idea that the firestorm was just beginning. In the space of a few days, he had become the most controversial person at Yale, and the most controversial white minister in the country. Nor had he expected to receive so much hate mail. Most came from the South, though he also got many nasty letters from the North. The viciousness of this mail showed what Americans could expect if they violated racial taboos. Coffin's critics used very few rationales, beginning with clear, powerful, vitriolic race hatred mixed with fear. In a bizarre coincidence, two young black men had been arrested for the rape and murder of two New Jersey society matrons the day Coffin's group was released from jail in Montgomery. The gruesome crime—confirming the worst psychosexual fears of white Americans—made the front pages of the *New York Times*, other New York papers, and others around the country. Some of the angriest letter writers attached clippings from their local papers. H. Gordon Rowe of New Haven clipped the photograph of Coffin being arrested to the story on the murder and scribbled on a card, "Have you a feeling of exaltation?" Another sent along a clipping, including a photograph of the two suspects, on which he had typed, "Two 'freedom riders' that you should have taken with you on your rabble-rousing tour of Alabama." Another note, from Louisiana, that reached Coffin was signed "Omega" and was addressed to "Rev. Rabble Rouser Wm. S. Coffin Freedom Riding Jailed Chaplain of Yale University, New Haven, Conn.":

THESE CLIPPINGS ARE FOOD FOR THOUGHT. ALL SORTS OF CRIME BY YOUR NEGRO STUDENTS
Negro Rabble Rousers like yourself has caused more trouble in my country U.S.A. than Lumumba has caused in Black Africa.

My Country has it's hands filled with foreign Communists and i think its about time to lower the Boom on you Devils.[38]

Along the same lines, a Florida man wrote that "down here in the South-land we know more about the Negroes' problems in a second than you'll learn in a lifetime start coddling one within minutes as he will do all the talking . . . how well they love white meat especially if its a female from 42nd St the painted kind." An M. Shapiro from New York City fulminated on a postcard: "You dopey nut mixing with niggers in this white world—what can you prove—only that niggers belong in the zoo with the rest of the animal freaks."[39]

Many correspondents attached clippings of a recent column by the conservative commentator David Lawrence attacking the Freedom Riders. One also sent along an article on the baby born to Sammy Davis Jr. and the white actress May Britt, with a little note, "Integration Leads to Miscegenation." An unsigned, typed note invited Coffin to "Come to New Orleans where we won't even allow you on TV. Better still, live by your last name—coffin!" And an anonymous Yale alumnus from Washington, D.C., suggested, "You may, perhaps have mulatto blood in your veins." For "it certainly is true that you have lowered yourself beneath the level of a 'Nigger' to disgrace the University which hired you to preach Christian religion." A Henry Dutton wrote of the distress he and his daughters evidently experienced in an integrated school in New Haven during the 1930s: "The nigger boys had a vice of grabbing the girls by the back-side and feeling of their breasts and suggesting indecent things to do." Another correspondent asked, "Do you want your girl raped by a filthy, lousy Negro who would probably leave her with her throat cut?"[40]

The second general line of attack accused Coffin and the Freedom Riders of stirring up trouble where they did not belong. Many southerners had been embarrassed by the mob violence directed at the Freedom Riders and vented their anger on the northern provocateurs for exposing this side of their culture. An anonymous "solid segregationist" from New Orleans wrote that the "real motive of the 'Freedom Riders' was to inflame local passions by deliberate provocation. . . . P.S. We thought you damned fools, all of you!" Coffin loved this argument, had already preached and written about it, and had a ready response organized around the "We don't want no trouble" line from Al Capone.[41]

Finally, many were offended and angry that a representative of Yale University had inflamed a complex situation. Yale alumnus E. H. Chapman of Darien, Connecticut (Class of 1920), a businessman who had spent ten years in Memphis, argued that "Northerners such as yourself who have limited experience or knowledge of racial problems down South should mind their own business at home, and not contribute to further unrest and violence. *Not* to mention the detriment to Yale itself." He ended with what soon became a shopworn threat not to contribute any more to Yale "if faculty members continue such actions as yours."[42]

Coffin responded to a large number of these correspondents, often trying to genuinely engage his critics. He clearly enjoyed the repartee and thought he could change minds, as in his exchange with John H. Doeringer, an alumnus of the university and the law school, who found it "embarrassing to see the faculty of my university engaged in causing public disorders, inciting riots or conspiring to incite riots, and generally using the tactics of street fighting also used by the nazis and the communists." Doeringer expected brotherhood to be achieved "through peace and harmony," not by agitation, and he worried about embarrassing "our country at a dangerous time."[43]

Coffin went straight for the heart of the matter: "As a lawyer have you not more concern for Federal law and Constitutionally guaranteed rights of American citizens?" He then exaggerated—"Your comparison of Martin Luther King to a Nazi stormtrooper also seemed a bit far-fetched"—and pulled the rank of experience: "Perhaps I have spent more time abroad than you. Wouldn't you agree that it is really segregation that embarrasses the United States rather than those who are fighting to hasten its end?" Coffin gave no quarter here, or on Doeringer's reading of the gospel: "What do you think Jesus meant when He said 'I come to bring not peace but the sword?' Surely He was a great disturber of the peace." "There are many forms of peace," he pressed on. "There is the peace of the lion that has swallowed the lamb, and the peace of the lamb that has just been swallowed by the lion."

But Coffin had undeniably "dragged" the Yale name into the controversy, so he had a standard reply to this charge: "Unlike other institutions, a university never speaks with one voice, and surely you would not want the Administration to deny its faculty members the freedom guaranteed them by the Nation!" He closed, as he did frequently to alumni, offering "to talk further about these matters" in New Haven.

By and large the Yale community rallied around its newly notorious chaplain.

Faculty and students raised more than seven thousand dollars in bail money. With Battell Chapel overflowing his first Sunday back, Coffin abandoned the sermon on infant baptism that he had prepared in the Montgomery County jail. As George Smith and his sister Inez sat in the front pew, Coffin preached a version of what would shortly appear in *Life*. He disclosed the phone call from "people in high places in the Attorney General's office" who "did ask us most circumspectly to reconsider our decision to make the trip." More pointedly, he asked why should "the Negroes be asked for a return to normalcy? Why shouldn't Governor Patterson be asked?" Coffin praised the courage of the black leaders: "They were like the first disciples—serene—just beyond anything anyone could do to them—profoundly calm because they were doing right."[44]

Coffin received his key support from President A. Whitney Griswold, whom he had carefully not informed of his plans. Even Coffin had "not expected," he wrote much later, "upon entering his office, to be met by [Griswold's] mischievous grin. 'Aha,' he said, 'Here comes our *enfant terrible*.'" Griswold had already written a form letter for irate alumni, which he showed Coffin. He acknowledged the "controversy and strong feelings" provoked by the protest, but "when Mr. Coffin decided to take part in this protest he did so in response to his convictions as a Christian and the promptings of his conscience as an ordained minister of his faith to make personal, public testimony to those convictions. . . . he was not officially representing Yale and Yale has taken no official position in this matter. He was acting independently. In so doing he was exercising a personal freedom which is guaranteed to all citizens and is not curtailed by their employment in universities. Moreover, he was acting in response to religious convictions which are equally immune to curtailment because of the institutional associations of those who hold them." Griswold's letter placed Yale firmly behind its chaplain, even as some alumni began their first demand for his head, using their donations as a threat.[45]

The alumni had company. Shortly after his return Coffin received a confidential letter from Provost Buck sounding a "discordant note."[46] He was particularly angry that Coffin had involved Yale: "It is however a fact that you cannot act as a private citizen. You are the Yale Chaplain, and in every newspaper account all over the world you appear, not as Bill Coffin, but as the Yale Chaplain." If Coffin intended to continue in this way "and devote your energies to outside activities, to the neglect of your more immediate pastoral duties," he should resign.

With Griswold on his side Coffin refused to retreat. He regretted that Buck "never attempted to argue the issue on Christian grounds, which after all are the only ones on which a University Chaplain can finally stand. . . . is it not my role as University Chaplain to serve the University by reaffirming to the best of my ability the Christian convictions on which she was founded?" Coffin never quite acknowledged that for all of his—and Griswold's—efforts to sidestep the issue, he was no longer a private citizen. His Yale post had become an important part of any public action he took; Coffin knew this, and used it.

He also continued to pay flattering, almost obsequious, attention to his president. As Griswold was about to leave on a vacation, Coffin wrote him that "Yale, and I in particular, are most fortunate that you are Yale's president. . . . Here's hoping you have a wonderful healthy restful summer and do remember from time to time how much you are loved and appreciated by your 'enfant pas trop terrible, j'éspère' . . . P.S. Please give Mary my affectionate best, too." Although Coffin could be impetuous, he also understood the art of political self-protection, and practiced it assiduously.[47]

The alumni controversy roiled on in one form or another for the next dozen years. Coffin had set off a political and cultural explosion in the staid world of the Yale alumni. And as long as he held the chaplaincy, alumni life never fully returned to its former placidity. The *Yale Alumni Magazine* printed twenty letters on Coffin in its July and October issues, sixteen in support, four suggesting that he be condemned or fired. The "anti" letters, mostly from older alumni, ranged from the overtly racist to the personally nasty. They seem to have provoked even more support for Coffin, who had made some alumni prouder of their alma mater.[48]

Faculty members, too, wrote Coffin of their support for and pride in his actions. The economist (and former OSS conduit) Elliott Dunlap Smith wrote him eloquently and at length, thoroughly endorsing the chaplain's decision to "live up forthrightly to your conscience." While attracting "public attention in the press on a controversial issue" could be "disturbing to some alumni and to some potential donors," Smith doubted that Yale would "be better off if its chaplains are known to be pallid trimmers than if they are known to be men who live and act carefully but boldly in accordance to what they believe is right." Smith understood that for Yale to produce men capable of leading modern society, it needed to engage their convictions and consciences as well as their intellects and concern for status. Yale University was never simply an institution of higher learning. From its origins it had prepared young colonists for leadership. In the late nineteenth century it had played a key role in the toughening and transformation of regional elites and the creation of a national ruling class.[49]

In the early 1960s Yale lay on the edge of another transformation, one that would open its doors further to Jews, to sons of the middle class, to public school graduates, and, at the end of the decade, to women. The more farsighted members of the Yale community, like Smith, saw that there were times when it was important to shake up what he called "this admirable, influential but all too easily complacent university." Thanking Smith for his "very moving" thoughts, Coffin wisely sent the letter to Griswold's assistant to help her with replies to unhappy alumni.

The experience changed Coffin, and it changed Yale as well. Like the Freedom Riders in the South, Coffin forced his community to choose between well-meaning complacency and principles "disturbing to the peace." If he had not foreseen the results at Yale, he nevertheless fully accepted—and thrived on—his new status as the center of argument, outrage, support, adulation, and vitriol. Aside from the threatening phone calls, some of which contained death threats that understandably upset Eva and his secretary, the incident had no downside. It flushed out his opposition, offered opportunity for serious dialogue on important issues, forced students who preferred abstract discussion to test their ideas against a tangible concrete reality, and pressed supporters into action. Tactically, in other words, Coffin's restlessness, impetuosity, and courage had successfully forced civil rights issues into the forefront of debate at a leading American university. Coffin had hit upon an issue he could get his teeth into, in a way that could galvanize his community and provide him with an even broader stage on which to test his talents. Magazine editors and book publishers who had been pursuing him for a year stepped up their requests. The files of preaching invitations grew fat, and in 1963 his secretary began a "declines" folder.

Coffin rose to the challenge of his new celebrity, "doing a lot of homework," working harder on quips and epigrams, all the while continuing to cultivate important people at Yale. He surprised himself a bit. "I didn't think I could suddenly drop a whole sermon and talk for thirty-five minutes about what it was like in a way that would really communicate in church that Sunday," he recalled later, "but I did. So I had just enough confidence that on my feet I could think fast enough and well enough to handle these situations." He felt powerfully the need to be prepared when called upon: "if you're going to be thrust into that role you want to know a great deal about it." As he put it, "You become quickly aware of the fact that the press and the country generally tend to value the sensational over the valuable. So you better cooperate gracefully with this and try to sensationalize what is valuable. And you better have that message ready. You better have done your homework." From watching Ralph Abernathy deflect and turn around the hostile comments of reporters and Attorney General Robert Kennedy, Coffin had learned that "boy, when they stick that mike in your face you better know what it is you want to say."[50]

Coffin's significance went far beyond Yale and his own career, however.

He made an important addition to the civil rights movement, for suddenly an articulate, photogenic, charismatic white Protestant leader in the North— blessed with impeccable class, educational, fraternal, and patriotic credentials —was ready to do battle for the movement. The movement needed these white northerners badly, for the plain fact was that national press paid far more attention to whites than to blacks, and especially to well-connected whites like Coffin. Black civil rights leaders had no qualms about inviting such men to raise the profile of their dangerous and often lonely struggles. The needs of the movement meshed perfectly with Coffin's own growing skills and pleasure in acting on a larger stage. Coffin had found his calling.

Preaching the Word: Coffin in Demand

"A Chaplain Worthy of Yale"

An important new figure on the educational and religious scenes of the early 1960s, William Sloane Coffin Jr. appeared to be everywhere. *Life* magazine designated him one of the "Red Hot Hundred" in a special issue in 1962 devoted to "The Take-Over Generation."[1] From television appearances and radio programs, from prep school lecterns and college pulpits, from national magazines, local newsletters, and newspaper headlines, Coffin preached a witty, quotable, provocative, prophetic Christianity. His photogenic and, more importantly, telegenic good looks—his handsome, square-jawed face, horn-rimmed glasses, slightly receding hairline, and athletic build—were about to become fixtures in American media for the rest of the decade. With a knack for stirring up controversy, Coffin created news. By 1963, he had become nothing less than a phenomenon.

Coffin's first move after the Freedom Ride took him in an entirely different direction. Back in March of 1961 Sargent Shriver had tried to recruit Coffin to organize and head a new training school for the Peace Corps—in a Puerto Rican rain forest. Though intrigued, Coffin declined and instead accepted Kennedy's invitation to join the Peace Corps National Advisory Council. Despite Coffin's criticism of the administration during and after the Freedom Ride, Shriver remained interested. In June he asked Coffin to take a four-month leave from Yale, set up the training camp in Puerto Rico, and stay on to run the first two training cycles. After four years of chaplaincy, Coffin—who had loved his training work in the army and the CIA—jumped at the chance to immerse himself in the physical world again.

Working with his friend Josh Miner from Andover, by then head of American Outward Bound, to hire an eccentric staff of rock-climbers and physical

More than any other preacher or activist of his time, Coffin (here at Union Theological Seminary, Richmond, Virginia, 1975) excelled at the art of the radio and television interview, turning conventional wisdom on its head and tossing off witty, provocative, quotable one-liners. Courtesy of William Sloane Coffin Jr.

educators, Coffin oversaw the creation of his training camp in a month. He inspired his staff and made the most of his apparent political pull to get enormous assistance from local units of the U.S. Army and Navy, who built latrines, tent platforms, a mess hall, and kitchen. In just a month, the camp was ready for the inaugural cycle of Peace Corps trainees, and a much-reported-on group of thirty-two male road builders and surveyors headed for Tanganyika. Since the volunteers had not been told about this rigorous training regimen, they rebelled at first, and Coffin used a combination of threats and inspiration to turn them around. More than sixty trainees, men and women bound for the Philippines, made up the next batch, and by then the camp was in full swing. Coffin was glad to leave the dense, finally "oppressive" forest after three months but missed the intensity of the work.

As he wrote to his colleagues ten days after returning to Yale, "I have been thoroughly unsuccessful in keeping my mind off Puerto Rico, not that I have really tried very hard. Quite honestly my heart is torn, and all of you are in it forever." As letters from the camp and from others attested, he provided the soul of the operation. Shriver offered an example of what Coffin had accomplished: "The Philippine Volunteers . . . began evaluating their program at

Penn State in terms of your leadership and inspiration and found everything suffered by comparison. . . . the camp has proven to be one of the best examples of what the Peace Corps has done to date." Shriver hoped that in the future they could keep "the Peace Corps a 'Coffin' kind of operation." Since his first involvement, Coffin kept his fondness for Outward Bound and the Peace Corps. The combination of the experiences confirmed his conviction that first-hand experience made the best education.[2]

When he first came to Yale, Coffin made relatively little use of his home pulpit because his predecessor had used it to bring famous preachers to Yale. Coffin followed tradition at first, preaching a little more than once a month while inviting such luminaries of American Protestantism as Reinhold Niebuhr, Martin Luther King Jr., and Paul Tillich; the chaplains of Harvard, Wesleyan, and Brown; deans of the Harvard and Yale Divinity Schools; his old professors from Union and Yale; and his friend John Maguire. He hosted leading European Protestants as well as church-connected activists such as Donald Benedict from Chicago's City Mission Society and Will Campbell, the white civil rights activist who staffed the southern office of the National Council of Churches.[3]

When visitors preached at Battell, Coffin usually took to the road, though he stayed for King and Tillich. His secretary kept a double-columned "Preaching Engagements" calendar that she gradually filled in during the year. The left column indicated Coffin's Sunday morning obligations; the right, those in the afternoon or evening. Most of his outside invitations during the late fifties and early sixties came from New England prep schools, colleges, and universities, though Coffin did travel as far as Stanford University in January of 1961.

As he made bigger waves abroad, however, Coffin began to preach more at Battell, gradually reducing the number of guests. Still, very little kept Coffin home Sunday afternoons or evenings. In the 1962 calendar year, Coffin had thirty-one speaking or preaching engagements out of town. By 1965 the number had grown to fifty-seven.[4]

To the surrounding culture, Coffin offered novelty. Few Protestant ministers projected such masculine affect (at six feet, two inches, and two hundred pounds), multilingual worldliness, and a taste for poetry, music, and sports. As a man who could delight unabashedly in beauty, use the word *love* in a myriad of contexts, and talk the core talk of Christianity, Coffin projected a more erotic presence than most of his brethren.

Coffin performed well in the spotlight. With President Kennedy on the platform to receive an honorary degree from Yale in 1962, Coffin's commencement prayer received notices (and excerpts) in the *New York Times*. Building his prayer around the theme of love, Coffin used for the first time the image of the "lover's quarrel": "Because we love the world we pray now . . . for grace to quarrel with it, O Thou whose lover's quarrel with the world is the history of the world." He invited his listeners to quarrel with "the worship of success and power," with "a mass culture that tends not to satisfy but exploit the wants of people," with those who "pledge allegiance to one race rather than the human race," and—riskiest of all, given the guest of honor—"with those who prefer to condemn communism rather than practice Christianity." Coffin made sure to praise the can-do ethos of the New Frontier, in the form of "men for whom the complexity of issues only served to renew their zeal to deal with them . . . men who were always willing to risk something big for something good."[5]

Even while performing the more mundane aspects of the chaplain's job, such as offering prayers at ceremonies and dedicating new buildings, Coffin kept to his main themes. At groundbreaking exercises for a new geology laboratory, for example, he warned that "science this day can greatly bless or wholly destroy" and urged his listeners to "remember that the acquisition of knowledge is second to its use." Several months later, blessing two new residential colleges, Coffin concluded by praying "that these colleges be dedicated to the increase of love: love of beauty, love of truth, and love of Thee and neighbor."[6]

When his sermons failed to cohere completely, they still included a rich mix of biblical exegesis, historical explanation, contemporary social criticism, barbs at conventional Christianity and unimaginative universities, and a powerfully felt and expressed faith in the glory of God. "It is really incredible," Coffin began a sermon on vocation, "that the Church, so concerned with how people spend their money, should be so indifferent to how they make it in the first place." Universities too, allowing their "moral concerns to be dictated largely by their public relations aspect . . . are much more concerned with sexual than vocational morality." For a "conscious Christian," he argued, "an important job clearly must have priority over an attractive one," a distinction that existed in every profession, even the ministry.[7]

After the Freedom Ride, A. Whitney Griswold faced heavy alumni pressure regarding his chaplain, and that fall he requested one of his few private meetings with Coffin. "As long as things were going well," Coffin recalled, "Griswold didn't ask to hear directly from me and he really wasn't that personally interested in religion or the chaplaincy," though he did usually attend Sunday services in Battell. But now Griswold tried to plant a seed: "He said to me, 'You know, Bill, you may well someday find that this place is just a little too dull for you.' And it never occurred to me—this will show you how naive I was—that he was suggesting that I might leave for Yale's sake. So I hastened to reassure him that I found it very interesting. And I was having a very good time and as always deeply grateful for the opportunity to be chaplain. I never caught on to what he was obviously saying." Even so, Griswold continued to defend Coffin and two years later recommended that the Yale Corporation reappoint him for another five-year term. The Corporation voted positively on April 6, 1963, setting Coffin's salary at $10,000 annually (roughly $56,000 in 2000 dollars), along with an entertainment allowance of $2,000 (approximately $11,000 to-day). Less than two weeks later, Griswold was dead.[8]

Coffin was reinventing the role of Yale chaplain and providing a new model for the American college chaplaincy. Throughout the Yale community, one could not help bumping into him literally or figuratively. The *Yale Daily News* clearly enjoyed such a nonstop source of copy. Each year Coffin wrote a form letter to all one thousand incoming freshmen, a letter so striking in the genre that the *Boston Globe* published it one year. He appeared at civil rights demonstrations, on Yale's radio program "Yale Reports," and he cut a striking figure on the squash or tennis court, as well as at official Yale events. Coffin's sermon on the Kennedy assassination got three full pages in the *Yale Alumni Magazine*. Not one of Coffin's best sermons—the occasion limited his wit and penchant for turning common notions upside down—it still articulated Coffin's conviction that God suffered with and cared for humanity "no matter how wayward." Coffin sought above all to comfort his flock, to help Americans understand that "recognition of their limits" ("We cannot even keep our President alive") might lead to maturity or profundity. At "his best," however, John Kennedy "exemplified freedom both at home and abroad," and Coffin suggested that "if we would be true to the best memory of this man we might now on his be-half . . . take up the unfinished business of freedom. America is not free, not in terms of the 14th or even of the 1st Amendment; our press is not free, it's private and far from free; many of our citizens are free only to sleep in the cold water tenement of their choice; and none of us are free of the greed, trivia and superficiality that mark so much of our national life."[9]

By spring 1964, his prayers had become gems: condensed, poetic, well-worked, occasionally self-quoting, always pointed. Coffin saw himself representing the realm of the heart in the land of the mind; his prayers consistently reminded his listeners that intellect needed a soul. When the news broke that Yale Provost and Acting President Kingman Brewster Jr. would become Yale's next president, Coffin's Sunday prayer paid tribute to one who had "graces rare among high administrators" and asked not for wisdom but for a "frame of heart fit for his new estate." Brewster had earlier offered an elegant affirmation of Coffin's right to act on his conscience. "If in order to be a Chaplain at Yale," he wrote the critics, "one had to agree to refrain from any public demonstration of conscientious conviction, then I do not see how we could expect to find a Chaplain worthy of Yale."[10]

At the same time, like millions of other Americans, Coffin felt change in the air and thought conservative old Yale needed to open itself to new cultural currents. Praying at the inauguration luncheon for Brewster, he asked: "In a world in which traditions need to be reshaped and purged as much as protected, O God, bless us all with uncertainty. Grant us grace not to find reasons to support what we already hold, but to seek a truth greater than anything we have as yet conceived. . . . And remind us that our neighbors suffer from injustices we too were born to correct, for the world is now too dangerous for anything but truth, too small for anything but love."[11]

At the Yale senior dinner Coffin prayed that the graduates "not be overcome by the inevitable contrast between what they expect and what the world intends. . . . we pray that thou wilt grant them grace to develop the habit of heroism, lest, looking back on their springtime fifty years gone, they say, 'Those were the days,' and be right." In his own way, Coffin was indeed blessing "every God-damned sewer in town"—taking every opportunity to provide a pointed Christian commentary on all of Yale's public events. He pressed his audiences to think "beyond knowledge and power, pride and certainty, on behalf of what lay beyond knowledge: truth and beauty, grace and love, dreams and justice."[12]

On the Road for Civil Rights: Baltimore, Birmingham, and St. Augustine

Coffin was developing a knack for flamboyant civil rights work. He could hardly have carried out the dangerous, shack-to-shack, hands-on organizing that young SNCC volunteers were undertaking in Mississippi and Alabama —and held onto his job, that is. Temperamentally, too, Coffin was made for the limelight. After the Freedom Ride, he brought media attention wherever he went, even when playing lesser roles.

He and Eva, for example, both got arrested in a large desegregation action at the Gwynn Oaks Amusement Park outside of Baltimore on Independence Day, 1963. A multiracial and multifaith group of a dozen clergy led the action and became the first (of nearly three hundred) to be arrested. The image of Eugene Carson Blake, head of the United Presbyterian Church and a former college football player, being arrested in his suit, hat, and clerical collar made front pages around the country.

Coffin, who did nothing to plan the event and did not join the dozen clergy leading the action, nevertheless received third billing in the *Times* story. The reporter saw Coffin trying to go to Eva's side after she had sat down inside the park. "'That's my wife in there,' he said as a policeman blocked him. 'Doesn't make any difference to me,' the policeman said laconically, putting him under arrest." The *Times* reporter understood the event's larger significance: "It was the first time that so large a group of important clergymen of all three major faiths had participated together in a direct concerted protest against discrimination." Coffin, his antennae ever alert, had picked an excellent moment to jump into the spotlight.[13]

By late 1962 something new had happened to white clergy in mainline Protestantism, Catholicism, and Conservative and Reform Judaism. First, in each denomination a few individuals, mostly northerners, were willing to speak out publicly on civil rights—within their congregations, their communities, and their denominations. This group included Coffin; fellow Presbyterians Blake and Robert McAfee Brown; Episcopalians Malcolm Boyd, John Morris, and Paul Moore; Catholic Philip Berrigan; Baptist Will Campbell; Reform Rabbi Balfour Brickner; and the preeminent Jewish theologian Abraham Joshua Heschel.

Second, the outrages of militant segregation—in Little Rock, during the Freedom Rides, and in the 1962 Ole Miss riot blocking the court-ordered enrollment of James Meredith—shocked many northern clergy into a sense of responsibility for African-American civil rights in the South. Simultaneously, civil rights leaders were calling increasingly on northern white clergy to come South, be willing to get arrested, and create the publicity that an all-black southern movement could not generate on its own.

Third, the more liberal clergy, including denominational officials, felt invigorated at just this time by "a new spirit of interfaith cooperation," in historian Michael Friedland's words, "demonstrated markedly by the Second Vatican Council and various proposals for Protestant denominational unions in the early 1960s." Although the ecumenical movement had older roots, Vatican II, by lifting the stigma of "Christ-killers" from Jews, paved the way for clergy of both faiths to work with others more easily. Since activist clergy represented such a tiny minority within their own denominations, social action on behalf of civil rights relied heavily on interfaith partnerships, which in turn further nourished the ecumenical spirit.[14]

In that spirit, a group of Catholic, Protestant, and Jewish denominational and interdenominational agencies organized a large national interfaith gathering in January 1963: the National Conference on Religion and Race. More than 650 delegates, laity as well as clergy, from sixty-seven denominations and organizations, gathered in Chicago to hear Rabbi Heschel join the civil rights struggle in his keynote address. The conference drew praise from the mainstream religious press and inspired smaller conferences emphasizing a wide range of desegregation and antidiscrimination issues in cities across the country.[15]

Suddenly Coffin had plenty of colleagues in civil rights work, though he remained the most controversial Yale activist. Whenever he made the papers, he made the *Yale Alumni Magazine* as well, attracting critics and defenders and provoking conversations throughout the far-flung network of alumni clubs and among thousands of alumni. Like many white sympathizers, he and Eva went to Birmingham, Alabama, in early May of 1963 to provide support to the SCLC's desegregation battle. Letters to the editor both sneered at Coffin for his undignified presence (he was reported wearing "sneakers" and running errands for Martin Luther King Jr. at the Gaston Motel) and offered "ten cheers" for his efforts.[16]

Coffin's report on Birmingham nearly ran in *Christian Century*, the principal national journal covering mainline Christianity, but when the editors received King's extraordinary *"Letter from Birmingham Jail"* they bumped Coffin's piece. Both men were responding to eight of the city's white clergy (including a rabbi) who had charged that King's demonstrations were "unwise and untimely." King's answer, an eloquent exposition of militant nonviolence, has become one of the classic statements of twentieth-century political protest.[17]

Coffin used his position in more traditional ways as well. The Sunday after his trip to Birmingham, Battell Chapel had no scheduled preacher, in favor of a "Service of Music." But Coffin could not resist an occasion made to order for his thoughts on the relationship between music and activist religion. He began the sermon conventionally enough, observing that church music played "as integral a part of the service as the reading of Scripture, preaching, or praying. It is worship become music." Why? Because, like revelation, music acted in mysterious "divers and subtle ways." Only music—in contrast to scripture, preaching, and praying—"first arouses the emotions and only then reaches the intellect."

And as Coffin loved pointing out in a university setting, the only thing that might be "more dangerous than emotions that are not clad in intelligence" was "an intellect untouched by emotions." Using one of his favorite vignettes, he told the story of the poet Heinrich Heine, struck with awe while regarding the cathedral of Amiens. "Tell me, Heinrich," implored his friend Alphonse, "why can't men build edifices like this any more?" "Cher Alphonse," Heine responded, "it's easy; in those days men had convictions; we moderns have opinions. And it takes more than an opinion to build a Gothic cathedral."

Instead of feeling the power in sacred music, "church goers sing their heads off in the bath tub or shower but in church drone dejectedly through 'A Mighty Fortress is Our God.'" In church, music "should be a means of unlocking us," he rhapsodized, "of bringing our hearts and minds into some alignment, of helping us express joy and gratitude, poignancy, tenderness, courage, and love —all the great religious feelings."

That is what he had just lived through in Birmingham, "the singingest week I have ever experienced": from Joan Baez and the Highlander Center's

Guy Carawan, to nineteen rabbis who "had three thousand Negroes singing in Hebrew, 'How lovely it is to live like brothers,'" to "of course everywhere, 'We Shall Overcome.'" Singing, which Coffin had always loved as performance, as expression of joy, as release of energy, and as worship, had also become an instrument of justice. "There was more light on the Negro faces of Birmingham than I have seen on faces in a long time," he told his congregation. "For these people were not only talking about human dignity and freedom, they were living it. And because they were living it, they just had to sing of it."[18]

After the Sixteenth Street Baptist Church bombing that killed four little girls in Birmingham, Coffin organized a special collection for the church's rebuilding fund, eventually sending more than five hundred dollars. He also had a flyer distributed on the Yale campus that suggested writing letters of sympathy to the families of the murdered children (he provided their addresses) in the hopes that "an outpouring of sympathy and support" would both "help to assuage the grief of parents and to relieve the understandable bitterness and frustration now oppressing the hearts of the Negro population in Birmingham."[19]

Overlapping with the Birmingham campaign, the civil rights action in St. Augustine, Florida, seemed perfectly suited to Coffin's gifts, and he made the most of it. St. Augustine first moved into the national civil rights consciousness in March 1963 as the little city prepared to celebrate its four hundredth birthday in 1965 and requested $350,000 in federal funds to underwrite the festivities. The local NAACP, led by black dentist Robert Hayling, drew the wrath of the white community by attempting to block federal support. Although blacks had been fighting segregation in St. Augustine since the 1950s, tensions rose dramatically, leading to a series of violent incidents. In March 1964 Hayling's group affiliated with the SCLC and invited northern college students and faculty to spend their spring breaks in St. Augustine doing civil rights work instead of sunning on the beaches.[20]

At Yale the Battell undergraduate deacons responded enthusiastically and announced the call in church on March 15. About twenty students left at the end of the week, accompanied by two assistant chaplains. Coffin preached Easter Sunday, March 29; the next day he, associate chaplains Arthur Brandenburg and Jacques Bossière, and Yale Medical School professor David Miller left New Haven, arriving in St. Augustine Tuesday, March 31.

The truly notable northern presence in St. Augustine that week, however, was that of Mary Elizabeth Peabody, the seventy-two-year-old Boston Brahmin, mother of the governor of Massachusetts, and wife of the retired Episcopal bishop of central New York. Mrs. Peabody had decided to accompany two friends (one black, both wives of senior Episcopal priests) who were responding to the SCLC call. Coffin got a phone call from a black colleague urging him to make sure that Mrs. Peabody got arrested for the media attention it would bring.

By the time Coffin's group arrived, the drama was in full swing. Police had arrested twenty-six demonstrators on Saturday, nine more on Easter Sunday (including the Yale students and a chaplain), and thirty-nine more the next day. On Monday, Mrs. Peabody's black friend Mrs. Burgess was arrested with Hayling when they tried to get served at the restaurant of the segregated Ponce De Leon Motor Lodge.

In Hayling's absence, SCLC staffer Hosea Williams was directing the action, preparing a group of 150 black high school students for a march to the motel dining room. Coffin swung immediately into an "effective, impassioned pep talk." At the end of their march, while most of the students were being arrested "by electric-cattle-prod carrying police-dog-leading police," in Miller's words, word came that Mrs. Peabody was "in trouble" at the Trinity Episcopal Church. Slipping into the church by pretending to be a tourist, Bossière found her surrounded by church members urging her to "give up her mission in St. Augustine." With some difficulty, he escorted her out of the church and to Hayling's office, where he, Coffin, and Hosea Williams sat down with her. "She appeared to have been brainwashed," Miller reported, having "decided that perhaps the white people were right, and that the trouble in peaceful St. Augustine may have been caused by bad Negro leadership."

Facing defeat, the three men put "considerable effort" into persuading their newsworthy companion of "the incredible oppression of the whites toward the Negroes." Coffin pointed out that "unless Mrs. Peabody went to jail with Mrs. Burgess, she would be letting her down and, with her, the Negro community in Massachusetts." Moral suasion had failed so far; it was time to bring "adverse national publicity" to bear on the town's tourist industry, and Mrs. Peabody's arrest would do the trick. Coffin's charm could have fallen on no more receptive ears than those of an elderly, liberally inclined, church-connected, New England upper-class matron—the Boston likeness of Catherine Butterfield Coffin. She "overcame her natural reticence," of course, "and finally agreed to go to jail." She did check first with her son the governor, who told her "to do what she thought best." That afternoon she went back to the Ponce de Leon with two Boston friends and some black women from St. Augustine, where she was arrested and carted off to jail.

Mary Peabody's arrest did indeed make the national news; Wednesday's *New York Times* carried a large two-column photograph of her being led off by a cigar-chomping St. Augustine policeman. The following day the paper covered her brief news conference on the steps of the county jail and ran an admiring profile of the courageous "Back Bay Crusader." Coffin got a piece of that day's headline, too, as he, his two chaplains, and David Miller joined four black women and got arrested at the Ponce de Leon. By the end of the day eighty-eight protesters had been arrested, bringing the total in five days to nearly three hundred. The police had been making a great show of their dogs during this entire action, and they put Coffin and Miller into the backseat of the cruiser with a "large, awake police dog." According to Miller, Coffin managed to pet the dog so skillfully that he rendered this "intimidation tactic" completely useless. Jail, while physically uncomfortable, lasted just one night. The Yale group soon posted bail, attended a large, lively mass meeting addressed by Coffin and Mrs. Peabody, among others, and left for New Haven.

St. Augustine's white leaders did not budge. In May and June, when King and the SCLC made a major push in St. Augustine and the city seemed on the verge of anarchy, even political pressure from the White House could not bring the crisis to a negotiated solution. Only passage of the Civil Rights Act of 1964 forced local businessmen, who feared the Klan even more than they did black marchers, to desegregate.

Coffin only needed tactical successes to keep going. He sent a letter to the *Times* the following Monday, sticking up for the high school students who had marched. Far from "being used," he argued, "their education took. They believe in the Declaration of Independence." He called on others "of the prominence and gallantry of Mrs. Peabody—bishops and archbishops, business men, labor leaders, artists and athletes" to show they cared about "the lives of those whose dignity they preach." "Who, then," he concluded, "is going to follow Mrs. Peabody to jail?"

A Boston lawyer (and Yale alum) wrote to thank Coffin for his efforts and mentioned that he had just seen "a delegation off for St. Augustine." Coffin also received thanks from a black New York University student who had been about to write a letter lauding Mrs. Peabody, and from a Long Island rabbi (another Yale graduate) who announced himself "prepared to join you on similar trips."[21]

In May Coffin wrote to congratulate a member of the St. Augustine celebration committee for making a public statement regarding race in the city. Sensing a crack in the formal edifice, Coffin peppered his second paragraph with tactical questions and ideas regarding the committee's private and public positions: were there going to be more statements? what about public resignations? is anyone trying to influence the president? In June, as Martin Luther King issued an "urgent plea" for clergy to "come with friends to St. Augustine," Coffin wrote an old classmate, a banker in St. Paul who was coming to stay for a night, and urged him to "live it up for a day and a night in St. Augustine, a marvelous Negro community, and then rest in the St. John [*sic*] County jail for a couple of days. Think of the issue you would be on return, and what an education therefore you could carry on!"[22]

Restlessly intelligent, eager to move, loving to talk the talk of civil rights and Christianity, Coffin was having terrific fun in the thick of conflict and action. From his Yale position he could write to anyone, and expect answers from most. He raised bail money for St. Augustine arrestees, probably with help from Eva, his mother, his children's recorder teacher, his brother and sister, his in-laws (a thousand dollar gift), and the wife of a wealthy Yale Corporation member (two thousand dollars from Mrs. John Hay Whitney). Coffin was learning how to use his skills and his position.[23]

A Theology of Civil Rights

Coffin was also learning to wield his Christianity with tremendous dexterity, developing a theology of civil rights action that sustained him for many years. To a Wellesley student who had written him about the relative value of education and action, Coffin maintained that, all by themselves, arguments were "rather useless because what is emotionally rooted is not intellectually soluble." Action, on the other hand, "makes you a pariah, but sometimes it wins a begrudging admiration if it is carried out without great self-righteousness or hostility. It may also take on meaning in retrospect. It may mean something to the Negro community, and it may inspire lives elsewhere. Who knows the influence, positive or negative, of one's actions?" Since one could not know for certain, one could only act, and hope that it would be for the best. With growing confidence in his instincts, Coffin was transforming his own impatience into a theory of political action.[24]

On the "Yale Reports" radio program in early 1962 Coffin explained how his views on race stemmed from his Christianity and sketched the ideas and phrases that would govern his thinking for years. First, as he never tired of repeating: "It is a fundamental, theological presupposition of the Christian Church that it is not because we have value that we are loved by God, but because we are loved by God that we have value." Very simply, then, "as regards race relations, there can be no graded scale of worth," since none of the ways we humans distinguish ourselves exist in God's eyes.[25]

As a demonstration of this truth, Jesus' ministry was "primarily concerned to discover the image of God no matter how torn or how distorted or how faded the image, in every derelict, whore, prodigal, or profligate with whom he [Jesus] came in contact." Coffin told a favorite story about a sixteenth-century beggar "brought to an operating table of some doctors in Italy." Speaking in Latin (which they thought he would not understand), they said, "Let us experiment on this vile fellow." Their would-be victim, "an impoverished student later to become the renowned scholar Marc Antoine Muret," answered, also in Latin, "You call vile one for whom Christ did not disdain to die." Not only a "humanistic" offense, discrimination was "blasphemy in the face of God."

The question of equality followed. Here, Coffin relied on St. Paul, for whom equality did not mean "equality of rights or equality of opportunity," but rather "oneness"—not sameness, but oneness. He then drew out the radical implications of what he had been saying: "if God loves, as seen in the life of Christ, all men indiscriminately," and "if as Christians we are followers of Christ," we are to love all men just as Christ did.

Coffin modified an aphorism of G. K. Chesterton (that, in a slightly different form, would become one of his most enduring sayings): "Christianity has not been tried and failed, it has very rarely ever been tried."[26] For Christians, "it is not enough for us to be tolerant—because tolerance is really controlled antagonism—it's an armistice, not a peace." The real test was love: "As Christians we are called upon to love, with the same type of love that God has shown for each man in the life of Christ. . . . We as Christians are not called upon to create the brotherhood of man, only to recognize it."

Coffin understood how systems nurtured racism but rejected wholly environmental explanations for this evil on the Niebuhrian grounds that "prejudice is most fundamentally an expression of man's inherent, his constitutional self-centeredness." Christianity, as a result, must be concerned primarily "not with social structures, nor with political parties, or any other type of social or economic or political organization," but rather with "the heart of every man." Because "the 'pretender' is seated so firmly on the throne in the heart," the church "needs a disturbing voice." From Moses speaking to Pharaoh, to Amos and Jonah and Jesus himself, prophets had to speak painful truths.

On the other hand, he pointed out, "Jesus did not direct His voice exclusively to the heart of every man, but challenged the unjust people who were governing the society in which He lived . . . which, of course, was why He was crucified." Was "it not contradictory," he asked, "for a Christian to show compassion to a Negro as an individual without at the same time being concerned with the structures of society which make him an object of compassion?"

As regarded law, Coffin admitted, "You cannot legislate morality" but retorted that "you can legislate conditions which are more conducive to morality." Coffin had few compunctions about breaking bad laws, even though such actions might "disturb the peace" and "invite, I don't say incite, I say invite violence." After all, Coffin pointed out, "if you look at the life of Jesus, you have to recognize that He was perhaps the chief disturber of the peace."

He closed his radio comments with a rare self-referential paragraph on the "dilemma of a minister," who must always strive "to balance in some responsible way his priestly [pastoral, sacramental] responsibilities and his prophetic ones." Since the church had been "remiss in its prophetic role," any error should be on the "compensatory side, on the side of the prophetic role." After all, "it is very, very dangerous philosophy or theology to try to improve on Jesus. We cannot forget that it was His prophetic role that ended His priestly role at the age of thirty-three."

Coffin's ideas on civil rights changed little over the next two years, but he hammered the words into tighter, more condensed and striking form. In a talk titled "Suburbia—No Hiding Place," Coffin displayed his newer, cadenced verbal formulas: "A man's value is not achieved. A man's value is received. God's love doesn't seek value; it creates value"; and, getting closer to Chesterton: "I also know that Christianity has not been tried and found wanting; it's been tried and found difficult." Finally, discrimination was "blasphemy in the face of the Creator" because "it's making distinctions which God himself doesn't make."[27]

Because the question of property rights loomed so large in northern civil rights conversations, Coffin concluded his discussion by asserting that "property rights should reflect human rights and not reject them." The entire speech was shot through with Coffin's by now trademark aphorisms: those describing the relative peace of the lion and the lamb, the meaning of "peace at any price," the Al Capone line "we don't want no trouble," "true peace" being "never the absence of tension but the presence of justice," and a conclusion that he used numerous times during these years: "Solon, the great law-giver of Athens was asked, 'When will perfect justice come to Athens?' He gave an answer which I think is pretty good for Americans today: 'When those who are not the victims of injustice feel just as keenly as those who are.'"

The talk was so wide ranging—from what churches and synagogues could do to integrate the ranks of real estate agents, to why, from a Jewish or Christian perspective, "there is no such thing as inter-racial marriage, for all marriage is inter-personal," to discriminatory unions and clubs—that the Connecticut Commission on Civil Rights published it in a special supplement the following July.[28]

The story about Solon and Athens perfectly described Coffin's own mission during these years. Based in a bastion of wealth and privilege, Coffin spent little time with the afflicted. He did, however, spend a lot of time with the comfortable, and knew how to talk to them—how to afflict them, how to push them toward feeling what Heschel called "the monstrosity of injustice."

In a speech to schoolteachers in Scarsdale, New York, on election day 1963, he rattled off a series of one- and two-liners: "From a Christian point of view," he argued, "our basic sin is that we are always trying to put asunder what God himself has joined together." He gave his pithy understanding of the Cain and Abel story—"Am I my brother's keeper? No, I am my brother's brother"— and followed with: "We are not called upon to achieve the brotherhood of man. We are only called upon to recognize it."

But now he had a better story on the environment and prejudice in a Niebuhrian take on *Winnie the Pooh:* "Bear goes to Rabbit's house for dinner and gets stuck in the doorway on his way out. Unable to extricate himself, Pooh says to Rabbit: 'Your door is too small.' Rabbit answers, 'The fact is, Pooh, you've eaten too much.'" Pooh played the environmental determinist, Rabbit the believer in sin. With a nod toward the environment, he preferred Adam and Eve's proof that "even in a perfect environment men can't resist the temptation to put themselves first."[29]

Coffin clearly enjoyed taking his message on the road. He occasionally appeared on TV host David Susskind's "Open End" talk show; whenever it aired, Coffin got mail. A Catholic woman in Woburn, Massachusetts, was typical, writing that she "could almost hear the electricity of your manner, humor, and opinions snap through the air of our living room." According to another, "You're so right about the suburban parish—but we wouldn't be floundering amid sugar-coated country club style spiritual mish-mash if our leadership came from more William Sloane Coffins!!"[30]

When a correspondent wanted advice about how to change her insular church, Coffin spilled over with ideas, from starting a study group to asking the minister why he shied away from civil rights. "If it divides the church," he prodded, "that may be all right. After all, Christ was the great disturber of the peace, and the peace of most churches needs badly to be disturbed if it can be done thoughtfully."[31]

No snob as to venues, Coffin published his ideas in *Mademoiselle* ("On the Roots of Prejudice"), *Parents' Magazine* ("Stand Up for What You Believe In"), and *Glamour* ("Do You Undervalue Sex?") (see Chapter 10). In *Mademoiselle* he encouraged his readers to learn courage, which could be acquired "only by risking, by daring to step out, abandoning the safe for the exciting, the useless for the more creative." At college this could mean "reading not only *Mademoiselle,* but the *New Republic, The New Leader, The Nation,* and all kinds of literature capable of overturning these beloved sheltering lies about ourselves and the world we live in." Courage could also mean "avoiding sororities, which are so reassuring to our anxious egos but so useless to any larger concern," and volunteering in a tutoring or voter registration program. He encouraged readers to consider "mixing it up—black with white, white with black—at all sorts of social occasions, parental and other objections notwithstanding." Courage might also mean "risking the Peace Corps or some other radical vocational choice. It probably means not joining both Junior League and country club." After all, was "it really necessary to be among 'one's own kind' all the time?" Instead, why not join the NAACP or CORE or a local political organization, "where accents to be sure are threateningly different, but where, accordingly, there is much to be learned?"[32]

While Coffin still relied on Reinhold Niebuhr for critique—of sin, self-righteousness, sentimentality—he followed a number of contemporaries into new territory as regarded the power of love in the struggle for justice. As Mark Silk observes, the heyday of neo-orthodoxy was passing in the early 1960s, partly because a new version of the much more optimistic Social Gospel seemed to be bubbling up in the civil rights movement and in a new interest in social action discernible in many Protestant denominations. Martin Luther King Jr. described this movement in his own theological evolution as overcoming his Niebuhrian doubts about the transforming power of Christian love—mainly through discovering Gandhi's notion of *satyagraha:* active, loving nonviolence that aimed to convert the opponent rather than defeat him. "As I delved deeper into the philosophy of Gandhi," King wrote in a *Christian Century* piece, part of a series called "How My Mind Has Changed," "my skepticism concerning the power of love gradually diminished, and I came to see for the first time that the Christian doctrine of love operating through the Gandhian method of nonviolence was one of the most potent weapons available to oppressed people in their struggle for freedom."[33]

Coffin occasionally quoted Gandhi but had not clearly been struggling with how to reconcile the optimism of the Social Gospel with Niebuhr's pessimism about human nature. Instead, he learned from the black ministers who led the civil rights movement, remarked often on the joy they brought to the practice of self-sacrifice, and already had a theological preference for the power of love from his divinity school days. Silk points out that the neo-orthodox theology "of man's utter distance from God, of the imperfectability of human affairs, could not make for a politics of social redemption." Niebuhrian prophecy had "more to do with the breaking of idols and the exposure of false prophets than with any summons to a promised land," which made it far less relevant to a very real movement issuing just such a summons to a people long enslaved.[34] Coffin responded eagerly to that call because it so perfectly fit his own aggressive Christianity, his energetic activism, and his fundamental personal confidence and optimism. Intellectually, Coffin remained a Niebuhrian; emotionally, he had joined the new movement. Although he never felt close to Martin Luther King Jr., he ended up one of King's most influential disciples.

EIGHT

Wading into the Big Muddy

The Dilemma of Dissent

Like most Americans, Coffin had little interest in the faraway country of Vietnam in the early 1960s. When editorialists or government officials mentioned the tiny nation that few Americans could have located on a map they generally invoked common, if inaccurate, Cold War pieties. "Communist guerillas" supported by "outsiders" (in this case North Vietnam as well as "Red China" and the USSR) threatened a "democratic ally" whose "freedom and independence" were vital to American interests. That this analysis served to describe the Philippines, Laos, Indonesia, or any number of other countries facing alleged "internal subversion" made it more readily deployed by officialdom, and more easily swallowed by the general public. This inattention to the realities of individual countries with distinct histories eventually proved extremely costly.[1]

By 1963, however, Vietnam had broken through into the public mind— or at least the public press—mainly because of the repressive and corrupt regime of President Ngo Dinh Diem. Along with his brother Ngo Dinh Nhu and flamboyant sister-in-law, Madame Nhu, Diem had managed to alienate both his country's Buddhist majority and his American patrons. The dramatic self-immolation of the Buddhist monk Quang Duc in June (the famous picture of which landed on the cover of *Life*) alerted Americans—officials as well as the public—to the possibility that "our guy" Diem had serious limitations. That fall U.S. officials let it be known in Saigon that they would not oppose a coup against him, a hint that became reality on November 1.

Beginning in the summer of 1963, and continuing through much of 1964, a number of American opinion-makers and public officials raised doubts about U.S. objectives and tactics in Vietnam. From the liberal magazines *The Nation, The New Republic,* and *Commentary* came serious questions about the viability of South Vietnamese "democracy," about the prospects for victory over the insurgency in the south, and even about the supposed costs of a Communist victory. From sources as disparate as the eminent columnist Walter Lippmann, the editorial pages of the *New York Times* and of smaller newspapers around the country, and the conservative *U.S. News & World Report* came more questions about American strategy and support for a negotiated settlement. Even senators began to worry publicly that a commitment to Vietnam might be unending.[2]

Religious figures, particularly mainline Protestants but also some Jews, began to raise concerns in *Christianity and Crisis* and *Christian Century.* In the wake of the monk's self-immolation, a group of thirteen clergy, most in New York City, formed a "Minister's Vietnam Committee," led by such luminaries as Reinhold Niebuhr, Riverside Church Senior Minister Harry Emerson Fosdick, Union Theological Seminary President John Bennett, Episcopal Bishop James Pike, and Temple Emanu-El's longtime rabbi Julius Mark. First the group took out ads in the *New York Times* and *Washington Post* protesting American sacrifices for the "unjust, undemocratic, and unstable" South Vietnamese government. Then, when Diem's brother used American-trained forces to raid and loot pagodas and arrest Buddhist monks all over Vietnam in August, they put another ad in the *Times,* this time declaring the support of "17,358 clergymen of all faiths." Even if they had inflated this number (roughly one in twelve American clergy), they had reached into the mainstream, an achievement confirmed when Union's Bennett wrote skeptically of administration Vietnam policy in *Christianity and Crisis* in July 1964.[3]

Still, support for the administration in general, and President Lyndon Johnson in particular, dominated most Americans' attitudes toward Vietnam —when they had them at all. And throughout the 1964 campaign Johnson effectively countered the bellicose Republican nominee Barry Goldwater by presenting himself as the peace candidate in Vietnam. The Gulf of Tonkin resolution, giving Johnson a virtual blank check for military action in Southeast Asia, had sailed through Congress in early August 1964, and both *Christianity and Crisis* and the *Christian Century* broke with their traditions and endorsed the president.

Johnson's overwhelming victory in November did not move him away from military options; no amount of public support would be enough to counterbalance his fear of being painted as "soft on Communism" by the right. In response to the administration's continuing hard line, opponents staged an antiwar rally at the Berkeley campus of the University of California that drew eight hundred, organized a thousand-person rally in New York City, published a large advertisement in the *Boston Globe* supporting a cease-fire agreement, sent an appeal from 105 Washington, D.C.–area religious leaders asking the president to seek a negotiated peace, and got five thousand academics to sign a letter to the president urging him "not to enlarge the scope of the war." Even earlier in the year small leftist and pacifist groups had held rallies and published ads critical of American Vietnam policy. Students for a Democratic Society (SDS) began planning for a Washington antiwar march the Saturday of Easter weekend, 1965.[4]

This was the early anti–Vietnam war movement: writers and journal editors, groups of religious leaders and intellectuals, professors and radical college students, occasional public officials and journalists, and old-line leftists and pacifists who were willing to raise questions, speak out publicly, rally, and march for negotiations and against the use of napalm and chemical defoliants and escalation. However small, these groups were becoming more active and more vocal, and they had access to existing liberal networks. They represented, in other words, a significant minority position against military escalation in Vietnam in 1964 and early 1965.[5]

Although Coffin followed public affairs closely and could not have missed newspaper and magazine coverage of Vietnam, he kept his distance, waiting more than a year before throwing himself into the public debate. This characteristic Coffin "pause," used to such advantage at New Year's 1945, when he chose to train troops rather than go to the front, and later that spring, when he missed his train and Chingis Guirey persuaded him away from the front, had become an important emotional tool that he wielded intuitively. Coffin paid little attention to Vietnam before 1965. He recalled being "stunned" to hear Johnson's commitment to Vietnam in the 1965 State of the Union message but also distressed that the president had fulfilled the gloomy predictions of Coffin's leftist friend Staughton Lynd, who taught American history at Yale. He had plenty to occupy him without entering such dangerous waters.[6]

Still, Vietnam was a growing issue during late 1963 and all of 1964. A succession of governments in Saigon highlighted the profound instability of America's ally, while the military situation in the countryside continued to deteriorate despite a gradually increasing number of U.S. military "advisors." From mid-1964 through early February 1965 the Johnson administration either sought or waited for provocations to widen the war. The Tonkin Gulf incident provided much of what Johnson wanted. Then, five months later, just as top American advisor McGeorge Bundy was preparing to end a fact-finding trip to Saigon, the Viet Cong gave Johnson the rest. On February 7, 1965, they attacked a U.S. installation near Pleiku, killing 8 and wounding 126. Within hours, Johnson had the approval of the National Security Council for retaliatory bombing attacks, soon transformed into "Operation Rolling Thunder," the sustained bombing of North Vietnam.

Caught unaware by the ferocity of the U.S. military response, Coffin prayed about Vietnam for the first time the Sunday after the Pleiku incident, questioning government actions. He hoped that "the conduct of this nation's affairs in South Vietnam may reflect political wisdom informed by moral sensitivity" and reminded his audience of "the obligation to put loyalty to truth above obedience to the national will, for the church is no mere echo of the state, and the university is committed to intellectual faithfulness." A simple opposition, however, would not do. His next paragraph invoked the Niebuhrian tragic sensibility: "Save us, O God, from all Utopian illusions, from any desire to stress the good at the expense of the possible, from any notion that any course of action would now be free of any moral distress. Save us, O God, from all vain hopes of an easy peace." Here, Coffin was retreating from arguments he made constantly on behalf of civil rights, an arena in which acts of witness and civil disobedience, he well knew, could change the calculus of the "possible" and "impossible." In correspondence with self-described civil rights moderates, he frequently challenged them to "stress the good at the expense" of the allegedly "possible."

He then returned to critique, praying to be saved "from all fighting creeds no longer in touch with the realities of the situation" and attacking the "madness" of war itself, in which "for every boy turned into a man . . . there are five human beings turned into animals." Finally, "O God, keep us human, obsessed with tenderness in the midst of all this inhumanity; through Jesus Christ, who showed us what tenderness was, who showed us how only the truly strong can be truly tender."[7]

By deprecating "vain hopes," "Utopian illusions," and "creeds no longer in touch," Coffin rhetorically established his own clearer insight, his realistic beliefs, and his complex, tragic understanding that moral distress could not be avoided. If the enemy seemed clear, the friend (other than Jesus, exemplar of tough-minded tenderness) appeared less so. In the absence of a position, the prayer adopted a pose—skeptical, committed to the possible, "realistic," "tough minded"—one easily recognizable as the mindset of the New Frontiersmen, the Kennedy "whiz kids" who now, in the Johnson administration, were talking themselves into the swamp of war.

The first teach-in on Vietnam took place March 24–25 at the University of Michigan in Ann Arbor, and Coffin made no reference to it. That month the New Haven Committee to End the War in Vietnam called on the Yale faculty to sign a petition opposing the bombing of North Vietnam, urging the president and Congress "to negotiate the immediate withdrawal of U.S. forces from South Vietnam." More than 150 faculty members signed, including many eminent scholars. A number of well-known faculty circulated a long "Open

Letter" to Lyndon Johnson calling for a negotiated settlement. Coffin signed neither statement.[8]

The Fellowship of Reconciliation (FOR) organized a Clergymen's Emergency Committee for Vietnam and published ads in the *New York Times* on April 4 and April 18, Easter Sunday. The first ad claimed the support of 2,700 ministers, priests, and rabbis calling on the president to, "In the Name of God, Stop It!" Two weeks later, in the wake of Johnson's own call for unconditional negotiations, the number had grown to 16,916 Protestant clergymen saying, "Initiate Negotiations *Now!*" Bennett, Martin Luther King Jr., and two Protestant bishops joined with the FOR group, named themselves the Interreligious Committee on Vietnam, and called for a Pentagon vigil Palm Sunday weekend, May 11–12. Although nearly a thousand clergy and laypeople showed up, Coffin, who recalled agonizing over whether to attend the SDS rally in Washington on April 17, ignored the vigil and the demonstration, indeed the entire subject of Vietnam, in his Good Friday and Easter sermons.

While many in the religious community had begun to take public stands, Coffin felt stumped. The February prayer suggested that he knew what he did not like (American policy in Vietnam) but not what he did like. He published a piece in *Life* magazine in late April titled "Don't Tell Them to Play It Safe," aimed mostly at university administrators, professors, and parents, that defended protesting students but never mentioned Vietnam. He also ended the piece with familiar language—a plea to "keep on loving," for "our quarrel with America is indeed a lover's quarrel, and we shall have nothing to contribute if it degenerates into a dirty and purposeless grudge fight." This argument had superficial rhetorical force, but this was not the only alternative open to a dissenter. One could be angry and still have much to contribute, if not as much as King or Gandhi. On the other hand, when a correspondent wrote to criticize student demonstrators, Coffin defended them: Vietnam protesters "are apt to be the same ones" who do low-profile, in-the-trenches work on behalf of the poor.[9]

Coffin may have been exploring different positions by criticizing those with which he disagreed. He wondered, for instance, to a presidential aide whether Johnson was "determined to drag all other countries of the world behind his chariot"—but did not say that the chariot was ill conceived. Alternatively, perhaps, Coffin's inability to stake out his own position left him at moral loose ends, so he freely criticized everybody else.[10]

In 1965, he wrote much later, he also had substantive qualms about the war's opponents. "Troubled" by the New Left's "fudging" on the question of Communist totalitarianism and by the increasingly anti-American rhetoric of SDS leaders, Coffin never felt comfortable calling the United States "imperialist" or marching to "such distant drummers as Ho, Mao, Che Guevara." Being in a "lover's quarrel" with his country structured Coffin's political activity, and he recoiled from harsher ideological language. Coffin had not easily opposed his government back in 1961, but he had done so in the name of American and Christian ideals. Marching under, or near, the flags of America's enemies was an entirely different matter. Here, Coffin made common cause with millions of Americans. Just twenty years after the end of World War II, in the midst of a Cold War that to most Americans had a clear right and wrong side, it was far easier to trust the American government and an immensely popular president apparently committed to a new Great Society. Fighting the military and foreign policy decisions of the government whose uniform he had worn so proudly would involve considerably more moral struggle than Coffin—and millions of his fellow citizens—had experienced by supporting civil rights.

Coffin also kept his distance from other people's positions and parades because, in private and public settings, he needed to be at the center of attention and the action. Unlike many political activists, Coffin did not find the enveloping presence of a like-minded crowd exhilarating. Joining a march twenty thousand strong met few of his psychological needs. Dating from his high school years, Coffin had admired the men of action, or those directing the action, but had rarely felt close to those in the trenches. Far from the leadership of the Baltimore civil rights action in 1963, he had pushed into the center of things—and the press—by rushing to Eva's succor. In St. Augustine, he had gotten himself into the center of the event by convincing Mrs. Peabody to get arrested. Coffin liked being on the inside, knowing what was what, leading the charge.[11]

Off the Fence

The day after the Pleiku attack, the musician (and Yale Music School student) Paul Jordan felt betrayed. "I voted for this man," he recalled, "because he said last fall that unlike Goldwater, who was proposing to bomb North Vietnam, he would not do that." An organist and a well-known recorder player, Jordan had been sailing back to the United States in June 1964 when a fellow traveler made a "very deep impression" on him by predicting that Vietnam was "going to lead to a horrendous impasse in American politics." Later that summer, Jordan heard the president's version of the Tonkin Gulf incident. While Johnson tried to "get us all revved up with anger at the North Vietnamese and ready to accept some sort of action on his part," Jordan recalled at the time, he felt there was "something not quite right here." Still, between the devious Johnson and the belligerent Goldwater, he easily voted for the president.[12]

As American bombers pounded North Vietnam, however, "my world sort of collapsed around me." He began gathering information on Vietnam, and fuming. His own pastor disliked controversy and distrusted Jordan's growing collection, worried that it might be Communist propaganda. So Jordan kept a hopeful, if generally disappointed, eye on Battell and Coffin. At last, just before summer 1965, someone told him that Coffin had preached a "very cautious sermon" on Vietnam in which he said, "This is an issue which we have to consider as Christians. We can't look away from it, but so far as I can tell at this point, it is an issue on which Christians can sincerely differ and in which there will be Christian arguments on either side."[13]

Jordan, already "furious" about the war, wanted more. So when he ran into Coffin on the street several weeks later, "I sort of accosted him with the audacity of youth and said, 'How come you're supposed to have given this sermon saying Christians could go either way on the Vietnam War? Do you really believe that?' And he said, 'Well, do you have any evidence that I should consider that might change my opinion?'" Jordan went home, retrieved his "bulging manila folder"—an assortment of documents, articles, editorials, brochures, speeches, photographs, clippings, and the like—and brought it to Coffin. The file, which Coffin plowed through much of that night, was an eye-opener, documenting "a history of corruption, of misperceptions and missed opportunities the likes of which I had never imagined."[14]

On August 1, Coffin joined a Connecticut "speak-out" against the war. He quoted his February prayer, warning that the "greatest casualty" of the war was "truth," but then swung into preaching cadences: "How can the American government continue to claim that Americans are defending the interests of the Vietnamese," he asked, "when clearly Saigon has lost control of most of South Viet Nam and clearly all efforts of the CIA to subvert the North Vietnamese government have failed miserably; when clearly if the U.S. were to withdraw its support, the whole South Vietnamese effort would collapse in a matter of a few days?"[15]

He and his family went off to Cape Cod in early August, but Coffin "couldn't shake the depression which came close to ruining everybody's fun." Convinced that he needed to do something, but genuinely confused about what that something was, he apparently floated the idea of getting a group of people to visit China. Staughton Lynd responded positively, including the information that "Bob [Parris] and Al L[owenstein] want a get-together to discuss the idea." Encouraged by this response—he had stirred the interest of the country's premier African-American civil rights organizer and the premier organizer of white students—Coffin got to work.[16]

He borrowed a typewriter and banged out a three-page proposal to "re-open the China debate." More concretely, he proposed forming an eminent, "national bi-partisan committee" to support U.S. recognition of the People's Republic of China, normalizing trade and travel with China, and admitting China to the United Nations. The nominal "hook" for the proposal would be the question of China's admission to the U.N., sure to be raised in the fall; the real hook was Vietnam. Coffin assumed that if relations with China could be normalized, other conflicts in Asia could be solved far more easily.

He sent the proposal off to "hot shots" like Bennett, George Kennan (at Princeton's Institute for Advanced Study), Walter Reuther of the United Auto Workers, Arthur Goldberg (then ambassador to the United Nations), and Jonathan Moore, a special assistant in the office of the assistant secretary of state, as well as to his mother and his brother, with a request for comments. "The only way to get the enclosed off my mind is to put it on yours," he wrote Bennett. The "we," in the draft, Coffin admitted, was "really me unable to enjoy a vacation, and still determined that something must be done." Bennett wrote back almost immediately, with encouragement and some suggestions for revision. He, too, thought the time was "ripe for a group which is not simply protesting but which is hoping to relate itself to new steps in policy." It appears that Lynd, Lowenstein, and Coffin (or at least the first two) met in late August to launch a new organization that soon became known as Americans for Reappraisal of Far Eastern Policy, or ARFEP.[17]

It may seem odd for men with the combined political astuteness of Coffin, Lynd, Parris, Lowenstein, and Bennett to have launched a group concerned about China rather than one focused on Vietnam. Coffin felt at the time, and maintained decades later, that ARFEP "was a way of getting indirectly into something that I felt and Al Lowenstein certainly felt, I'm sure, we couldn't simply attack frontally." There wouldn't be sufficient support "so that your weight could be felt," Coffin argued. "There wouldn't be that much understanding." Unlike university issues, where "you just stormed into the President's office," or civil rights, which "was pretty easy" ("After all, King was in there!"), "it wasn't that easy to get into the Vietnam situation."[18]

This retrospective analysis combined historical inaccuracy and tactical insight. First, as a public issue in mid-1965 the admission of China to the U.N. paled beside Vietnam. Second, by this time the antiwar movement was already well under way. Tens of thousands of Americans had taken the leap of dissenting from Cold War orthodoxy and demonstrated that they were publicly concerned about Vietnam and were willing to march, sign petitions, pay for expensive newspaper ads, organize teach-ins, hold rallies, and even cause a flap at the White House, as the poet Robert Lowell did in June 1965 by publicly declining the president's invitation to a White House Festival of the Arts.[19]

Vietnam, in other words, had already become a significant issue in the academic, religious, and foreign policy circles in which Coffin traveled. At the University of California at Berkeley, for example, thirty thousand attended a Vietnam Day teach-in on May 22, 1965; unlike its predecessors, this gathering did not pretend to even-handedness and featured the novelist Norman Mailer, who predicted that demonstrators will hound Lyndon Johnson "into nightmares and endless corridors of night without sleep." Coffin read newspapers and magazines, followed the exploits of Staughton Lynd, saw student petitions, and associated, at least briefly (as in Lowenstein's Encampment for Citizenship), with more radical young people.[20]

So in reality it was not that difficult to get into the "Vietnam situation" for many intellectuals, pacifists, religious people, and civil rights activists. King himself had been making critical comments about Vietnam, an increasingly disturbing issue for him, since late 1964.[21] By mid-1965 Coffin would have known about King's views.

On the other hand, Coffin's insight lay in his recollection that it was far easier to rally big names and establishment figures on behalf of a flank attack rather than for a frontal assault. Few prominent mainstream Americans (intellectuals and civil rights activists did not fall into this category) had concluded that U.S. military action in Vietnam should be halted. Even if they had, they would have felt uneasy saying so directly. It is a measure of the power of the Cold War consensus that Coffin's back-door proposal met with such positive response. King, for example, came under heavy criticism—from the administration and colleagues within the civil rights movement—for continuing to speak in favor of a negotiated settlement in Vietnam in mid-September 1965, so much so that he decided to "withdraw temporarily" from the debate "so I can get on with the civil rights issue."[22]

Finally, since Coffin had waited so long to get involved in Vietnam matters, he would have been joining someone else's show. Temperamentally, he committed much more easily to an effort he was leading rather than following.

Coffin's targets for his idea responded variously. Bennett, his fellow minister, offered the most encouragement. With one prominent exception, those in the administration humored him, endorsing his well-meaning energy while condescending to his lack of knowledge. For example, U.N. Ambassador Arthur Goldberg responded promptly, combining personal warmth with a short lecture on the well-known intractability of the Chinese Communists. Jonathan Moore had spoken to some people and felt "interest is very strong" but sent along "some select materials on China, and a general packet on Vietnam." Ambassador-at-large, Cold War architect, and recent Assistant Secretary of State for Far Eastern Affairs Averell Harriman, however, cut Coffin no slack: "I can assure you that the program that you have for [ARFEP] will only play into the hands of the Chinese communists," he wrote, not at all fooled by Coffin's effort to sneak up on Vietnam. "Normally I am all for discussion groups among university graduates," wrote the "wise man" who would later occupy the position of senior U.S. dove, "but when our country is engaged in the kind of conflict in which we are today in Viet-nam, I firmly believe that it is irresponsible and against our country's interest to undertake the type of activity that you describe in your letter and its enclosures. Its only effect will be to encourage North Viet-Nam and delay the cessation of fighting." Harriman, who later claimed —falsely—that he had always opposed intervention in Vietnam, concluded by declaring that he "completely share[d] President Johnson's conviction" that the lesson of Munich was being taught again in Vietnam.[23]

George Kennan sent what Coffin characterized accurately in a letter to Bennett as a "long, rather sad letter," arguing that "it has become impossible to confront the issue of policy towards China today without confronting simultaneously the problem of Vietnam." Coffin did not mention the elaborate self-dramatizing and mannered tone of Kennan's decision to withdraw from "any sort of participation in the discussion of contemporary political problems" on the grounds that his views carried no weight. Ned Coffin, while endorsing the general idea of educating Americans about China, objected to the entire thrust of his brother's proposal, particularly insofar as it argued for a "moral or emotional appeal."[24]

Coffin hit pay dirt when Lowenstein called, saying he "would help translate the idea into immediate action." Coffin was willing to redraft and revise to bring some influential people on board, but his main interest was in finding people to move with him. Still, he did pay attention to Ned. His next version had shrunk to one page (from four), contained little attempt at emotional or moral suasion, and no longer resembled a sermon. Perhaps that is why Ned sent a check for fifty dollars.

The last week of September, ARFEP organized formally on the Yale campus. Within its first forty-eight hours, Coffin wrote to new correspondent Norman Thomas, the group had located an office, hired full-time and half-time secretaries, and raised seventeen hundred dollars, five hundred from Thomas himself. That week, Coffin asked Bennett formally to serve on the national committee of the fledgling group. He also dispatched letters to likely members of the Yale faculty, as well as others he knew in academic and religious circles, inviting them to serve on the committee and letting them know about ARFEP's "crash program" to launch discussions on fifty campuses October 24.[25]

This very program had been outlined in the August 29–30 meeting that might have included Coffin. That group had decided on a "a target date of

October 24, UN Day, for an opening shot of symposia, teach-ins, lectures, movies, panels, seminars, in at least 50 universities and colleges across the nation." Three of the four points of the proposed organization ended up in ARFEP's program: a call for a cease-fire in Vietnam, "unfreezing" the question of "Red China" in the U.N., and U.S. reconsideration of recognition of China. The quick consensus, the brisk set of plans, the interest in "organization of a student movement linked to a national executive committee pressing for a more realistic Asia policy," and the mention of a "regional structure to prod schools in specific areas" all bore the stamp of Al Lowenstein, who specialized in putting together student-based organizations to carry out targeted actions. Within days of receiving Coffin's meandering sermon-length proposal, Lowenstein had boiled it down, rendering out the religious rhetoric, to a moderate program easily stated and easily grasped. The final point, too, was pure Lowenstein: "Absolutely no civil disobedience in the name of this organization."[26]

Coffin and Lowenstein made a dazzling combination. Coffin accurately described Lowenstein as "the best student organizer in the country," as well as "the finest stand-up orator I had ever heard."[27] Like Coffin, Lowenstein knew the importance of cultivating key older supporters along with students. Coffin brought his own impressive credentials: he had become the best-known, most passionate, and most influential university chaplain in the country. He had already preached hundreds of sermons, at baccalaureates, commencements, retreats, "religious emphasis" weeks, "ethics weekends," prep schools, colleges, and universities, from coast to coast. No other mainline preacher so regularly riled up campuses about values and issues.

The qualification is important because there was another kind of campus preacher, the kind who led revivals on fundamentalist campuses, black as well as white, across the country. And there was Martin Luther King Jr., who preached and lectured throughout the country. But King's effect differed from Coffin's. King did not speak in small groups to students; he had become a more distant figure, more absorbed by the larger national public, constantly balancing the needs of the civil rights movement, of his organization, and of national-level political pressures and press (and FBI) scrutiny, all under the ever-present threat of assassination. With his salary assured, his office provided for, and his staff left pretty much to their own supervision, Coffin could act far more independently.

As Lowenstein hit the road in September organizing campus chapters of ARFEP, sometimes two a day, and the organization was heading toward its big splash on October 24, Coffin at last felt that he was *doing* something about Vietnam. Energized by the activity, Coffin unleashed a torrent of correspondence from his office to potential supporters and national committee members.[28]

By the time he went to press with the brochure announcing the U.N. Day action—more than twenty campuses sponsoring rallies, speakers, films, and seminars keynoted by a nationwide telephone hookup—he had persuaded an eclectic group of academics, journalists, lawyers, and public figures to lend their names: Bennett, *Texas Observer* editor Ronnie Dugger, the Harvard China scholar John Fairbank, the critic and editor Irving Howe, Yale professors John Hersey and Mary Wright (a Chinese historian), the psychologist Rollo May, and founder of the American Civil Liberties Union (ACLU) Roger Baldwin. Avowing moderation, the brochure's cover featured quotations from McGeorge Bundy favoring "discussion and review by private individuals of any aspect of our foreign policy, and particularly our policy toward the Peiping regime" (a witty barb aimed at Averell Harriman), and Pope Paul VI admonishing the United Nations in early October to "study the right method of uniting to your pact of brotherhood, in honor and in loyalty, those who do not yet share in it." "This day," the copy read, "is not a day of civil disobedience, but one of education."[29]

Even so, the Sunday before the national ARFEP event, Coffin broached the topic of civil disobedience directly for the first time. Preaching on Acts 5:27–39, especially the sentence, "We must obey God rather than men," Coffin explored the dilemmas of two students who had come for counseling regarding the draft and Vietnam, one an ROTC senior who had concluded that the war was "immoral." Congratulating the students for their "courage in wrestling" with their dilemmas, the sermon suggested that Coffin did not feel entirely at home in his middle-of-the-road organization. He pointed out rationally that "the principle of no compromise is no higher than the principle of compromise . . . that must be accepted by those who elect to work within society." But he also posed a striking rhetorical question: "Is it not incredible, for instance, that not one Divinity School student here or elsewhere has given up his 4-D exemption, refused the draft and gone to jail, given the sentiment against U.S. policy in Viet Nam that we know exists among seminarians today?" The sermon bristled with the aphorisms people were beginning to call Coffinisms:

> —No, as power corrupts the strong, so lack of it corrupts the weak.
> —And therefore we can say with a fair degree of accuracy that while the rich have given us our standards of taste it has generally been the poor who have told us what is right and wrong.
> —Our sin is that we are constantly trying to put asunder what God himself has joined together.[30]

The impressive ARFEP program—the speakers, the sponsors, and the campuses—drew national press. Bennett opened the event, which included presentations by *Saturday Review* editor Norman Cousins, Michael Harrington,

Fairbank, and Thomas. The *New York Post* headline declared "25,000 Students Tune in on Teach-In" and called it "one of the largest 'teach-ins' the country has seen." The *New York Times* reported participation by thirty campuses and highlighted the ARFEP pledge to demonstrate "not by civil disobedience but by education." Moderation played well; the *Times* reporter paraphrased Bennett extensively to the effect that "the new organization wanted to distinguish itself in two respects from recent demonstrators against United States policy." First, "pickets and draft-card burnings," he said, "may have reached the point of defeating their own purpose: they are hardening the opposition." Second, ARFEP wanted to "get away from the exclusive attention to Vietnam, and get to the broader problems of Asia."

Though a brand new group with a skeleton structure and a thin program, ARFEP immediately struck a nerve. Even *The Nation*, whose politics lay to the left of ARFEP's, characterized the new group as "more mature, less vulnerable, and probably longer lived" than some "new left" groups. In particular, the national committee "is so studded with well known names . . . that the J. Edgar Hoovers, Eastlands, Dodds, *et al.*, will be hard put to redbait it into silence."[31]

ARFEP's inaugural event appeared all the more attractive coming the weekend after the International Days of Protest, in which twenty to thirty thousand protesters marched in New York City and Oakland, and smaller groups demonstrated in sixty cities across the United States and fifteen other countries. On Friday, October 15, a young pacifist demonstrator stood before a crowd at the New York City induction center and declared his intention to burn his draft card in protest. Whether it was due to the attention-getting draft-card burning, the geographic spread of the protests, or the range of liberal, pacifist, and leftist organizations marching under one umbrella, public officials and mainstream media lashed out at the dissenters. *Time* headlined its coverage "Vietniks— Self-Defeating Dissent," while Attorney General Nicholas deB. Katzenbach hinted that his department might have to prosecute "some Communists" among the marchers. FBI Director J. Edgar Hoover suggested that most protesters were "halfway citizens who are neither morally, mentally nor emotionally mature." The influential *New York Times* columnist James Reston opined that protests were "not promoting peace but postponing it."[32]

ARFEP benefited, not completely innocently, from the negative publicity given to the more outspoken and dramatic protests by eschewing civil disobedience and holding fast to an explicitly "middle-of-the-road" position. Bennett appeared to be criticizing the antiwar protests the previous weekend. As Coffin wrote to Mary Wright after the U.N. Day event, "I think we have got to keep going, or nobody right of SDS will be opposing the President."[33]

Coffin exaggerated. The summer 1965 issue of the literary and cultural journal *Partisan Review* ran an antiwar petition from such respected liberal intellectuals as Richard Poirier, Martin Duberman, Alfred Kazin, Norman Podhoretz, and Stephen Marcus. In June the *Christianity and Crisis* editorial board —including Niebuhr, Bennett, Harvey Cox of Harvard Divinity School, and Robert McAfee Brown of Stanford—came out against the war. Coffin knew about the respectable face of dissent. Perhaps he remained concerned about the tactics of some demonstrators, which were beginning to escalate; a few days later, an American Quaker, Norman Morrison, immolated himself in front of the Pentagon to protest the war. As Coffin told Lynd, ARFEP had ruled out civil disobedience "only for ourselves, and only as a tactic to persuade obtuse middle-of-the roaders."

Coffin stayed close to Lynd, encouraging him personally as well as politically, thanking him for participating in a service at Yale, as well as for a lengthy letter to the *Times* on the subject of negotiations. Coffin kept a relatively open mind regarding his friends, acquaintances, and colleagues. He continued to correspond with men in the administration. And because he knew how to charm donors, he kept up a close correspondence with Norman Thomas and the poet Lenore Marshall, a philanthropist of left-wing causes.[34]

Yale ARFEP put a full-page advertisement in the *New York Times* on December 10, asking, "Are we prepared to live in the same world with China?" According to one Yale professor, this was the first time "2,000 Yalies had signed anything except a petition for co-education." Coffin lent the group five thousand dollars to pay for the ad and some office expenses. The advertisement attracted a good bit of interest, both on the Yale campus and further afield. Several hundred faculty members signed, ranging from junior acting instructors up to assistant deans, college masters, and nationally eminent scholars holding endowed professorships.[35]

The ad brought checks and encouragement, as had *The Nation* editorial in November. Convinced that he had hold of a tiger, Coffin, with the help of Norman Thomas, tried to persuade Al Lowenstein to become ARFEP's permanent national secretary. When Lowenstein was organizing chapters, ARFEP grew. When he stopped, ARFEP slowed. National committee members had lent their names, not their energies. ARFEP needed a full-time staff person who could take hold of the fledgling organization and give it national structure and direction. But the peripatetic Lowenstein had other ambitions. In late November he "parachuted," to use his biographer's word, into the Democratic primary race for the Nineteenth Congressional District in Manhattan.[36]

Having excited student (and some faculty) activity on a couple of dozen campuses, ARFEP's program stirred up interest in Asia that translated into study groups, public forums, newsletters, speaker series, and the like. This kind of interest and activity soon transferred to the subject of Vietnam directly. That ARFEP grew at all, and that individual chapters held forums and informational sessions all through the spring of 1966, testified to the unease with Vietnam policy that a significant minority of students and faculty around the country felt. But without Lowenstein and without a growing crusade, Coffin changed direction, and ARFEP soon petered out.

Although most histories of the period ignore ARFEP, its brief story carries significance for two reasons. First, it showed that campus organizing on foreign policy issues could spark interest, raise money, and unite faculty and students. It is worth remembering that even though students and faculties divided later in the decade, on civil rights and in the early antiwar movement, these two constituencies worked in tandem more often than not. At many colleges and universities, faculty preceded students into dissent on Vietnam, a fact that student radicals conveniently forgot later in the decade.

Second, the experience was personally important for Coffin, who discovered much in the process of thinking up and launching ARFEP. He realized once again how much he enjoyed a crusade, for at its beginning ARFEP fully engaged Coffin's appetite for activity as well as his interest in being at the center of the action and in charge. Next, he learned that he could attract the strong support —political, emotional, and financial—of older activists, academics, and church-connected people for moderate political aims. He recruited John Bennett, for instance, while remaining friends with Staughton Lynd. He raised substantial sums from Harold Hochschild, Lenore Marshall, and Norman Thomas. Here, the Coffin charm clearly helped.[37]

Coffin also learned that his ideas could not break into policy circles. Harriman attacked, while his Washington acquaintances patronized him. The ARFEP experience recalled his late-night phone calls to McGeorge Bundy and Harris Wofford outside Ralph Abernathy's house in Montgomery back in 1961. They took his calls only because of who Coffin was. Coffin's insights in these matters were tactical rather than substantive. He sensed, correctly, that liberals were prepared to hear and respond to modest dissent in the service of liberal internationalism and great power "realism." The energetic and quotable fashion in which he articulated his ideas seemed fresh to many listeners, and he benefited from being able to speak from deep within the American educational, religious, and political establishment.

When Coffin spoke and wrote in religious terms, he offered more striking images and deeper insights. Inspired by ideas alone, his words were less supple, strained more for effect, fell flat more often. Inspired by a biblical text, there was little he could not do from the pulpit. As the secular ARFEP began to fade away, Coffin's antennae extended, listening for a different kind of crusade, one that could engage the full range of his talents. Over the Christmas break in 1965, he found it.

Into the Fray

No matter how little Americans knew about Vietnam (and a significant, though diminishing, minority did not even know there was fighting in Vietnam at this time), they nevertheless supported their government's position overwhelmingly. Few were prepared to question a fight against Communism. At the same time, a growing minority of Americans, many of them connected to liberal Protestantism and liberal Judaism—along with historic peace churches and pacifist groups, civil rights organizations, antinuclear groups, Old Left socialists and Trotskyists, as well as New Left groups (mainly SDS)—had begun to question or oppose American Vietnam policy. Detailing all the national and local vigils, fasts, rallies, marches, teach-ins, forums, and letter-writing campaigns would take pages. That the mainstream press had begun covering antiwar sentiment helped ratify its existence.[38]

By late 1965 a vigorous, multifaceted, uncoordinated movement of people who wanted to bring the fighting in Vietnam to an end had emerged. While these groups and individuals differed on tactics and on the desired outcome in Southeast Asia, most supported a diplomatic and negotiated solution to the conflict, an end to the American bombing, and some kind of cease-fire. By the end of the year the United Church of Christ; American Baptist Association; Union of American Hebrew Congregations (UAHC), the largest group of Reform synagogues; the National Council of Churches (NCC); and *Christianity and Crisis* had made statements "at least mildly critical" of American policy. Most also defended their right to protest Vietnam policies. Smaller groups called for outright withdrawal. And as the administration prepared to increase draft calls, some groups had also begun to target the draft.

While public support for the president worked against the antiwar movement, the government's heavy-handed treatment of critics could backfire as well. The sheer nastiness of administration and press attacks on the October antiwar demonstrators prompted a broadly based group of clergy in New York City to hold an ecumenical forum on U.S. foreign policy in Asia. That group announced its intentions at a press conference on October 25 (the day after the ARFEP event) that featured the world-famous Rabbi Heschel (professor of Jewish Ethics and Mysticism at Jewish Theological Seminary), as well as a twenty-nine-year-old Lutheran pastor active in civil rights, Richard Neuhaus, and the Catholic priest Daniel Berrigan, a protégé of Thomas Merton and a founder of the Catholic Peace Fellowship. Heschel, renowned as a scholar, not as an activist (though publicly committed to African-American civil rights), startled his colleagues by announcing unilaterally that the group would continue as an organization. Without realizing it, they had founded Clergy Concerned About Vietnam (CCAV).[39]

New York City, home to the new organization as well as the pacifist Catholic Worker movement and the Fifth Avenue Peace Parade Committee, probably hosted more antiwar activity than any other city: draft-card burnings, vigils, and rallies, and even an American self-immolation, the third that year. In this fertile ground, CCAV invited five thousand area clergy to a study conference on Vietnam on Sunday, November 28, the day after a large Washington march organized by the liberal Committee for a Sane Nuclear Policy, known as SANE.

Daniel Berrigan had already been probing for the limits of what the Jesuit hierarchy would allow him to do. When he gave a sympathetic eulogy for the young man who had burned himself to death, he discovered them. Within a week his superiors had transferred him to a three-month assignment in Latin America and ordered two of his Jesuit colleagues to end their involvement with CCAV. The consequent uproar caught officials by surprise. Seminarians, the more liberal Catholic press, and students and faculty at Catholic colleges protested what the liberal Catholic magazine *Commonweal* called a "disgustingly blind totalitarian act," while Fordham students picketed the cardinal's residence. Non-Catholics joined in, as *Christian Century* objected to the "high-handed exercise of ecclesiastical authority." Worried about the damage to their ecumenical organization, Neuhaus and Heschel blasted the "offensive" exercise of ecclesiastical power.[40]

The CCAV conference drew four hundred to a Park Avenue Methodist church. The *Times* featured Coffin, an invited speaker, near the top of its story. In a dramatic gesture of solidarity with their missing Catholic colleague, CCAV placed an empty chair on the stage. (The pressure paid off. When Berrigan was allowed to return in March, he was permitted to pick up his peace activity as well.)[41]

The gathering galvanized CCAV leaders. As Neuhaus wrote Coffin ten days later, enclosing an honorarium check, "There is no lack of things that can, and even must, be done." With "leads on a couple of very competent people who could give full time to this for a couple of months," the group was "exploring the financial possibilities." Convinced that CCAV had stumbled on an important entry point for national antiwar activity, John Bennett called a meeting for January 11 in his apartment to consider expanding the New York group into a nationwide organization. The group included Bennett's wife, Anne, Neuhaus, Heschel, Coffin, Harold Bosley (whose church had hosted the fall meeting),

David Hunter of the NCC, and Rabbis Maurice Eisendrath and Balfour Brickner (president and director of Interfaith Activities, respectively) of the UAHC.[42]

Calling themselves the National Emergency Committee of CCAV, participants decided to call on the president to extend the Christmas bombing pause he had begun December 24, to halt further escalation, to "negotiate an end to the war," and to give priority to "economic development for humane purposes at home." More importantly, they decided to become a genuinely national governing committee and to establish local committees of clergy throughout the United States that would organize local support for these positions and communicate them through letters, telegrams, and phone calls to the administration and Congress. Coffin, on a break between terms, offered to give a week to make calls around the country to organize chapters, if the group could provide a couple of offices, several telephones, and a WATS line (an unlimited long-distance phone line, an expensive—six thousand dollars a month—rarity in the mid-1960s). The offices never materialized, but desks in the NCC offices at the Interchurch Center at 475 Riverside Drive (known in religious circles as "the God Box") did, along with student volunteers from Union and Jewish Theological Seminaries, both around the corner.

Building on what he had learned from creating ARFEP chapters, Coffin and his volunteers used time zone differences to call across the country each evening for a week, starting on the East Coast and ending up with California, Oregon, and Washington around one in the morning. They employed a simple strategy. Using lists of likely sympathetic clergy provided by CCAV members and friends, callers would "locate by phone two or three clergy in communities in every state, put them in touch with each other, urge them to go to work and ask them to report back in a week what they had done." With a goal of "one hundred pins on the map by week's end," Coffin had found the precise niche he had been seeking for months.[43]

Even before the organizing push, Coffin had found himself so compelled by Vietnam work that he canceled a lucrative series of lectures he had promised to deliver at Goucher College. Apologizing to a furious religion professor after his week in New York, Coffin could not stifle his excitement. After pointing out that the "blood brother of apathy" is an "incapacity to give priority to what is important," Coffin pointed out accurately, "I just happen to be gifted in organizing emergency efforts."[44]

Working almost exclusively among religious professionals—and therefore using biblical language—and on a first-name basis with some of the best-known, most sophisticated religious figures in the country, Coffin was having great fun. He had the persuasive skills, personal charisma, intellectual liveliness, and physical stamina of few others, so he was immensely valuable to the group.

His Yale pulpit made him useful for many reasons, not least of which was Yale's status as the *Times's* favorite—that is, most reported on—Ivy League university. His name carried weight throughout mainline American Protestantism, he had a gift for turning a phrase, and he had a shrewd sense of how to play the limelight. Finally, as he explained to the Goucher professor, "The response of the clergy has been overwhelming in its enthusiasm."

As the acting executive secretary of the organization, Coffin led the New York City press conference announcing the formation of the National Emergency Committee a mere week after the meeting in the Bennetts' apartment, and the *Times* covered it on page three, "Vietnam page" that day. Coffin announced a forty-one-member national committee and 150 chapters in forty-three states. *Christian Century* featured the new organization on its cover and in a sympathetic lead editorial that listed the names and affiliations of every member of the committee, which included the magazine's editor, Kyle Haselden, as well as Associate Editor and University of Chicago Divinity School Professor Martin Marty.

The impressive list included Methodist and Episcopal bishops; seminary presidents, professors, and deans; editors; high-ranking denominational executives (such as Eisendrath, Eugene Carson Blake, Unitarian Universalist Association President Dana McLean Greeley, former NCC president Edwin T. Dahlberg, and Rabbi Jacob Weinstein, president of the Central Conference of American Rabbis, the organization of Reform rabbis); and Martin Luther King Jr. While Catholic priests and faculty signed on, the group was able to find only one cardinal—Cushing of Boston—who soon withdrew.

This list was as revealing for who was not on it as for who was. The dearth of high-ranking Roman Catholics pointed to the Catholic Church's alliance with American nationalism and its unwillingness to rock the foreign policy boat during the first two decades of the Cold War era. The list included almost no parish-level clergy, who would have been answerable to their congregations or their local bishops. Editors, executives, tenured professors, and Coffin himself, a chaplain, had considerably more freedom, had to account to fewer "regular folk," and tended to be more politically liberal than the members of local churches and synagogues.

Why was the group so successful so quickly? At first, CCAV made very modest concrete proposals. It applauded the president's bombing halt, endorsed his "peace offensive," and stood behind the Great Society efforts that were threatened by increased military expenditures. It sought, as the *Times* put it, to "counteract pressures" on Johnson to resume the bombing, thus implicitly drawing a distinction between the "best and the brightest" advisors—Secretary of State Dean Rusk, Secretary of Defense Robert McNamara, McGeorge Bundy

—and the president himself, whose sincerity went unquestioned. As one chapter put it, they were providing a "witness of support to President Johnson for his efforts to achieve a negotiated peace in Vietnam."[45]

While not explicitly eschewing civil disobedience, CCAV emphasized traditional legal educational and pressure techniques—forums, letters, phone calls, press conferences, telegrams, rallies, marches—rather than direct-action nonviolent tactics such as sit-ins, sit-down strikes, or draft-card burnings. And given how tactics were beginning to escalate among antiwar protesters (as well as among counter-demonstrating supporters of the war), this restraint appealed to clergy, few of whom felt comfortable being lumped with "radicals" or "draft-card burners."

CCAV reflected Coffin's own internal struggles regarding what he should have been doing about Vietnam. His instincts meshed with those of many clergy who had been searching for an appropriate framework through which they could express their reservations about the war. Few were eager to climb out on such a treacherous limb by themselves; together, hundreds, and soon thousands, were willing to state what they considered the obvious: that military victory was both elusive and unlikely to produce the stated goals of American policy, that real negotiations made more sense than intensified military pressure, and that both of these positions had solid religious backing. CCAV clergy could intervene in the debate so dramatically because they had waited. The bombs had stopped for a religious holiday, and they could entreat the president on behalf of peace: of extending the bombing halt, of stopping the *escalation,* not the war itself. "The moment is crucial," Coffin warned at the press conference, "for it may well be that morally speaking the United States ship of state is today comparable to the *Titanic* just before it hit the iceberg. If we decide on all-out escalation of the war in Vietnam, then to all intents and purposes of the human soul we may be sunk. We plead therefore with our fellow clergy to support our government's effort to negotiate an end to the war and to prevent its further escalation."[46]

In the next few weeks Coffin appeared to be everywhere, using his speaking schedule to carry the CCAV message. He was well prepared. Even the first words of his January 18 press conference he had first tried out in a sermon on January 9, the Sunday before the meeting in the Bennetts' apartment, before his weeklong organizing drive, before the birth of the National Emergency Committee. In that sermon, titled "The Spirit of Lamech," Coffin had organized his theological and political indictment of the war as well as his analysis of what to do about it. Impatience suffused the entire sermon.[47]

He began by quoting the hymn (Andover's) that had such personal significance it became the title of his memoir: "Once to every man and nation comes the moment to decide / In the strife of truth with falsehood, for the good or evil side." It was time, he argued, for Christians to "cease being so concerned with free love and so indifferent to free hate. We must make peace our major religious responsibility, and Vietnam our immediate one." Months of caution and hanging back, of exploration and waffling, of reading and pondering, were at last bearing fruit.

Early in Genesis, Lamech, a descendant of Cain, celebrates killing one man and wounding another. "Today," Coffin warned, "the spirit of Lamech is moving over the face of our land." As a country, the United States was naively assuming that "God is automatically on the anti-communist side." Instead of doing God's will, he lamented, recalling his statement of faith, and Reinhold Niebuhr, "this nation is separating itself from God." Since separation from God was Coffin's definition of sin, he had leveled a heavy charge at American foreign policy.

Coffin then deftly moved into history, pointing out American mistakes first in aiding the French, then in undermining the 1954 Geneva accords, and, finally, in backing the series of unpopular Saigon regimes. "The unpleasant truth," he concluded, "is that we are backing a mediocre jockey on a losing horse." Even so, he stopped well short of arguing for an American withdrawal, on the grounds that "what morally is demanded and what politically is feasible are two different things. . . . What Christians in particular must remember is that moral outrage is a wonderful motivator but no formula for a solution." Withdrawing immediately "would be to betray an obligation to people we have promised to defend, to prove our commitments a paper tiger, and to give the green light to the National Liberation Movement in Thailand and elsewhere." That is why neither the Vatican, nor the NCC, nor the UAHC had called for withdrawal, while all thought "that of the three basic alternatives—withdrawal, negotiation, escalation—escalation would be the worst."

Coffin also used paradox to bring a fresh perspective to the argument, claiming, "To seek military victory would be to court political and moral defeat." For "the real horror" lay in the conduct of the war itself, "being waged in a fashion so out of character with American instincts of decency that it cannot help but undermine them." Here, Coffin argued, "the picture is clear: frustrated and humiliated by setbacks, and unwilling to expend the lives of our own men, we have resorted to indiscriminate killing—their women and children instead of our men."

He then ratcheted up the intensity of his language: "But the essence of the spirit of Lamech is the guise of goodness with which it cloaks evil. . . . Just because we do not seek territorial expansion does not mean we cannot be corrupted by pride and power." Coffin displayed his Niebuhrian roots throughout

the sermon, focusing on American "pride," the self-righteousness of the assumption that if one's country does a deed, it must be a good deed. "O America,"
he lamented, paraphrasing St. Augustine, "thy pride-swollen face hath closed
up thine eyes. Thou hast become as Lamech."[48] He then returned to Lamech's
"song" of murder and concluded with a wail: "O America, my country, my
country."

Coffin had timed this powerful performance—in effect launching his next
crusade—to make the fewest possible waves at Yale, which was still on winter
break. Students did not fill the pews, many faculty were away, and the *Yale
Daily News* did not publish during these weeks. Still, "I feel that I heard Amos
returned," wrote visiting Harvard Divinity School Professor George H. Williams,
who felt "privileged to have been passing through."[49]

By the following Sunday, however, Coffin's sermons had begun to raise
hackles. Two students wrote long letters complaining about the "anti-Vietnam"
thrust of the services on the ninth and sixteenth. Coffin replied personally to
both, thanking them for airing their thoughts, disagreeing crisply with their
analyses of the services, pointing out that the prayers were either utterly "balanced" or had nothing to do with war, and inviting them for a visit. He even
predicted "sermons in the future, perhaps even one of my own, which will
have little relevance to the great political dramas and I would say tragedies of
our time." He had no intention of backing down.[50]

In Philadelphia at the end of January, just before Johnson resumed the
bombing, Coffin reaffirmed his warning about the United States being like
the *Titanic,* taking out the qualification "may well be." His three-page statement
addressed Secretaries Rusk and McNamara directly, accusing Rusk of "putting
us on this collision course with disaster" and calling McNamara "a brilliant
administrator but just as consistently a mistaken prophet."[51]

On the eve of the resumption of bombing, the CCAV position differed
from that of the administration in three broad areas: the history of the conflict,
the nature of the combatants, and the conduct of the war. According to the
administration, the United States was defending the independence of democratic
South Vietnam, which faced internal subversion from the Hanoi-directed National Liberation Front (NLF, or Viet Cong) and external attack from Communist North Vietnam, assumed to be closely allied with the Communist bloc,
particularly China and the USSR. CCAV's version of the history stressed the
legacy of colonialism; the nationalism of Vietnamese resistance to the French;
the American sabotage of the Geneva accords (which had called for elections
and reunification of the temporarily divided country by 1956); the relative independence of the NLF, especially in the early years of the war; and Vietnam's
centuries-long distrust of China. In this version, the conflict in Vietnam was

a civil war (since South and North Vietnam were temporary artificial constructs) rather than an example of Communist aggression.

War opponents highlighted the brutality, corruption, unpopularity, and fragility of the successive South Vietnamese regimes, in contrast to the allegedly consistent support the peasantry showed the NLF. Supporters emphasized the NLF's use of terrorism. Opponents focused on the enormous destruction—to people and the countryside—caused by bombs, artillery, defoliants, and napalm, while supporters stressed the need to use powerful weapons against guerrillas, who knew the land intimately and coerced villagers into providing food and shelter.

Finally, the administration and its critics differed over negotiations. While everyone claimed to support negotiations, the principals disagreed about who should have a seat at the table. The United States and South Vietnam argued that they should negotiate with North Vietnam directly (since the NLF was a creation and tool of Hanoi). Ho Chi Minh disagreed, arguing that the NLF was the true representative of the South Vietnamese people. Though the general public considered this dispute the height of diplomatic silliness, it actually carried tremendous symbolic and political weight. The administration claimed to offer completely "unconditional" negotiations; in fact, the United States refused to bargain with the NLF.

The last weekend of January CCAV sponsored rallies and meetings "all over the country," according to the *Times* account of the New York gathering on the thirtieth where clergy called for "gradual military disengagement" from Vietnam, an "indefinite cessation" of the bombing, and—this was new—"exemption from military duty of all who 'conscientiously' oppose a particular war." Since the bombing halt had lasted thirty-six days by January 30, they had begun to hope that their efforts were having some effect, or that the administration had decided to extend the pause on its own. In either case, the pause looked promising. When Johnson ordered the bombing resumed on January 31, the CCAV people were crushed. At Stanford University, Coffin spoke out very sharply, acknowledging later, "I was pretty bitter."[52]

The CCAV steering committee issued a statement "deplor[ing] resumption of the bombing." Though "shocked at the intransigence of the Hanoi government," the group remained "unpersuaded that our own government has exhausted every possibility for peace." Still, the principals were unwilling to abandon the president entirely and welcomed his "turning to the United Nations." SDS and the War Resisters League, as well as other pacifist and leftist groups, reacted swiftly to the resumption of bombing, as demonstrators were arrested at Times Square and U.N. Plaza the next day. Coffin keynoted a Yale Law School rally—receiving "lengthy applause" and a standing ovation from "about half" the crowd of six hundred—the same day. The Vatican issued a statement supporting U.N. mediation, while Senator J. William Fulbright supported reconvening the 1954 Geneva Conference. Vietnam could no longer be considered a simmering pot on anyone's back burner.[53]

Coffin, true to what he wrote his student critic, did not even mention Vietnam in his next sermon. Instead, he preached mostly about Abraham Heschel's *Man's Quest for God*. Coffin had been much affected by meeting and getting to know Heschel during his week in New York City. Not only one of the world's greatest living theologians, with his massive, unruly white hair and beard, Heschel appeared to have stepped directly out of the Bible. Like the rest of the CCAV group, Coffin called him Father Abraham and fell under the spell of what Robert McAfee Brown called "the saintliness and the compassion of this really great man."[54]

Coffin loved being able to match wits and talk theology with Heschel, who also met Coffin's psychological need for an older man in his life; this one he could even call "father." Always the impetuous son, Coffin nearly offended Heschel at their first meal together, responding to Heschel's opening theological gambit by calling him a "shrewd old Jew." Fortunately, Coffin had a quick enough wit to recover, and Heschel had a generous enough spirit not to take offense.[55]

Coffin loved having an elder in the movement. Heschel often sounded like his good friend Reinhold Niebuhr. Heschel's insistence on the God "who transcends all" gave Coffin Niebuhrian and Jewish language to stand outside the church and criticize the "exclusiveness of church people" who did not understand that Christ "died not for the church but for the world." Coffin's preaching also began to refer more to "Christians and Jews" as opposed to Christians alone. As Heschel put it, and Coffin quoted, "To equate religion and God is idolatry." This line from Heschel became part of the Coffin repertoire; in his McCormick Seminary graduation speech in May, Coffin simply incorporated the idea without attribution.[56]

Coffin's new life in the antiwar movement combined great demands and great rewards. As the acting executive secretary of CCAV, he was receiving frequent national attention the way he had around the time of the Freedom Ride. Among clergy, few of whom had national political experience, he stood out even more than he had among civil rights workers. At press conferences or rallies, recalled fellow CCAV leader Brown, "He was the one we could count on to come and either get the thing going or sum it up. And he was extraordinarily good at this kind of thing."[57]

In February 1966 the influential veteran Senator Fulbright, chair of the Senate's Foreign Relations Committee, held hearings on Vietnam that have achieved legendary status. Televised live, they featured eminent and respectable critics—George Kennan and retired General James Gavin, for example—as well as top administration spokespeople: Secretary of State Dean Rusk and Chairman of the Joint Chiefs of Staff Maxwell D. Taylor. Angry at being snubbed socially and institutionally by the president, his old friend and former colleague, Fulbright turned the hearings into a searching exploration of the origins and conduct of the war.

They provided a forum, and political cover, for liberal senators who had private qualms about the war—Mike Mansfield, George McGovern, Frank Church, Joseph Clark, Eugene McCarthy—to begin speaking out publicly. The hearings, in other words, helped legitimize dissent regarding administration policy at the highest level of the legislative branch. Given the solidity of the consensus regarding Vietnam just a few years earlier, that was no mean feat. Even so, no one who testified at the hearings advocated a flat, immediate withdrawal from Vietnam.[58]

A month later CCAV principals received a boost from the National Inter-Religious Conference on Peace. Five hundred clergy and laity assembled in Washington, D.C., for speeches and workshops on a variety of global issues. While no single workshop focused especially on Vietnam, three of them easily lent themselves to the hottest foreign policy issues facing the conferees: "Confronting the Changing Communist World," "China and the Conflicts in Asia" (for which Coffin was an invited discussant), and "Forms of Intervention: Moral Responsibilities and Limits." Many of the participants had cut their activist teeth in the civil rights movement and were beginning to transfer these skills to the new issue of Vietnam. They could not easily be ignored.

President Johnson sent good wishes, U.N. Secretary General U Thant did likewise, and Vice-President Hubert Humphrey, who had recently defended administration Vietnam policy at the twenty-fifth anniversary dinner for *Christianity and Crisis,* gave a short speech in favor of peace. Participants saw that the administration was condescending to them and did not like it. Despite the large number of participants with many different perspectives, their final declaration came very close to repeating the initial CCAV position.[59]

By this time the CCAV steering committee knew it needed staff. Within a couple of weeks Coffin had recruited, and the steering committee had hired, a young and talented campus minister from the University of Pennsylvania, Richard Fernandez. The group also formally decided to stay in existence until the end of the war, committing members of what had begun as an "emergency committee" to genuine organizational duties (such as supervising and paying staff) and to a much longer term than any had first imagined. Finally, they changed their name to Clergy and Laymen Concerned About Vietnam, or

CALCAV. This last decision dramatically enlarged the organization's potential membership base, allowed clergy to recruit within their own congregations, and helped laypeople to pressure their own clerical leaders to take a position against the war.[60]

Coffin worked better as a public figure than as a staffer, and once the organization was in the hands of a capable executive secretary, he could consult, speak, write, and raise money while someone else handled the details. Unlike many in such work, Coffin never minded asking people for money, sometimes lots of it, and donors responded generously to his entreaties.[61]

Fernandez immediately took charge of the organization, getting real office space from the NCC, developing a budget, communicating with existing chapters, and organizing new ones. As a result of his skills, the eminence of his steering committee, and the escalation of the war—and despite persistent financial problems—CALCAV grew from eight chapters in May to seventeen in September and sixty-eight by April 1967. Throughout the country, religious people were coming together to express their distress about American Vietnam policy and to press for genuine negotiations.[62]

Between 1965 and early 1967 a large and varied antiwar movement was taking shape, one that, while including many different types of people and a wide range of political and tactical perspectives, nevertheless began to demand an end to the American intervention in Vietnam. This growing movement relied on increasingly independent sources of information. Journalists, for example, reported massive destruction in the South Vietnamese countryside, far outstripping the careful warfare described in the daily Saigon military press briefings. Visitors to North Vietnam likewise reported that American bombs were falling on civilians, even in Hanoi proper. What Coffin had called the "bloodstained face of war" was beginning to be brought home to American audiences in pictures and words that caused many to avert their eyes.[63]

Since most accounts of the war, and of the sixties, for that matter, give little attention to the religious community, much clergy and lay activism has in effect disappeared from historical view. By creating opportunities for liberal clergy to oppose the war, CALCAV played a key role in stimulating local, community-based antiwar activity. This grassroots activism frequently took place below the radar of most historical accounts of the movement. Only Coffin, the Berrigan brothers, and occasionally Coffin's CALCAV steering committee colleagues received the kind of secular press attention that elevated them to national political prominence. Nonetheless, they had influence far beyond their numbers, partly because some clergy—like Coffin—had high-level connections in the American political establishment and partly because policymakers had been raised during an era in which mainline ministers, at least those connected to large northeastern churches or famous seminaries and universities, could still lay claim to elite status.

Coffin could discuss Vietnam with an assistant secretary of state for Far Eastern affairs who had wide responsibilities for Vietnam policy because William P. Bundy sat on the Yale Corporation. William's brother McGeorge advised his president in June 1965, according to writer Tom Wells, that "articulate critics" in churches and universities had "stimulated extensive worry and inquiry in the nation as a whole." Richard Neuhaus referred to these clergy as the religious "establishment" because they often held leadership positions in regional and national denominational structures, organizations, or educational institutions. They had "better access to the media" than the laity and were "in control of the larger, more 'intellectually respectable' publications and of the interdenominational bureaucracies," as well as "the more prestigious theological schools."[64]

In other words, antiwar clergy had more resources, considerably higher profiles, and correspondingly more influence than the average parish pastor or rabbi. The crucial variable was the individual cleric's freedom of action. In hierarchical systems (Roman Catholics, United Methodists), clergy are assigned to (or moved from) their positions by their superiors, generally local bishops or their equivalents. In congregation-based systems, on the other hand (the United Church of Christ, Reform and Conservative Judaism), local parishes employ clergy and therefore have the power to fire them. Since congregations tend to be more politically conservative than their clergy, and nearly always prefer their religious leader to pay more attention to them than to the larger world, clergy interested in holding onto their jobs generally exercise considerable care with respect to their more overtly "political" activities. Like corporate or nonprofit executives, denominational executives have considerably more autonomy the higher their position. Similarly, tenured professors had no fear for their jobs no matter what they said or signed publicly.

Although most chaplains reported to college and university presidents (and did not have tenure), they did have freedoms that their parish colleagues lacked. The Yale Corporation issued and reviewed Coffin's contract. Yale President Kingman Brewster Jr., though chosen by the Corporation and reporting to it, had considerable influence over its decisions. Coffin was lucky to have the two presidents he did, as both were profoundly committed to the version of liberal culture that Yale represented at its best. Nevertheless, he wisely cultivated both of them (and Corporation members) carefully. Griswold had come from the faculty and suffered alumni fools without pleasure. When the "Old Blues" harrumphed and demanded Coffin's head, Griswold chuckled, swore good-naturedly, and wrote them an Olympian letter. Brewster, a former law professor, was temperamentally more suited to reasoned discourse, as well as thoroughly committed to the academic and intellectual freedom of his faculty. He also genuinely enjoyed the intellectual give-and-take he could have with his chaplain.

In 1964, for example, Brewster showed Coffin a speech he had given to an alumni group soon after his selection as president. Coffin criticized Brewster's defense of conservatism and his reverence for Yale. Brewster's response was prescient as well as personally revealing:

> Anyhow, you are my exhibit "A"; . . . You are a distinctive product of this institution. You might have happened elsewhere, but not bloody likely. Now you are having an impact on your generation and those to follow which is precisely in the Yale tradition which I proclaim and which you deny. Finally, we have an exchange of thoughts (some) and words (many) which I doubt would be found in the Presidential files of any other institution.
>
> It's great! Let's keep it up.[65]

It seems fair to grant Brewster his point. As much as he disliked having to defend Coffin—and he certainly complained about this chore—few others took the trouble to engage him so frequently, or so tellingly. In May 1966, for example, Coffin challenged Brewster's "consistent public attacks" on Staughton Lynd, even while he found "admirable your consistent defense of Staughton's right to speak and act according to the dictates of his mind and conscience." (Brewster had referred to "improper actions" and "reckless epithets.") Coffin pressed Brewster on whether it was "proper for you to take a stand on another man's words and deeds without taking a stand on the situation that prompts them? And if the situation is as serious as many of us believe then the epithets of an assistant professor may not be as reckless as the silence of university presidents. Yet Staughton has never attacked you."

While Brewster did not retreat on Lynd, he took up Coffin's challenge, confessing that "it is more the result of quandary than of official inhibition," since he simply did not know what the United States ought to do about Vietnam. Still, "it would do me a great service to continue our exchange of views about all these matters." Coffin thanked his boss for the thoughtful answer and arranged to send him John Kenneth Galbraith's most recent comments on Vietnam.[66]

Through a combination of flattery and intelligent engagement, Coffin kept his most important constituent in his corner. Since the more conservative alumni periodically mounted protests against his outspokenness, often around reunion time, Coffin wisely kept as many political fences mended as possible. For his part, Brewster, a reserved, lawyerly Anglophile, attended Sunday services at Battell Chapel whenever he was in New Haven. Indeed, in what may be one of the more remarkable statements of a university president in the past half-century, he once confided to Yale Divinity School Professor B. Davie Napier that his attendance at Battell was the most consistently rewarding experience of his presidency.[67]

Since early 1966 SANE director Sanford Gottlieb had been trying to get Vietnam into the electoral arena. Now Gottlieb asked Coffin to run for Congress as a "peace candidate." Coffin declined, after admitting "to a certain amount of political blood in my veins," but did agree that spring to be co-chairman, along with Norman Thomas, of SANE's "Voters' Pledge" campaign, an effort to get voters to commit only to candidates that pledged allegiance to a program similar to CALCAV's. Sponsors included some of Coffin's old ARFEP committee (John Hersey, Roger Baldwin, Rollo May, and Lenore Marshall) as well as CALCAV leaders Harold Bosley and Heschel. This campaign showed how quickly moderate opposition to the war could attract a stable of big-name sponsors. That SANE asked Coffin to assume the ceremonial leadership role showed how important his name had become to the moderate wing of the antiwar movement.[68]

But Coffin's own frustration was clearly building. Even though his political position did not change, his rhetoric became more intense. In a spring letter to his old friend Browne Barr, who had taken up the pastorate of the First Congregational Church of Berkeley, Coffin opined that "politically I imagine you are a loss." Barr tweaked him back, hoping that Wesleyan (where Coffin was due to receive an honorary degree) would "settle you down a bit and you will be able to absorb, as I have, some of the values of tradition and the reflective life." Coffin quickly shot back that he "couldn't be more anxious to walk beside the still water, but you know it just isn't easy when all that drowning is going on out beyond."[69]

In his prayers at the end of the school year in 1966, Coffin reached for less poetry and more prophecy. At the annual *Yale Daily News* banquet, for example, he prayed "especially" for those "who are increasingly giving priority to what is important at Yale, not ducking the difficult nor rationalizing the unacceptable; . . . and writing in the spirit of those who know that all men have more in common than in conflict." Recycling his baccalaureate prayer from the previous year, Coffin revised passages to stress the strength needed for conflict. His appeal in 1965 that God "help us . . . to become who we are" became, in 1966, "grant us thy strength, lest we lose the will to fight and attempt instead to forget."[70]

In his annual commencement prayer, which the university sent to the media each year, Coffin's rhetoric took on a more apocalyptic tone. "[G]rant us grace to understand that in this era we have nothing to lose but everything," he began. Beseeching listeners to "not stand comfortably aloof from the fury of our history, nor sit on little liberal fences with our fears on either side, nor out of love for the oppressed sow the seeds of a terrible new hate," Coffin's words echoed the Beat critique of consumer society. He worried about a "life where promises enclose emptiness, where cheerfulness is but a disguised and painted indifference, where America has become a nation of armed Babbitts, and where on every side men climb upon the cross to be seen from afar, trampling on the one who has hung there so long." Still, he reached, poetically, for a future world "where the din of war has given way to the clatter of doves waging peace in the sky."[71]

At Wesleyan, as Coffin received his honorary degree in 1966, he gave the commencement prayer as well, pushing even more strongly for a commitment to peacemaking. "Keep us on the stony, long and lonely road that leads to peace," he prayed. "O God, may we think for peace, battle for peace, suffer for peace. Convince us that patriotism now, like brotherhood, must be all embracing to be at all; and may we live as if the life of all mankind were at stake —as indeed it is."[72]

Coffin's rhetoric intensified in direct proportion to his inability to see a way out of the Vietnam quagmire. In a long letter to a former student skeptical of Coffin's activism, he failed to find a solution to his dilemma: "You don't have to get out. You don't have to be shoved out. You just don't escalate. I know it's a bit messy, but it can be done." The point would be to guarantee elections, which would probably go to Buddhists, who might be able to establish independence from the United States and from North Vietnam. That solution, Coffin noted correctly, sounded "pretty iffy." Another would be to offer the South Vietnamese generals a lot of money (twenty thousand dollars "or more") and a passport; maybe half would disappear while the other half would divide down the middle, with one group willing to set up a coalition government with the NLF. Coffin was "prepared to take that chance, prepared to see Viet Nam united under Ho Chi Minh, prepared to do everything possible to do the one thing needful—namely to keep the united Viet Nam independent of China." Coffin knew U.S. diplomacy did not work that way. He was floundering because he was running out of ideas. Even his deft public formulations—"we are not against our boys in Vietnam, only against their being there," he told a Memorial Day rally in New York City—could not hide this fact.[73]

The key stumbling block for most Americans remained the near certainty that without American military force defending any Saigon regime, Vietnam would end up under some sort of Communist rule. For all of their efforts to skirt this problem, the war's opponents in fact had very few choices. The first, which Coffin tried, was to say that Communism was no longer monolithic, that (North) Vietnam and China had a long history of antagonism that would trump their shared commitment to Communism. The second, which Coffin also tried in a letter to a correspondent, was to point out that the country itself had to decide on its own future: "In any case, I feel this is basically a civil war and we should interfere in other people's civil wars only very tentatively and with great reluctance." Third, one could point out, as Coffin did, that a commitment to keeping "a country ever from going Communist—by any means" differed greatly from helping a friend repel an outside attack. The latter would be a "military commitment of limited scope," not an "ideological one of unlimited scope," and would lead to eventual failure. The problem was that Communism was on the table no matter what.[74]

Negotiations would inevitably lead to NLF participation in a solution, which is to say Communist participation in a new government in South Vietnam, precisely the goal the United States was fighting to avoid. So while Coffin had it right that refusing to negotiate with the NLF was asking them to accept a military defeat they had not yet suffered, that was precisely the point of the American position. War opponents might make their case in a myriad of ways, but their unenviable task was to convince most Americans that a Communist Vietnam would not be all that bad, or that if it were bad, it would not be as bad as what the war was already doing to Vietnam and the United States. Until they could do so, the administration would hold the upper hand.

Even the struggle against the war could not keep Coffin in the country during July and August. He ground out a rash of letters his last week in the office, apologizing to colleagues, acknowledging his divided feelings. "On the one hand I am determined to be a family man and to lead the life of reflection," he wrote Bennett. "On the other hand I am so fighting mad that I want to barnstorm the country protesting the sickening syrup of the President's pietistic self-righteousness."[75]

On his last day in the office before leaving for Europe, Coffin wrote angrily and despairingly to William Bundy. "I am sitting here with a heavy heart," he began, perhaps unintentionally imitating Johnson's common locution, "retching at the sickening syrup of the President's piety," which was "filling the air with fighting creeds no longer in touch with the realities of the situation" (here he quoted from his prayer of February 1965). Like Billy Graham, the president was "delivering his simple message to simple people in simple times, when in fact neither the message nor the people nor certainly the times are that simple." Complexity was less the issue than Communism, but Coffin's prophetic conclusion hit the bull's-eye: "History is going to judge us harshly, Bill."[76]

Coffin did take up his role as a family man, even if the life of reflection eluded him. After a few weeks in Paris, he and his family ended up at the Rubinstein family home in Marbella, Spain. The day Coffin arrived for a month-long stay he was still nursing a twisted ankle from an accident in Paris. But he still had his fighting energy. The very first day he climbed the mountain behind the house.[77]

Gospel Tactics: Christianity to the Fore

Being on vacation gave Coffin the emotional space to dream up new projects. The previous August on Cape Cod had given birth to ARFEP. With a little free time Coffin hunted for new ways of dramatizing the inhumanity of the war. Never as engaged by policy alternatives as by moral perspectives and Christian principle, he struggled to find, in action, the equivalent to one of his aphorisms—a concentrated, finely honed, deceptively simple yet thought-provoking act.

His first effort consisted of a plan to send medical supplies to war victims in North Vietnam, South Vietnam, and Viet Cong–controlled areas of South Vietnam and became known as Vietnam Relief. A joint project of students, chaplains, and faculty, this initiative aimed to send money for "humanitarian relief" to the Canadian Friends Service Committee (CFSC), which had established connections with the North Vietnamese for such a program. But because the U.S. government controlled shipments to North Vietnam through the Treasury Department, Coffin and his group applied for a special license from the Foreign Assets Control Bureau, announcing their intentions publicly the first Sunday in October. Surprisingly, approval came in a week, and the story appeared on the front page of the *New York Times*. Licensed to send just $300, on a Russian ship that was leaving within days from Toronto, the group quickly raised $140 in Battell on Sunday, the remainder in Yale's residential colleges and the graduate school.[78]

This odd little episode demonstrated how a deftly wielded Christianity could at once burst through political barriers, draw public attention to a small act, thrust Coffin into the limelight of controversy, and drag along just enough respectable opinion to change some minds. As Coffin put the Christian argument in Battell, "All men have more in common than in conflict. And it is precisely when what they have in conflict appears overriding that what they have in common must be affirmed." Even Kingman Brewster declared his support for "a good cause which rises above opinion about national policy."[79]

Headline writers all over the country disagreed, and had a field day. As the *Times* put it, "U.S. Letting Yale Group Send Medical Help to Foe in Vietnam." The story never referred to the group's explicit intention to direct supplies to war victims—nor to the Treasury Department's understanding that the aid was "intended for the relief of civilians injured as a result of the current hostilities in Vietnam." The New Haven papers published headlines like "Yale Group's Aid to Viet Reds Approved" and "Salmona [a GOP congressional candidate] Slaps Yale Aid to Reds," while other papers typically ran headlines like "U.S. OK's Medicine For Reds" and "U.S. OK's Medical Aid to VC."

Coffin may have known what a hornet's nest he was stirring up. New Haven newspaper publishers disliked Coffin and editorialized against the effort, while New Haven Representative Robert Giaimo and U.S. Senator Thomas Dodd, attentive to the four thousand petition signatures collected by a New Haven insurance agent asking the Treasury Department to rescind the group's license, pressed the Treasury Department on why the permission was granted in the first place. The government engaged in some politicking of its own, announcing that the CFSC had "told the Treasury it was negotiating with North Vietnam and the Vietcong to have Quaker observers check on the distribution of the supplies and at the same time get access to United States prisoners of war."

According to the CFSC, however, U.S. officials completely fabricated the story about prisoners of war, knowingly "jeopardizing the possibility of our ever going in to Hanoi in any capacity." Moreover, the treasury license conditions were designed to damage the Yale group in two additional ways: first, they specified that the shipment had to travel on a Russian ship leaving within days (so the effort was even more strongly linked to the image of Communism— there were, after all, other countries trading with North Vietnam); and second, they allowed only a negligible sum (three hundred dollars), thereby requiring a second license—with more difficult conditions—for a significant contribution.

News of this effort traveled far—at least to the Okinawa *Morning Star* and the military newspaper *Stars and Stripes*—and a number of soldiers and their wives sent objections, in varying shades of anger and disgust. Coffin may have been surprised by the virulence of the reaction—he wrote one woman that the article she had seen "must have distorted considerably our intentions" since it had "produced a pile of hate mail"—but he dutifully answered several very harsh critics, including some stationed in Vietnam, and never retreated from the idea. To one Marine in Okinawa he argued that in the modern context of "total war," it was "surely right that we should try to send a very token sum to try and patch up the wounds of civilians killed on all sides. Of course it may stray into the hands of the military, but it is certainly not a large sum if it does, and I would rather take that chance than to do nothing."[80]

Coffin's achievement in this affair was to move the discussion from foreign policy, where government authorities spoke with more power, to the arena of morality and religious principle, where he and other clergy were more skilled. The entire effort represented a theoretically simple Christian act—"to love one's enemy"—that ran smack into an offended, powerful conventional political wisdom. The idea of sending "humanitarian aid" across battle lines has always given many people pause. For while Coffin himself risked nothing by taking the chance that the aid would end up in North Vietnamese medical units, the same could not be said of his soldier correspondents.

The basic Christianity of the gesture drew support from the eminent Yale church historian Roland Bainton, who explained to the *New Haven Register* how the talk of treason simply missed the point of the policies of the Red Cross, the ethics of the medical profession, and the fundamental principles of Judaism and Christianity. "Is there no limit to inhumanity in war?" he asked. "If we answer that there is not, who then are the barbarians?" Coffin used Bainton's points as he answered a local skeptic, "I think political aims have always to be limited by religious considerations," he argued. "I suspect you too are not for bombing hospitals, even though it is there that they are patching up people who are going to come back and fire on our boys."[81]

Other Christians responded to his efforts as well, including the Connecticut denominational executive of the United Church of Christ. He confessed to "the usual bourgeoise [*sic*] reaction to your long hair, sloppy sweater, and to your furtive fan club that tippy toed in silently to see what treatment the establishment was going to accord to the prophet," but was nevertheless so "impressed" with the fundamental idea behind the relief effort that within days he wrote to the president of his denomination proposing a large-scale, multi-denominational effort to provide purely humanitarian relief to victims "on both sides of the fighting line." Despite the noncommittal response, he still wanted Coffin's participation ("sweater, and all!") in another "project of importance," concluding, "God bless your ministry."[82]

As this episode demonstrates, Coffin had converted the Yale chaplaincy into one of the great pulpits in the country. It was not only that he could preach what he wanted. He had learned to make the office work on behalf of his issues. On almost any controversial issue he could be sure of drawing attention from the larger public, and when he provoked controversy, he stood a better than even chance of mobilizing powerful support not only from Yale students, but from the faculty, which included some of the most respected academics in the country.

He had done it with a keen and aggressive sense of public relations, catchy and challenging rhetoric, apparently limitless energy, a gift for thinking on his feet, an ability to make biblical argument compelling to a general audience, and excellent reasoning skills. When pressed to justify a controversial position,

Coffin could either respond logically at some length or deflect the question with a quip. He had successfully cultivated his bosses. He had also provided enough inspiration to his staff and to the students involved with the chaplain's office that they took up the slack when he was on the road or in front of the cameras.

Yale University had few institutional rivals in the world of scholarship; it had even fewer in its centuries-old mission of assembling and educating the young men who would exercise political, economic, religious, and cultural leadership over the United States. Under Coffin's leadership Yale's chaplaincy had become an institution without peer in the educational world for raising and articulating fundamental religious principles, and a genuinely uncomfortable gospel.

While he continued to raise money for CALCAV, attend meetings when possible, give encouragement to Fernandez, and speak on behalf of the organization, Coffin had little interest in the nuts and bolts of building organizations and organizing chapters. That CALCAV was chronically short of money, skating close to the edge of insolvency during most of 1966, would not have made the steering committee meetings very attractive to him.[83]

Coffin was more interested in dramatic gestures, especially since he felt that "the political acceptability of escalation will be much greater after the election." He wrote to A. J. Muste—whom he had heard might be traveling to North Vietnam—about "a sort of 'hostage' system whereby five or ten clergymen at a time might stay in Hanoi on a revolving basis." Thinking of CALCAV's moderate image, Fernandez did not thrill to the idea, while for Coffin it must have recalled the Freedom Ride, drawing national attention to well-known white Americans voluntarily in harm's way, instead of unknown southern blacks or faceless North Vietnamese civilians.[84]

Coffin also showed interest in an idea that had come in a letter from Colin Eisler (Yale '52), a New York University art historian who complained about "damned dull" advertisements and marches that present little "more than a touching tableau of liberal Scarsdale in Washington on a sunny afternoon." While he served in leadership positions in peace organizations, Eisler had been impressed by Coffin's medical relief idea, for his own groups (the Fellowship of Reconciliation and the Jewish Peace Fellowship), "unlike you, are not delivering the goods as yet." Eisler proposed a "great memorial Death March . . . with effective props and sounds," possibly even "directed" by Robert Brustein, dean of the Yale Drama School. No record survives of Coffin's reply, but about a month later Coffin himself asked Brustein what he thought of "the idea of a mammoth death march" in Washington, a "highly dramatized version of outrage and anguish." It took several years, but this was very likely the origin of a similar march on the eve of the huge Washington demonstration in 1969.[85]

CALCAV kept its organizational distance and independence from other peace groups, but some kind of national gathering did appeal to Coffin's colleagues, and in December 1966 the executive committee called for its own "Education-Action Mobilization" on January 31 and February 1 in Washington. Called "Viet-Nam: The Clergyman's Dilemma," the event would bring antiwar clergy together for training, for lobbying (of government officials), and for conducting a White House vigil.

The mobilization succeeded far beyond the expectations of the organizers, as nearly twenty-five hundred clergy—Jews, Protestants, and Catholics (though no bishops, despite enormous efforts)—came to Washington from forty-seven states, packed into the New York Avenue Presbyterian Church for speeches and worship, conducted a silent vigil in front of the White House, and vigorously lobbied senators and representatives on the Hill. Robert McAfee Brown arrived early to draft a common statement for the participants. CALCAV distributed the completed statement, "The Religious Community and the War in Vietnam," to the delegates and throughout the country in ensuing months. Coffin gave the opening remarks and helped lead worship the first evening. The closing session featured speeches by Senators Wayne Morse, Ernest Gruening, and Eugene McCarthy. Heschel concluded, sounding, according to Coffin, "like Jeremiah himself as he lamented over the sins of the nation he loved."[86]

The mobilization made a splash. In addition to extensive print and radio coverage, including a *New York Times* story, all three networks covered the vigil on the evening news, providing "balance" by showing the two-hundred-strong counter-demonstration alongside CALCAV's vigil of two thousand. Both Brown and Coffin were interviewed. The following day all three networks covered the mobilization's call for a "Fast for Peace" to begin on Ash Wednesday.

One group of CALCAV leaders met with Walt Rostow and S. Douglass Cater, while another—Coffin, Bennett, Heschel, Neuhaus, Brown, Jacob Weinstein, and Stanford-based Catholic theologian Michael Novak—garnered a meeting with Secretary of Defense Robert S. McNamara. Clearly clergy, even those on record as critical of administration policy, still commanded some respect from high government officials, if only of a backhanded sort. "To ignore them might hurt our public relations," one Rostow aide warned his boss. The encounter with McNamara, which Coffin chaired at Heschel's request, featured an emotional Heschel outburst and McNamara's unconvincing reply that he represented the embattled voice of restraint within the administration. Coffin and the others left "disconcerted" by the secretary's apparent decency, which could nevertheless do "so much evil."[87]

The Washington mobilization vaulted CALCAV into a new level of visibility, growth, and influence. Catholic leaders began to inch out of the woodwork, and when Martin Luther King Jr. decided that the time had come for him to tackle Vietnam head-on, and to do so from a pulpit surrounded by the "respectable"—that is, non-leftist—opposition, he came to CALCAV. Against the advice of most of his advisors, and even the SCLC board, King had agreed to speak at the April 15 spring mobilization. In order to mute the criticism he anticipated from that appearance, King wanted "his" kind of surroundings, which CALCAV could provide. Historians and participants disagree over who wrote which parts of the speech King delivered. According to Fernandez, Andrew Young and Al Lowenstein wrote the draft, which was edited by Fernandez himself and Fred Sontag, the CALCAV publicist. But according to King biographer David Garrow, Vincent Harding wrote "large segments," while Andrew Young and John Maguire wrote "smaller portions." Harding recalled that the speech was "[e]ssentially . . . what I drafted." The collective effort bore exquisite fruit: King's speech—at Riverside Church on April 4—may have been the single most powerful indictment of the Vietnam War of the 1960s. Combining King's experience in the civil rights movement, his perspective on national priorities, a thorough grasp of the history of the conflict, his religious faith and sense of calling as a minister, his Nobel Peace Prize, and his visceral conviction that the war needed to be stopped, he—more than any commentator or activist of the decade—combined criticism of the war with a critique of domestic and international racism that staked out new territory in Vietnam dissent.

He had thought long and hard about this step and had explored more tentative versions of this position for the previous year. Now he took national prophetic leadership on the issue—as no other American could have done—and received what most prophets receive in their own land: thundering disapproval, from close colleagues and friends as well as from supporters, journalists, critics, and enemies. He also began the last year of his short life. As Harding recalled poignantly much later, "I have not been able to forget that Martin was assassinated one year to the day after that speech. . . . The road from Riverside to Memphis seems very direct." Within a week King had accepted CALCAV's offer to co-chair the organization, and the most influential American preacher of the twentieth century joined the struggle against the war in earnest, giving the movement the single biggest boost it had received since its birth.[88]

In his speech King raised a concern destined to become one of the linchpin issues over which Americans fought the war at home. "As we counsel young men concerning military service," he explained, "we must clarify for them our nation's role in Vietnam and challenge them with the alternative of conscientious objection. I am pleased to say that this is the path now being chosen by more than 70 students at my own Alma Mater, Morehouse College, and I recommend it to all who find the American course in Vietnam a dishonorable and unjust one. Moreover, I would encourage all ministers of draft age to give up their ministerial exemptions and seek status as conscientious objectors."[89]

Back in November, Coffin, too, had begun thinking more about the draft. As he sought new tactics with which to build and dramatize opposition to the war, Coffin indicated to A. J. Muste that he was "impressed by the number of students who may decide finally not to cooperate with the draft." He had determined to "do what little we can to help them." In short order that "little" came to dominate Coffin's life.[90]

Moments of Truth: Civil Disobedience and the Draft

New Tactics: Going After Conscription

Over the next few years, William Sloane Coffin's personal confrontation with the Vietnam War pushed him to the forefront of the antiwar movement and to the pinnacle of his fame and influence. In one of the most celebrated political trials of the decade, the U.S. government tried, without success, to imprison Coffin, Dr. Benjamin Spock, and three others in a show trial meant to intimidate those resisting the draft. Coffin and his office became one of the key centers of antidraft and antiwar activity in the country, attracting an enormous amount of attention—positive as well as negative—from politicians, the media, college students, Yale alumni, and clergy and laity nationwide.

As the war widened, the Johnson administration expanded the draft dramatically. From 1963 until the second half of 1965 draft calls varied, but on average the army inducted roughly ten thousand men a month. Then the number shot up, to more than twenty-seven thousand per month. By the second half of 1967 that total had become more than thirty-four thousand. Because the great majority of young men who received draft notices either did not pass the physical or mental exams or were eligible for other exemptions, the Selective Service System sent out roughly five times as many draft notices as eventual inductees.[1]

When draft calls and inductions escalated along with the war, the selective service system became a major target of antiwar organizing. More and more potential draftees applied for conscientious objector status, normally only granted when an applicant could demonstrate his long-standing religious opposition to all wars; some refused induction and went to jail; some left the country rather than be drafted. In an only partially organized manner, a number began sending back their draft cards or pledging to resist induction directly.

The CALCAV principals hesitated much longer to take up civil disobedience in opposition to the Vietnam War than they had with respect to civil rights. To begin with, draft law was federal. From Montgomery, through the Freedom Rides and Birmingham, civil rights organizers had used federal laws and the U.S. Constitution to trump state segregation laws. That the Selective Service System made no provision for conscientious objection to specific wars meant that draft resistance could land violators in federal prison. Resisters needed greater confidence that their civil disobedience indicated loyalty to a higher law.

Moreover, civil disobedience during wartime would expose protesters more directly to the charge of treason—"aiding and abetting the enemy"—and to the Communist label. While by the 1950s and early 1960s millions of Americans had concluded that racial segregation violated American, religious, and humanitarian principles, far fewer had come to believe that American foreign policy in the Cold War era was fundamentally flawed or that American policy in Vietnam was basically misguided.

Finally, while extralegal civil rights actions focused attention on racist practices in particular places, like an amusement park or motel restaurant, no American targets represented the war in Vietnam so concretely. The Pentagon, object of much antiwar anger during these years, oversaw far more than Vietnam; so did the White House. Selective Service offices became the targets of more serious and violent protests because they bore obvious responsibility for sending young men to Vietnam.

Nevertheless, Coffin's personal path, and the choices of a growing sector of the antiwar movement, were beginning to converge on the issue of the draft. An increasing number of adults and young men were concluding that resistance to the draft should be the linchpin strategy with which to battle the Vietnam War. This movement, known in the literature of the Vietnam War as the change from dissent to resistance, came from a variety of sources, including the clear unwillingness of Congress to challenge Lyndon Johnson, despite the antiwar feelings of many representatives and senators. For Coffin, a visit to an antiwar senator in January 1967 had been both depressing and infuriating, as the senator explained that even his dovish colleagues feared—and therefore chose not to engage in—a battle that Johnson refused to lose. "In retrospect," he wrote, "I think it was the passivity of Congress as much as anything else that pushed me and many like me toward civil disobedience."[2]

Like most of the adults who helped young men grappling with the draft, Coffin became enmeshed in their struggle out of admiration for their courage and a sense of obligation to the younger generation. By virtue of his chaplaincy, he also became their unofficial pastor, the country's key religious figure on the draft and the one most trusted by young men opposed to the war. While

Coffin's critics called him a Pied Piper, leading youth to legal slaughter, it is more accurate, as journalist Jessica Mitford argued a quarter of a century ago, to think of Coffin and fellow adult antiwar activists as led by the young.

As Coffin and his CALCAV colleagues struggled to find a way to dramatize their opposition to the war through the draft, they looked for tactics that would put them directly in legal jeopardy. Otherwise, they opened themselves to the charge of manipulating the young on behalf of an adult agenda. At the Washington mobilization in early 1967, therefore, Coffin and Richard Neuhaus resolved to develop a concrete proposal on civil disobedience and the draft for CALCAV. They had begun to think that the draft represented an easier target than administration Vietnam policy. It was a shrewd choice. Hundreds of thousands of young men and their families would be facing the draft, which would bring the reality of the war home far more powerfully than any flyer, article, or sermon. By distinguishing between "just" and "unjust" wars, potential draftees tried to cast debate about the war in moral terms. The history of selective service had included a religious tradition of conscientious objection that offered the possibility of a dignified refusal to cooperate.[3]

A few weeks later in Washington, Coffin debated retired Supreme Court Justice Charles E. Whittaker on the subject of "Law, Order, and Civil Disobedience."[4] In front of reporters and television cameras, Coffin threw down the gauntlet on the related issues of civil disobedience and the draft. He invoked the "Puritan Fathers" who "refused to surrender their conscience to the State" and took pride "that many Americans whom we now hail as heroes were in their generation notorious lawbreakers." After all, Washington, Madison, and Jefferson were "traitors all until success crowned their efforts and they became great patriots," while many abolitionists "ended up behind the [sic] bars" in the previous century.

Coffin no longer held that one man's witness could stop the war, even though it might "do wonders for that man's conscience." Instead, "What about deliberately attempting," he asked, "to organize massive civil disobedience in opposition to the war?" Since "there were no easy or written answers," the war's opponents needed to make sure that they had done their homework, that they were fighting a truly great evil, that they had either exhausted legal remedies or could not afford the time to pursue them, and that many innocents would suffer. Since such ultimate questions could be answered only partially, "we have to proceed even as the government is now proceeding—to act whole-heartedly without absolute certainty." Along the same quotable lines, Coffin argued, "While no one has the right to break the law, every man on occasion has the duty to do so." He proposed that seminarians and young clergy opposed to the war "surrender their draft exemption in order to make it count on moral grounds." Then, "older clergy should publicly advocate their doing so in order that all be subject to the penalties of the Selective Service Act."

Coffin's next step allied him with hundreds, if not thousands, of young draft-eligible men who had begun organizing themselves into groups of draft resisters—and landed him in institutional hot water: "I would love to see one, two, or five thousand students and others of draftable age opposed to the war gather on some specified date this spring in some ten or twenty urban centers throughout the country, there with a moving simple statement to surrender their draft cards at previously designated federal buildings." This suggestion, coming from an antiwar moderate, placed Coffin in the front ranks of the nascent draft-resistance movement. Coffin sensed the degree of conflict he might be provoking, for he concluded by warning his audience, "Whenever God is taken seriously divisions always follow." Still, he believed that "it is a fundamental religious conviction that all men . . . have more in common than they have in conflict."

Whittaker's position, that the law was the law, made no news. But with forty reporters and TV cameras in the room, Coffin made great copy. His efforts to build an argument, to make a distinction between what he urged clergy to do and what he hoped students would do on their own, disappeared in the press coverage. The *Chicago Tribune* Press Service led with "The Yale university chaplain tonight proposed mass demonstrations, organized by the clergy, in which thousands of college students would simultaneously turn in their draft cards"; "Mass Draft Card Protest Sought by Yale Chaplain," ran a typical headline. Most papers, including the *Yale Daily News,* reported Coffin as having issued a call for clergy to "mobilize students to turn in their draft cards in a massive burst of civil disobedience."

Kingman Brewster had been out of town when Coffin spoke in Washington but could not help but see the press reports. He knew what Coffin had gotten him into again. On his return he fired off a note marked "Personal," requesting "for the record and in order to answer any questions from my colleagues on the Yale Corporation" a "clear-cut statement . . . as to whether and to what extent it is your intention to urge or organize disregard of legal obligations as a form of protest against the war in Vietnam." He enclosed a draft of the letter he intended to send to alumni.

Fortunately for Coffin, who promptly forwarded his speech to Brewster, he had not proposed that the clergy organize mass draft-card turn-ins. He did, however, revise the key paragraphs for further distribution, mainly by adding two sentences. The first, "My chief concern is with the clergy," preceded his suggestions about clergy deferments. The second, added just before his sentence beginning "I would love to see . . . ," made a similar qualification: "Then I think it would be a good thing if the students organized themselves." Coffin also composed a letter to the *Yale Daily News* and sent it to Brewster with obsequious flattery: "Yours is a beautiful letter and I hope my corrected paragraph and letter to the *News*—both enclosed—will justify your sending it." A part of Coffin's charm lay in his ability to apologize after going out on a limb. His letter to the *News* even nibbled uncharacteristically at humble pie, apologizing for "my own lack of clarity" and inviting people to pick up a copy of his speech —"my own poor best"—in his office.

Brewster's damage control efforts consisted of drafting a telegram ("COFFIN'S COMPLETE TEXT IS QUITE DIFFERENT FROM IMPRESSION CREATED BY PRESS REPORTS. AM SENDING IT TO YOU WITH LETTER EXPLAINING MY VIEWS ABOUT IT. THANK YOU FOR YOUR UNDERSTANDABLE CONCERN"), preparing a careful analysis of Coffin's position, and compiling a packet for the Yale Corporation. He praised the speech as "a thoughtful and eloquent sermon on the dilemmas a man faces when his conscience is in conflict with the law." He also differed: "While I strongly disagree with Mr. Coffin about the propriety of civil disobedience when it is primarily motivated by the desire to call attention to an evil rather than by conscientious non-compliance with a law of questionable constitutionality, he puts the case fairly and well."[5]

Since the alumni letters had started up again, Coffin also offered an explanation to skeptics through the *Yale Alumni Magazine*. He sent an advance copy to Brewster, with a note hoping that this would "help clear the air." More revealingly, he asked, "Didn't you ask for a copy of everything I wrote?" Given how much Brewster had to defend Coffin, he had taken a wise precaution.

Coffin focused on the primacy of individual conscience (as opposed to the power of the state). If a man had "conscientiously done his homework on Vietnam" for years, and to no effect, "does he then tuck his conscience into bed with the comforting thought" that he had done his best while "the President continues to escalate the war, and the law of the land is clear?" Coffin stressed that he was not advocating violence and that he was "against draft card burning, which I consider an unnecessarily hostile act." He still did not "advocate withdrawal. I am against withdrawal," he maintained, and "for negotiation."[6]

However much the lawyer in him disliked Coffin's vagueness and "volatility," Brewster derived a certain satisfaction from defending him. He clearly enjoyed sending a condescending letter criticizing the general manager of the local television station who had aired an anti-Coffin editorial, on the grounds that the editorialist had not seen a copy of Coffin's text—even though the editorial quoted Coffin accurately.[7]

Brewster was being brought to new insights by heading a great university in the midst of social turmoil, partly because one of the instigators of the turmoil worked on his own campus. Coffin did more to keep Yale close to its traditions of public, religiously based service than an entire alumni club full of lawyers and stockbrokers. Coffin also kept Yale closer to its students. As Brewster had written an irascible correspondent several years earlier, "I think he is the best chaplain I have known or have heard about. This is not because I agree or disagree with him, but because he has a capacity to communicate with the highly motivated members of the younger generation more effectively than almost anyone my age or older."[8]

More recently Brewster had related a remarkable (if suspiciously sentimental) anecdote to an alumnus he evidently knew well. At the Gridiron Dinner in Washington in 1967, Brewster had talked to two "much-decorated enlisted men," telling them, "I was a college president and that I had students, faculty members and a chaplain who were active protesters against the war. I said that the Chaplain even urged those who opposed the war to stand up and be counted, even to turn in their draft cards. I asked what I should do about these types. Their answer was speedy and unequivocal: 'Nothing.' They made it clear that these people's education must have been deficient; but when I asked whether I should fire or censor such people, they both said, 'Of course not, that kind of freedom is what we're fighting for.'" So, Brewster concluded, "there is little, timid patriotism; and there is the larger patriotism which believes in the risk of freedom as well as its armed defense."[9]

When Coffin next preached, on the parable in which Jesus heals a paralytic man (Mark 2:1–12), he picked up his critique of university life, titling his sermon "On Learned Paralytics." Jumping from theme to theme, Coffin sought to explain, in turn, American ideological rigidity, the failure of technology to bring true freedom, the character of Jesus' love, and, pointedly, the tendency of education to drive "a wedge between thought and action instead of enabling action of a higher kind." But he was most interested in what ailed the paralytic and what it took to heal him: what, in other words, did it take to change people's minds so they could act? "Here," he emphasized, "we see the eternal disseminator of God's freedom [Jesus] confronting the eternal paralysis of the human will."[10]

Coffin had hit upon excellent metaphors for Congress and the American people confronted with the war, as well as for a messenger desperate to get his message heard. In the parable of the paralytic, when Jesus forgives the sins of the sick man, he sees that the "teachers of the law were sitting there, thinking to themselves, 'Why does this fellow talk like that? He's blaspheming.'" Coffin pointed to the "terribly important quality of Jesus' authority," especially in light of the philosopher Hannah Arendt's recent observation that "truth has not only a persuasive but a coercive nature." This was indeed "a profound warning," as Coffin acknowledged, for when "piety becomes fanaticism, then faith becomes arrogance, and almost inevitably goodness turns to cruelty."

Coffin needed to take care that his own piety did not slide over into fanaticism, into a rock-solid conviction that he was right. As he was developing that very reputation, this sermon may have been a warning to himself. To his credit Coffin understood the danger signs and tried publicly to embrace Jesus' way. For "Jesus is no fanatic, no tyrant. To be sure he confronts people with his and their beliefs." But "no doubt it was this combination of authority and tenderness" that drew people to him.

Comparing himself to Jesus was a risky strategy. Coffin was surrounded above all by "teachers of the law" (in one translation of Mark) or "scribes" (in the one he used)—in other words, professors and lawyers. Coffin had changed the parable slightly in his sermon title, making "paralytics" plural and adding the word "learned," suggesting that the attending scribes might have been the true paralytics. Coffin enjoyed tweaking professors who questioned the authority of anyone other than God or themselves to pronounce on the most important issues of the day and lawyers who fretted constantly about risk and precision and careful formulations. Kingman Brewster had been a lawyer and a professor and still had not pronounced himself on the war.

When Coffin needed a Vietnam sermon later that spring, he returned to this parable, concentrating on the possibility that "America the beautiful has become America the fearful, that her citizens, far more than most are aware, are severely paralyzed in thought and action." "The eternal disseminator of freedom can free us from our fearful paralysis," he concluded powerfully, "free American eyes to see things as they really are, free American hands to extend aid where help is truly needed, free American feet to walk where once they walked with greater frequency, in paths of justice and peace."[11]

Scenes from a Movement: Two Vignettes

Coffin's high-profile moments led to some low-profile ones as well, in which his sincerity and compassion were both tested and displayed. He could have a powerful effect on young men he did not know at all. A New Jersey mother wrote in anguish to Coffin in the fall of 1966, for example, because her son, an Oberlin student, had heard Coffin speak, and "proceeded to mail his draft card back to the Selective Service Board" along with "a letter giving his objections to the war in Vietnam." Though they admired "his courage to stand up for his convictions," his "heartsick" parents feared for his future. They flew him home to talk these matters over, but when they saw how "firm his convictions" were, they "promised to back him one hundred percent even though we don't approve of what he is doing." She appealed to Coffin "as a minister of God to take a moment and give us some reassurance. I just can't seem to find any rest."[12]

"Deeply touched" by her letter, Coffin wrote, in her shoes he would be "as moved as you, and probably in as many directions." In his own one-on-one counseling with students, he explained, "I have always been exceedingly careful not to push anyone into civil disobedience, for fear that he might have regrets later and become disillusioned and bitter." So far, this was a conventional reply. "On the other hand," he continued, in an important rearrangement of the conventional wisdom, "I have been equally careful not to push anyone away from civil disobedience, for what is worse for a lad than to face his moment of truth and miss it? We all know how easy it is to miss the second, third, and fourth moments after missing the first. In short, this has to be an eminently personal decision."

Coffin then gave some practical advice. Since the future was at issue, "unless he were headed for the CIA, I would not be as concerned as you seem to be." After all, many conscientious objectors, even some who refused cooperation with the draft in World War II, were "doing very well, and not only in the ministry." More important, "it is widely recognized that a man cannot surrender his conscience to the State." He invoked the "Pilgrim Fathers" as well as the Nuremberg principles, which were likely to be "increasingly recognized again in this country as history judges our participation in this war more harshly." Ten years from now, Coffin speculated, "[your son's] action may seem very impressive."

The son claimed to remember little of those years. "I had always been a religious sort of person," he recalled. "Looking back on it I'm not entirely sure why I became so impassioned about the war. I was very impassioned about it." He did not go to jail. "I think when he realized how upset I was he got another draft card," his mother recalled in an interview. "He asked for it back, and they gave it to him." He was able to serve in the Peace Corps, as planned, "with no punishment."

But rather than get drafted, after he finished his stint in the Peace Corps he enlisted in the Air Force, where he spent four years. Coffin's letter had not reassured his parents. Thirty-five years later, his mother insisted on anonymity to discuss the issue because she wanted to forget about the entire affair. She mostly remembered the era as a "horrible period for parents." After all, "he had been such a perfect son, never got into any trouble . . . he did so many outstanding things."

When asked whether she found her son's action "very impressive" years later, as Coffin had predicted, she replied, "I think I admire him that he stood up for his convictions. After it was all over I think I did admire him." As for Coffin, "I can't say I blame him," she allowed. "I think people who go into the ministry do so because they have strong convictions. Maybe we'd all be better off if we had the courage to do that."

Several weeks after interviewing the son, the author received a packet of photocopied documents fleshing out his story, beginning with his eloquent explanation of why he turned in his draft card, written shortly after the fact. "I cannot compromise with what I consider to be the most important fact about myself," he declared, "that I have an obligation to be my brother's keeper, or as Rev. Coffin so well said, my brother's brother."

The rest of the documents detailed an episode in mid-1971, while he was stationed at Bolling Air Force Base in Washington, D.C. There, he became involved in the Concerned Officers Movement, a group of antiwar servicemen who sponsored a Memorial Service for the Indochina War Dead in Washington Cathedral in April 1971. He tried to distribute a leaflet—a two-sided reprint of the *Congressional Record* from May 13, 1971, consisting of a speech by Representative John Sieberling describing the memorial service and including the sermon Coffin gave at the service—on his base. At first his base commander refused him permission. When Senator Sam Ervin, chair of the Senate's Constitutional Rights Subcommittee, protested on his behalf, the Pentagon first granted permission to the young airman to distribute the leaflet and then initiated "emergency honorable discharge" proceedings against him, a procedure that Ervin also thwarted.[13]

It is impossible to measure Coffin's full effect on this family, none of whose members he ever met. The mother tried to push the entire episode out of her mind, so Coffin's counsel appears to have gone for naught. As for the young man, it seems clear that the dove who, inspired by Coffin, took flight at Oberlin never became comfortable with the wing-clipping administered first by his family and then by the Air Force.

Two years after his Oberlin speech, in November 1968, Coffin spoke at a New Haven antiwar rally and concluded with the prayer attributed to St. Francis of Assisi, "Lord, make me an instrument of thy peace." Exceptionally moved, a young man who had driven down from Hartford with a group of friends, stood, held out his draft card, and said, "My name is Gordon Coburn and I'm a sophomore at the University of Hartford and I'm doing this because I'm a Christian." Three of his friends turned in their cards along with perhaps a dozen others.[14]

The next day Coburn telephoned his parents, who hit the ceiling. His father, Ralph Coburn, a Harvard-educated lawyer and veteran (an admiral in the Naval Reserve), wrote Coffin a few days later lamenting his son's "foolhardy act" and demanding to know what consequences Gordon would face for his "draft card action for which, I submit, you must bear the major responsibility." Coffin acknowledged "a father's agony" but apologized neither for himself nor for young Coburn, on the identical grounds he had given the distraught New Jersey mother two years earlier. Since "turning in one's draft card is an eminently personal decision," he argued, "one should not push somebody into it, nor necessarily deter him from it. In the first instance a man might have second thoughts, become sour and embittered for some time if not for life. On the other hand, is there anything worse for a man than to feel he had his moment of truth and missed it?"

Coffin admitted that if Gordon Coburn had planned on joining the CIA or getting "a sensitive post as a physicist working for the government, then obviously he has jeopardized his future. If he wants to be a lawyer, it is more questionable." (In fact, Coffin often tried to talk future lawyers out of such acts.) If he wanted to be a minister or a teacher, however, "he will probably be a better one for having the gumption not to let the government confiscate his conscience."

"That whole experience changed my life," Coburn recalled in a telephone conversation thirty-two years later. "I hadn't planned to turn my draft card in. None of us had." But they felt challenged by the others turning in their cards, and by Coffin, especially his use of St. Francis' prayer. "Bill was inspiring. It seemed at the time that I could do no other. [Consciously or unconsciously, he quoted Martin Luther here.] This was an act of conscience, an act of spiritual conscience. This was Thoreau's majority of one" (a quotation from Henry David Thoreau's essay "Civil Disobedience"). He continued: "I remember walking back to the car and the wind whistling through the trees and the tall buildings and feeling the entire weight of the U.S. government about to fall on me, and also knowing that I'd done the right thing. It was very powerful, and also very, very scary; all of a sudden I was on the other side."

Gordon had some stormy times with his father, who felt Coffin had "aided and abetted" Gordon's decision, although the son insisted on his own "full responsibility." Ralph Coburn, though he disagreed profoundly with his son's choice, eventually came to the conclusion that the war was a "tremendous mistake." But even that fall, according to Gordon, a couple of weeks later, his father picked him up in Hartford, drove him to the Harvard-Yale game in Cambridge, and "we talked, and my father listened. He wanted to know what was going on. To his credit he listened to me."

As he expected, Coburn was reclassified 1-A—immediately eligible for the draft. He requested a hearing at his draft board, which he received the following spring: "They convinced me that I'd be better off applying for status as a conscientious objector; they thought that's what I was. . . . I agreed that night to file for status as a c.o., filled out the application, got letters of recommendation, and began building a file." Then, as a college senior in 1971, he went to the draft office in New York City and "flunked the physical." Classified 4-F, he was never drafted; nor did he ever receive conscientious objector status.

The decision, which he never regretted, "was a crossroads for me." In career terms he ended up choosing a "different route, a road dictated by conscience, by a sense of ministry." He had been training as a draft counselor when he turned in his card and later attended an Episcopal seminary in Berkeley for a while. A recovering alcoholic ("sober for a dozen years"), Gordon Coburn eventually earned degrees in English from Middlebury College and in psychology from Antioch University and was licensed as a marriage and family therapist specializing in treating addiction. In 1992 he had occasion to meet Coffin and thanked him for his speech that day in New Haven. According to Coburn, Coffin said, "I didn't do anything. I just spoke my conscience." Coburn replied, "Well, you recited the prayer," which Coffin parried: "Well, let's give St. Francis credit then."

Both of these young men gave Coffin credit at the time for inspiring them to turn in their draft cards and otherwise intensify their opposition to the war. Neither case brought Coffin publicity or glory. His letters to their parents used consistent, nearly identical language and probably did little to persuade them that their sons would survive their (possibly impulsive) acts. And clearly Coffin deeply affected their lives. In a matter of weeks the former airman unearthed thirty-year-old documents that referred to Coffin and testified to his religious persuasiveness. Gordon Coburn will remember Coffin and the date he turned in his draft card (which date immediately tripped off his tongue) as long as he has memory.

These two small episodes help illuminate one aspect of Coffin's influence on his time—his effect on young men of draft age. In fact, to measure Coffin's full contribution to his society would require excavating thousands of similar stories. Inevitably, a very few illustrative examples must stand for the myriad that will remain beneath the historical radar.

Escalation on the Home Front

Coffin's replies to the parents also showed him working over the material of his own experience, even if unconsciously. For Coffin had missed his "moment of truth" first that night in December 1944 when he effectively removed himself from combat; then the following spring, when he allowed Guirey to shanghai him not into a foxhole but into Russian Language School; and finally in February 1946, when he failed to stand up against the bureaucracy of repatriation.

For the next thirty years, Coffin sought out such moments of truth. He joined the battle against Soviet Communism in the CIA and the battle against segregation in the South. His antifraternity efforts at Williams turned out to provoke a usefully dangerous response. During the 1961 Freedom Ride Coffin put himself voluntarily into the most dangerous battlefield of his life.

In March 1967, leaders of the loose-knit network of draft resisters becoming known as "the Resistance" had begun organizing toward a national antidraft action on October 16. First announced during the spring mobilization demonstrations in April, the date gained credibility from a Resistance leaflet passed out at the San Francisco rally and the nationwide travels of organizer Lennie Heller. But the reality was that activists in disparate communities throughout the country began having similar ideas.

In Boston, for instance, Harvard graduate students Michael Ferber and Bill Dowling got together with Alex Jack, a graduate student at Boston University, and began talking about a local action for October 16. Their little band grew to seven or eight, and their organizing efforts took off. As Ferber reflected several years later, "Proof that individuals make history only when history is ready to be made seemed to grow daily, as only half a dozen of us easily galvanized a dozen organizations and five thousand people into action for October 16." He speculated correctly that the Resistance struck a chord "due in part to the same factors that led resisters to turn in their cards in the first place."

The war was widening and killing more people with no military end in sight; the political world offered no alternatives to President Johnson; public support for the war had not waned substantially; and many in the antiwar movement doubted that protests would remain nonviolent. Many Americans were beginning to feel that the existing political system had become thoroughly nonresponsive. The antiwar movement was attracting more militant members. Black ghettos in American cities burst into flame during the summer. Confrontational tactics were becoming more widespread on college campuses, and SDS grew rapidly. Allard Lowenstein hatched the audacious, outrageous, but increasingly attractive idea of organizing Democrats to get rid of Lyndon Johnson as the party's 1968 nominee. In the context of apparent stalemate on the one hand, and the felt need for new tactics on the other, the Resistance appeared "new, confident, and brave, respectable yet audacious, nonviolent (or at least unviolent), and full of energy. It dropped like a crystal into a supersaturated atmosphere. For a year or so, in Boston, we were the center of attention."[15]

As student activists organized, their elders wrote declarations. By the summer, Neuhaus and Coffin had outlined a statement pledging to violate the selective service law, Section 12 of which held that anyone "who knowingly counsels, aids, or abets another to refuse or evade registration or service in the armed forces" could face up to five years in jail or a ten thousand dollar fine. "We hereby counsel, aid, and abet these men in their decision to refuse service in the armed forces," the statement read, "knowingly violating Section 12 of the Selective Service Act of 1967, and thereby risk the same penalties they risk. If these men are arrested for failing to comply with the law that violates their consciences, we too must be arrested, for in the sight of that law we are now as guilty as they."[16]

"Throughout the country that spring, a thousand statements bloomed," according to Ferber and Staughton Lynd, "declarations, manifestoes, calls for support, confessions of 'complicity,' and appendices to We Won't Go Statements. . . . Everyone was confused, not least the resisters who were the intended bene-ficiaries of all the verbiage: there seemed to be as many drafts as draftees." Jessica Mitford called them the "prized brainchildren of literary prima donnas who didn't want a single word changed." Finally, however, one declaration "emerged pre-eminent in scope, publicity, and political impact," that drafted by Arthur Waskow and Marcus Raskin at the Institute for Policy Studies, a liberal think tank in Washington, D.C. They had seen many of the other state-ments and set out to incorporate them into theirs. By early July 1967, "A Call to Resist Illegitimate Authority" had attracted about a hundred signatures.[17]

Coffin now became involved in these events. Hunting for adult supporters of the Resistance, writer Mitchell Goodman, author of an earlier manifesto, had first gone to see the MIT linguist and social critic Noam Chomsky, who directed him to Coffin. When Goodman visited Coffin in late September, Coffin came up with the idea of collecting the draft cards turned in on the six-teenth and turning them over to the Justice Department around the time of a big march on the Pentagon scheduled for October 21. Goodman took on the organizing work.

News of "A Call to Resist Illegitimate Authority" began to seep out. On October 2 Coffin chaired the press conference at the New York Hilton that formally released the manifesto, with its 320 signatures of eminent intellectuals, professors, clergy, writers, and artists. Coffin introduced the impressive group of speakers: Chomsky, Goodman, Robert Lowell, Raskin, Benjamin Spock, Waskow, and the critics Paul Goodman, Dwight Macdonald, and Ashley Mon-tagu. That Coffin ran this event confirmed his relatively new status as a key antiwar leader on the national stage.

The "Call" made a national splash, running in *The New Republic* and the *New York Review of Books* in early October. Although Coffin thought it more eloquent than the statement he and Neuhaus had written for CALCAV, by asserting the signers' belief "that our statement is the sort of speech that under the First Amendment must be free, and that the actions we will undertake are as legal as is the war resistance of the young men themselves," the "Call" stopped short of proclaiming its signatories' liability to arrest and prosecution. Coffin made up for that at the press conference, where he tied the "Call" to the Resistance-inspired acts of civil disobedience in eight cities beginning October 16, including the mass draft-card turn-in in Washington, D.C., on October 20.

He also exploded a political bombshell, offering Battell Chapel "as a sanctuary from police action for any Yale student conscientiously resisting the draft." The *Times* headline—"War Protesters Promised Churches as Sanctuary" —referred only to this pledge while the story quoted Coffin saying that "any man who asks asylum in a church will be given it," all but inviting federal agents to enter religious buildings to make such arrests. "If a further mockery of American justice is not to be made," he continued, "we [the clergy] must be arrested too."[18]

Brewster quickly summoned Coffin to explain himself to the Yale Corporation. Coffin only recalled meeting with some Corporation and alumni types "and letting them blow off some steam before they went over to Mory's [pub]" and congratulated themselves on having "told off" the chaplain. "Sometimes that was the best way to handle those guys."[19]

Brewster's follow-up letter, on behalf of the Corporation, went through four drafts by the next day, gradually becoming more critical. Aghast at the idea of Battell becoming a sanctuary (a term that had had no legal standing since the twelfth century) for resisters, Brewster noted pointedly that "Battell Chapel as a University building is ultimately the responsibility of the President and Fellows [of the Corporation]." Deeply skeptical of the "propriety" of an older person urging draft resistance on younger men, Brewster added his "very real doubt about the propriety of urging or exploiting conscientious objection for political ends," and repeatedly attacked Coffin's interest in "dramatic potentialities for public effect." Coffin disagreed profoundly with this concern, but no record survives of his reply. Until resisters showed up in Battell, he could escape the consequences of his offer.[20]

Coffin had already agreed to join the Resistance in a liturgically dramatic fashion. The Boston Resistance group had organized a rally on the Common for October 16, to be followed by a service at the historic Arlington Street Unitarian Church, during which draft cards would be turned in. The group invited Coffin to preach and receive the cards, and he was delighted to oblige them. "No sooner had I hung up," he remembered, than he called NBC news reporter Sander Vanocur in New York and baited the hook. Always alert to the public relations aspects of events, Coffin "could see the picture in Sandy's head—long haired young men, their cards in hand, streaming forward toward an altar. That would be news all right." Coffin made still more news by meeting with undergraduate leaders and Yale divinity students, asking them to consider turning in their draft cards in Boston. "This was no pressure I put on them," the *Times* quoted him. "It's my job as chaplain to raise issues that are issues. I called them in simply to point out that civil disobedience is a possibility they must face." That his remarks could be considered disingenuous evidently did not occur to Coffin.[21]

Five thousand people rallied on the Boston Common October 16. At the end, led by a hundred clergy and two hundred Resistance members, the crowd marched into the Arlington Street Church.[22] TV cameras stood at the ready. Coffin's sermon elaborated on his recent suggestion that churches and synagogues offer a form of sanctuary to young resisters by daring the forces of law and order to arrest young men inside their buildings. In the event of such arrests, members of the congregation could demand that they be arrested as well for "aiding and abetting." He challenged institutional religion frontally: "Are we to raise conscientious men and then not stand by them in their hour of conscience? And if there is a price to pay, should we hold back?" How "fitting" that these men would take their action within two weeks of the 450th celebration of the Reformation. "For what we need today is a new reformation, a reformation of conscience." He concluded with Martin Luther's own words: "Here I stand, I can do no other."

George Williams, Hollis Professor of Divinity at Harvard, spoke last and most dramatically. As he called for the cards, he pointed meaningfully at the candle burning on the altar below. It was William Ellery Channing's own candlestick, he thundered; it had illuminated his writing as it now illuminated the faces of the resisters. (Channing, the outstanding voice of antebellum Unitarianism, had served this very congregation for four decades.) Coffin's heart sank as he suddenly realized that many of the young men would now burn their draft cards in "the sacred flame of Channing's candle." Coffin had opposed card burnings, and he feared that they would overpower the service as well as the far more important TV coverage. But liturgical solemnity won out. While 67 resisters burned their cards, 214 handed theirs to Coffin and two other clergy. Participants broke bread, and Coffin took great pleasure in the closing hymn, "Once to Every Man and Nation," a useful condensation of his approach to his antiwar activity: "Once to every man and nation / Comes the moment to decide / In the strife of truth with falsehood, / For the good or evil side."

Coffin and the Resistance could not have had better press coverage. The *Boston Globe* gave them page one play. NBC's evening news featured the service, the draft-card burnings, and Coffin's remarks; then the protesters hit pay dirt, as anchor John Chancellor remarked, Coffin remembered, "If men like this are beginning to say things like this, I guess we had all better start paying attention."

Only half over, October had already been quite a month for Coffin—a national press conference announcing the "Call," a tense meeting with the Yale Corporation, and a nationally televised mass draft-card turn-in. There was more to come, as Coffin now traveled to Washington, D.C., days later to hand the collected draft cards to the U.S. Department of Justice, and stride even further into the jaws of federal law.

Mitchell Goodman had recruited hundreds of writers, artists, professors, clergy, and draft resisters from all over the country to participate in this political drama and had secured their appointment with a Justice Department official. Coffin served as spokesman. The most astute description of Coffin's performance the morning of Friday, October 20, in front of the Justice Department came from Norman Mailer.[23] Mailer did not know Coffin and had wondered who the "well-knit man about thirty-five" (Coffin was forty-three) was, with "the well-balanced grin of a man who is as confident with an audience as an executive of regular habit is with the morning shower." Mailer even caught Coffin in one of his quick put-downs of the less graceful—"You'll be able to hear me better just as soon as Mitch Goodman gets his foot off the microphone wire" —and described his manner as "hard, quick, deft, and assured, his remarks purposeful, even salient—yes, he would be the kind of man who would know how to talk to reporters. He had a voice which sounded close to the savvy self-educated tones of a labor union organizer, but there was the irreducible substance of Ivy League in it as well." The group, perhaps five hundred in all, marched from a church to the Justice Department. Coffin took the bullhorn and explained that, after some speeches, resisters would deposit their cards, and the cards they had brought with them from around the country, into a bag. A delegation would enter the department to turn in the cards. Unsure whether the delegation would be arrested on the spot, Coffin sketched several possible scenarios. Then he gave his speech.

Even painfully hung over, Mailer displayed his keen eye and ear. Coffin's "sentences had a nonpoetic bony statement of meaning," he wrote, "which made them exactly suitable for newspaper quotation." He wondered whether Coffin had come from a "long line of New England ministers whose pride resided partly in their ability to extract practical methods from working in the world" and mused that he had "one of those faces you expected to see on the cover of *Time* or *Fortune,* there as the candidate for Young Executive of the Year." Coffin, of course, had already been featured in *Life* years earlier as one of the "red hot hundred." Mailer had been uneasy all morning with the evident virtue of the pacifist-leaning, New England and Quaker sensibilities on display around him; his discomfort led him to see in Coffin the young executive's "flint of the eye, single-mindedness in purpose, courage to bear responsibility, that same hard humor about the details in the program under consideration, that same suggestion of an absolute lack of humor once the line which enclosed his true Wasp temper had been breached." But Mailer also gave Coffin the highest praise he could offer: to the novelist most obsessed with carrying on Ernest Hemingway's legacy in print, Coffin "was one full example of the masculine principle at work in the cloth."

Coffin's speech, as good as any he had given in a secular setting, was indeed eminently quotable.[24] He used some of his Boston sermon but also found new ways of honoring the young men who were taking this enormous step. He even injected humility into the proceedings. "What we are here to do is not a natural, easy thing for any of us," he began, not entirely accurately. "We are writers, professors, clergy, and this is not our 'thing.'" He had worked on his rhetorical flourishes—"In our view it is not wild-eyed idealism, but clear-eyed revulsion that brings us here"—but stayed focused on the consciences of the resisters: "We admire the way these young men who could safely have hidden behind exemptions and deferments have elected instead to risk something big for something good. We admire them and believe theirs is the true voice of America, the vision that will prevail beyond the distortions of the moment." Almost parentally, he confessed, "We cannot shield them. We can only expose ourselves as they have done."

Coffin wanted it understood that he and his colleagues were breaking the law by counseling these young men "to continue in their refusal to serve" and pledging "to aid and abet them in all the ways we can. This means that if they are now arrested for failing to comply with a law that violates their consciences, we too must be arrested, for in the sight of that law we are now as guilty as they." A masterful rhetorical mixture of alliteration and assonance, cadence and repetition, Coffin's concluding paragraph offered a quotable epigrammatic analysis, and a striking vernacular promise: "Still, to stand in this fashion against the law and before our fellow Americans is a difficult and even fearful thing. But in the face of what to us is insane and inhuman we can fall neither silent nor servile. Nor can we educate young men to be conscientious only to desert them in their hour of conscience. So we are resolved, as they are resolved, to speak out clearly and to pay up personally."

Then a group of eleven—Coffin, Goodman, Spock, Raskin (a late addition, as Coffin and Goodman thought Mailer looked too hung over), Waskow, Professors R. W. B. Lewis (of Yale) and Seymour Melman (of Columbia), and four representatives of the resisters—proceeded inside to their appointment with

Assistant Deputy Attorney General John McDonough. The meeting itself proved a collision of political cultures, as the stiff, formal bureaucrat tried to manage the mostly sober delegation of moralists, professors, activists, and resisters, but which also included one antic Berkeley-based African American, Dickie Harris, who acted just bizarrely enough to keep McDonough and his staff on edge.

Coffin's group made their statements; McDonough responded with a prepared statement of his own. Then the resisters and McDonough engaged in a comic exchange about whether he was going to accept the briefcase containing the draft cards. McDonough pulled back from the briefcase, Coffin wrote, "as though it contained hot coals." Since the entire event had been organized for the purpose of committing an illegal act, one that exposed the resisters and their supporters to arrest, Coffin and his colleagues were at first puzzled, then stumped, and finally furious. Waskow exploded at the functionary, demanding that he perform his oath of office. Instead, McDonough sat unhappily while the group marched out.[25]

Coffin explained to the crowd what had happened. "Here was an officer of the law facing clear evidence of an alleged crime," he announced, "and refusing to accept that evidence. He was derelict in his duty." Mailer noted the "contained anger in Coffin, much like the lawyer's anger, as if some subtle game had been played in which a combination had been based on a gambit, but the government had refused the gambit, so now the combination was halted." Apparently misunderstanding the purpose of the meeting, McDonough told reporters he refused the cards because he wanted to avoid creating the impression that "in doing so we had accepted the notion they had the right to turn these things back and in doing so to free themselves from the obligations of the draft." In any event, the FBI wasted little time. Even as the Saturday demonstration continued, agents were busy sorting the cards and making plans to interview some of the resisters. Agents quickly began speaking to members of the draft boards of a number of the young men who turned in cards.[26]

The rally and demonstration the next day—fifty thousand at the Lincoln Memorial and thirty thousand later at the Pentagon—confirmed many protesters in their new stance of "resistance." As peace activist David Dellinger said at the rally, "This is the beginning of a new stage in the American peace movement in which the cutting edge becomes active resistance." Civil rights leader John Lewis led a chant of "Hell no, we won't go!" Coffin, after speaking briefly at the Lincoln Memorial, headed back to Yale.

Most of the demonstrators, however, marched to the Pentagon, where yippie Abbie Hoffman (a former civil rights organizer) had promised to levitate and exorcise the symbol of American military might. Instead, several hundred radicals rushed the building (twenty-five even got indoors before being arrested), and a long, nasty confrontation began to take shape between demonstrators and the troops called out to "defend" the Pentagon. Late that night military police and troops attacked the unarmed sitting protesters. Headlines across the country stressed the violence that attended the rally. Some demonstrators, like Dellinger, were convinced that more militant tactics had brought larger crowds. Others found themselves dispirited by the yearning for confrontation among the young radicals, as well as the willingness of the authorities to use brutal force. No one could miss the new level of conflict.[27]

Back at Yale the draft card action received more press than the demonstration, both because Coffin had led it and because the largest single group of draft cards came from Yale: approximately twenty-five from divinity students, sixteen from other students, and six from faculty members. The *Yale Daily News* ran Coffin's speech on the steps of the Justice Department on a full page, along with photos of the action.

Monday morning, Yale Divinity School student George Stroup had just returned to his dormitory after breakfast. As he reached the ground floor entryway, Stroup recalled, he heard a voice on the second floor, where he lived, saying, "We are agents of the Federal Bureau of Investigation and we would like to see George Stroup about the violation of a federal law." Stunned by the reality of FBI agents at his home, Stroup walked quickly down to the basement, which was completely dark. There, he sorted out his feelings and decided to go see the agents, who were waiting in his room. He talked to them for about an hour, "and it was a classic case of good cop, bad cop." The older man, a Presbyterian elder, focused harshly on the five-year prison term Stroup was facing, while the younger man was "nice and friendly." But it "soon became apparent that they had no interest in me whatever. They were after Bill [Coffin]. They wanted me to say in some kind of unequivocal fashion that Bill had influenced me or persuaded me to return my selective service card." Later that day he went to their New Haven office and signed a statement about why he had turned in his card, "but I refused to say I was influenced by Bill Coffin. In fact my decision was not influenced by Bill."[28]

FBI agents were "all over the campus" that day (though it did not take many to seem like a lot), interviewing students who had turned in their cards and stirring the indignation of fellow students and professors. They raised the most excitement at the divinity school, where students posted a sign quoting Proverbs 25:17. "Dear FBI," it said, "'Let your foot be seldom in your neighbor's house, lest he become weary of you and despise you.'" The dean promised to tell agents that they were trespassing on school grounds and invite them to leave, while law professors, including Dean Louis Pollak, advised students they were "under no obligation to say anything to the FBI agents." The CBS nightly news covered the story Tuesday.[29]

Coffin turned up the heat even further. On Wednesday, October 25, in Detroit, at an NCC meeting, CALCAV finally released its statement on draft resistance, pledging "active support to all who in conscience and through non-violent means decide to resist" the draft. The statement contained the key paragraph exposing its signers to arrest: "We hereby publicly counsel all who in conscience cannot today serve in the armed forces to refuse such service by non-violent means. We pledge ourselves to aid and abet them in any way we can. . . . if they are now arrested . . . we too must be arrested, for in the sight of that law we are now as guilty as they." CALCAV and Coffin had led eighteen denominational executives, bishops, editors, and theologians to declare themselves subject to arrest over the draft. Another fifty participants at the NCC meeting signed on as well. This was, by almost any measure, an extraordinary development, one with no parallel in the twentieth century and probably no analog since the 1850s and mass resistance to the Fugitive Slave Law. Its importance may not have been fully grasped at the time, or even much later. Dozens of well-known, very highly regarded clergymen—including such eminent figures as Heschel, Brown, Truman Douglass, UAHC President Rabbi Balfour Brickner, Harvard's Harvey Cox, and the University of Chicago's Martin Marty—placed themselves on record in direct violation of federal law, daring the U.S. government to send them to federal prison.[30]

To top it off, Yale's annual Parents Weekend began two days later, and Kingman Brewster had trouble. His chaplain and his students had publicly violated federal law; FBI agents had been intimidating his students (and calling some of their parents), while his divinity school dean had all but tossed them off his campus. His law school dean had told students to stonewall the authorities. Coffin had been splashed all over newspapers and TV the previous weekend, and on the national news this week—when the men and women who paid the tuition bills were coming to campus—he was pushing draft resistance. Brewster knew he had to address recent events; he also knew that he could not afford to alienate this most important constituency.

So, giving Coffin no advance warning when he spoke to the parents on Saturday, Brewster freely criticized the "strident voices which urge draft resistance as a political tactic."[31] He reiterated his (and Yale's) intention to "honor and respect those who would, not for political effect but for personal, private reasons, witness their conscience by a willingness to pay the price of their disobedience." In attendance, but not on the podium, Coffin winced as Brewster criticized the chaplain's "efforts to devise 'confrontations' and 'sanctuaries' in order to gain spot news coverage," which seemed "unworthy of and to detract from the true trial of conscience which touches so many of your sons and preoccupies so many." He disagreed with Coffin's position and then used a phrase that stuck in Coffin's craw for a decade: "and in this instance deplore his style."

But if he disagreed with Coffin's actions, why did he not "forbid them?" Here, Brewster gloried in his element—the defense of liberal education—criticizing "conformity in the name of patriotism" and "timidity in the name of public or alumni relations" and standing up for the intelligence and ability of Yale students to "make up their own minds." Finally, he offered a powerful endorsement of the religious and moral energy that Coffin had brought to the Yale campus: "Thanks in large part to his personal verve and social action, religious life within and without the church reaches more people at Yale than on any other campus I know about. More important, the rebellious instinct which elsewhere expresses itself so often in sour withdrawal, cynical nihilism and disruption, is here more often than not both affirmative and constructive, thanks in considerable measure to the Chaplain's influence."

A decade later, Coffin remained stung by the surprise attack and, as he put it in his memoir, the fact that "Kingman had not been totally wrong in what he said about my style." The elderly Reinhold Niebuhr had told him, he admitted, that he reminded Niebuhr of "my youth—all that humor, conscience, and demagoguery." Coffin acknowledged that he "found it hard to resist a bit of rhetorical showboating" and that when he got angry, he also got "strident."

His substantive disagreement lay in Brewster's insistence that draft resistance remain a personal matter, while for Coffin the personal violation of selective service law had public consequences and therefore needed to be drawn into the light of the public world. And Coffin was living in that world more and more. Since "the press would love the prospect of a good fight and be clamoring for a response," he wrote, he quickly "ducked out" and headed over to Brewster's office. His first words to Brewster—"Can I tell the press that you are willing publicly to debate these matters with me?"—showed the constituency he was thinking most about. (Brewster allowed Coffin to say that he was "seeking a proper forum for further discussion.") Then Coffin wrote out his own statement, made copies, and handed it to the "grinning newsmen" camped in front of his house. In Coffin's account the nameless press resembled a Greek chorus commenting on the events played out on the stage, occasionally intervening as the voice of the audience: "Hey, Bill, where does it hurt? What have you got to say?" And after reading Coffin's studied reply, "Come on Bill, . . . that's no good. Haven't you got something more to say?" Coffin had reached the point of having to think about his life as though it were being lived in front of reporters most of the time.

The following weekend Coffin got his turn and showed that however much he appeared to have taken up residence in the world of the press conference and the one-liner, he lived, thought, and felt most deeply when he stepped into the pulpit. True, even in Battell he could toss off quips, but by and large, Coffin's engagement with a biblical text produced deeper and more vulnerable insights. He took great pleasure in being able to preach about Martin Luther on the 450th anniversary of the Reformation and offered, with varying degrees of indirection, an analogy between his own activities and Martin Luther's, and therefore between Brewster's and the pope's.[32]

"No man," he led off, "does anything in this world for one reason alone." So if we wait for our motives to become pure, we will have a "good excuse to do nothing. . . . when we hope to avoid issues by criticizing the motives of those raising them we are engaging in an irrelevant and often brutal strategy." Even the "man who 450 years ago nailed his ninety-five theses to the Church door" had probably had "motives as mixed as our own."

Coffin now had some fun: "The Pope to say the least deplored Martin Luther's style, and the Pope was right." Battell erupted in laughter, and Coffin looked over at Brewster, sitting on the dais; the president grinned widely. ("If you could do it with wit," Coffin recalled, "Brewster took it well.") He continued gleefully: "Luther was far from the first religious leader to lack taste and tact," proving his point by conjuring up images of the prophets attending dinner parties: "that dirty bearded sandled shepherd Amos," the unpredictable Ezekiel, and Hosea "bringing along his harlot wife." While the pope represented "success, also gentility," Luther "had more truth in his little finger than had the Pope in all the Vatican." More laughter from the congregation.

Then Coffin broadened his sights and insisted on the lesson the Reformation had to teach the present day: "Truth is always in danger of being sacrificed on the altars of good taste and social stability . . . for what the Church was to Luther American society may be to the American Christian today." Coffin quoted from Luther's letter to his confessor Staupitz, to whom "Luther lacked taste and tact; also a concern for stability. But to Luther, Staupitz lacked courage." No one in Battell that day could have missed the allegory of Coffin and Brewster. "This is not a time to cringe," Luther had written, "but to cry aloud when our Lord Jesus Christ is damned, reviled, and blasphemed." Coffin concluded with a ringing defense of his own prophetic role (on the edge of self-congratulation): "So what the Christian community needs to do above all else is to raise up men of thought and of conscience, adventuresome, imaginative men capable like Luther of both joy and suffering. And most of all they must be men of courage so that when the day goes hard and cowards steal from the field, like Luther they will be able to say 'My conscience is captive to the word of God . . . to go against conscience is neither right nor safe. Here I stand. I can do no other. God help me.'"

Events accelerated at Yale. Some of the students who had turned in their draft cards in Boston and Washington began hearing that their draft boards had reclassified them. The day after Coffin's sermon on Luther, George Stroup's draft board in Tulsa, Oklahoma, notified him that he had been reclassified 1-A-D, or "delinquent," which placed him at the very top of the draft rolls. Even though he had carefully considered his actions, he "was pretty shaken" and called Coffin, "looking for a pastor."[33]

"I got right in to see Bill," he remembered with surprise. "He was an extremely busy man. It's remarkable that I goååt to see him." After the preliminaries "he asked me what I intended to do, and I told him I intended to pursue this wherever it led." In Stroup's recollection, Coffin promised to "stand by you in this whatever you do. It's very important that we get this before the American people. I will stand with you on the steps of the Tulsa courthouse and defend what you have done." But instead of sensing that Coffin felt any "empathy about my spending five years in prison," Stroup ended up with "the feeling that Bill was already planning the press conference after my conviction." When he told his roommate David Bartlett (then on the staff of the Yale Religious Ministry) what had happened, Bartlett wrote Coffin, distressed that what he had admired—Coffin's "ability to combine a genuine prophetic zeal with a genuine pastoral concern"—was coming unraveled, forcing students to "choose between having you as our leader and having you as our chaplain."

Coffin responded quickly and soon got together with Stroup, Bartlett, and their friends (and fellow students) Ron and Janet Evans. He "went out of his way to apologize," Stroup recalled, "to say that that was not his intention, that maybe he had come across as more interested in how it would look for the movement, and did everything he could to try to make amends for what he had said." Stroup was persuaded.

Later a professor of theology at Columbia Theological Seminary in Decatur, Georgia, Stroup held no grudge: "Bill was passionately caught up in this movement. The risk in this always is that you lose sight of the individuals." Though it was "painful" at the time, he and Bartlett had concluded "that this was the risk that prophets run. In this case I think Bill performed an enormous contribution for the church and for larger public life. I thought it then and I still feel it."

As for the prison term, "what happened to me is what happened to all of us." The divinity students joined a class action suit that became known as the Oestereich case. Eventually decided by the Supreme Court in late 1968, the suit successfully challenged the directive (of October 26, 1967) from Selective

Service chief General Lewis Hershey authorizing draft boards to reclassify holders of deferments as punishment for antiwar activity.

In the meantime, more Yale students, joined by students from other Connecticut and Massachusetts universities, planned public events around their own draft-card turn-ins. Because of Coffin, because of Battell Chapel, and perhaps even because of Kingman Brewster's principled respect for students' trials of conscience, Yale became the key northeastern university site for draft resistance. Following a downtown rally on Monday, December 4, twelve hundred students and faculty packed Battell for a "Service of Conscience" supporting forty-eight resisters: twenty-one Yale students, along with students from Harvard, Boston University, the University of Connecticut, Wesleyan University, and New Haven College. As the service ended the group marched the few blocks to the steps of the U.S. courthouse, where the resisters presented their cards to Coffin and to Rabbi Robert Goldburg of Temple Mishkan Israel in nearby Hamden.[34]

It was a measure of Yale's centrality to the national media that the following Sunday, when Brewster and Coffin finally debated civil disobedience, the draft, and the war, they did so on national television—"The David Susskind Show"—joined by Yale Corporation member (and former NCC president) J. Irwin Miller. The antagonists broke little new ground. Though Brewster did refer to the "horror and outrage at the war as it is," he nevertheless repeated what he had written Coffin months earlier, that he would not know what to do about the war if he were in power. Coffin, despite his intensifying activism, remained muddled regarding a resolution to the conflict, arguing that "his duty as a private citizen was to protest, not make solutions."[35]

Indictment

Coffin had defied the law too long in the limelight. From all over the country young men were sending their draft cards into the Selective Service office. His hate mail increased, as did telephone threats. Coffin began to sense "some kind of showdown" on the way, an impression confirmed when two FBI agents came to his office to inquire about "some of your recent activities." Three weeks later, on Friday, January 5, 1968, the U.S. government charged Coffin and four others—Dr. Benjamin Spock, Mitchell Goodman, Marcus Raskin, and Michael Ferber—with conspiracy to violate aspects of the draft law. Building its case around a few very public acts—the "Call" press conference, the October 16 draft-card turn-in, the Justice Department events—the government connected the defendants and all of the actions by use of a conspiracy charge. Because Department of Justice staff had handed the indictments to the press the same day they mailed them to the defendants, all five men learned of their indictments first from reporters. The indictments were front-page news across the country. Already the most controversial—at once the most admired and the most hated —white minister in the country, Coffin found himself at the center of a political firestorm.[36]

Coffin knew he had been courting legal action. That had been the point of his—and other CALCAV principals'—public declarations. They wanted to share the burden carried by potential draftees. But the government complicated matters by charging them not with violating the draft laws, but with conspiracy to do so.

Before the indictment, Coffin had imagined going "straight to jail" instead of challenging the legality of the war in a trial. After all, CALCAV had "always stressed the moral aspects," and a legal battle would shift public attention from the real subjects: the war and the draft. So when the reality hit, Coffin began by imagining himself and his "co-conspirators" pleading guilty and taking up residence behind bars, their presence a challenge to many more of the war's opponents to join them, "our silence more effective than our words." Then he had second thoughts. As he wrote later, when "going to jail seemed very imminent—and inevitable if I pleaded guilty—I was suddenly assailed by feelings of guilt vis-à-vis my family." Though Eva and the children would have been "well cared for by the Yale community," he could not shake the feeling that he was "deserting them, in part because I was suddenly beginning to wonder if I hadn't already deserted them too often."[37]

Coffin sought legal advice, the first time he had consulted lawyers regarding his political activity, and soon found himself extolling the virtues of "packed jails" to a distinguished group of Yale Law School professors: Dean Louis Pollak (who had defended him during the Freedom Ride case), Alexander Bickel (the renowned constitutional lawyer), Abraham Goldstein, an expert on the conspiracy law, and Elias Clark, Coffin's neighbor and master of Silliman College. They had little patience for Coffin's ideas. To a man they found the conspiracy charge so dangerous—Bickel called it "a worn-out piece of tyranny that has to be resisted"—that they wanted Coffin to fight the charges as an act of citizenship. A skeptic could argue that once Coffin brought in the lawyers he had made up his mind to plead not guilty. How, after all, could eminent lawyers be expected to endorse their friend and colleague going to jail, particularly when his case offered the chance to challenge what many regarded as one of the most sweeping and pernicious weapons in the prosecutor's arsenal? "I was persuaded," Coffin told the *Times*'s Fred Shapiro, "that fighting this indictment would be the best support we could offer to those who are resisting the draft. Unchallenged, the precedent it would set might make it much too easy for the

Government to indict anybody for conspiracy, and this would diminish the possibilities of dissent and the exercise of the rights of conscience."

In later years Coffin reflected with chagrin about the "ease with which they persuaded me" to give up his initial impulse. They knew "next to nothing about religion," after all. "Why then did I allow myself to be so quickly shifted off the ground I knew best, the ground on which I had always tried to stand? I wasn't out to fight conspiracy laws no matter how evil; it was the war I opposed and on moral grounds." The answer seems clear. Coffin knew enough about jail to know that he would have had a very difficult time with the regimen, the inactivity, and the lack of an audience. Coffin made his living with words. Enforced silence might have been an important Christian "witness"; it would also have taken a serious toll on the garrulous, hyperkinetic minister accustomed to nonstop public speaking and preaching.

He also wanted to keep his job. "You know, people who say that even now I'm not really as vulnerable to conviction as the boys I'm supporting don't take into account what I really could lose," he argued to Fred Shapiro of the *New York Times*. "Yale has been wonderful to me and I just happen to love this job. . . . it's no small consideration to me that if I go to jail I could well lose it all." If he went to jail Coffin would almost certainly have lost his Yale income; if he were sentenced for years he could expect his contract not to be renewed. Eva and the children would probably have to leave the chaplain's house, and while she had access to money through her family, the Coffin family life would have gotten even more complicated. As Coffin told Shapiro, jail would not "be easy on my family. . . . My wife faces it intellectually, but it is another thing to face it emotionally." There were, in other words, plenty of reasons to avoid jail. "Consequently," as he put it in his memoir, "I was more than usually receptive to the arguments for a plea of not guilty."

The day after Coffin's legal consultation, all of the defendants convened at the home of famed defense attorney Leonard Boudin in New York. (Coffin brought along Abe Goldstein.) As the only "conspirator" who knew all the others, however slightly, Coffin performed the introductions. The discussion repeated much of the ground Coffin had been over the night before. Goodman, Raskin, and Spock all wanted to challenge "the government's right to put us in jail," while Ferber, the Resistance activist, with "the least to lose," expected to go to jail and shared Coffin's "preference for a simpler moral stance." But Ferber spoke up the least and went along with the majority, just as Coffin did: "I had no desire to split the group."

The lawyers took care of that. They argued successfully that each defendant should have his own legal representation, so as not to appear "conspiratorial" to a jury. The defendants were aghast, since "what might look good to a jury

Coffin, accompanied by his wife, Eva (in the foreground), on his way to the federal courthouse in Boston, January 29, 1968, where he and his fellow defendants all pleaded innocent to charges of conspiracy to violate the Selective Service laws. Despite the trial judge's rulings banning discussion of the Vietnam War, the "Boston Five" trial further discredited the U.S. government. Courtesy of AP/Wide World Photos.

would look bad to the peace movement." But they deferred to the lawyers. More in his element back at Yale that weekend, Coffin used the public knowledge of his indictment to avoid preaching about it explicitly. His meditation "On Hope" assumed added resonance in light of his indictment.[38]

The government's strategy of intimidation backfired as public relations. The case attracted enormous press attention, much of it sympathetic. Courtesy of the government, "the five of us had become celebrities. At universities, where before I had addressed hundreds, now there were thousands." Coffin appeared on "Meet the Press" with Spock, while the *New York Times Magazine* published an admiring profile. Like thousands of his listeners, reporters fell under Coffin's charm. He was such an engaging talker, and so much the establishment figure, that most writers discussed his impressive résumé before getting to his more controversial actions. Like Spock's baby doctor fame, Coffin's background helped legitimate his ideas. The "impeccable credentials," the CIA bona fides, the Russian liaison experience with real Soviet Communists, along with the astonishment that a man of the cloth could be so witty and athletic, so interested in the Super Bowl, and such a reckless driver all at once, clearly seduced Fred Shapiro.[39]

Coffin also received tremendous backing from the Yale community. Faculty members quickly circulated two letters on his behalf. One, signed by fifteen who had been part of the October demonstration in front of the Justice Department, expressed "solidarity with the young men who have chosen to resist" the draft and invited indictment by pledging to "aid and abet them in any way we can." The other, a general letter of support in the form of a petition circulated to the entire Yale faculty, was initially signed by law professors Clark, Pollak, Bickel, and Goldstein, as well as the psychologist William Kessen, political scientists Robert Dahl and James David Barber, psychiatrists Theodore Lidz and Robert J. Lifton, and historian C. Vann Woodward. Eventually, 362 signed.[40]

He frequently received a kind of equivocal backing from Catherine, who sometimes sent cautionary messages through their mutual friends. While she generally contributed to Bill's causes—and to his bail—she was "always," as Coffin remembered, "far more concerned about what others would think." So instead of telling Kingman Brewster "how lucky he was to have me as a chaplain," she was "constantly telling me how lucky I was to have him as a president." She frequently told him, "I hope, son, you're awfully grateful [that] so many people are behind you." Coffin recruited professor friends to call her "and just say how're you doing and isn't it just wonderful that Bill is doing so well." Catherine remained a presence in Bill's adult life, but he had grown behind her influence, if not entirely beyond her criticism.[41]

Draft-card turn-ins continued apace, and thousands of Yale students and New Haven residents were forced to confront the issues Coffin was raising simply by virtue of his presence at Yale in New Haven. Kingman Brewster, for instance, whatever his distaste for Coffin's antidraft rabble-rousing, had to issue a statement in the wake of Coffin's indictment. As he explained very carefully to an annoying correspondent, he did so only after he "had consulted and obtained the approval of all available members of the Corporation's Prudential Committee and two or three of the Alumni Fellows, including Bill Martin, [New York City Mayor] John Lindsay, and [former Pennsylvania Governor] Bill Scranton." Moreover, the civil libertarian in Brewster was offended by the notion that an accused defendant should be treated like a convicted criminal: "Respect for due process of law, however, requires that anyone who is accused is presumed to be innocent until he is found guilty under a constitutionally valid law. Therefore the fact of indictment itself does not warrant any change in Mr. Coffin's status at Yale." That Coffin managed to retain his position while under indictment meant not only that Yale publicly affirmed a key tenet of criminal law, but that thousands of students received a first-hand education in the practice of a principle normally honored in word more than deed.[42]

Like current Yale students, faculty, and staff, and like New Haven residents, Yale alumni also found themselves affected by Coffin's notoriety. They faced questions, comments, and criticisms in their daily newspapers, from their friends and family, and from their fellow alumni. Hundreds wrote Brewster, while dozens wrote letters to the *Yale Alumni Magazine*. Brewster's correspondence just after the indictment clearly favored dismissing Coffin, while the magazine printed many from impassioned supporters, including former and current military officers.[43]

The case, however, reached far beyond New Haven and Yale graduates, serving a similar function nationally. Many Americans who dismissed most antiwar protesters as traitors or dupes or charlatans found it more difficult to ignore this group of defendants. By far the best known of the group, Dr. Benjamin Spock was an institution by 1968, despite his long-standing activism on nuclear disarmament. His *Baby and Child Care* remained the all-time American best-seller—after the Bible. Raskin had worked in John F. Kennedy's White House; Ferber, a bespectacled Harvard graduate student, looked no more threatening than a choir boy; anything but an upper-class dandy, Coffin combined "regular guy" interests in sports and motorcycles with his Yankee pedigree. By becoming a topic of frequent conversation in religious, political, and educational circles, Coffin and his indicted colleagues pushed millions of Americans to confront the morality of the war and the draft in new ways.

The defendants all pleaded not guilty at their January 29 arraignment in Boston, where the government had decided to try the case (even though only one of the specified "overt acts" took place there). Presiding was the eighty-five-year-old District Judge Francis J. W. Ford, the oldest serving federal judge in the country, a crusty, authoritarian former federal prosecutor whose sympathies lay so clearly with the prosecution that he occasionally anticipated—and granted—prosecutorial objections before they had been made. Each defendant had his own lawyer, which meant that the defendants offered no joint strategy and had little sense of comradeship as the trial grew close.

According to Goodman, the lawyers "had a terrible effect on us. They began to separate us." After a brief service a few days after the arraignment, they "never even saw each other" until the pretrial hearings, "when we just met in the courtroom. The lawyers prevented us from taking our case to the people, into the streets, holding demonstrations and picket lines, or from any sort of public collaboration with the Resist groups." On unfamiliar grounds, the defendants never even tried to organize themselves for a different kind of strategy.[44]

Coffin's indictment on conspiracy charges added to his stature at Yale and around the country. More than five thousand people crowded onto the New Haven Green Saturday, March 2, 1968, to hear Coffin and playwright Arthur Miller (right) criticize administration Vietnam policy and endorse Senator Eugene McCarthy's candidacy for the Democratic presidential nomination. Courtesy of AP/Wide World Photos.

At pretrial motions in April, Judge Ford dashed the defendants' hopes to bring up the legality of the war and the draft by holding these issues irrelevant. Once the larger legal and moral issues had been severed from the case, each defendant became even more subject to the strategy hatched by his own lawyer. All except Spock's lawyer, Leonard Boudin, wanted their clients to keep a lower profile during the trial. Michael Ferber generally ignored his lawyer's advice, while Coffin also escaped this straitjacket to some extent. He continued to preach at Battell and address other audiences, and he even led the largest anti-war demonstration in Connecticut history in early March.[45]

Coffin received about twenty-five letters a day. His case did not exactly polarize the country (there were plenty of events to help out with that), but his correspondents rarely had lukewarm opinions. The hate mail could be shocking, even to one accustomed to the spotlight. One writer sent a preprinted circle (from the "Minutemen") with crosshairs, under which a paragraph titled "Traitors Beware" suggested the range of people (the milkman, auto mechanic, insurance salesman) who might be planning to kill the recipient: "Even now the cross hairs are on the back of your necks."[46]

Interlude: Coffin, Brewster, and Yale

The mail that mattered most to Coffin's future, however, went to Brewster and his colleagues on the Yale Corporation. Had not Brewster already gone on record supporting Coffin's right to believe and preach as he wished, Coffin's job would surely have been in danger, especially since his five-year appointment came up for renewal that spring. Brewster was the Yale official most sensitive to the currents of politics, finances, and public—including alumni—relations. Coffin had caused him the kind of problems presidents dislike intensely. The steady stream of criticism following Coffin's public acts, particularly those that got him into the clutches of the law, cannot have been welcome for Brewster. No other member of the Yale community provoked a tenth as much negative ink. Even though Coffin never spoke for Yale, he had come to symbolize the institution everywhere.

Brewster prepared for the Corporation meeting on Coffin partly by asking Coffin's faculty deacons, through historian Harry Rudin, whether Coffin "was fulfilling his obligations as chaplain." The other chaplains, Rudin reported, "explained to me that he was a tremendous power in the religious life of the campus. Each one told me that Bill talked with more students, graduates and undergraduates, than they did." According to one, Coffin did so "in large part because he does his work long into the night." Rudin was surprised that Coffin "adhered to a religious orthodoxy when chaplains on many university campuses go for the newest thing to attract undergraduate attention." The deacons, too, even with some "very strong objections on religious grounds," all supported Coffin's reappointment on the grounds that "he is so great a religious asset to Yale that everything should be done to keep him." Brewster's handwritten note on the letter read, "Hold for April Corp meeting."[47]

In the spring of 1968, Brewster, his colleagues and staff, and the alumni activists working on class reunions and fundraising campaigns, found themselves in the middle of an alumni revolt. For Yale was also in the midst of a transformation that was dramatically reducing the number of alumni children (and prep school graduates) admitted to Yale. Since 1966, alumni had been feeling that pinch, especially those whose sons had mediocre academic records. A sizable group had just learned of these rejections in mid-April.[48]

Much about the late sixties strained Old Blues' traditional relationship with Yale, but Vietnam played by far the largest role. "They tended to be patriotic," remembered Paul Moore Jr., former Corporation member and Episcopal bishop of New York. "Most of them had been in World War II, and therefore this Vietnam peace movement scared them very deeply. I think Coffin symbolized all that stuff. He was leading their kids down the primrose path and sullying the name of Yale, which was an old, wonderful patriotic institution: for God, for country, and for Yale."[49]

Staughton Lynd's Christmas 1965 trip to Hanoi with SDS leader Tom Hayden had drawn howls for his scalp from Old Blues, and Brewster had spent an "inordinate" amount of time defending Lynd's academic freedom. With his chaplain awaiting trial on conspiracy charges, with the alumni fundraising effort in full swing, with Yale being featured frequently in news reports as a center of draft resistance activity, and with heavy negative mail—he could have made his life much easier by firing Coffin.[50]

Instead, as Brewster reported in a personalized form letter (which he published in the *Yale Alumni Magazine* as well), the Corporation voted "by an overwhelming majority to reappoint the Chaplain" indefinitely, though he remained "subject to termination by vote of the Corporation" with at least a year's notice. They reasoned first that Coffin was "outstanding" as a "preacher, and in his attention to the religious life of the University generally, and to his student parishioners in particular." Second, "to the majority there was no doubt that if the church and if religion were to be important to undergraduates . . . it had to be actively involved in current social and moral issues." Third, Coffin was neither "exploiting" his Yale position nor using his counseling function to persuade students to follow his example. Last, while Coffin's indictment could not "in and of itself justify failure of reappointment," the Corporation might want to "review the appointment when the lawsuit was finally terminated, if it seemed that the final judgment or the factual basis for it had some bearing on the Chaplain's fitness for his duties." For all of Brewster's care in his letter, Paul Moore remembered the decision as a virtual rubber stamp: "There was never any doubt—I mean Kingman was behind him, and we were."[51]

In retrospect, it is difficult to decide which is most remarkable: the fact that Coffin kept his job, the skill with which Brewster handled criticism of Coffin, or the principled stand taken by a politically cautious, personally reserved, liberal Republican Ivy League university president whose main political ambition was to be U.S. ambassador to Great Britain. Brewster's biographer argues persuasively that through a variety of initiatives, most prominently the change in admissions criteria, he had undertaken to "redefine the purpose of first-rank national institutions like Yale, and to advance a subtle struggle within the American establishment pitting traditionalists against modernizers." As Brewster once put it memorably, "I don't want Yale to become the finishing school for Long Island Sound."[52]

Brewster's support for Coffin played a role in his effort to make Yale a more dynamic source of leaders for American society in the latter twentieth century. Over and over, to critics and supporters, Brewster set out his larger agenda for Yale students; Coffin figured prominently in these thoughts. While he thoroughly disapproved of civil disobedience as a political tactic, Brewster wrote one alumnus in January 1968, he remained "eager to encourage, not destroy the capacity for moral outrage and conscientious courage as personal traits. Most of all I do not want this generation to think that Yale is so afraid of any sincerely advocated idea that it would protect its students from exposure to it." He had "mounting respect" for the current crop of undergraduates, for whom "to a remarkable degree Yale has remained a place where disagreement does not fester into distrust, and where dissent has not slopped over into disruption." Where did Coffin fit in all this? "I think our chances of keeping it that way are probably better if we counter but do not censor the Chaplain."[53]

Six months later, in the midst of Reunion Weekend, and in the middle of Coffin's trial, Brewster answered a question about Coffin's status. "This is sufficiently difficult and serious," he acknowledged, "so I don't want to toss it off with a quip." The truly important issue was the quality of Yale itself, and how it went about developing "educated citizens as well as intellects." Coffin, he concluded, had "done for this community what has been so difficult to do in the nation: that is to preserve a respect for the process, to preserve a respect for your fellow man, to preserve a positive outlook on the processes of freedom rather than the rebellious, cynical opting out which has characterized other campuses." With Coffin as a bellwether, Brewster could attract the kinds of faculty and students that made a more engaged and relevant university, graduates of which would exercise principled leadership in the nation and the world. He told people he wanted the next Martin Luther Kings to be Yale students. How could they be expected to attend Yale if the university could not make room for someone of Coffin's evident talent—and loyalty to Yale?[54]

Though never close friends, Brewster and Coffin made a remarkable— and much remarked upon—duo. A proper, impeccably dressed Anglophile who had raced sailboats as a boy and specialized in antitrust law, Brewster enjoyed reasoned debate and quiet recreation. Coffin, the ebullient, sloppily dressed Russophile, played competitive squash and tennis, swearing so much that one alumnus still remembers his undergraduate ears burning at the chaplain's language.

While they socialized some, Brewster could not have been very comfortable at a Coffin dinner party, with the chaplain the center of attention, playing the piano and singing Russian folk songs. At the president's house, the hyperactive Coffin would naturally have taken over the relatively sedate gathering. Given their differences, the two best-known Yale men in the country were almost necessarily competitive whenever they were in a room together.

By virtue of their competing styles and views of the world, and the unique historical moment they shared, these two proud men were also tremendously *useful* to one another other, so much so that they could not truly admit the debt each owed the other, and certainly not face to face. Coffin described their relationship as "tiffy," though their disagreements usually occurred in private. In one small meeting, however, Brewster lost his temper and shouted, "Your remarks are certainly ungrateful addressed as they are to one who spends an inordinate amount of his time defending you to Yale alumni." Coffin replied, at the same volume, "The amount of time you spend defending me to the right, I spend and more defending you to the left, and I'd be more worried if I were in your shoes." Brewster "stormed out of the room," but returned minutes later, "as cool and collected as ever."[55]

Brewster may have backed his way into supporting Coffin. He found the experience of worship in Battell Chapel to be consistently satisfying. Moreover, according to his biographer, he had been tutored to tolerate and value Coffin by his own mentor, ACLU founder Roger Baldwin. From Baldwin, Brewster had learned not only that "change—even far-reaching change—was possible to achieve through the system," but also that "society was strengthened rather than weakened by the troublesome agitator." Brewster reaffirmed these values when Yale conferred an honorary degree on Baldwin in 1969: "'In your life,' Brewster told his old mentor, 'Tom Paine and Henry Thoreau have lived again.'" Coffin could hardly have had a better ally.[56]

For Coffin, who had been cultivating Old Blues, and especially his presidents (and their wives) since he arrived as chaplain, Brewster's usefulness was obvious. Not that Coffin's approach to Brewster was entirely calculated, though his flattery verged on the fawning. Coffin had little anxiety about keeping his job, knew that Brewster liked what happened in Battell, and understood that a quick wit and seriousness of purpose went a long way toward calming his boss's concerns about his notoriety.

Judging from Brewster's files, his decision to reappoint Coffin drew much more support than disapproval, including the backing of such key donors and eminent alumni as William S. Beinecke (who had earlier urged firing him) and Henry P. Becton, for whom a new engineering building would soon be named.[57]

Coffin's friend Robert Raines, minister of the First Methodist Church in the Germantown section of Philadelphia, was "never prouder of my university than I am today." The president of Vassar reported on a speech Coffin gave "to a packed Chapel" in which he "said the nicest things about his chief. You should be very proud of him." The Dartmouth chaplain wrote his "personal appreciation" to Yale for Coffin "and the magnificent leadership he provides for our profession." According to the former chaplain of Amherst College, Coffin "served as a model of what the man of faith says and does in a revolutionary church and world." The Chief Class Agent of the Class of 1946, then working at *Newsweek,* offered his "commendation" to Yale for reappointing Coffin, pointing out, "I, for one, think that he is representative of Christianity in action and that his active involvement in the problems of today does credit to Yale."[58]

The most eloquent letter of all came from Mary Shepard of St. Paul, Minnesota, a trustee of Macalester College and the mother, daughter, aunt, wife, sister-in-law, and daughter-in-law of Yale graduates. Since her father-in-law had signed an anti-Coffin petition, she wanted to put her family on record differently. She had followed Coffin's career since his undergraduate days, and while she had "wished he could be less abrasive," she knew his preaching too well and appreciated its effect on her sons too much to wish him to change his spots. She had worried that both her sons had a "skepticism [that] bordered on cynicism" and that they would simply reject Coffin's ideas. Instead, after listening to what they said about Coffin, she had come to believe that "if there were not a few Bill Coffins in the world I am afraid the coming generation would succumb to unabashed cynicism. His example and his faith may be all that stands between many young people and despair. There is no question that he has affected the lives of two of my family in a way for which I feel profoundly grateful."[59]

Brewster's strategy worked. Coffin, the dissenter whom the establishment could love, kept his job and his loyalty to Yale. And Brewster kept an ally on his left who could help defuse the antiadministration sentiment that swept American college and university campuses in the late 1960s.

Co-Conspirators on Trial

Wholly politically inspired, the prosecution's case intended, according to Justice Department attorney John Van De Kamp, to provide a "graceful way out" for Selective Service Director Lewis Hershey, whose October 26, 1967, letter to draft boards—suggesting reclassification of resisters—had drawn widespread criticism even from within the Justice Department. In the wake of the unfavorable public reaction to Hershey, the department formed a special unit in the Criminal Division to speed up investigations and prosecutions of draft law violations. The Spock-Coffin case was the unit's first, largely, according to Van De Kamp, its director, because "there was so much evidence available on film. They made no great secret about what they were doing." Jessica Mitford, who elicited this candid admission, remained appropriately skeptical that a U.S. president as concerned with image as Lyndon Johnson would have left the decision to indict one of the most revered men in America (Spock, not Coffin) to underlings in the Justice Department.[60]

While prosecutors may have thought they were merely going after the easiest targets, the trial seems to have been designed to accomplish what most political trials are intended to do: to intimidate or otherwise disrupt the opposition. Moreover, since Coffin, along with many others, had been inviting the authorities to charge him, officials could well have felt, justifiably, that not taking action would be perceived as weakness on the part of officialdom. The U.S. government had to do something about public draft resistance. It could not allow men of Coffin's and Spock's prominence to defy the law publicly, on the steps of the Justice Department and on national news, and not respond.

The government's odd response, however, did not fully succeed: either by gaining new respect for the law or by completely derailing the defendants. The conspiracy charge attracted sympathy for the defendants because it seemed so silly on its face. After all, these were not secret plotters; their acts took place in public—and they did not all even know each other. But since conspiracy charges needed to be fought on legal, not moral, grounds, the proceedings proved expensive and contrary to the spirit of the antiwar movement.

Beginning May 20, 1968, the trial of the Boston Five offered some interesting confrontations, some humor from time to time, and showcased at least three very well-known lawyers: Leonard Boudin ("a sort of Clarence Darrow of the appellate bar," in Mitford's words, but with little trial experience) representing Spock; James St. Clair (a top Boston trial attorney with little experience in civil liberties cases), who took on Coffin's case; and Telford Taylor (the distinguished chief Nuremberg prosecutor), who defended Raskin. But for the most part the proceedings fit Coffin's contemporary description: "dismal, dreary, and above all demeaning."[61]

Once the judge barred the key issues—free speech, the draft, the war—the trial became a legal sparring match in which lawyers and witnesses argued over minutia and spent much time laying groundwork for appeals. Since the defendants had so clearly sought prosecution, even a sympathetic reporter found it strange and "humiliating" to watch them on the witness stand denying what they plainly believed, as when Coffin tried to argue that he "would not seek to get converts to my view." St. Clair even elicited from Coffin (with a straight face!) the bizarre notion—which he repeated in his closing argument —that Coffin's involvement in draft-card turn-ins actually sped up the conscription process by moving resisters to the head of the line.[62]

The trial provided occasional theater for the defendants, for their families, for journalists, and even for the antiwar movement. Coffin, for example, had long been scheduled to preach Wellesley College's baccalaureate sermon. Since he was occupied in court, thirty-five of the graduates came to the courthouse in caps and gowns, wearing "omega" pins (the symbol of the Resistance). Instructed by court personnel to remove their ceremonial garb in favor of street clothes, the young women did so; three got into the courtroom. During the morning recess, Coffin gave an abridged version of his sermon in the hallway. Coffin's stand-in at Wellesley dedicated his sermon to Coffin, saying, "He has stood with Jesus, with Socrates, and with Moses. I do not mean to say that I am merely sympathetic with his plight. I mean to say that I endorse all that he has stood for."[63]

Catherine Coffin stayed with her daughter Margot (who lived near Boston) and came to the trial every day. According to Mitford, she "invited many a niece and nephew, handsome prep-school boys in Brooks Brothers jackets, elegant debs in Italian knits, to come and hear Uncle Bill testify. Before court opened, she went around greeting them: 'My dear, how lovely to see you. *Isn't this nice?*' One could hear Spode teacups clinking in the background." Margot brought pew cushions from her church for the defendants' families. Defendants cracked jokes to relieve the boredom. Impressed by the strikingly short miniskirt of the young British journalist (later a distinguished economist) Emma Rothschild, for example, the twenty-three-year-old Michael Ferber composed an "Ode to Emma's Legs," which Coffin confiscated.[64]

Jessica Mitford argued that by the time of the trial, press attention had waned, with the notable exceptions of the *Boston Globe* and *Washington Post.* But Mitford was writing very close to the events, in 1968 and 1969. In fact, regular coverage by these two papers mattered a great deal; spot coverage continued, and the *New York Times* ran numerous articles on the trial.

Now it is also easier to see that 1968 was an extraordinary year in American history, surely the densest single year in the decade, likely in a generation and possibly longer. Aside from Vietnam and the pursuit of the presidency, no story could hold center stage for long. Historians have called it the "pivotal year" of the decade, the "hard year," the "fulcrum year," a year that included the assassinations of Martin Luther King Jr. and Robert Kennedy, the riots following King's murder, Lyndon Johnson's withdrawal from the presidential race, the rise of Eugene McCarthy and the disastrous Democratic Party convention in Chicago, the election of Richard Nixon, the student uprising at Columbia University, and the Ocean Hill–Brownsville strike in New York City. Abroad, the year included the French student-worker uprising, the Soviet invasion of Czechoslovakia, the Tet Offensive, and the siege of Khe Sanh. Time seems to have speeded up in 1968, as historians Nancy Zaroulis and Gerald Sullivan put it: "It was a year in which events happened so quickly, hammer blow after hammer blow, that in retrospect it seems astonishing that the national psyche remained intact. Perhaps it did not."[65] To some, electoral politics seemed all-consuming during the spring and summer, as the insurgent candidacies of McCarthy and Kennedy mobilized antiwar protest into electoral channels. Others lived for street-level confrontations, as the far left abandoned nonviolence and came to every antiwar demonstration prepared for violent altercations with uniformed authorities. The formerly "paranoid delusions" of protesters became reality as the U.S. government infiltrated and spied on liberal and radical groups. Next to the extraordinarily rapid pace of dramatic events all over the world, the surprise is that a tedious trial in Boston—from which all political and moral issues had been expunged—still drew such strong press interest.

After a four-week trial and just eight hours of deliberation, the jury acquitted Marcus Raskin and, to no one's surprise, found Coffin, Spock, Ferber, and Goodman guilty of conspiring to aid and abet draft resistance. In a departure from normal practice in a criminal trial, Judge Ford had, as part of his charge, given the jury a series of questions clearly designed to guide them toward a guilty verdict. The verdicts made front-page news, as did the sentences Judge Ford handed down two weeks later: two-year prison sentences for all four, five-thousand-dollar fines for the older three and one thousand dollars for Ferber. The defendants all gave notice that they intended to appeal, and the judge freed them on their own recognizance.[66]

Coffin returned to Yale during the trial to take part in the baccalaureate service for the senior class. "When he came to the rostrum to give the invocation," recalled Brewster aide Charlie O'Hearn, "the entire senior class, attired in their academic gowns, got up as one and applauded him. To my knowledge this has never happened to anyone at Baccalaureate where no one is applauded, even the President when he gives the main address." At the president's house afterwards, even those graduates who disagreed with Coffin "admired and respected him as a person and said they were proud of Yale for retaining him as chaplain."[67]

Coffin had hired an expensive lawyer for his trial and an even more expensive one for his appeal, former Supreme Court Justice Arthur Goldberg, then a partner in the eminent New York firm Paul, Weiss, Goldberg, Rifkind, Wharton & Garrison. St. Clair's initial bill topped $39,000, but Coffin talked him down to $25,000. Goldberg charged a flat fee of $25,000. Abe Goldstein, who worked with St. Clair on the trial, donated a large portion of his time but also charged nearly $8,000.[68]

Coffin and his friends, family, and supporters raised all of this money. While the government's legal strategy undoubtedly strained the antiwar movement, the collective effort of raising money for the defendants became an important organizing effort within the movement, again pushing friends and supporters of the activists to decide what they believed. Coffin's neighbor, law professor Elias Clark, managed one William Sloane Coffin Defense Fund; Coffin's young friends Ron and Janet Evans ran one called "Bucks for Bill"; and the NCC ran a third. Yale faculty sent an appeal to their colleagues, friends hosted fundraising parties, and even an article in *Parade* magazine drew $5,000 in small contributions. Fundraising continued through 1969, and the defense funds paid off the lawyers in early December. By January 1970, Coffin was returning checks.[69]

In early July 1969, a 2-to-1 decision of the First Circuit Court of Appeals set aside all the convictions but ordered new trials for Goodman and Coffin. Ford's unusual instructions to the jury had been prejudicial, the court held. And while Ferber and Spock could not have conspired to do what the government charged, Coffin and Goodman could have; hence the new trials. Typically, Coffin learned of the verdict from a reporter, while playing tennis. Coffin called the acquittals a "great victory for free speech," if only "medium good news" for himself and Goodman.[70]

Soon Goldberg telephoned the Justice Department to find out whether the government intended to retry Coffin and Goodman and learned that it would drop the charges "as quietly as possible." Coffin wrote Ferber in September that "according to Goldberg, the Government is not champing at the bit to bring Goodman and me to a new trial." The following March, St. Clair wrote Coffin that the solicitor general had "said that he had 'just disposed of my case.' I am not sure what he meant, but it could be good news." Incredulous, Coffin marveled that "such a stickler for clarity" could have let the "statement go unclarified." It took the Boston U.S. attorney's office until April 15, 1970, fully eight months after the appeals court verdict, to formally dispose of the case.[71]

With the whiff of martyrdom about them, Coffin and Spock had made excellent defendants despite their effective muzzling in the courtroom. The mere fact of such famous men being prosecuted for their beliefs helped damage the credibility of a government whose credibility on the war was already unraveling. Because Spock was so widely admired, and because Coffin had built such a large constituency among liberal students, parents, and clergy, their stature increased during the prosecution, trial, and appeal. Even though the trial absorbed energy and money, the ultimately unsuccessful prosecution added to the defendants' standing as peace movement celebrities and consequential moral figures for supporters—and notorious subversives for opponents. Coffin's mail on both sides hit new peaks after his indictment, during the trial, and at "news bumps" in the trial: TV appearances, the conviction, the appeal, and the appeal results.[72]

In a front-page editorial in *Christianity and Crisis* after Coffin's conviction in 1968, John Bennett argued, "In the academic community and among his fellow clergymen he has grown in influence while under indictment. There is no more persuasive spokesman for those who seek to make the Christian message meaningful for the issues of our time."[73] From the president of Union, this was an extraordinary statement about Coffin's importance to practicing mainline Christians. Bennett could have made it only after King's death three months earlier. For while Coffin did not inherit King's mantle, neither did any other preacher. The preeminent voice of theological liberalism and a refashioned Social Gospel, King had spoken to and for white and black Christians. Coffin's influence lay far more with whites.

An unusual leader, Coffin headed no organization outside of Yale. He accepted invitations to give speeches and sermons all over the country. He occasionally wrote articles for the national press, but he did not have a reputation as a writer. A consistent Democrat since he had voted for Harry Truman in 1948, Coffin sometimes publicly endorsed candidates (McCarthy in 1968, McGovern in 1972) but never ran for office. He often said (quoting Amos 5:24) that it was the "preacher's job to call for justice to roll down like mighty waters. The politician's job was to work out the irrigation system." Yale distributed his prayers but not his sermons. What made him a leader, in Saul Alinsky's famous phrase, was the fact that he had a following. And that following, made up of draft-age young men, college students, Yale faculty and alumni, liberal clergy and laypeople—Jews and Catholics as well as Protestants—consisted of millions of Americans.

Coffin had such a following precisely because he articulated a gospel that spoke to and for the political and theological liberals who had risen to the ascendancy in mainline American Protestant denominations as well as in Judaism and Catholicism. At the ecumenical level, the National Council of Churches (the voice of organized Protestantism) continued to take a leadership role on a host of liberal issues, moving more to the left as the decade wore on. At the level of the ministry and the laity, the mainline Protestant denominations—Presbyterians, Methodists, Episcopalians, Lutherans, Disciples of Christ, American Baptists, and the United Church of Christ—became more involved in the social issues of the day, reviving a version of the turn-of-the-century Social Gospel. These largely white denominations, almost entirely run by men, began opening seminaries and the clergy ranks to African Americans, Hispanics, and women.

At the level of liturgy, younger laity, as well as younger clergy, pushed for and introduced more contemporary music—folk, jazz, and rock—and more informal modes of interacting in church. Roman Catholic liturgical modernization, in which the Latin Mass gave way to English, found its analog in the United States as Protestants participated more in prayers, restored the "passing of the peace" as part of new intimacy in worship, and brought guitars along to accompany the hymns. Abraham Heschel had excoriated the "pomp and precision" of 1950s services that had everything but "Life." Social action now became the watchword of liberal clergy and their parishioners—on behalf of civil rights, the urban poor, and the peace movement.

Theologically, the currents of sixties Protestantism flowed away from the apparently rigid certainties of earlier generations. "Death of God" theology suggested to many that morality could substitute for God and faith, that denominational or religious boundaries mattered not at all, and that traditional religions had little of relevance to say to the modern world. Among many liberals, questions of faith gave way to discussions of ethics.

In the midst of these transformations, Coffin remained theologically and liturgically orthodox. He explicated biblical texts, and never tried to make God or Jesus less than divine, into informal "buddies." The music in his services, true to his training and Yale's musical resources, remained classical. Though his hair grew fashionably longer, and his penchant for dressing down landed him in the fashion mainstream during the blue-jean era, Coffin, unlike the Berrigan brothers or Episcopal Bishop James Pike, drew little inspiration from the cultural phenomena of "the sixties." His musical ignorance of his surroundings during the heyday of rock and roll made him an embarrassment to his children; as master of ceremonies at antiwar demonstrations, he needed much on-site assistance. He did not smoke marijuana, experiment with psychedelic drugs, or claim to be hearing the personal voice of God. He continued to wear horn-rimmed (not wire-rimmed) glasses and a black robe in the pulpit.

The gospel he preached, and the morality he articulated, spoke to the liberals, not to those scandalized by the changes in church and youth culture. "Principles are signposts, not hitching posts," went one of his most-repeated sayings. Principles could help guide one's actions, in other words, not direct them. Coffin's emphasis on the sacredness of individual conscience as regarded the war and the draft further undermined the authority of institutional morality, even as he hearkened back to Martin Luther and the Reformation.

Coffin provided inspiration and an example for his constituency, even when they did not always agree with his stands. Brewster, for example, saw that moral and religious life at Yale owed much of its vigor to Coffin's leadership. And all over the country, it seemed, Coffin touched Americans deeply. Soon after his conviction, for example, Coffin received sympathy and an offer to contribute to his defense from Louis "Bo" Polk (Andover '49, Yale '54), then a vice-president of General Mills. "I just want to tell you," he wrote, "how much I deeply admire your willingness to search deep within yourself as to what you really believe in and then commit yourself to a course of action in terms of that belief. . . . I don't feel I would have gone as far as you have gone, but by God we need Bill Coffins in this world."[74]

TEN

Marriage and Family Life

Scenes from a Marriage

Through all his activism in the political and social spheres and the controversy he engendered, Bill Coffin was also a man with a family, who inevitably had to live through the activism and controversy with him. True to her word and to 1950s domestic expectations, even in the artistic world, Eva Rubinstein had left Broadway to marry Coffin and move to Andover in December 1956. Whatever their personal domestic expectations, she and Bill confirmed the conventional wisdom about the difficulty of the first year of marriage.

Coffin had worried that the move from Broadway to a little New England town would bore Eva. "After all this is a pretty glamorous actress in New York, and that's the way all of Andover looked at her," he remembered. But "that wasn't the way it turned out at all." Because she had not been to college, she ended up feeling "inferior to everyone else." Life with the overbearing, hypercritical man Coffin occasionally called King Arthur had damaged her more than anyone realized. Moreover, Bill had not entirely resolved his own ambivalence about the marriage. An Andover friend wrote him later about "that first year—your doubts and problems outweighed by deep conviction and joy— her too intense devotion and immaturity—and loveliness. What help is that? —none!"[1]

Eva's own doubts, temporarily suppressed, soon resurfaced. "I could not have put words to it then," she recalled, "but I knew I was very unhappy. I didn't really know why, maybe I couldn't admit it to myself." Much of what she remembered of those years is quickly recognizable as "the problem with no name" identified by Betty Friedan in *The Feminine Mystique* in 1963: a powerful feeling of general dissatisfaction, the half-articulated sense that the housewife's lot—cooking, cleaning, raising children, caring for a husband—

failed to provide the fulfillment it should have. A beautiful and accomplished dancer and actress, Rubinstein had simply walked away from a career coveted by millions of girls and young women for the role of minister's wife. If life in the footlights could not replace the sense of self so depleted by her father, it had provided much more public adulation than life as "the chaplain's wife" at a prep school or a small isolated college.

But in the late fifties unhappily married women rarely left their marriages. Like many women in her situation, she began having children. "I wanted so badly to get pregnant," she remembered, "that I would call Bill and say 'Now! Come home this minute! Now, now, now!'" By April 1957 she was pregnant, and Amy was born in mid-January 1958. Eva's stitches had not completely healed when she found herself pregnant again; they moved to New Haven over the summer and Alexander Sloane was born in mid-December, during Christmas break at Yale. David Andrew followed fifteen months later. By late March 1960, the Coffins had three children separated by just twenty-six months. "It never occurred to me to prevent them from coming," she said of the boys, "but they were total surprises."

Marriage to William Sloane Coffin Jr. had certain rewards, especially once he became chaplain at Yale: prestige, a lively social life, involvement in important causes, exposure to famous and interesting people. It also had serious drawbacks. Eva Coffin had entered a physically and emotionally grueling period. The arrival of children did not draw her closer to her husband. Three quick pregnancies had been hard on her back. Running a household with little children could strain the strongest and happiest mothers; Eva was neither. And like most men of his generation, Coffin knew nothing about caring for babies and was expected to be fully engaged by his chaplaincies, not his domestic life.

The presence of Catherine Coffin, by then a well-known "grand dame" and cultural hostess in New Haven, did not make life easier. "To me," Eva recalled, "she was like criticism incarnate. She made me feel every single thing that I did wrong a hundred times over." Not that Eva herself was less than a "handful" when she arrived in New Haven in the fall of 1958. "I had to see to the redoing of the entire [chaplain's] house, twelve rooms. . . . And Amy was six months old and I was five months pregnant." Until the house was ready they lived with Catherine while Bill was off getting used to his new duties. Later, "I had someone in the house to help because I couldn't take care of a twelve-room house and three kids under three, you know."

By the summer of 1960, when Bill had gone to Guinea and Catherine needed an eye operation, the relationship had deteriorated so much that even Eva seemed anxious to repair it. Along with Coffin's sister, Margot Lindsay, and John Maguire, she stepped in to help her mother-in-law with transportation and company, even reading her Lawrence Durrell's *Alexandria Quartet*. "It has been a joy to me to spend time with her these last few (10) days," Eva wrote her husband. "I feel as though I were given a second chance to straighten out a relationship and I intend to do my utmost to right it." Catherine either concurred or put on a good show. Eva, she noted briefly to Bill, was "a born nurse too and is thoughtful in countless ways which have made these past days pleasanter in every way." Maguire also wrote Coffin about the rapprochement, rhapsodizing about Eva's "radiant . . . buoyancy" in discovering that she could handle three children with her husband gone, her mother-in-law ill, and Eva's own mother rushing through town after the death of Eva's grandmother.[2]

Abandoned by her husband to her convalescing mother-in-law, three little children, a maid, and her husband's best friend, Eva cannot have been having very much fun. For all of their loving and upbeat tone, her letters illustrated the struggles of a young wife dealing at once with a critical mother-in-law, an unsatisfying marriage, complex relationships with Coffin's colleagues and friends, her own demanding parents, and a generally low opinion of herself. Maguire, Eva, and Catherine each referred to these troubles, even as they announced their (not entirely convincing) success at overcoming them.

Reading racy novels to Catherine while living a celibate summer, Eva ached with physical yearning: "I love you and kiss you and long for your sweet warm darling self," she gushed, "all around me, and on me, and in me!" She wondered at the effect of "those chocolate skinned 14 year olds whipping off their scarlet bras in a whirling frenzy. God—I could almost (almost, nothing!) <u>feel</u>, let alone <u>hear</u> the drums."[3]

Amid exclamations of love—"I love you so very much my own darling!! [followed by a heart]"—Eva offered commentary on other marriages and her own. She wrote Coffin about a couple they knew: "He makes not the remotest effort to meet <u>any</u> of her needs—emotional, physical or any other—that she is almost cracking up." Her own need was palpable: "I can't wait to have you again to touch you and love you—my whole being just cries for you—<u>body</u> [triple underlined] and <u>soul</u>. I don't think I could ever let you go like this again." Her hopes for their reunion in Paris at the end of the summer pointed to a good bit of previous tension between them, as well as her own internal struggles: "Let us meet again <u>allowing</u> [double underline] ourselves <u>and</u> each other to be New Beings if we feel so—and <u>really</u> embody the whole question of forgiveness and acceptance, which I am finally <u>beginning</u> in all humility to understand! <u>Not by ignoring</u> our own or each other's faults and shortcomings but in a way by <u>absorbing</u> them with our love for each other—does that make any sense?"[4]

She referred to an earlier playful suggestion that they assume new identities in a romantic, faraway place—"when we meet in Paris let's pretend we're someone else"—an effort to find a different role, a new way of being a happy wife. The effort had backfired, as her husband worried about what she might be saying about their marriage. Eva now apologized for proposing it so "stupidly and clumsily." Bill had probably realized that he had made a terrible, unchangeable mistake. A year and a half later, he wrote to a former student to "just remember the problem in life is not marrying the girl you love but loving the girl you marry."[5]

She felt consistently beneath the women who might have been her friends, she recalled, "because I was a bad wife, I was uneducated, I didn't finish college. And all the bloody wives from Andover on, you know, had degrees and they were so smart and they ironed their children's clothes." The contemporary record confirmed these recollections. "I am rapidly getting over all my guilt-ridden burden of feelings of hopeless inadequacy and uselessness," she wrote in the summer of 1960. "I am even almost convinced that I could be one hell of a good wife to you! (Imagine that—what nerve!)"[6]

So she cooked for the dinner parties, as her mother still did for the maestro's post-concert suppers, since "I had to find little areas where I didn't feel inferior." Intent on conversation, however, her guests, including her husband, rarely noticed the food.

Visitors could see that things were not working out. "It was clear that they weren't communicating," Bill Webber recalled. There was no "mutual partnership, sharing and taking care of the kids and stuff like that." He remembered Eva as needy, "self-centered," used to "being taken care of." Maguire noted her great charm, but "if Eva just felt bad or was mad about something, everybody knew it." Eva knew she was hardly all sweetness and light. "I was always pissed off at him for something," either at his clothes or at the "mess" his things were in. "There was a student who always used to call me Groucho."[7]

Bill Coffin had no idea what was bothering her. She recalled pleading with him to talk to her, to which he responded, more or less, "What's the matter with you? You've got three healthy children, the sky is blue, everything is fine, what more do you want?" After a day of "listening to other people's troubles," he told her once, "It would be so neat to come home and find you smiling in the kitchen! I said, well, I'll try."

The sociability of their life helped hold the marriage together. As Eva put it, they just felt "better off when there were other people around." At the end of the summer of 1960, for example, when Eva finally met Bill in Paris at her parents' otherwise empty apartment, the very first night some of the students from the Crossroads Africa group showed up wanting money or information. They traveled for four days with a "whole bunch of them, going to Chartres with this gang." Instead of resenting it, she realized that "he was just nicer to be around when there wasn't just the two of us. There was more of him."

In other ways they had a genuine partnership. "I liked a lot of the life," she recalled. "I believed in the things that Bill did." She encouraged him to go on the Freedom Ride: "I said, you know, I'm kind of scared. Keep in touch. Let me know what happens." She "spent a lot of time raising bail." And Bill asked her opinions about his sermons, which he worked on for several days before the Sunday chapel service. He read portions he was unsure about out loud to her. "I enjoyed it because I did it well," she remembered. "I couldn't make it right, but I could tell him what was wrong."

The problem remained that she was, in her own words, "very needy," while Bill did not know how to meet her needs. He enjoyed the flow of emotion in his direction, whether from individuals or from groups, and he could accept the social and emotional favors offered by those who adored him. He found it far more difficult to reverse the flow, to respond emotionally over the long term to individuals who needed him. In the short term, however, individuals who were the object of his attention also felt tremendous warmth. Coffin had the ability, common among politicians and actors, to make an individual feel like the most interesting person in the world. Then he moved on, and it could feel as though the lights had been turned off.

While Coffin responded more reliably to larger groups, to audiences, Eva wanted what she thought of as one-on-one intimacy. "I always felt that Bill's personality would sort of disappear along with the audience," she explained. "The smaller the audience got, the less of him there was, until finally there was just me, and there was nobody there at all! And that's who I got to go to bed with."

Eva began going to see her husband's assistant, Associate Chaplain David Byers, first as someone to talk to and then because she was attracted to him. In Eva's account, Bill confronted her with his suspicions just before Easter 1963. She admitted seeing Byers. Bill wanted to know whether she was sleeping with him. She had been tempted, but "I said, 'no.' He said, 'Why not?' And I said, 'the day I do, we're finished.'"

Eva recalled that Bill's response "blew me away." First, she remembered him "marching up and down the room, pounding his fists on the walls as he reached them, saying, 'He doesn't have the scope! He doesn't have the scope!'" Struck that she had so wounded his pride, Eva was flabbergasted by what came next: Coffin's revelation that he had had an affair with his secretary in Puerto Rico two summers earlier.

This rejoinder, whether meant as a defensive counterattack or confession to clear the air, misfired badly. Eva wondered at her ex-husband's "incredible naiveté, in terms of what I was actually feeling," for instead of leading to any reconciliation, his admission opened the "floodgate" for his emotionally and sexually frustrated wife, who promptly gave up on the marriage and sexual fidelity. "Starting then," she recalled ruefully, "I was unfortunately extremely available. And I would end up in a lot of extremely bad things. Bad things. Which were not very satisfying either. Because it was just anger and frustration."[8]

Coffin, Christianity, and Sex

What Coffin knew of his wife's extramarital activities must remain conjecture. No relevant correspondence survives, he claimed to know little, and he appears not to have discussed the issue with his friends. Like poets and novelists, Coffin used his own and others' experience as the raw stuff of his sermons. What he thought about virtually any matter—emotional, theological, or political—came out in his sermons, the receptacles of his most intense and focused intellectual energy.

The 1960–1961 school year had seen a very public sex scandal at Yale, known as the Suzie affair, in which a large number of students were disciplined (some expelled) after having had sexual contact with a drunken sixteen-year-old New Haven girl. Even without such an incident, however, new questions about sexual morality and sexual experimentation pervaded college life. Ten-year-old *Playboy*, with its glossy pictorial mix of mostly nude women and high-end stereo equipment, along with publisher Hugh Hefner's libertine "philosophy," sold well to male college students. The birth control pill was rapidly making its way into pharmacies, medicine cabinets, and the national consciousness; more women were attending college (which is to say, living unmarried while unsupervised by their parents); and the national divorce rate had started to climb.

Coffin first preached on sex, love, and marriage in May 1962, endorsing sexual love and sexual pleasure as God's creation, even as he stressed the limitations of bodily love. "For sex alone," he preached, "is like the rainbow arch, beautiful perhaps to behold but lacking in substance."[9] His text, Ephesians 5:25, spoke of love, not of desire: "Husbands, love your wives, even as Christ also loved the church, and gave himself for it." The point for husbands (following Tolstoy) was not even to lust after one's own wife because such men were "continually plagued by lustful feelings for other women." He offered words "for husbands to say daily: 'I have bound myself for life, I have made my choice. From now on my aim will be not to choose a woman who pleases me, but to please the woman I have chosen.' That is, daily to court her, to surround her with care and reassurance." As contraception became more widely available, and recreational—as opposed to procreational—sex more likely, Coffin the preacher remained skeptical of passion and stood foursquare for responsibility.

But if Coffin understood (at least in theory) how husbands ought to treat their wives, he also offered a critique of marriage at odds with the domestic ideology of his time, as well as his own wife's desires. Just as he criticized sexual desire for not looking high enough, he pointed out the shortsightedness of domestic romance. Because sex always tempted a husband and wife into the self-centeredness of "us two," he argued, "the best marriages are therefore between those who *can* get along without each other in the sense that they are not totally dependent on each other for security, for forgiveness, for the 'courage to be.' . . . only a great and common purpose can finally keep people together in life and death." His emphasis on the "great and common purpose" could become a way of avoiding the many small negotiations that constituted daily life in a marriage. As Eva complained, "Bill would say things to me like, 'you're only as big as what makes you angry.' And boy, does that make me feel small."

He took up the "problem of premarital sex" in early 1964, less than a year after the blow-up with Eva over Byers.[10] He hoped to avoid, he joked, "both the pious bilge that flows from so many reverends and the juiceless jargon that doesn't flow at all from the so-called sexologists." Since everything in the natural world, including sex, was part of God's creation, he held conventionally, to consider sex "evil would be blasphemous." Here, Coffin joined the mainstream of liberal—and liberal religious—thinking on matters sexual. The National Council of Churches had endorsed "mutually acceptable" methods of birth control in marriage, and commentators everywhere touted the "naturalness" of sexual expression. On the other hand—and here Coffin argued against the tide—people ran the risk of undervaluing sex by simply calling it "natural." Only if we then say "Yes, and isn't nature fabulous," he maintained, could humans avoid losing a "sacramental view of creation."

The sacramental view of the world was continually threatened by "our bureaucratic age," by the "mechanical, impersonal mediocre lives" lived by so many, who sought a purely physical "escape through sexual release." Coffin described the psychic ordeal of a participant in the Suzie affair who had escaped punishment at the time and "had felt no shame," but now, years later, wanted to turn himself in. "Suzie" had sent him a Christmas card, and the boy's defenses had crumbled. He had finally understood that "people are to be loved and things are to be used," contrary to "our gadget minded, consumer oriented society," which "is encouraging us to love things and use people." Here, too, Coffin joined the mainstream liberal critique of the consumer society of the 1960s.

Finally, Coffin popped the question: if "two people are deeply involved with and committed to one another, to all intents and purposes are engaged to be married: if proper precautions are taken is premarital sexual intercourse wrong?" "The Bible," of course, "finds a lot of other things worse." The real question was not "whether the love of two such persons is genuinely mature enough to be consummated; rather the question here is whether or not their love is socially responsible," whether lovers collapsed into an "egoism à deux," in which they forgot "relations with parents, friends, society in general." Here, Coffin echoed his Puritan forebears who, despite their reputation for sexual repression, thoroughly approved of an active and pleasurable conjugal life— as long as it did not interfere with the worship and glory of God. "So what have we come up with?" he asked, infuriating parents and conservatives with his reply: "Certainly no rules. Rules at best are signposts, never hitching posts. . . . And if we exalt freedom as Christians we must remember that freedom is grounded in love. . . . Though setting no outer rules, love exacts much from within. . . . So let others say, 'Anything goes.' The Christian asks, 'What does love require?'"

The discipline of sexual morality, in other words, lay in the theological realm of love's discipline, a discipline that could also demand sacrifice. "The life of love," he argued, "is a life of tension," whose "symbol is the cross. Release from tension for release's sake has therefore always been un-Christian as it has always been bad psychology. Sexual chastity then," he announced, doubtless disappointing many of his listeners, "may be a legitimate cross of unmarried youth."

Coffin had queried a Catholic priest about how he could bear "his cross of chastity." The priest pointed to the words on a crucifixion painting—"and greater pains than thine has He endured"—and said, simply, "That inscription helps." "And so I pass it on to those of you who are trying to . . . live your unmarried lives as Christians."

For Coffin only Christianity gave meaning to sex *or* chastity, a point of view that frustrated young people who wanted to know what to do. Instead, Coffin offered advice about how to think about what to do. He sent copies of these sermons to correspondents and preached a similar message from a variety of pulpits. He also began suggesting that "preceremonial" sex (between the announced engagement and the wedding) "is something we shouldn't be too concerned about." A minister making such an argument accounted for the statement being picked up by the press.[11]

In the eyes of some parents and students, this was dangerous advice. A woman in her seventies, a United Church of Christ minister, still nursed a thirty-year-old grudge in 1993 as she recalled Coffin's presentation on the "new sexual morality" at Pembroke during the fall of 1964 when her daughter was a student. According to her daughter's report, Coffin suggested to his audience that they would be better off on their wedding nights if they had slept with their boyfriends well in advance. Fourteen Pembroke students became pregnant that pre–*Roe* v. *Wade* year, the woman remembered, including her own daughter, who announced her pregnancy in a postcard citing Coffin's advice.[12]

In a March 1964 sermon in Battell, Coffin appeared to be dealing, at times very directly, with his own marriage difficulties.[13] The text, the famous passage in which Jesus confronted the woman at the well, lent itself to such meditations, which some preachers in his situation—but not Coffin—might have shied away from. The key to the biblical passage, Coffin argued, was the simultaneous wisdom and compassion in Jesus' observation and injunction: "Neither do I condemn you; go, and sin no more." He repeated this line six times to make the point that Jesus "never confuses the virtue of compassion for the sinner" ("Neither do I condemn you") "with the vice of condoning the sin" ("go, and sin no more"). Jesus knew what sin was, and forgave it.

Coffin agreed with an observer who claimed that "the craving for married life and the craving for sexual satisfaction outside of marriage have the same roots"—feelings of inadequacy and unmet need not solved by "mutual attraction and a wedding." In his own home Coffin had heard a good deal about inadequacy and unmet need, even if he had not understood it. The line he quoted so approvingly could have been aimed directly at Eva, who had made it plain that her needs were not being met in marriage and had begun to satisfy them elsewhere. Coffin likely suspected something about Eva's affairs.

He did not, however, understand her distress: "Marriage is hard, as those of us who are married know—particularly those who marry preacher types because everyone has a pastor except the pastor's wife!" Still stung that his wife could have taken up with his assistant, he implied—mistakenly—that Eva's need for a talking partner was in fact her need for a pastor. But marriage was difficult for preachers' wives (or, for that matter, the spouses of doctors, social workers, or therapists) for a different reason: because their husbands gave most of their attention and caring at the office, and had little left for their families.

"Marriage is hard," Coffin declared from the pulpit, "because we want from each other more than we need, and because what we need more than anything else is to have our sense of need submerged." This quasi-aphorism may have expressed his own feelings, but as an analysis of marriage it paled next to his understanding of the Bible. Eva wanted more from him than he felt she ought to have needed.

Three decades later, she agreed with him. "I was asking him to do things that he wasn't set up to do!" Coffin must have wondered more than once why she could not "submerge" her sense of need. "Good marriages are therefore between those who *can* get along without each other," he repeated from his sermon a month earlier. And Coffin could get along without Eva, much better than she without him. Rather than confess his own inability to provide what Eva wanted, he put the onus back on her and her unreasonable need.

Invited by *Glamour* magazine to write a "Letter to College Women" on the subject of whether traditional moral values were outmoded, Coffin responded with an article he titled "Do You Undervalue Sex?" which repeated most of the key arguments he had made in his sermons, without the explicit Christianity.[14] "I suspect that our deepest trouble stems from our need to escape from worries about esteem and status," he wrote, as though he were describing Eva, "from feelings of failure and cowardice." Instead of love meaning "the gift of one's self," our "new interpretation" is that love "fills an unmet need."

He took a pastoral tone, sympathizing with the "great pressure" girls faced from boys, "who may be looking for their reassurance in sexual prowess as you may be looking for yours in being sexually attractive." He allowed that if sexual relations were genuinely "personal," they could help provide the "reassurance of plain, simple affection," needed by so many. On the other hand, "if sex is impersonal, if we are out to satisfy a desire rather than create a real relationship, then I think the answer [to whether it could provide this reassurance] is 'no.'"

Coffin refused "to offer any hard and fast rules" but pressed his readers to consider whether their love was "socially responsible" as well as romantically satisfying. That good marriages were based on independent people only "points up the importance of developing, while at college, before marriage, a true independence, the ability of giving of one's self. This aim is seldom furthered by sexual experimentation." While refusing to rule out premarital sex, Coffin gave his female readers plenty of permission to say no.

He received hundreds of letters and many requests for reprints. The residential staff at Mary Washington College thought "so highly of it" that the dean of students requested prices for bulk amounts. Most letter writers felt that the article gave them strength to remain virgins in the face of temptation and unrelenting pressure from boys. Sex was the principal topic among college students, they reported, and as virgins, they felt very much in the minority. Among the self-identified nonvirgins who wrote, many felt degraded, even fallen because they had slept with a boy. The writers, who included mothers and older women, nearly all referred to the great majority of boys in identical ways: they wanted all they could get; they would drop you after getting it; they were unfaithful.[15]

Coffin's replies to the often troubled young women could show compassion and sensitivity, but sometimes displayed his lack of experience counseling girls and women and a tendency toward the flip. A twenty-two-year-old, writing earnestly—and a little self-righteously—on behalf of herself and her roommates, wondered why there weren't articles "that might encourage the virgin that she is on the right road to a successful marriage and a good sex life" and asked Coffin to "talk to the young men of our generation." Coffin replied argumentatively—"I shall try to talk to them, but they will probably be more impressed by what you say"—and with odd sharpness: "However, I think there is only one basis on which a girl can talk, namely, that she admits to herself that she hides in her heart the desire she condemns in her dates." A first-year student at Smith College thanked Coffin, explaining that the article had given her the "moral stamina, courage and conviction to keep on 'fighting'" for a "meaningful relationship" rather than give in to sexual pressure from her dates. Coffin jokingly invited her to drop in, for "I cannot help thinking you must be unusually beautiful to be so hotly pursued."[16]

This occasional glibness pointed to the relative unimportance of sex in Coffin's own life. Coffin himself had not sought "sexual release" energetically while in the army and in fact kept his virginity until the night he arrived in Europe, where he was separated from his mother by an ocean and a war. While he had pursued female companionship and enjoyed the attentions of women, he appeared almost as happy to be with the family of his Georgia girlfriend (during basic training) as with her and with the sister and father of Manya as with the young actress herself.

His sexual opportunities far outdistanced his actions. A young, red-blooded male in a series of army camps, he did not patronize prostitutes, though he did negotiate prices for his fellow G.I.s in Paris. He wrote risqué letters to his mother. His sexual energy, in short, found release in playfulness, in the boisterous gaiety of Russian dancing, say, rather than in concentrated, intimate attention. Coffin's gift for human relationships lay not in one-on-one privacy, where sexual intimacy occurred, but rather with the group, in which he loved to be the spark and the life of the party.

Coffin was a sexual whirl, not a sexual partner, which confused and disappointed Eva and helps to explain why she felt he did not enjoy sex very much. Perhaps his "cursed upbringing" was really at work for much more of his life than he had thought. And perhaps, too, the fact that Coffin himself seemed less a slave to his desires than many other extremely masculine men of his time made it possible for him to be relatively detached on the subject, lacking in sustained jealousy, apparently indifferent to the fact that, as Eva remarked dramatically, of all Coffin's friends only George Bailey never made a pass at her.

A number of Coffin's acquaintances, as well as more distant observers, have addressed this confusing part of Coffin's nature by wondering whether he might be gay. Coffin has always had powerful feelings for his male friends and has probably felt more himself in their company than in the company of women. Like most men, when he has striven to prove himself in the world—as a musician, soldier, preacher, or athlete—he has measured himself against men more than women. But to argue, therefore, that Coffin was either hiding or sublimating same-gender sexual feelings goes far beyond any documentary, direct, or indirect evidence.

Coffin turned forty in the summer of 1964. While the civil rights movement focused on the voter registration effort that became "Freedom Summer," Coffin accepted an invitation from the State Department to undertake a speaking tour in India. He begged off several invitations to come South, pleading the long-standing commitment to Ambassador Chester Bowles and to Eva, who was accompanying him without the children in an effort, she explained, "officially, supposedly, to try and mend the rift in the marriage."[17]

Stopping in Greece on the way, Eva and Bill took a bus tour of classical sites and ended up at Delphi, home of the oracle but near the location of the ancient Olympics as well. Coffin recalled being urged by Eva to enter the town's daily race over the original two-hundred-meter course. She recalled him challenging two twenty-year-old traveling companions to the race: "He beat the hell out of them," of course, "and I remember making a crown out of some leaves and placing it on his head. Everybody thought it was adorable." Coffin wrote that "word spread" that a forty-year-old had won, and "that night I was a hero all over town." The experience, he wrote later, "helped me through the trauma of turning forty." Eva only marveled retrospectively, "He had to win! He had to win all the time."[18]

Winning the race proved far easier than relating to Eva, for his attentions lay elsewhere. On the way to India their plane stopped briefly in Teheran. While Eva slept, Coffin sneaked off the plane and scrawled a note he gave to a French officer to deliver to Manya Stromberg (by then widowed but still working in the French embassy and well-known to the French community), suggesting a rendezvous in Paris at the end of the summer. Unaware of this remarkable maneuver, Eva wondered all during the trip why her husband seemed even more distant than usual. They visited temples with erotic sculptures and she would go in while "he would sit on a wall and talk to the coconut gatherers or something." Instead of mending the rift, "there was almost nothing going on between us that whole time." When she finally read Coffin's account of this episode in his memoir, the summer finally made sense. "For a forty-year-old man," he had concluded accurately, "I might be fleet of foot but I was also very confused." He did see Manya in Paris. He had "carefully" planned to see her only with Bailey. At "the last moment, however," he went "an hour early, alone." Their reunion rekindled the distant torch Coffin had been carrying for nearly two decades.[19]

Coffin did not act further on this encounter, though it suggests the extent of his marital trouble. Marriage was hard, he knew from experience, and by the following March Coffin was warning his congregation against giving into "the anger that rises out of personal grievances." He revealed more than he meant to, trying to justify his own position within his family, as he pointed to the way a Christian only "'speaks the truth *in love,*' speaks if to speak is edifying, not if it is destructive. Every man doesn't have to know everything about himself, his wife, his children."[20] Eva Coffin wanted Bill to know her better and care about her more. As she understood much later, he simply "did not have it to give."

As Coffin traveled the country on behalf of civil rights and the nascent antiwar movement during 1965 and 1966, and reached for broader appeal and greater power in his preaching, he may have paid a large price. For his emphasis on a transcendent God far beyond the machinations of humans drew him farther away from understanding individual human beings. In his otherwise exceptional 1966 Easter sermon stressing "the cosmic victory of seemingly powerless love over loveless power," in which he coined a much-repeated saying—"Christian faith is not so much believing without proof as trusting without reservation" —Coffin provided an unintentional glimpse into his own, rather loveless, love life.[21] God's everlasting love "cannot of course be explained," he declared, "for love is personal and only the impersonal in this world is susceptible to explanation. When you stop to think of it the more personal anything is the more limited has to be our description of it."

This argument was at best odd, at worst silly. Coffin knew that for many people, describing the "personal" could be a virtually unlimited exercise. Bringing intelligent description to bear on human relationships made marriages and families work. Coffin's easy condescension to the "idolatry" of the family— students and parents fight over allowances and use of the car but not over "choosing an important rather than an attractive job"—simultaneously showed great insight into the big issues and little grasp of daily life.

His theological understanding, in other words, hurt his personal relationships. God was huge, transcendent, the source of all, the force with which humans ought to try to empathize, to which they ought to bend their necks: "*thy* will be done, thy Kingdom come," as he often put it. But there was something profoundly impersonal, if also majestic and "cosmic," about this vision. For if God was so big, and humans so small, why invest human relationships with the big emotions? Public life, engagement with God, beckoned even more strongly than marriage and family ever had. Coffin ended the sermon with an inadvertently bleak image of death and resurrection: that of a dying Antarctic explorer who left a note for his wife pinned to his tent. The note focused on their joint love of God rather than for each other.

Eva Coffin sank into depression: "I was miserable. I was suicidal." She was taking large doses of Librium "to get through a normal day, getting the kids to school and I would forget to pick the kids up at school, I would have total irresponsibility. . . . I was ready to be put away for a while, actually. Because I was really going nuts."

With little to boost her sense of self, she relied on the traditional standby of a beautiful woman: her sexuality. Eva recalled that she felt no compunctions at all about sleeping around: "So I don't know if I just had a banner around my head saying 'Come and get me,' or, probably, you know, one gives out vibes, and the vibe was, 'here I am.' . . . I wasn't going to dry up and die."

Her emotional and sex life became almost as tumultuous as her husband's public life. She fell "profoundly in love" with a nineteen-year-old freshman. They waited until he had finished his first year of college and then carried on an intense, three-and-a-half-year-long affair. He visited the house frequently and sometimes sat for the children; an actor, he pretended to be gay to allay suspicion. Coffin claimed not to have known about these goings-on. "Maybe, perhaps, I'll never know, I wanted him to catch me," she mused. Maybe "I wanted him to stop me, I wanted him to get upset about it. . . . I was practically doing it under his nose! I was literally screwing somebody in the laundry room while he was in the study writing his sermon!"

Still, Eva kept up her public role as the chaplain's wife. During the trial of the Boston Five in 1968 she appeared often in photographs with her husband and at the courthouse. In reality, however, as the trial wore on, Eva and Bill Coffin were contemplating the end of their marriage. While the jury was deliberating, they were trying to figure out how to factor in the possibility of Coffin going to prison and who would care for their children. As she had previously during Bill and Eva's courtship, Harriet Gibney, now divorced, entered Coffin's life. Bill had "got mixed up with Harriet again," in Eva's words, and "that sort of gave him somewhere to go" emotionally. By the end of the summer of 1968—"the worst summer spent by either of us," he described it later—they had agreed to split up.[22] "I think he was more eager for the whole thing at that point," she recalled. "And I was ready to go to a sanitarium. But I decided, maybe divorce would be healthier than getting locked up."

Eva's parents offered to help her financially, so at the end of the summer Eva Coffin moved into a tiny New York apartment "to try a new life" as a photographer. The children stayed with Bill. "It totally wiped me out," she explained, but "I could not take the children to New York." After all, "the fact that I was impassioned [about photography] didn't mean that there were going to be any results. . . . How was I going to go to school to learn?—I just couldn't figure it out." The children visited weekends.[23]

Life with Father

Even though he had had no marriage to speak of for years, Coffin appears to have been comforted by the mere fact that he was married and that Eva had responsibility for the children. He knew the Christian justification for divorce, and had counseled many couples with marital problems, but he could "hardly say the word." So if he had indeed wanted divorce as much or more than Eva, he had to confront his own desire and guilt. The combination proved daunting. No longer able to pretend, Coffin lost his way.

He went to see Kingman and Mary Louise Brewster in the fall to tell them of the divorce and to offer his resignation as chaplain. Brewster, to Coffin's great surprise, told him of his own parents' divorce, rejected his resignation, and offered him a room in his house. Coffin had begun his education about the realities of divorce.[24]

He dreaded the public and private failure, though many of his friends were, like Browne Barr, "surprised they stayed together as long as they did." As he wrote later, he was afraid of "failure itself" and worried that this particular failure would damage his authority from the pulpit, and his ability to speak out against the war. Coffin wangled a session with the psychoanalyst Erik Erikson (to whom Harriet had introduced him), who allayed his fears on this count with the example of Gandhi, "an extraordinary public figure but something less than an ideal husband," as well as with the reminder that "there were ideal husbands who were dreadful public figures." More to the point, his good friend Richard Sewall told him that if he had "suffered from anything, it is from an aura of too much success. A little failure in your personal life can only improve your ministry." Coffin knew that all men and women were sinners; accepting this truth about himself proved as difficult as accepting his much earlier insight about accepting the full meaning of "the Lord giveth." It was easier simply to feel guilty, because, as he wrote later and worked into an aphorism, "guilt is the last stronghold of pride."[25]

Coffin was also intimidated because even more than most public men, he was a domestic ignoramus. Eva recalled the time, in 1968, that *Life* magazine was doing a story on Bill at the house and she cut her finger by accident. When Coffin asked, "Where are the Band-Aids?" she let him have it, out loud, in front of the reporter and the photographer: "You've lived in this house for ten years and you're asking me where the Band-Aids are?"

Coffin's three children—aged ten, nine, and eight—needed attention, much more than they had been getting from Eva. Bill could neither cook nor clean. He knew nothing of paying the bills or shopping for groceries or dressing children or parent-teacher conferences or driving to music lessons. He did not even know the things he knew nothing about. So when a friend suggested he hire a housekeeper, he agreed quickly and hired Bertha Lynch, who (he wrote) "may have taken half my paycheck, but she saved my life." Lynch lived with the Coffins Monday through Friday, and did the cooking. ("Whenever my father had to cook," David Coffin remembered, "it was corned beef hash right out the can, ketchup.") At the same time there were some disturbing violent incidents around his house on Wall Street. Someone had hauled his children's bicycles over the fence and into the street and flattened them. Someone also had hung a dead cat in a nearby tree, possibly with a threatening note.[26]

One afternoon just after Eva had gone Coffin poured out his distress to Ron Evans, a divinity student and draft counselor he knew. The next day he invited Evans and his wife, Janet, to move into the house to "help look after the children and so forth": bills, meals, transportation, laundry, and general household maintenance. Reluctant at first and a little stunned ("why us?"), they nevertheless accepted.

Even with three live-ins, the household breathed chaos. On the one hand, it was "very exciting," Janet Evans recalled, "because that was where the action was and you felt as if you were absolutely at the center of the universe. Everything that was happening in 1968 was happening right there in that living room at that time and so you felt like you were absolutely making history. Literally by opening the front door." On the other hand, "there was simply never a moment of peace. . . . And to try and hold that household together in some semblance of order, and particularly on behalf of the children who had obviously been through a very difficult, stressful time . . . was a real trick."

The children, whom Coffin described as "hellions," had to deal with a guilty mother who had left them (as they understood it) to pursue a career in New York; a guilty father who lived in the public eye when he was at home, but who was also on the road constantly and who therefore attended few games, recitals, or teacher conferences; a series of adults who cared about them but who changed from time to time; large numbers of friends and strangers passing through the house; and their grandmother Catherine, who expected them to come to Sunday dinners at her house scrubbed, dressed, and ready to behave as though they were attending high tea.

The Evanses described it as a "circus," as "exhausting." Coffin had never been in more public demand, and the threat of prison still lay over his head. He felt tremendous pressure to raise money for his legal bills and to continue his role as spokesman for the antiwar movement. Beyond feeling called to the public role, Coffin also loved it and chose to continue it, knowing that he was missing recitals and school programs. "And then," according to Ron Evans, "the children would act out." David evidently had a learning disability and a good bit of anger toward his mother that surfaced in difficult ways. As a team, Amy and Alex terrorized baby-sitters and frequently escaped the house in search of nocturnal excitement, becoming well-known to the campus police for their pranks. David remembered getting caught trying to steal "a teeny pack of gum" from the pharmacy where his father bought pipe tobacco: "I think I probably had a sign that said, 'Catch me, please.'" Bill Coffin was stuck in a serious dilemma, one that could have been resolved only by giving up on one or the other of his roles entirely. Since he did not consider this an option, he instead shuttled back and forth between them, spending more time in public and feeling guilty about his children.

Though most observers agree that Coffin began to take his role as a father much more seriously during this period, he still remained fundamentally clueless about domestic life. Ron Evans remembered the large Bertha Lynch confronting Coffin on the subject of the children's shoes as he came out of the shower one morning. "Mr. Coffin, which of these shoes are we going to have to disappear?" "Bertha, I don't have time for that." She blocked the doorway; "Mr. Coffin, which of these shoes?" Janet Evans recalled with amazement that "he would schedule a meeting for Halloween night!"

"I was keenly conscious of the fact that I was not an adequate father," Coffin recalled. He knew things were not exactly in control. "I thought I was just awful. . . . I just had too much to do . . . and I just sort of felt I'm not on top of this thing, you know. And I didn't see how I could just drop the peace movement at that point and chaplaincy at Yale."

When he was around, however, he communicated his infectious physical energy to the household and to the children—more than he realized. He played soccer and football with the boys, competitive board games with the whole family, and sang and played the piano. "There was always music in the house," according to David. Bill paid attention to Amy's piano lessons. "I remember getting to the point where we could actually sit down and do four hand" piano, Amy Coffin recalled. "Which was fun." The children occasionally dropped by his office, and sometimes Coffin took a walk with them on the Old Campus, the freshman quadrangle outside his office. Coffin communicated physically and through his energy and verve and voice. David Coffin fell in love with church music, the organ and the choir, and eventually became a professional musician. There were times that he felt "the most fathered when I went to church. I didn't listen to a word he said during the sermons . . . it was the sound of his voice I was concentrating on."

Bill and Harriet

Already involved with Harriet Gibney when Eva left, and feeling almost unbearable pressure, Coffin sought a quick replacement for his first wife and looked neither far nor wide. Rationally, Harriet seemed a good choice. He had, he said later, "a genuine attraction to Harriet, largely based on what I perceived to be strong psychological insights; [she] was good company, we never lacked things to talk about." An editor at Children's Hospital in Boston, Harriet had expertise in the one area Coffin most needed it—children. As Janet Evans put it, "She had a piece of understanding that was very important to Bill at that point." Coffin agreed: he "was impressed by her psychological perceptions," and "the kids really needed attention. Needed a mother."[27]

Much more psychologically sophisticated than Bill, Harriet had strong intuitions about him, a public man who was uncomfortable probing his interpersonal relationships. She nevertheless found herself charmed and attracted to the outsized figure that Coffin cut at the time: "I recognized . . . someone here who was very effective, very talented and very playful, but was avoiding altogether intimacy, in what I called the microcosm. . . . I told Bill that I had everything I wanted in Cambridge. I had kids, a lovely house . . . the only thing that I was missing in my life was a close, intimate relationship. But I wasn't sure that he was interested in that sort of thing." Which was fine for him, she thought, but not for her. "And then he said that he just didn't know much about the microcosm, and so forth, that he'd like to learn if I'd just teach him. You can hear him talking, almost, in his persuasive way."

Harriet had two children from her previous marriage (Margot was named for Coffin's sister, while the boy, Alex, was known as Tiger). She got on very well with the Coffin children during a Christmas skiing trip, and at the end of the trip ten-year-old Amy asked her father, "'When are you going to marry Harriet?' And that just, pow! That decided it in my mind," he remembered, adding with the clear vision of hindsight, "Very irresponsible, on my part." Coffin asked Harriet to marry him, and she agreed.

However little Bill Coffin appeared to need intimacy, he was nonetheless lonely—and had been so for some time. As he confided to his friends Robert and Sydney Brown during the summer of 1968, "When I go home, it's cold and empty." As his old friend Bailey put it, "The fact of the matter is that William has to have a woman. That's all there is to it. He can't live without one." Coffin hoped that if he married Harriet, the chaos of the year after Eva's departure could be stilled, and he could bring more warmth and stability to his home life.[28]

Harriet also went against what she later thought of as her better judgment.

She figured she would need Bill around more in the first year as they tried to put the two families together, and she wanted an agreement from him that if something went wrong, they would "seek joint help." She "thought it would be fun to be married to Bill, provided this area got cleaned up. Well, of course none of that—I should have known. Well, no, it was a very high-risk thing. And I knew it was a very high-risk thing."

Coffin's kids liked the idea a lot. "I remember my dad picking me up from school," Amy remembered, "and said, 'I've got a surprise for you!' And I knew right away for some reason. 'You and Harriet are gonna get married!' 'Yes!' 'That's great! Let's go tell Alex!'" They were married in September 1969 on Marsh Island, the Muscongus Bay (Maine) island that Harriet owned with a friend. Sidney Lovett and Robert McAfee Brown performed the ceremony, as more than a hundred friends and family members gathered to celebrate the occasion.

At first it seemed to work. "I still think," Coffin argued, "initially in many ways, she brought some real order and stability to the family." Harriet quickly saw that they would need a larger house, and Yale provided one, on Trumbull Street. "My three kids got along famously with her two," Coffin remembered. Accustomed to working, Harriet nevertheless decided "not to work the first year because I would be needed too much to sort of try to pull the family together." The first year or two they seemed to get along. "They both liked to have fun," according to Harriet's daughter, Margot Gibney; they shared an "adventuresome spirit" and communicated that spirit to the children. "We'd be playing around, rough housing," she recalled of her stepfather. "He really does have a love for life in that way. . . . And we would do outings and that was a lot of fun."

Problems soon began to surface, however. Bill Coffin continued to rely completely on Harriet to manage the household and the family. He did not cut down his schedule and did not fully realize that, having been a professional woman before marrying him, Harriet would approach married life very differently from Eva, who had been much younger and more naive when she married Bill. Harriet felt the combined burdens of a complex domestic life, an uprooting from her home of many years, and a nationally famous husband who was both adored and reviled. She soon wanted to work, she hoped within Yale, but was not welcomed with open arms.

When Harriet Coffin came to New Haven, moreover, Yale was in the early stages of another large transition. In the spring of 1969 Yale University had broken with 168 years of tradition and admitted five hundred women to its freshman, sophomore, and junior classes. The women arrived that fall. It would be hard to overstate the tensions associated with this change, coming at the beginning of the 1960s revival of American feminism. At all of its levels—from bathrooms to the boardrooms—the university's culture announced its masculinity, often in terms quite antagonistic to women. In that culture professors and poets and deans and athletes and artists and musicians were men, while women were secretaries and librarians, kitchen workers and nurses, and graduate students (occasionally), junior faculty (in rare cases), and senior faculty (almost never). They were, above all, wives, girlfriends, and "dates." Nearly all women at Yale experienced this culture, to varying degrees, as condescending, cold, indifferent, or downright hostile.

Temperamentally disinclined toward passivity, Harriet Coffin struggled against this masculine culture, and its representative in her own family, in ways that endeared her to few of her husband's friends and colleagues. Bill Coffin was accustomed to being the center of attention. "I think she was resentful of that," said Janet Evans. "He was always the one everybody wanted to see. Who wanted to see Harriet?" As Harriet reflected much later, "I think to live with Bill, or when I was living with Bill anyway, you have to be pretty much of a caretaker and stay very heavily in the background." She had not signed up to be a caretaker but had missed the signals that would have alerted her to the danger.

Harriet could not find a way out of her dilemma. Bill was not much help to her as she looked for work. She wanted to teach writing and eventually landed a course taught through a residential college. She became a sounding board for some of the undergraduate women who were having a difficult time dealing with Yale. She competed with her husband conversationally at social gatherings and did not win points for it. It is a measure of the sexism of the culture that Coffin's social competitiveness was simply taken for granted by those who knew him; they saw it as natural and integral to his personality, even when they did not like it. Harriet, as the new person in the equation, received little understanding from the principals in her new environment. As one put it, Harriet wanted "to be on a platform with him—a podium of equal height with his. And Bill just doesn't function that way." According to John Maguire, "Harriet fancied herself a journalist and she wanted to match Bill. If he had a comment on the passing parade, she wanted to be right there with her comment and to be recognized by everybody. Not only is everything I said valid, it's as substantial as what Bill said." Maguire unintentionally showed what Harriet was up against.[29]

She occasionally rebelled against her role as domestic major domo as well. "I kept trying to think of ways to get out of being the witch and also being the manager," she recalled. "I didn't want to sort of run things." So, she suggested that he—or his secretary—handle the bills one month. Bill agreed, but did nothing else, and the electricity was turned off before he paid the bill. Or there was the Monday morning (the housekeeper's day off) that five rabbis showed up at the door, explaining that they had been invited to breakfast. Harriet brought them in, told Bill ("Oh! I forgot all about it!"), and went back to bed. "Then people would say, for instance, that I wasn't willing to take care of the rabbis." She fought what she referred to as "the tyranny of the spontaneous," but she did so intermittently, and since Bill Coffin was not going to change, she was caught in a no-win situation.

Whether it was the strain of her life as wife of the Yale chaplain, or the added pressure of finally having a course to teach in Yale's high-pressure environment, or a physical tendency, Harriet began to drink—and to be noticed for it. Bill Coffin, of course, had been a well-known vodka drinker since his days in the army, and Yale was a hard-liquor-drinking culture, especially among faculty. He was known to be able to "hold his liquor" like few others. Harriet was not similarly blessed.

The combination of factors ate away at the marriage. Harriet wanted them to be partners in the public world as well as Yale's. They wrote side-by-side articles for *Vogue* in 1971 titled "Your New Self-Image," for which Bill recycled a sermon on Adam and Eve in which he criticized the need for male and female sex roles. Harriet's piece resembled many articles during the early seventies about the need for men and women to give up on destructive and rigid sex roles in family and work. The magazine pictures told a different story about their relationship. In one a needier, dependent Harriet rested her head on her husband's shoulder; in another she clasped her arms around his neck from behind.[30] Much later, Harriet reflected that she had "underestimated how much I needed to be dependent. . . . I was not as strong as I thought I could be."

Coffin disliked Harriet's competitiveness and did not enjoy collaborating with her, but he could not confront her: "She wanted to go on the road, and we would talk together. That's what she wanted, and I did it once. A male and female something. I really should have put my foot down. I'm such a coward. . . . And it was just a big mistake. And I should have known it. I mean I did know it, but I didn't have the courage to say, 'This is crazy. We're not going to do it.'"

"I did not like being around Bill and Harriet," Maguire admitted. "When you drink a lot, by the end of the evening you become lugubrious or sexy or something. In their case . . . it just got vicious, verbally." By the summer of 1971 it was obvious to a recent college graduate who was living in the house and working as Harriet's assistant that "she didn't hold her liquor terribly well and I think she drank a little too much than was good for her." The Evanses agreed. She occasionally spent nights at a friend's house, whom she expected to provide her with a bottle of bourbon. The same friend said, "She was vicious. Particularly when she had a few drinks."[31]

As the marriage deteriorated her temper showed more and more. "Sometimes I'd blow my stack," she remembered. "I did throw a clock out of a window once, I got so mad. . . . I was not very pleased with myself for some of the behavior." Unappreciated by Bill's friends, she would sometimes just not come when the two of them were invited, or leave early. She occasionally made him late for events, changing her clothes at the last minute, forgetting her keys, undecided about whether to come. "I saw her provoke him to the point, where if I had been he," recalled Rabbi Arnold Wolf, Yale's Jewish chaplain in the early 1970s, "it would have been the end of the marriage."[32] What Coffin remembered of that time was "that tightening of the stomach as the plane came down in New Haven."

The problem for Coffin was that when Harriet drank she wanted even more to talk with him, in the way she knew how to be intimate. These matters intensified when Bill took a sabbatical year starting in the fall of 1973. He and Harriet moved to Marin County, California, and he began writing his memoir. Harriet not only had encouraged him to write it, she had a separate contract with the publisher, Atheneum, to edit the book. On the one hand, he found himself greatly moved by writing about his distant past and seems to have enjoyed exploring a number of "human potential movement" approaches to understanding the self. On the other hand, he resented how much access Harriet was getting to his new interior life. Harriet continued to drink, according to Coffin, and demanded what she was missing from her marriage. "She just couldn't stop, she just couldn't call it off," he recalled. "She'd just follow me around, all around the house—there was no getting away. Out in California I spent I don't know how many nights in how many different motels on Route 101 just because there was no way I could stay in the house."

At the end of the school year the Coffins spent the summer on Marsh Island, where under Harriet's direction they hauled driftwood and lumber and built cabins. There, too, she sometimes pursued him, trying to get him to talk. "You see," she explained, "two things were happening at once around this book. One is, I was trying to get him to make it three-dimensional. So I was after his vulnerable spot. Poking around. Then personally, I was trying to get toward that intimacy that he said he would work on." Coffin could not confront her to stop these conversations. "He never griped!" Harriet said in amazement. He saved his conscious anger for larger issues and as a result could not express anger in more intimate settings.

Instead, he said, "I'd go off, I'd take a sleeping bag and try and find a place in the woods and she'd get a flashlight and come out" looking for him. Finally, when Harriet found him in the middle of one night, Coffin snapped. Unable to respond verbally, and feeling himself at the end of his emotional rope, he reacted primitively, physically. "I used to be a big judo guy," he explained twenty years later. "In the army I taught judo. So I know that the easiest way to take somebody out is to hit them very nicely right across here [indicating the center of the forehead, just above the bridge of the nose]—a nice sharp blow like that." He referred to this as "a gentle way of taking them out." "I felt absolutely miserable," he remembered. "Then I carried her back and put her in bed and went out in the woods. . . . And she felt very penitent about it all" in the morning. But Bill Coffin had crossed a dangerous line.

Back at Yale that fall Harriet gave him very astute criticism on his manuscript. She pushed him to make certain emotional themes more explicit, particularly the conflict in his life between the WASP expectations of the Coffin side of the family, symbolized, she thought, by Uncle Henry, and the more emotionally expressive side symbolized by Russian and Manya and Chingis Guirey. Harriet easily got inside her husband's emotions. The problem for her was that he did not want inside hers.[33]

Late one night in November 1974, they clashed again: "I said 'Bill, I am scared tonight. Please talk to me.' 'I will not talk to you.' 'Just sit and listen.' But I was hitting right at his most vulnerable spot. I said I wanted to talk, and I wanted to talk about how I felt, and so forth and so on. And I pestered him. 'Please, please talk to me. Please, please talk to me.' And he went in the other room. And I came in and woke him up again and I said, 'Please, talk to me.' . . . I was pretty persistent. I mean, I can't say that I wasn't provoking."

They had been scheduled to see a counselor the following day, Harriet remembered, "And he refused. And that's when he clobbered me."

He remembers that it was about three in the morning, that she was drunk, and that "she broke a door down to a room where I was trying to sleep. . . . So I said, 'What the hell, I've got to do this again.' Only this time it was dark, and I guess I didn't take quite enough aim." He understated. He took her to the hospital in the morning. His one judo chop had given her "a huge black eye," she remembered. "My whole face was swollen." He had also given her a hairline skull fracture.

Coffin told his friend Arnold Wolf; he told Ron Evans; he told others. Wolf, who could not stand Harriet, said, "We all wanted to hit her. My then wife wanted to hit her." But when he and Coffin talked, he said, "Coffin, you can't hit anybody but you certainly can't hit your wife. You've got to get out of the marriage if that's the way you feel. Divorce yes. Abuse no." But Coffin did not fully understand the gravity of the situation. He did not think Harriet needed to go to the hospital. "I didn't hit her very hard," Wolf remembered him saying in his own defense.[34] To Ron Evans, he was "so terribly remorseful that he had allowed this . . . to get to a point where he'd struck out."

It was a measure of the loyalty Bill Coffin inspired in his friends—and Harriet's isolation—that some were willing to give him the benefit of the doubt. For Miriam Horowitz, the question was simple: "When I said, 'How did this happen?' She said, 'I asked for it.'"[35] When Janet Evans heard about it, her first reaction was, "If Bill had hit Harriet I'm sure he had good reason." She had seen Harriet "in some situations where . . . if somebody has had a lot to drink and they're being impossible and difficult you just say tchew, you know, out of here! So that's my fantasy." But the complicity of friends could not hide the fact that Bill and Harriet Coffin were in deep trouble.

ELEVEN

Activist Episodes

The rhythms of the church and academic calendar continued to give basic structure to William Sloane Coffin Jr.'s life during the late 1960s and early 1970s. He preached most Sundays during the school year, gave baccalaureate and commencement prayers, counseled students on personal and draft-related issues, performed weddings and funerals for members of the Yale community, wrote recommendations for students, played tennis and squash—extremely competitively—and took Augusts off to spend with his new family on Marsh Island, Maine. He traveled a great deal, driving all over New England after church on Sundays as well as during the week, and flying to the Midwest, California, and the South. He collected honoraria to supplement his salary, for his legal bills, and to help support his larger family once Harriet moved to New Haven with her children.

Because of Coffin's consistently compelling preaching, his famous legal confrontation with the government, his ease in the limelight, and his ability to speak to and for young people, the cultural and political tumult of these years continued to catapult him into the national spotlight with some frequency. As big events, like antiwar demonstrations, rumbled into being, or national political developments took a new turn, or controversy erupted at Yale, Coffin got invited to speak, to comment, to sign statements, to give invocations, to march, to serve as a figurehead, to act as master of ceremonies. His life took on an even more episodic quality during this time, as he was called into brief periods of intense public action and then subsided into the routine chaos of everyday life.

National antiwar activity reached a crescendo in the fall of 1969, with the nationwide, locally based "Moratorium" on October 15 and the Washington "Mobilization" on November 15. Though candidate Richard Nixon had promised to bring the war to an end and to withdraw American troops in the name of "Vietnamization," under President Nixon the draft continued to call young Americans in large numbers. From January through September of 1969, the army inducted an average of more than twenty-eight thousand draftees per month, roughly ten thousand per month *more* than every month since June 1968. While the war continued, covered by the media, and the Paris peace negotiations dragged on interminably and, to most eyes, irrelevantly, millions of frustrated Americans, including more mainstream groups than ever before, participated in Moratorium marches, teach-ins, and rallies. In New Haven Kingman Brewster gave his first antiwar speech, joined by Democratic Mayor Richard Lee, to a crowd of fifteen thousand. One hundred thousand gathered on the Boston Common. New York City Mayor John Lindsay declared a day of mourning and ordered flags flown at half-staff.[1]

Richard Nixon counterattacked on November 3, with his famous "silent majority" speech: "North Vietnam cannot defeat or humiliate the United States," he declared. "Only Americans can do that." Speaking at a Jewish temple in Providence, Rhode Island, the next day, Coffin argued that Nixon had "polarized the nation very badly," increasing the likelihood of violence between Americans. Unintentionally, Nixon forced what months of negotiations had been unable to do: he got the different factions of the antiwar movement to cooperate temporarily on the November 15 Mobilization, which became (at the time) the largest Washington gathering in American history.[2]

The evening before the Mobilization, he helped lead the March Against Death, in which forty-five thousand protesters walked in a solemn funeral cortège four miles long, from near the Arlington National Cemetery across the Arlington Memorial Bridge, down Pennsylvania Avenue past the White House, and then on to the Capitol. Carrying a lighted candle and placard with the name of an American killed in Vietnam, each marcher spoke aloud the name of a dead soldier and filed toward the Capitol, where open caskets received the placards. Later that evening Coffin took part in a CALCAV-sponsored service at the National Cathedral; one condition of the group getting permission to use the cathedral was that neither Daniel Berrigan nor Coffin could preach.

With Benjamin Spock, Coffin co-chaired the enormous Mobilization and emceed the rally but did not find it a happy experience. The two politicians, Senators George McGovern and Charles Goodell, were booed by too many in the crowd. Even Coretta Scott King could not command "undivided attention." Protesters seemed more interested in the music (which some likened to an inspirational antiwar Woodstock), which was deafening from the stage; worse, for Coffin, he had to introduce musicians and speakers he knew nothing about. "I didn't know who the hell Richie Havens was," recalled this child of the forties. Finally what brought Coffin's spirits low was the fact, obvious from the stage as Weathermen threatened to rush the platform, that the peace movement could not stay nonviolent, that some marchers relished a violent confrontation with the authorities.[3]

In these years Coffin preached and spoke increasingly about the question of violence. Clearly concerned to avoid the routine denunciation of black militants and the New Left for their threatening rhetoric, confrontational styles, and occasional violence, Coffin sought a different language with which to embrace the passion for change, and offer it guidance at the same time. As always, he went to the Bible, and on opening Sunday in September 1968 he preached a biblical version of Bob Dylan's "The Times They Are A-Changin'": "And it is deadly to try to put the freeze on history, whether one's own personal history or the history of institutions, nations, and the world." After all, "in remembering Christ we are remembering the most uprooting revolutionary force in all human history." Here, Coffin parted company (as he always had) with a pacifist position. Since the presidential candidates and university presidents seemed to think that "all violent change is automatically deadly," he wondered how they would justify the American Revolution and the current American violence in Vietnam. For "personally, I think it is dangerous to condemn violence unless one condemns indifference more harshly."[4]

By the spring of 1969 he had begun using a new formula, distinguishing between insurrection—in which one hates evil—and resurrection—"only because you so love the good." "Without love violence will change the world; it will change it into a more violent one," he preached in June. Or, put a little differently, "When men merely hate evil and do not love the good, they simply become damn good haters." He had found a way to combine militancy with nonviolence: "Insurrection says we must become twice as militant. To which resurrection says yes, and twice as nonviolent. In short, the order for the day reads twice as tough and twice as tender." Coffin dealt with his own despair, and tried to help the despair of others, by returning to the key Christian message of death and resurrection. "Let us be honest enough to recognize," he told numerous audiences, "that it is a Good Friday world, that we live under skies eclipsed by evil." But the promise of resurrection could give us the ability "to live in a wintry world like the first swallows of a new summer."[5]

Influenced by Harriet, Coffin had begun thinking more psychologically. He might also have been affected by the arrival of women undergraduates at Yale in the fall of 1969. For the first time, Coffin began questioning the kind of manliness enshrined in American mythology, the kind he himself embodied. Referring to former Secretary of State Dean Rusk's famous line about the Cuban missile crisis—"We were eyeball to eyeball and the other fellow blinked"—

Coffin argued that if "High Noon encounters with nuclear weapons represent manliness, then we simply have to reinvent manhood." Then he made a powerful connection between nonviolence and masculinity. "And this I think is what nonviolence is really all about—a new kind or perhaps a New Testament kind, of manhood, patterned after the person of Jesus." Even though he had "only begun to think about this," he was ready to draw some important conclusions: "We should avoid words or acts which inhibit the awakening of a decent response and only confirm us in our self-righteousness and self-pity." As a result, "Such words as 'pig,' 'nigger,' 'honky' are not helpful." Like King, and Gandhi before him, Coffin felt he had to explain that "nonviolence has nothing to do with passivity; it has everything to do with resistance." He could hardly have guessed that soon, his careful formulations about violence and nonviolence, law and morality, inflammatory words and a new form of manhood, would be tested as Yale University became the target of black militants and student radicals.[6]

May Day 1970

For many thousands of Yale students, faculty, and staff, as well as New Haven residents, "May Day" became the accepted shorthand for the unprecedented series of pronouncements, fantasies, demands, meetings, marches, negotiations, speeches, rallies, confrontations, secret plans, and terrifying rumors that surrounded the beginning of a New Haven murder trial in April 1970. May Day was a watershed for Yale: the institution and the community. It confirmed Kingman Brewster's reputation as the most skillful, and possibly the most visionary, university president in the country. While Coffin's knowledge of the students and his intuitions about dealing with crowds helped Brewster enormously, the episode damaged Coffin's reputation outside the university, as a liberal too willing to give in to militant blacks.[7]

It began, oddly enough, with a speech at Battell Chapel by Bobby Seale, national chairman of the Black Panther Party, on May 19, 1969. The Black Panther Party, the 1966 creation of Oakland-based militants Seale and Huey Newton, became the best-known—and most notorious—late-1960s black militant group. Combining street smarts and paramilitary chic, "revolutionary" Marxist-Leninist and black separatist rhetoric, the Panthers preached and practiced armed self-defense for African Americans, and paid heavily when local police and the FBI reacted with campaigns to wipe them out. The Panthers' willingness to fight back (with guns) against police harassment, the literary or oratorical skill of some spokesmen (Seale, Newton, Eldridge Cleaver), and their consequent ability to portray themselves as victims of a racist establishment simultaneously made them romantic heroes to a portion of the Left and objects of fear and hatred for most Americans, including many black civil rights activists. The official counterattack was largely successful. By the end of 1969, the Panthers claimed that police had killed twenty-eight of their members; Newton was in jail; and the Panthers' infighting had become legendary (and occasionally deadly).

After Seale's speech that night in Battell, he apparently went to New Haven Black Panther Party headquarters, where, according to police, members were "trying" and torturing an accused informer, Alex Rackley, before shooting him to death and dumping his body in a river late the next night. In the next week police arrested eight Panthers; during the summer they arrested four more who had fled; and finally, in August in California, police arrested Bobby Seale, implicated by a Panther turned prosecution witness.

Seale's legal troubles were complicated because at that point he was about to stand trial in Chicago on conspiracy charges connected to protests at the 1968 Democratic National Convention. When Judge Julius Hoffman severed Seale's case from that of the others, the Chicago Eight became the Chicago Seven, Seale returned to San Francisco, and the following March Governor Ronald Reagan ordered his extradition to Connecticut. Seale's arrival in New Haven focused national radical attention on the upcoming trial, and on Yale.

In late March and early April 1970, a combination of groups in shifting interactions with each other—the small New Haven chapter of the Panthers, the New Haven Panther Defense Committee, the Black Students Alliance at Yale, as well as individual Yale faculty members—pressed the university, and Yale students in particular, to take a variety of stands and positions in support of the Panther defendants in general, and Bobby Seale in particular. These ranged from a call for a moratorium on classes, to a demand that the Yale Corporation immediately contribute $500,000 to the Panther Defense Fund, to a call for Yale to establish a $5 million revolving loan fund for low-income housing in New Haven.

On April 14, the trial judge gave unusually serious, six-month contempt sentences to two Panthers observing the trial who got into a scuffle with a court officer. Yale students called a meeting for the next night, at which several hundred students voted overwhelmingly in favor of a class moratorium in support of the Panthers. On April 15 Chicago Seven defendant Abbie Hoffman announced that on May 1 radicals would convene in New Haven to "burn Yale," and Kingman Brewster's ears perked up. He began planning, making contact with local law enforcement officials and putting together his own committee of trusted advisors, headed by his special assistant Henry Chauncey Jr., known universally as Sam.

For his part, Coffin was struggling for the right attitude toward the Panther trial; his sermon of April 19 acknowledged his own "sharply divided" feelings.[8] The sermon was Coffin's complex, carefully balanced attempt to chart a moral course through the thicket of conflicting opinions and emotions. He started where the Panthers themselves never did, with the prisoners and their families as human beings in need of comfort, encouraging listeners to write to the prisoners and raise money for their families. Coffin criticized the "oppressive" rather than "impressive" rationality of the Panther slogan "Off the Pigs"— "Enough of all these efforts to enhance one segment of our population by scape-goating another!"

Then, as he moved to the heart of his argument, he quoted one of the jurors in his own trial, who had "found us legally wrong but morally right." Like the juror, Coffin proclaimed, "I am prepared as an anguished citizen to confess my conviction that it might be legally right but morally wrong for this trial to go forward." Despite the qualifying "might," he went on to make the general case—in religious and political terms—that nothing could be gained by continuing the trial. After all, while the defendants may be proved guilty, "in the eyes of God all of us conspired to bring on this tragedy—law enforcement agencies by their illegal acts against the Panthers, and the rest of us by our immoral silence in the face of these acts."

Coffin took Christian morality to the edge, asking whether Jesus' "verdict to these defendants, and to us their co-defendants," might not be "neither do I condemn you. Go and sin no more." Since he knew nothing would stop the trial, and violent opposition would only cause Seale's jailers to "bolt the door more firmly," he proposed a nonviolent march from Battell Chapel to the courthouse on May Day, where marchers could engage in civil disobedience and submit to prearranged arrest. Finally, Coffin warned that the "days ahead will be rough," that "it will be difficult not to oppose evil with evil, not to fight hatred with hatred, but we must refuse to do so." Pointedly, Coffin concluded not with "power to the people," a slogan he despised, but with "all power to Almighty God."

As far as the media, students, and the public were concerned, the sermon made news for one reason: a Yale dignitary had said that the trial should be stopped, that it was "legally right but morally wrong." The *New York Times* editorialized a few days later (under the headline "Murdering Justice") that Coffin had "stood moral principles on their head" and was "doing his best to guarantee moral confusion among his student followers." For his part, Coffin knew that his idea for a nonviolent march—with arrests—in which participants could have no "illusion that one is going to succeed" had not caught fire with students and that "there were a lot of people who really felt that probably I was a bad influence, that the march was against a more militant stand." As he explained to an interviewer a year later, however, "The original intent seemed fairly good: it would have dramatized what was going on; it would have given expression to a lot of energy. It would have been a way of expressing solidarity with those in jail and seemed to me also another way to set a tone for the non-violent weekend which, hopefully, was to come." Much later, Coffin thought the "legally right but morally wrong" formulation was "too flip."[9]

Events moved too quickly for a march called five days earlier. That same Sunday an evening mass meeting at Battell featured a rousing speech by the captain of the New Haven Panthers, Doug Miranda, who electrified his Yale audience by saying, "There's no reason the Panther and the Bulldog can't get together! . . . That Panther and that Bulldog gonna move together!" For days the campus buzzed with anticipation of a strike. Brewster formed an advisory committee that became obsolete almost immediately. Informal meetings seemed to happen nonstop across the campus as the Yale community prepared for a campus-wide gathering in the thirty-five-hundred-seat hockey rink Tuesday night. The faculty, particularly the black faculty, prepared for their own momentous meeting two days later.[10]

When on Tuesday the trial judge released the Panthers he had jailed for contempt (including national Chief of Staff David Hilliard), many believed that their pressure had been successful. Four thousand five hundred members of the Yale community crowded into Ingalls Rink that evening, some for a strike vote, some to learn more about what was happening, some just to watch. Coffin interrupted the proceedings near the outset to put in a plug for his choreographed nonviolent march; he appeared very much out of step with the collective mood, irrelevant to the business at hand.

But finding relevance at the meeting turned out to be difficult indeed. After being greeted with a standing ovation, David Hilliard squandered this goodwill with a rant against the courts, against "pigs," and against Yale students themselves when they booed him for saying, "There ain't nothing wrong with taking the life of a motherfucking pig." In the middle of Hilliard's speech, a confused white man made his way toward the podium; Hilliard's bodyguards intercepted and beat him. A well-known black Yale philosophy professor, Kenneth Mills, intervened and took control of the podium. He let the man say a few words, whereupon the psychologist Kenneth Keniston came to the microphone and led the dazed young man away. The meeting ended inconclusively and unsatisfyingly shortly afterwards. Many students returned to their residential colleges, where gatherings in nine (of twelve) voted in favor of the strike. Two more followed Wednesday.[11]

Wednesday afternoon, after much internal debate, Coffin canceled the march he had announced on Sunday, at least partly because it could appear inflammatory in a situation that appeared to be calming down. He did not enjoy disappointing the five hundred students who had come to Battell to plan the march, or Brewster, who had all but endorsed it the previous Sunday afternoon. He was not even certain he had the power to call it off. But as he reflected much later, sometimes it paid to go against type. He remembered that his sociologist friend Kai Erikson told him, "You know, I've admired you for a lot of things, but for nothing more than for calling off a demonstration."[12]

The faculty assembled Thursday afternoon, April 23, in one of the most remarkable meetings in its history. After the black faculty presented their resolution in favor of a "suspension of normal academic functions," the meeting adjourned briefly to allow an address by black student leader Kurt Schmoke (later mayor of Baltimore and Corporation Fellow), who astonished the faculty by addressing them humbly as "our teachers . . . the people we respect" and pleading with them to provide "guidance and moral leadership." The faculty gave him a standing ovation.[13]

Brewster entered the fray with a prepared statement. While Yale could not contribute financially to the defense of any individuals, he argued, "No principle of neutrality should inhibit the university from doing whatever it can properly do to assure a fair trial." Nor should it "inhibit any one of us, in his individual capacity from declaring himself on the issues of the trial and its fairness." Brewster then stunned his own faculty with the only statement (besides Coffin's and the slogan "Free Bobby Seale") to outlive the events of May Day: "I personally want to say that I am appalled and ashamed that things should have come to such a pass that I am skeptical of the ability of black revolutionaries to achieve a fair trial anywhere in the United States. In large part the atmosphere has been created by police actions and prosecutions against the Panthers in many parts of the country. It is also one more inheritance from centuries of racial discrimination and oppression." Having never heard their president take such a strong political position, the faculty gave him "thunderous applause."[14]

Even after this personal endorsement, Brewster had a difficult job ahead of him: getting a unified position out of the faculty. It took all of his skill to forge a compromise that could be passed by the four hundred attendees. (Anyone who has observed a college faculty debate a contentious issue will appreciate the magnitude of his task.) At last the faculty voted in favor of a directive that "the normal expectations of the University be modified," that faculty "should be free to suspend their classes" in the interest of allowing "all concerned and interested parties a chance to discuss the issues and ramifications of the issues, to plan what direction we should take in this crisis." The strike was on, and in a remarkable exception to nearly every other student strike of the decade, it had the support of the faculty and the president of the university. The next day, Brewster announced that Yale would welcome May Day weekend guests and that the university—through the residential college system—would plan to house and feed thousands of demonstrators.[15]

The Yale community united behind Brewster even further when his "skepticism" statement hit the news, and commentators across the country—from Connecticut's Senator Thomas Dodd to Governor Dempsey, to politicians and television commentator Eric Sevareid—attacked him and the students at once. Tuesday night, Vice-President of the United States Spiro Agnew joined the feeding frenzy, calling for Brewster's replacement. Nothing could have been better designed to bring Yale students, faculty, and administration together than an attack by the despised, anti-intellectual vice-president; the next day students presented Brewster with a supporting petition signed by three thousand students. Hundreds of faculty did likewise, while Corporation Fellow William Horowitz released a nasty public letter to Agnew, objecting to his "unjustified, irresponsible, and serving comments . . . I frankly do not believe that your experience as a president of a P.T.A. Chapter qualifies you to evaluate the contributions to education by the most distinguished University President in the United States."[16]

Coffin continued to play a key role in trying to plan for a peaceful weekend. He assembled a Student-Faculty Monitoring Committee that met with all of the interested parties, from the Panthers to the police, and facilitated communication among groups that were not talking to each other. The group relied on Coffin's very wide network of contacts and became an indispensable source of reliable information in a situation awash in rumors, many of them frightening.

As May Day approached, two realities predominated. On the one hand, every major actor in the drama—the Panthers, their support groups, the town police, the Yale administration, the Chicago Seven (who were coming for the weekend)—all made public commitments to a peaceful weekend. On the other hand, bizarre rumors about stolen guns and discovered explosives and one hundred thousand radicals coming to New Haven to "burn Yale" made for a climate of fear and enormous tension. As many as a third of the students left town for the weekend, while many store owners boarded up their windows and shut down Thursday afternoon, April 30.

Brewster and his aides and a few confidants (Coffin, Corporation Fellow Cyrus Vance, some other faculty) established very close communications with the New Haven police chief and with the Chicago Seven, particularly Tom Hayden; David Dellinger (Class of 1936), the titular head of the demonstration; John Froines (Yale Ph.D., 1967); and Anne Froines, of the Panther support group. Unbeknownst to the demonstrators, or to the Yale students, these principals all tried to make sure that the weekend did not produce a riot. Brewster,

Sam Chauncey, and a few others monitored the rally from a secret command post in the Alumni House less than a block from the New Haven Green. Police Chief James Ahern had been training his men for weeks in successful crowd control that would also minimize the possibility of violence between demonstrators and the police. After complex negotiations with the mayor, the governor, and the state commander of the National Guard, Ahern also prepared to deploy National Guardsmen as backups to his force.

These preparations proved remarkably successful, given that ten to twenty thousand demonstrators who cared little for Yale University—including all sorts of white radical sects eager for violent confrontation—came to New Haven the weekend of May 1–2. Students and staff made and ladled out tons of granola and brown rice and green salad in residential college courtyards. The daytime rallies and workshops drew peaceful crowds, and the warm, sunny spring weather cooperated fully. Both evenings, however, less peaceful groups gathered on the Green; provocateurs and protesters bent on confrontation got a taste of the action they wanted—despite the efforts of student marshals to separate the groups—when police fired tear gas on them. Even so, these efforts of student marshals and the police paid off: no one was injured and no property damaged.

Brewster circulated through the colleges Friday evening where the Chicago Seven were giving speeches; at one of them Abbie Hoffman gave him a bear hug and, according to Coffin, "introduced him grandly as 'the sartorial showpiece of the people's revolution.'"[17] Coffin himself stayed on the move throughout the weekend, helping to defuse tensions wherever he could. As there were moments of danger and drama, there were also comic elements to the affair. At one point Friday night Coffin borrowed a bullhorn from Chief Ahern and gave it to Panther Doug Miranda, who—obscenely but effectively—moved most of the crowd off the Green and away from a confrontation with police. Later that night, working with Kenneth Mills, Coffin tried unsuccessfully to talk some white gas-masked radicals out of a confrontation with police.

Fortune was smiling, however, on Brewster, on Coffin, and on Yale. Just before midnight an explosion ripped through Ingalls Rink, soon after the last of a crowd of fifteen hundred had left it. Magically, almost, no one was even injured, and partly because Sam Chauncey asked the local media to downplay the incident that night, few protesters learned about what could have been seen as a terrible provocation until the next morning.

Saturday, Coffin continued to circulate with student marshals as a kind of rapid response team. Richard Sewall, master of Ezra Stiles College, recalled a confrontation that had begun almost outside his window on Broadway between protesters and some of the National Guard troops stationed along the street. He called headquarters, and "within four minutes Bill [drove up] in an automobile with three marshals (students with armbands), walked out and Bill just shouldered his way into that tussle which was just about coming to blows and I heard him say, 'I'm Reverend Coffin. What's going on here?' And everything quieted down. And they soon dispersed." Sewall came out to the street, and Coffin himself called headquarters, probably Chauncey, and urged him to "take those soldier boys out of here. . . . If you hadn't had them, nothing would have happened." The guardsmen soon received orders to move to a less provocative location. But Coffin was not done. "Let's go around and see those guardsmen," Sewall recalled him saying. "They don't like this anymore than we do." Coffin's pastoral instinct—and perhaps his wartime training—hit the target. "Thanks a lot, Reverend Coffin," one of the guardsmen said. "You came just in time." Later that evening there were more confrontations and more tear gas, but no violence.[18]

Since protesters began leaving town on Saturday, the leaders canceled Sunday's program. In Battell Chapel Sunday morning, with the taste of tear gas still in their air, Coffin rejoiced at the victory for nonviolence: "We did a hell of a job. We did a Christian job. We practiced Christianity. We took a Christian chance, and it paid off. We licked 'em with love." Two members of the congregation spoke about the events of the weekend. Harry Rudin criticized the strike as foolishly and dangerously anti-intellectual. Kurt Schmoke argued emotionally, if wearily, that students had a responsibility to more than their classes. In truth, however, Coffin felt "far from elated." The "emotional energy expended on preventing violence that weekend was sure to leave everyone too exhausted to deal with the conditions Kurt so rightly deplored." Moreover, the victory in New Haven paled before the widening of the war in Vietnam signaled that weekend by President Richard Nixon's invasion of Cambodia. Excoriating Nixon's concern that the United States not become a "pitiful, helpless giant," Coffin declared that "President Nixon set a dreadful tone when he suggested that manhood is for a giant to behave like a giant. That is the most perverted notion of manhood that has been heard from high places in a decade."[19]

In the midst of an extremely complex, constantly shifting situation with immense stakes, Brewster and Coffin provided extraordinary leadership in keeping Yale intact while encouraging Yale students to engage issues of principle. Far from close comrades during the events, they were nevertheless indispensable to each other. Coffin's stature, and his position to the left of Brewster, provided space for the president to maneuver. Coffin's insistence on nonviolence, even when it seemed out of step with many Yale students, meant that someone with authority, a following—the largest student following of any Yale figure until Agnew attacked Brewster—and access to the media was constantly promoting humane interactions and trying to undermine the most physically confrontational tactics and defuse the tensest situations. Many radicals did not like Coffin's religious and moral language and leadership. They saw, quite accurately, that Coffin drew students away from slogans like "Off the Pigs," away from the careless suggestion of a "revolution" against "fascism," and away from nasty or hot-headed confrontations with the authorities. Coffin's physical presence and evident fearlessness added to his ability to deal with police, guardsmen, and radicals bent on mayhem.

For his part, Brewster worked at the peak of his own skills and reaped the results of a brilliant presidency. By strengthening the residential college system, he had helped to create a humane learning community for undergraduates who felt unusually well connected to their university. By drawing more undergraduates from public schools he had moved the political center of the student body to the left—while boosting its academic profile. Unlike most of his counterparts at the time, Brewster genuinely liked his students. He made himself accessible to ordinary undergraduates, making a point of walking around the campus, greeting students by name when he could, and engaging them in conversation. As a former campus activist himself, he remembered—and respected—what it had been like to be fired by youthful idealism. Despite his apparently stuffy Anglophilia, Brewster was hard to dislike: extremely intelligent and quick-witted, he enjoyed the riposte of quip and argument and never gave the impression of feeling threatened by protesters of any kind.

In this era Brewster's tactical sense was unmatched. While S. I. Hayakawa became the darling of the right for yanking out the wires of a radical sound truck in the middle of a demonstration, Brewster worked to make sure that he was rarely the object of a student demonstration. Yale was the last of the Ivy League campuses to experience a revolt, after the serious confrontations at Columbia in 1968 and Harvard and Cornell in 1969. To revive a sixties term, Brewster knew how to co-opt dissent. The best-known Yale radical of his time, Mark Zanger (immortalized as Megaphone Mark by Garry Trudeau in the comic strip "Doonesbury"), told an interviewer in 1990 that Brewster "would never do the stupid thing that would put everybody on our side . . . I spent a lot of time trying to fathom this guy in order to be able to embarrass and defeat him. And I really did come to admire his cleverness."[20]

But beyond his shrewdness, by sticking with Coffin when many wanted him fired, Brewster guaranteed that important moral issues would be discussed seriously on his campus. At the very least, the chaplain's office served as a safety valve, absorbing energy that in less open institutions would have expressed itself in building takeovers and hostile confrontations with administrators. Under Coffin, Battell Chapel and the chaplaincy had become far more: the spiritual and moral center of the university campus and the entire Yale community.

Once Brewster made up his mind, he stuck with his position. In the case of his "fair trial" statement, which critics frequently misquoted and took out of context to make him appear to be less careful and more radical than he was, Brewster refused to back down. To one correspondent Brewster went further, charging that the real "fault for the uproars on our campuses and streets does not lie with the young and the blacks. If it lies anywhere it lies with us, with our generation," who too often "delude themselves about the quality of existing institutions and hence put off and put down those who seek orderly change."[21]

Such sentiments, rare among college and university presidents at the time, go a long way toward explaining why Yale never exploded during the 1960s and 1970s, and about the fondness that many Yale students and graduates of that era had for their university—and its leadership—during a time when it was far more fashionable to despise one's university administration.

Mission to Hanoi

Relatively few American troops remained in Vietnam in the latter part of 1972; only fifty thousand Americans were drafted that year, and the American involvement consisted principally of massive bombing. The spring and summer had seen a massive North Vietnamese offensive and a furious American counterattack that included mining Haiphong Harbor, blockading North Vietnam, and launching round-the-clock B-52 bombing raids. By late summer, compromise was in the air.[22]

In that context the North Vietnamese decided to release three American prisoners of war: Lieutenant (j.g.) Norris Charles, Lieutenant (j.g.) Markham Gartley, and Major Edward Elias. Their delegation in Paris asked Coffin's friend Cora Weiss (head of Women Strike for Peace, which Weiss had founded in the 1950s to oppose aboveground nuclear testing) and David Dellinger (who had accepted previously released POWs) to assemble a small delegation to travel to Hanoi to accept the captured pilots and escort them home to the United States. Weiss invited Richard Falk, a professor of international studies at Princeton, and Coffin, who, frustrated and "fed up with the war," welcomed the chance to take part in a humanitarian act. He also expected to "have my passions rekindled by the bomb damage."[23]

Given the hostility of the U.S. government toward a group of peace activists traveling to the enemy capital to receive American POWs, the public relations aspects of the trip were complex, especially because the North Vietnamese had agreed to the Americans' proposal that a family member of each POW come along as well. Both sides clearly wanted to use the release for propaganda purposes. Gartley's mother and Charles's wife eagerly accepted; Elias's father, however, gave in to Pentagon pressure not to legitimize the American delegation. American press and public opinion had not been kind to previous visitors to North Vietnam, so even such secure congressmen as Ron Dellums, John Conyers, and Father Robert Drinan turned down invitations to join the group.

Like most Coffin adventures, the two-week trip combined risky public relations, sobering confrontations with distressing realities, important human contact, and a certain level of humorous hijinks. Ever curious and gregarious, Coffin engaged people everywhere: the children who gathered around him, Prime Minister Pham Van Dong (who unexpectedly summoned the group to his residence for an interview), and a small group of priests and Protestant pastors.

Beyond the simple task of accepting prisoners, however, Coffin and his colleagues hoped they would be able to use the occasion—and perhaps the released POWs themselves—to make a strong statement against the war while they had the attention of the world press. They wanted to rebut President Nixon's position that he was continuing the war partly to get the POWs home when it was quite clear to them that the North Vietnamese would release all of the POWs when the war ended. As a result, much of the trip was taken up with calculations about how best the delegation and the POWs could remain independent of U.S. military and political officials, who would want the released prisoners to return quickly to the military fold.

Greeted by an air raid alert almost as soon as they arrived in Hanoi, the American delegation often had the experience of taking shelter against American bombers. Coffin and his friends wanted to see the bombing damage outside Hanoi as well, and their hosts asked whether the three pilots would accompany the delegation on this tour. "We responded," Coffin wrote later, "that hard as it might be on them, we thought it only proper that they should be [with us]. Whether they chose to speak of what they had seen when they got home was up to them, but at least they should know the truth." The North Vietnamese clearly approved and announced that the pilots would be freed that night. For several days the larger group went sightseeing in Hanoi.

In the provinces, into which they drove at night, the Americans saw enormous destruction: a bombed-out hospital, bombed-out churches and schools, bridges, pagodas, and the like. Vietnam's third largest city, Nam Dinh, lay three-quarters in ruins. Further south, in the city of Ninh Binh, formerly home to fifty thousand, "two buildings were left intact."

Coffin was most interested in the interactions between "enemies": how the North Vietnamese felt about the Americans; how the pilots felt about the damage they and their comrades had rained down upon the country. After all, he preached often enough about how much human beings had in common even though they might be arrayed against each other by war. The Vietnamese astonished him by not even guarding the released pilots. He finally asked a local village leader how he felt about "offering hospitality" to men responsible for this destruction. "The victors must always be generous to the vanquished," came the stock, smiling reply.

At least two of the pilots were willing to talk about what they were seeing. But mostly, Coffin realized, they were feeling guiltier about leaving their buddies behind. The entire group realized that the return trip was going to be complicated, most of all for the newly freed men. The last time prisoners had been released, in 1969, the American military had immediately taken charge of the men in Laos and put one on a "road show to tell horror tales he later confessed were untrue." Since that performance could have scotched releases in the previous three years, the men decided to come home with the escort delegation and cabled President Nixon their desires. This was a brave request on their part, and probably influenced by Weiss, Coffin, and Dellinger, for most military men would have naturally given themselves over to their superiors.

When they received no reply from the White House, they figured out an elaborate return route to allow the men their own press conference in Copenhagen before they flew to New York. At the same time, press reports made quite clear that U.S. officials planned to intercept the men as soon as they landed in Vientiane, Laos, on their original route. Many reports incorrectly but conveniently blamed the North Vietnamese for interrupting the group's departure.[24]

They flew first to Beijing, where they talked to no one, and then to Moscow, where American Chargé d'Affaires Adolph Dubs tried to take charge of the three pilots. Coffin, Dellinger, and Falk blocked his way at first while the pilots stayed back with Cora Weiss. Before the confrontation escalated in front of reporters, the parties agreed to talk elsewhere. In an Aeroflot office, the American officials tried to talk the airmen into staying at the ambassador's residence and taking an American military flight back to the States. Each refused, preferring, on behalf of their imprisoned comrades, to stay in an Aeroflot hotel and return home on a civilian aircraft—through Copenhagen—with their original escorts. The story made the front page of the *Washington Post* and received intense coverage in papers across the country. Coffin was widely quoted as having first called Dubs's behavior "threatening"—and then backing down when asked whether Dubs had made an explicit threat. But there was no mistaking Dubs's effort to use his authority to pressure the men back into the official fold. Secretary of Defense Melvin Laird also chimed in, publicly declining to rule out the possibility that the men might be subject to court-martial for statements they made in captivity.[25]

The next day the group left for Copenhagen, but not before Coffin and Dubs tangled again. This time Coffin accused Dubs of being "so indifferent to the plight of those pilots in North Vietnam." He was referring to the miniaturized spy equipment that the Pentagon had apparently tried to send the prisoners hidden in "care packages" that the North Vietnamese had shown to Coffin and the others. "How dare you," Dubs interrupted loudly. "Oh come off it," Coffin replied (according to the UPI report), continuing, "Now shut up and you listen to me for a change. It's quite clear who's using whom this time." Clearly stung and furious, Dubs said, "with slow measured tones, 'Don't address me in those terms. Just don't address me in those terms.'" Coffin got the last words, telling him to "get off your hind legs and come down off your high horse."[26]

The government did better than words. Two embassy men boarded the flight to Copenhagen and finally got a chance to talk to the pilots away from their escorts. "I have no idea what they said," Coffin wrote later, but the entire group had just learned about Laird's unsubtle threat. Journalist Peter Arnett, who had accompanied the delegation, correctly surmised that the embassy pair had brought uniforms for the men.

Coffin and his fellow activists had pinned large hopes on the press conference that the freed prisoners had agreed to hold in Copenhagen. All the circuitous travel and all the risk of bad press and the disapproval of the U.S. government had been on behalf of this one opportunity for the former captives to speak freely to the American public. Coffin knew by then that Gartley and Charles had enormous misgivings about the war and about the bombing campaign in which they had taken part. Charles's wife, Olga, opposed the war quietly, while Gartley's parents had become antiwar activists in their own right. If either of them would describe how they really felt about the war, or the bombing damage they had seen, "the war effort would be dealt a serious blow." On the other hand, Coffin saw that the pressure had grown too intense and the men simply did not have the experience to take the risk that they could be seen as "brainwashed" or "traitors" to the American cause and to the five hundred prisoners still in North Vietnam. Had they been critical of Hanoi, they felt they could be jeopardizing further prisoner releases; had they been critical of their own government, they risked even more.

Under this kind of fire, Charles and Gartley showed real courage. "If you really want to bring these men home you can do it," Charles declared. "If you really want to end the war you can do it. I call on you to help me bring the men home." Gartley announced that "whichever policy will bring the men home the fastest is the one I support the most." Implicitly, these statements rebuked the president's Vietnam policy; some headline writers interpreted the men's statements as asking for an end to the war.[27]

When the delegation finally arrived in New York, military and Defense Department officials took nearly immediate charge of the former POWs. Cora Weiss called it "a recapture scene, one incarceration replacing another." Some of the men's family members were indeed bitterly disappointed by the Pentagon's speed in whisking them off to military hospitals. "Dispute rages at takeover of POWs by U.S.," ran one headline, while the *New York Times* noted that Gartley, who knew many prisoners from his four years in captivity, was prevented from speaking to a group of current POW wives and parents who had come to meet him; the *Times* also editorialized about the "Ungracious Welcome" provided the released prisoners.[28]

Coffin wrote a series of five articles (for national syndication) about the Hanoi mission. He and the others had hoped that the prisoner release would provide an opening to change minds on the war, too—or at least help make for a quicker end to the savage endgame. They did gain some publicity for their cause and may have helped add to sentiment against the bombing campaign, but by 1972 most Americans knew what they felt about Vietnam; even if they opposed it, the majority refused to vote for the presidential candidate who had promised to end it quickly. While Coffin returned from Hanoi "filled with new anguish, with much to report on the horror and futility of the war," he found that outside antiwar circles—and his parishioners at Yale, who packed Battell Chapel his first Sunday back—not many really wanted to listen. Even the liberal *Newsday*, which published Coffin's articles, also ran a cartoon accompanying one article showing the "peace activists" as a puppet master, dangling strings from which the three POWs had escaped.[29]

Helping to release captives held a biblical resonance that—along with a skin thickened by many previous controversies—overcame any misgivings Coffin might have had about being branded an agent of Hanoi. "Love thine enemy" meant something powerful to Coffin, especially since, as he wrote about Pham Van Dong, he "should never have become an enemy." Coffin's use of a different moral calculus, one derived from the Bible rather than from politics, invited Americans to challenge their casual beliefs about enemies during wartime. After all, without Cora Weiss's connections to the North Vietnamese, the POWs would very likely not have been released.

Winding Down

Little could console American liberals in the fall of 1972 and the spring of 1973. Weeks before the election of 1972 Coffin preached a sermon on despair and how to overcome it that could have been meant for himself as much as for his congregation. Quoting Lincoln—"I have often been driven to my knees out of a sense of no other place to go"—Coffin insisted that despair was "healthy if it makes us search for deeper remedies." Before going to Hanoi he had begun thinking about the question of amnesty for opponents—and prosecutors—of the war once it was over. In the spring of 1972 he had chaired the drafting committee of an interfaith conference that supported amnesty for all those "in legal jeopardy because of the war in Southeast Asia," except for "those who had been convicted of violence against persons," though even these deserved "their cases reviewed individually." He had preached on the subject in April, and in the fall he tried to build public support—on religious and secular grounds—for amnesty for draft resisters, draft evaders, and deserters, as well as for those who had committed horrendous war crimes, like Lieutenant William Calley at My Lai.[30]

His argument was simple. Historically, American presidents from George Washington to Andrew Jackson had pardoned an assortment of rebels and deserters. Abraham Lincoln—"the spiritual center of our country," Coffin called him—had faced the greatest rebellion of American history, and instead of suggesting punishment, he delivered his plea "with malice toward none, with charity for all" in his Second Inaugural Address as the Civil War wound down in early 1865. Despite the twentieth century's "lamentable" record on this score, Coffin argued nonetheless that Israel might have done better, after having tried Adolph Eichmann and "gotten out all the information," to have simply released him to be tried "at the bar of history." Coffin failed to stir up much interest in amnesty.

Then in one of the great electoral college routs of American history, Richard Nixon crushed George McGovern's bid for the presidency with the largest margin since Franklin D. Roosevelt had destroyed Alf Landon in 1936. American soldiers continued to leave Vietnam while American bombers rained unprecedented firepower on the North. When the Americans and North Vietnamese finally signed the Paris Peace Accords in January 1973, the only people who really felt like celebrating were the families of the POWs still held by Hanoi. By the end of March they had all come home. Everyone else awaited the eventual defeat of the government of South Vietnam.

For despite secret American promises to South Vietnam's President Nguyen Van Thieu that the United States would help defend his regime with food and bombs, the combination of Congress's increasing rebelliousness and Nixon's decreasing power and credibility meant that South Vietnam was on its own. Increasingly absorbed by the growing Watergate scandal during the spring and summer of 1973, official Washington wanted little to do with Vietnam once there seemed to be a way out of the war. Even though the Paris Accords, originally touted by Nixon and Henry Kissinger as finally bringing peace with honor, brought neither to Vietnam, they provided diplomatic cover for final American withdrawal.

Coffin found little to celebrate in the end of the war. He spoke at a national conference on amnesty that spring and argued "that the vast majority of American people, and it grieves me to say this, but we might as well face up to it, do *not* want amnesty."[31]

In May 1973 Coffin received the prestigious Edwin T. Dahlberg Peace Award of the American Baptist Churches at the biennial convention of the 1.5-million-member denomination.[32] (The first recipient, in 1964, had been Martin Luther King Jr.) But by that spring Coffin was ready for a change, and possibly even a rest. Brewster granted his request for a sabbatical for the following academic year. He and Harriet made plans to move to Marin County, California, in the fall, where he planned to begin writing an autobiography.

The "Watergate summer," however, produced a bizarre incident that drew Coffin back into the public eye. On June 14, 1973, Jeb Stuart Magruder, former deputy campaign manager for Richard Nixon's 1972 reelection effort, testified before the Senate Watergate Committee and implicated Attorney General John Mitchell, both in the plan to bug the Democratic headquarters and in the following cover-up. Magruder, who had been a student and friend of Coffin at Williams during 1957–1958, blamed the chaplain. "We saw continual violations of the law done by men like William Sloane Coffin," he told Senator Howard Baker. "I saw people that I was very close to breaking the law without any regard for any other person's pattern or behavior or beliefs. . . . we had become inured to using some activities that would help us in accomplishing what we thought was a cause, a legitimate cause."[33] The *Times* invited Coffin to write an op-ed piece, which ran the following week under the title "Not Yet a Good Man."

Coffin reminisced about Magruder at Williams, whom he had warned, "You're a nice guy, Jeb, but not yet a good man. You have lots of charm but little inner strength. And if you don't stand for something you're apt to fall for anything." He analyzed Magruder in the context of 1950s education, when "students were agreeing their way through life" and most professors were "morally asleep." Coffin wished that he—and "all of us who taught him"— had done a better job of helping Magruder to develop a self that could be loyal to the Constitution instead of to the current boss. Clearly, in order "to do evil in this world you don't have to be evil—just a nice guy, not yet a good man."[34]

Magruder wrote Coffin promptly, apologizing for having renewed their contact on national television: "I think your response was excellent," he admitted, "and you certainly have not lost your touch in both sensitivity and understanding." He and his wife hoped to sit down with Coffin, who shortly called and invited the pair up to New Haven. Magruder remembers Coffin suggesting that he could "make adjustments in your moral and ethical structure. You can benefit from this or you can be destroyed by it."[35]

This odd couple, the minister and his Watergate conspirator former student, stayed connected for a while longer. *Harper's Magazine* ran a conversation between them moderated by the interviewer Studs Terkel in October, and Coffin reviewed Magruder's autobiography the following year. In these interactions Coffin kept pushing Magruder to see the moral forest instead of the factual trees, to see that when he defended John Mitchell as a humane boss he was insisting on "the littleness of loyalties, at the expense of great loyalties" like the Constitution. Magruder could not see it. He told Terkel that Coffin "revels" in confrontation with people, which Coffin denied: "I'm forced into it by a bunch of people like you, who are so suave you can't confront things. . . . Maybe the truth is confrontational." Magruder still appeared slick, admitting to wrongdoing but unwilling to look at larger issues. The following year Coffin's words had apparently begun to sink in. As Magruder wrote Coffin from what he called "the slammer," "I thought your various reviews were fair, particularly after I got in prison and was brought face to face with the horror of the system." Since 1981 Magruder has been an ordained Presbyterian pastor.[36]

In California Coffin launched himself into writing his memoir. Despite the predictions of friends that the "inactivity of a sabbatical year would drive me crazy," Coffin appears to have had plenty to occupy him. He kept a modest speaking schedule; friends visited from time to time; and he valued the time he spent unearthing memories and setting down his experiences. Harriet and Marin County, and Erik Erikson, who lived nearby, provided a more psychologically oriented environment than Coffin had ever lived in. Harriet had wanted to be in the Bay Area to explore the "human potential" movement of those years: Esalen and Werner Erhard's est and Zen Buddhists and others. Coffin joined her in some of these, finding himself much more intrigued than he expected to be.

Engaged in more sustained reflection than ever before in his life, the forty-nine-year-old Coffin began to think seriously about the future as well as the past. He wrote Brewster, asking his opinion on "whither Coffin?" Brewster took the question seriously and wanted to talk about it seriously in person. In the meantime, he advised Coffin: "First, whatever you decide to do, do it with enthusiasm for itself, not as a means to some other end. Second, if you could see and feel yourself fully enthused about the Yale Chaplaincy—not as a base-camp, but as an absorbing dominant focus for life—you can be sure that Yale and especially her president, want you back." The "important thing is to make the 'right' decision—above all the one that is right for you. Now," he concluded, warmly, "having been so neutrally statesmanlike, let me just say personally how much we miss you and how much we look forward to your resuming the partnership." Still, Coffin had held the post of chaplain for a decade and a half, the fifteen most tumultuous, change-filled years in Yale's history. It might be getting time to move on.[37]

Interregnum

Dilemmas and Decisions

By the fall of 1974, when he returned from his sabbatical, Coffin had tired of Yale. Vietnam offered little grist for the prophet's mill, as Americans seemed ready to forget about the devastated little country across the globe. Yale had changed, too, by the mid-1970s. Students had narrowed their vision as the U.S. economy stagnated, and the fundamental optimism of 1960s higher education, the innovative energy often shared by faculty, students, and administrators, had begun to dissipate under the pressure of budget-cutting and "belt-tightening." Absent the frequently excruciating moral choices posed by the war and the draft, undergraduates showed less interest in unconventional thinking about their futures and homed in on career paths such as law and medicine as never before. An associate Yale chaplain during the latter 1970s described students' problems—roommates, boyfriends and girlfriends, parents, getting into medical or law school, finishing dissertations—as endlessly repetitive and almost entirely devoid of religious content or moral conflict.[1]

Yale may have tired of Coffin, too. With the arrival of undergraduate women, campus controversies often turned on male-female issues: safety, health care, sexuality, gymnasium use, the male-female ratio, and the integration of women into a previously all-male institution. Coffin was considerably less engaged by the women's movement than he had been by the war or civil rights —not least because Harriet had so visibly staked out that territory. As much as he enjoyed the company of women—and women generally enjoyed his as well—Coffin had been schooled in a more masculine time and found it harder to incorporate feminism into his style and his work.

Like many fifty-year-old men, he had worked shoulder to shoulder with other men, thought of his colleagues as male, and resented the pressure from his wife to broaden his point of view. He also had a hard time seeing the many ways that Yale's profound maleness made women feel like second-class citizens. Now that Yale students had become less crusading, more careerist, less passionate, and less male, they had less interest in Coffin, and he in them.

On the other hand, coeducation and feminism had changed him since the early seventies. Deborah Kaback, a recent Yale graduate who worked for Harriet and lived in the Coffins' Trumbull Street house during the summer of 1971, recalled a three-way discussion on the deck about a book Harriet liked that dealt with "the female within all of us." Kaback had a "beautiful Parisian umbrella with flowers on it, frilly and . . . super femmy," she remembered. "We were in this conversation and at a certain point I guess Bill just had enough. So he takes the umbrella and he opens it up and he twirls it around and he promenades up on the deck and he says, 'You see? I'm showing my feminine nature!' And we just all howled!" Well, not exactly. Harriet "laughed because I laughed," Kaback admitted, "but she was pissed off. She didn't appreciate the joke, she really didn't." Mocking Harriet's earnestness, Bill showed his discomfort with the topic.[2]

Three years later, however, from the pulpit he mentioned the "sexist presuppositions that have invested Biblical and English language so secretly and fatefully." He began to make changes, including women in his sermons more, opening up American history and religious perspectives to the formerly excluded half of humanity. Preaching on patriotism during the upcoming American bicentennial, for example, Coffin listed a series of American heroes—Abraham Lincoln and Frederick Douglass, Herman Melville and Ralph Waldo Emerson, John Jay and Alexander Hamilton, Jonathan Edwards and John Winthrop, "not to mention a host of American women who like that gallant early Quaker lady, Mary Dyer, said calmly to her persecutors, 'Truth is my authority, not authority my truth.'" He told an interviewer from *People Weekly* magazine that "the so-called feminine virtues are things I think we need more of," that "churches will profit enormously" from women entering the ministry, and that the presence of women had changed Yale "for the better. Students are kinder to each other. There has been too much of this macho stuff."[3]

Trapped in a deteriorating marriage, Coffin felt bored and restless. Lacking a great crusade, his ministry had less fire. So he launched a Yale Hunger Action Program. But Coffin had never been capable of igniting a movement; he could bring a movement to Yale, interpret it to liberal and moderate students and faculty, and raise its issues biblically through his sermons. When Coffin told *People* that he found the hunger fight "mesmerizing" because it involved "almost every other crisis: inflation, armaments, multinational corporations, our own personal life-style," he was clearly overstating his own feelings. Like most of his fellow preachers and chaplains, Coffin had not figured out how to excite the hearts of students or faculty in this new time.

So he preached about his dissatisfaction with Yale. In September 1974 he took on the question of what constituted a liberal education, noting, "I seem to be afflicted with a love-hate relationship with Yale, and with the academic world as a whole, whose intensity constantly surprises me." The subject pushed him to acknowledge how much of his own humanity he owed to the education he had received at Yale. On the other hand, he found that he increasingly preferred preaching to fellow clergy, to whom he did not "have to explain Biblical language." At one time the "thought police were over on the church side" and academics were needed to enlarge the thinking of the church; "it's now the church's turn to turn around and say, 'you, my dear friends in the academic community, are avoiding the realities of the human condition by denying that there are any more questions.'"[4]

By January 1975 Coffin had found what he really wanted to talk about: the deficiencies of academia, the meaning of biblical freedom and security, and the assumption of vulnerability. He began, in effect, a sermonic assault on the moral narrowing of the university in the face of global insecurity. "Why at great universities," he asked rhetorically, "is the main debate still the rather peevish one between service and scholarship?" Where were the intellectuals who believed, with Nietzsche, in "bloody truths?" Had intellectuals become, he asked with withering contempt, "academics who like their truths *in vitro* instead of *in vivo*, who believe not so much in right thinking as in rational control, insisting that the cognitive is intrinsically divided against the emotional, spiritual, and active dimensions of human existence, to use the juiceless jargon that is the opiate of the repressed?" Where, in short, were the truly "Wise Men" of the Christmas story, who "made themselves vulnerable; [who] took off from security, not even sure where they were going, going at night, nothing but a little itty bitty star, over what?" In working out his own feelings, Coffin found his prophetic voice: "Vulnerability: the precondition to wisdom. Vulnerability: freedom, wholeness. What a place Yale would be if we defined education as a process to help youth mature into vulnerability."[5]

When an old friend had come to visit late in the fall of 1974 and accused him of engaging in "maintenance, man, just maintenance," Coffin had been ready to hear the wisdom in his words. If Yale were no longer going to be in the forefront of a movement, Coffin was not going to be fully engaged preaching to and counseling students and faculty. He no longer felt compelled by his own pulpit. In reality, Coffin was preaching as though he had already decided to leave Yale.

In late January he broke the news to Brewster, who, not entirely surprised, agreed to announce Coffin's decision at the next Corporation meeting. In a note for Brewster to distribute, Coffin thanked the Corporation for its support over the years. "That for some members of the Corporation this support has occasionally been difficult to extend," he acknowledged, "makes me all the more grateful for it." He explained his decision: "I know that growth demands a willingness to relinquish one's proficiencies. So I want to become more vulnerable, or as the old pietist phrase goes, 'to let go and let God.' What's to come is still unsure—and that's the way it should be!"[6] At the end of the next Sunday service in Battell, Coffin told the world he would be leaving at the end of the calendar year.

The announcement "stunned the Yale Community," according to the *Yale Daily News,* and made news across the country. Publicly, Coffin appears to have felt freed by the decision, though it is not at all clear what he thought he or his family would do after he left. And despite his expressed gratitude for his years at Yale, Coffin's decision seems to have tapped into a sharper, more critical, more judgmental streak toward his world that he had reserved formerly for segregationists and warmakers. In an interview in *People* he freely lambasted academics (for being "too academic"), academia (where "too little of real consequence for the future [was] taking place"), and students who lacked "moral courage" and whose interest in religion was "for bad reasons, to get more security." Once Coffin made the decision to walk away from his own institutional security, he lost patience with those who were still seeking theirs.[7]

In his first sermon after announcing his departure, Coffin picked up the same themes—this time using Jesus' words in Matthew 6:25: "Do not be anxious about your life."[8] How indeed? In an extended meditation on secular insecurity, and the source of Christian security, Coffin quoted a favorite line of Thornton Wilder's, with which the playwright enjoyed taunting other writers. He had asked Coffin once whether, in writing out his sermons, he had left "room for the Holy Spirit." Coffin, who wrote, and rewrote, his sermons out word for word over a period of days, confessed that "it was at least five years after coming to this beloved place, however, before I could ever depart from the text, let alone allow any opening. I was just too anxious about my life." His love-hate relationship with Yale burst into full flower: "In the mindscape of scientific rationality that is Yale, . . . to make room for the Holy Spirit, we have to loosen our rational grip or, more accurately, our irrational white-knuckle grip on life." He assailed academic tenure as a system that, though it once provided a "safeguard for controversy," now "represents an assurance of superiority which cultivates a dependence on social position and financial gain."

Psychology, too, had little to offer the anxious. "One of the great illusory promises of psychotherapy," he claimed, jabbing at Harriet, "is that once you know everything about yourself you will be more secure. What arid nonsense!" He mocked Freudian language: "Suppose you do know that that's penis envy and that's a castration complex, that as everybody knows is clearly Oedipal and any idiot can tell you that that's polymorphous perversity!"

He may have been rediscovering his bearings. With no job ahead of him, having chosen to be "vulnerable" with a marriage on the rocks, Coffin was trying to put his faith where it belonged. "For if the world does not give us what we want," he assured his listeners and, perhaps, himself, "God gives us what we need—and probably what we really want anyway . . . namely freedom, a thumb-nosing independence from all the powers of death militant that want to do us in." With "heavenly tenure," he concluded, "who cares about the earthly comforts of an armored life! 'No room for the holy Spirit?' Veni, Sancte Spiritus. Come Thou Holy Spirit." A tour de force on a fundamental Christian principle, this sermon took up his only true theme in the year or so before he left Yale: that true security, real life, genuine love, and true immortality were to be found only in God, and faith in God. Coffin's personal decision for a modicum of insecurity gave him the freedom to preach it so powerfully. "He really preached for himself," his secretary recalled twenty years later.[9]

It may not have been only the security he felt as a child of God that enabled him to preach these liberated sermons. After all, he could still rely on secular securities, as well as the security of well-off siblings and a well-off mother who could help out in a pinch. He owned roughly $86,000 in stocks and bonds, worth close to $270,000 in current dollars—though he surely did not know the total—which were managed by his friend William Horowitz. He rightly pointed out that the Bible says little positive about holding onto financial security, but he was not in fact giving up his worldly possessions to follow Jesus. Nor did he acknowledge what was obvious to his listeners, that his well-known skill and reputation would unquestionably land him a decent job.

At baccalaureate ceremonies in 1975, Brewster paid tribute to Coffin explicitly and at length. "You are lucky to have been here when he was," he told the graduating seniors. "So am I. We have had our moments of disagreement —even mutual disapproval. They have been rare. They have been good for both of us." He teased Coffin gently about his "overweening modesty," his refusal to be "deterred, or even perceptibly influenced, by the prospect of political failure." But Brewster's real subject was the way the "enviable Chaplain" had lived a life truly "integrated around a sense of moral purpose, a feeling of usefulness." Especially in the years of a shrinking and competitive job market, Coffin's "obvious enjoyment" of his life was "the best witness to my point, his example the best clue to the pursuit of happiness."[10]

That August, however, happiness was in short supply. Bill and Harriet went to Marsh Island, but the tension was palpable. Harriet felt Bill's stiffness and distance, while Bill waited for events to decide the fate of his marriage. They had conversations about the fall, the coming transition in their lives as he left Yale. Like most men who had difficulty expressing their feelings directly, Coffin probed by asking questions, by asking Harriet for guidance. "Do you think we should separate?" she recalled him asking. She did not want to. On the other hand, she was concerned about the fall, and remembered telling him, "I think it's better that you go now than if you're thinking of going later." According to her, Coffin denied all. "So again, it was a challenge, I think, to him that somehow he had to conquer this."[11]

Coffin may also have been tempted by a proposal some friends came to make that same month. As Bill Webber, president of New York Theological Seminary, told it, he, his wife, and Don and Anne Benedict, all vacationing in Maine, had the idea of putting Coffin on the road: "And so we said, let's go down and tell Bill Coffin that he's got to become the [mainline] Protestant Billy Graham." They arrived in the shore town closest to Marsh Island, and "we run into them right there in town—they're on their way back. So we go back, the four of us get in their boat and go back out to the island and sit down with Bill and Harriet and tell Bill that's what his great gifts are. To do something like that." Coffin was intrigued: "Well, that's sort of his fantasy too," Webber remembered him saying, "but he didn't know how to give it shape." In fact, this idea seems to have been floating around a number of Coffin's friends for a year or two, and it is possible that Coffin even wrote out a version of the Webber-Benedict proposal, for a "preaching and teaching mission for a just and global future."[12]

Farewell

Back in New Haven Coffin spent his last few months continuing his "lover's quarrel" with Mother Yale, preaching for students and for himself. Still jobless, he hammered away at security and the final inadequacies of education as opposed to faith. "While education mocks human pretension, it is improperly hostile to human aspiration," he told his opening Sunday congregation. Like Jesus, religious faith "takes our deepest longings and turns them into expectations." He took up the message posted in front of the Career Advisory Office —"Is there life after Yale?"—and, implying that life at Yale represented a kind of death, swung into full antiacademic mode. He attacked the familiar target of tenure, which, by "protecting people against themselves," tended to turn "first-rate people into second-rate people." The problem, as Coffin saw it, was the "insurance mentality" that seemed to blanket the Yale campus (as well as

Christianity), boosting applications to medical and law school, preventing students and Christians from seeing life as a "risk exercise," despite St. Paul's assurance that nothing "can separate us from the love of God." In his sermon just before Thanksgiving, Coffin zeroed in on the scribe in the parable of the Good Samaritan (Luke 10:25–37), who grilled Christ on "what should I do to inherit eternal life?" He turned the parable into a critique of academic life— where the question, "What must I do to be smart?" took precedence over "What must I do to be good?"[13]

Five hundred well-wishers gathered for Coffin's early December farewell dinner, which featured toasts and roasts and a booklet of "Coffinisms" at each setting. Coffin directed the Glee Club, sang with the Russian Chorus, and, with his family, gave gifts to his mother, neighbors, and colleagues. Coffin's friend—and tennis and squash partner—Richard Sewall focused first on Coffin's squash game, which Sewall had taught him and lived to regret, then on his tennis, in which the older man still prevailed: "'The winters,' he told me, 'are good for my morale and your character; the summers are good for your morale and my character.'" "Let me confess," Sewall continued, "you woke me up to more than the inadequacies of my squash game. You gave me —you gave this community—new meaning, new purpose, new life. We had been simmering. Hero-like, you brought us to a boil."[14]

Once Coffin got to be alone at the podium, he picked up his guitar and played a Russian song about a boy leaving his girlfriend, explaining that he had "always thought of Yale as feminine, and any quarrels I have had with Yale are lover's quarrels. I hope that's not sexist. In leaving Yale I feel I am leaving the kind of friend which is irreplaceable." The choice, apparently impromptu, revealed more than he wanted. It stamped him irrevocably as a Yale man of the old school, by referring, however unintentionally, to the well-known fresh-man handbook advice (removed soon after coeducation, but not before) that Yale students treat their university as a good woman: "leave her when you must." The Russian twist inevitably recalled Manya, the Russian girlfriend he had left decades earlier, and might have been thinking about anew.[15]

His last sermon, which he delivered three days later, on December 14, to a fully packed Battell Chapel, stressed what one reporter called his recent "reve-lation, man's need for vulnerability." If "it were in my power to give all Yale people a farewell gift, it would be God's gift of vulnerability, which I hope I would also have the grace to accept myself."[16]

On New Year's Eve, Brewster wrote Coffin a personal farewell.

> As someone once said, sadness is only for those left on the shore. So . . . those you leave behind at Yale will be saddened.

What we—or I at any rate, <u>never</u> the representative man!—will miss most is the exhilaration which you breathed into all of us, in play as well as work, in dreams as well as thought.

<u>Enthusiasm</u>, as you have so often preached and practiced.

Happily, though, what you have given cannot be taken away. While I hope we don't coast on it, thanks for the momentum.

Cheers to you and for you in whatever lies ahead.

Affectionately,

King.[17]

For nearly a year, Coffin had been treading water. He had given up a position he had held for seventeen years and not sought to replace it. In interviews during that year he had talked vaguely about doing something with respect to world hunger and perhaps the arms race. He had been preaching more about global—as opposed to mainly American—problems. He had also been preaching his way to secular insecurity and personal vulnerability on behalf of trust in God, and the only plans he and Harriet had made were to spend a "secluded month in Mexico," where they would finish Bill's memoir and he would study Spanish and travel through Latin America. (Yale was letting them keep the house until the school year was over.) In early December he sent a deposit for a cottage in Barra de Navidad, Jalisco (Mexico), for a month beginning February 5.[18]

The truth was that Coffin did not know what to do next. He wrote later that during the "public farewells and Christmas festivities I was privately going through a time of agony." His fights with Harriet "were getting worse," and he felt caught between "necessity and guilt. I knew I had to leave Harriet, and felt it was wrong." His friend Arnold Wolf came to a kind of rescue and invited him over. They made small talk, and "Arnie was looking kind of distressed," until Coffin asked, "What's up?" Wolf got to the point: "How are you and Harriet getting along?" Taken aback, Coffin recalled answering, "Well, as a matter of fact, not too well, but how would you know?" Wolf: "Because you're an actor. A good one, but still an actor." Coffin: "So it's that obvious, huh?" Wolf: "All I want to say is, get out of that marriage, or one of you is going to be dead. I won't say which one." Coffin remembered that "to have my deepest feelings validated that directly was one of the most wonderful things that could have happened. And I'll always be grateful to Arnie for that kind of directness."

"After that encounter with Arnie," Coffin reflected, "I realized, I can't go off with her to Mexico. It would be ridiculous. So I just told her, I was just going to have to go off by myself." According to Harriet, Bill simply told her "I'm going off to think about my marriage," the day before "we were supposed to leave for Mexico to finish his book. I knew I'd never see Bill again."[19]

Harriet did not know where he had gone. "When we were first separated," she recalled bleakly, "he just disappeared." In fact, Bill first went to his sister's, just outside Boston. Then in February, he went to visit Inge and Arthur Miller (with whom he had become friends during the antiwar movement) in Roxbury, Connecticut. As Miller put it humorously many years later, Coffin came for the weekend and stayed six months. Finally, in late November, still in 1977, he ended up in the little town of Strafford, Vermont, in a room in his brother Ned's barn.[20]

In the spring of 1977 Amy Coffin was finishing her senior year of high school in New Haven, and her brothers were already away from home: Alex was living with a family in Mexico while David continued boarding at the Wooster School in Danbury, Connecticut. At first, neither Harriet nor Amy knew that Bill had gone for good. Amy wrote Alex a few days after the fact, indicating that she had not heard anything from him and that a genuine separation or divorce could be in the offing. This was clearly not the first time the subject had been raised, but now she was worried. In early February David needed a knee operation and his father came back briefly, as did Eva, unaware of the breakup. The stress of being titular head of the household did not help Harriet's drinking, as she felt she had been left "homeless, jobless, townless, childrenless, husbandless."[21]

Still, Harriet kept the household going, and when she and Bill resumed contact they corresponded and quarreled about phone bills, credit card charges, medical bills, and the like. Harriet's claim that Coffin frequently botched these matters seems reasonable, given Coffin's well-known inability to keep money in his pocket or handle bills or any kind of paperwork at all. Uncashed checks (from Harriet) remained clipped to her letters a quarter century later. On the other hand, he did send her some expense checks in the spring. He seems to have offered little without being asked.

Coffin's canceled checks from 1977 indicate occasional gifts to David and Amy, and at least one check to Harriet, but no large or regular payments that could be construed as child support, especially when contrasted with the numerous checks to doctors, stores, and utility companies in Vermont. Harriet recalled none. When the separated couple finally got to a divorce proceeding in 1978, Harriet sued for substantial economic support, accusing Coffin of providing no money for support since his departure. She also claimed that she needed to care for his three children until June, when two of them were mostly away from home, and their father claimed that graduate students were looking after Amy in return for room and board.

However bad the marriage—and it appears to have been very bad indeed at the end—Harriet had been left in a town she had never much liked, taking care of some portion of her absent husband's children, needing to leave the house at the end of the school year, with no employment, no good prospects, the nearly universal disapproval of the Yale community, a drinking problem, and a fairly high level of physical and emotional stress. Over the course of the spring Harriet packed up her belongings, leaving Coffin's for him to take care of after she left. That summer she took the children to Marsh Island again, while Coffin continued working on his memoir at the Millers'. Coffin later claimed—disingenuously—that "nothing could be more natural" than for Harriet to take his children to Marsh Island for the summer, where they worked for her.[22]

Coffin was surely depressed for a while, but the fact that his children had places to stay (with Harriet, at school, and with other family), the kindness of his family and friends, the pull of his writing project, and the occasional speaking and preaching engagement, and the comfort of women, helped his normally irrepressible nature to surface. By the end of the summer, he had begun to move on. He wrote about his life with great energy and read portions of it to his hosts. In the meantime, Ned had mentioned Bill to a younger female friend, Randy Wilson, the spunky manager of the local general store. She only vaguely recognized the name but told Ned, "Well, if he ever shows up, ask me to dinner and I'll come." When Coffin arrived one weekend, Ned asked Randy, and she came to dinner.[23]

Virginia Randolph Wilson had not been having an easy time of it. A native of South Strafford, she was losing family members to death, had recently ended her own marriage, and had almost no money to support two little children. "I had an enormous amount of stuff going on, and a very unsettled sort of situation," she reflected. "And on all fronts was struggling like crazy. . . . I'd sort of had it with men for the moment," though she did have an undemanding boyfriend at the time. But she enjoyed the evening's intense conversation immensely: "to have a conversation with somebody who just sort of—I call it duking it out—would duke it out with me—was great fun."

The next day, on his way out of town, escorted by Ned, Coffin stopped by her store, and in a brief conversation asked her if she would see him again (or go out with him—their memories differ) if he came back to town. Coffin meant the question simply. Randy saw it as "very weighted" because she immediately—and wisely—saw that a relationship with Coffin was not going to be simple: "I just thought, Oh God, this is going to be complicated. I just needed to see if I was up for it or not. And decided I was." So the next time Coffin came up to Strafford they first went to a discussion at a local restaurant and then escaped from their chaperones and went out to dinner. By then they appeared to have been smitten with each other. After that dinner, when Coffin went back to the Millers', having invited her for a weekend visit, Randy Wilson did some more serious thinking—and worrying: "I had to decide whether I was going to get serious about this . . . it was going to be all-consuming, I knew that. I could just tell. And I had two very small children and no money and . . . [was] scared to death, and Bill was without a job and still married and had three kids all over the world and didn't know what the hell he was doing. He was a big mess."

But she was already in love. It took her about two weeks to put "her affairs in order," to break up with her boyfriend, and prepare herself emotionally for a new life. Then she called Coffin at the Millers', told him that if he still wanted her to come she was ready, and within a few days, the weekend before Thanksgiving 1976, she boarded a bus to Connecticut. Coffin seems to have been taken as well. From New York, where he had gone to see his editor at Atheneum, he wrote "dear sweet Randy" a gushing love letter in which he mentioned having "no excuse to leave Strafford for several months." Since he was living in Roxbury at the time, this seemed to represent a decision to move to Ned's barn.[24]

Bruised by his editor ("compared to him nails are soft and cuddly"), who wanted Coffin to expand the personal sections of the book and build more conflict and drama into it, Coffin asked how much longer he needed to write. "For a start," the editor answered, "think the Ides of March." Having begun work on it during his sabbatical two years earlier, having already written steadily since January, this was not good news. On his way back to the Millers' and "back to the 'fuckin' ' book," Coffin confessed, "I don't know, sweetheart, if I could do it without you. But with you I know I can." He concluded, "Tell me you miss me. You can see how it is with me! I love you."[25]

Randy Wilson had not been to college, had not paid a lot of attention to newspapers or politics, and barely knew Coffin's reputation, but she did know who Arthur Miller was and therefore was already intimidated. When Coffin met her at the bus station, she discovered they were going to Inge Miller's book party. Horrified, dressed in "something god-awful," she made Coffin take her to a bar, thinking, "'I can't do this. I can't handle this. I don't have the skills for this.' And he gave me a scotch and water, maybe two, and said, 'It's a piece of cake. You can do it.' So I did . . . it was awful. I was scared to death the whole time." But the weekend was different, and the Millers made her feel welcome. Coffin had been staying in a cabin apart from the house, but Randy apparently did not join him there. Still, the following Tuesday, he began his letter "Randy, my sweet," and ended with "I love you."[26]

Coffin had lived for nearly a year without a domestic partner, and Randy thought him "coarse" when she met him: "Raggedy. Very raggedy. Depressed. . . . I mean Bill at any given moment can get up and talk. But once that's over, then there was this raggedy, depressed piece of work. Who just, I don't know, he never brushed his teeth. He didn't take care of himself. He didn't wash his clothes. He didn't eat well. He was just a mess. He drank too much. Didn't know where he was going, or what he was doing."

He was, in short, a man in need of caretaking. Randy Wilson was twenty-two years younger than Coffin, lively, independent, sure of her instincts, inter-ested in the world, and uneducated in the ways of cosmopolitan political, artis-tic, and intellectual life. When she decided to get involved with Coffin, she committed herself totally to the relationship. She could not tell where it was going to lead, but she sensed that he was complicated enough, and vulnerable enough, that "screwing around with him" would not have worked. "So I was totally, absolutely faithful," emotionally as well as sexually, from the very begin-ning. Even that level of commitment did not make it easy.

For one thing, Coffin did not get along with her two children, ages five and four, who shuttled back and forth to their father's place in Strafford every other day. When they were in their mother's home they wanted her, not Coffin, who knew next to nothing about little children. "They were horrible to him," she recalled, "and they were so horrible to each other that I finally said, 'Bill, you may not come to this house when I have the children. I will see you without my children at your house.'"

Secondly, Coffin was thoroughly engaged in writing and rewriting his memoir. His luck lay in finding a woman who was "hugely interested" in his work. It may have taken her a while to discover just how absorbed Coffin was in his own work, and how utterly uninterested he was in domestic matters. But the facts soon became clear, and Wilson accepted the developing bargain. "If I had been a man," she argued, and allowed to do the things that men were, "I would have wanted to do what Bill did." So she listened to his chapters and suggested the same kinds of revisions as his other listeners and readers: to put more of himself into it, to probe more deeply. Coffin, who simply did not know how, took as little of the advice as possible. On the other hand, Randy argues, without her the memoir would have even less of Coffin in it than it finally did.

Coffin also remained angry with himself for the failure of his second mar-riage, however convinced he was that he needed out of it. For a man not inclined to emotional commitment, the prospect of another serious relationship could easily have been quite threatening—assuming that he thought about it. On the other hand, in the words of his son David, Coffin "needed someone to take care of him," and at a certain level was not especially choosy.[27] Again, he got lucky. Few women could have offered him the energetic, flat-out commitment of Randy Wilson. She loved her children, and she loved Coffin's children. She knew and lived country domesticity, from cooking and cleaning and paying the bills to stoking the furnace, hauling water, and cutting firewood. And she became passionately committed to what she called Coffin's "work," his engagement in the struggle for social justice.

Coffin seems to have understood only dimly what Randy was offering him. He even felt embarrassed mentioning his new love to his children. "He never told Alex about me!" she exclaimed in wonderment nearly twenty years later. To Amy "the line was, 'I have met a woman who is a cook and a comfort to me.' I almost killed him when I heard that. Almost killed him." There can be little doubt that Coffin needed a comfort—and a cook. Without someone to care for his domestic needs, he would work at the expense of everything else; he would be, in Randy's blunt summary, a mess.

"It was a very hard time" for Coffin, she pointed out, even though "Bill never said so, never complained, never uttered a word of despair, or [gave] any indication whatsoever verbally that everything wasn't absolutely hunky dory. Ever." Coffin continued to court Randy Wilson—with his charm, with his seriousness of purpose, and with his playfulness. During the winter their relationship deepened. As Coffin recalled, "In the middle of the night I'd be down there in the store helping Randy get the clinkers out of the boiler. It would be minus fifteen. At that point I got a little introspective. I said, 'Either it's invincible ignorance that keeps me here in this freezing weather or I must be in love.' . . . And I decided I was pretty well smitten. Indeed I was. So I hung around and went into the summer."[28]

The Coffin children had stayed in touch with their father by mail and phone, and occasional visits. David continued at the Wooster School, and Amy and Alex had gone to Spain on an educational program—and then to Paris to stay with Eva's parents over Christmas. At the end of the school year, they would need a place to stay, so during the summer of 1977, Amy and Alex Coffin came to Vermont while David worked as a counselor at a summer camp. They each brought a friend, and with Randy Wilson's children the two families lived in an old summer camp that belonged to the Wilson family. Amy worked in the general store, while Alex painted houses.

Coffin finished his memoir, and he and Randy began thinking about the future. They found a little two-story house across the town green from Ned Coffin, two doors away from the Congregational church. Coffin sold enough stock during the summer to put sixteen thousand dollars down on the thirty-two-thousand-dollar house. Wilson signed for the mortgage. It was an odd step toward domestic stability, for both he and Wilson knew that Coffin's sojourn in Vermont, along with his unemployment, were coming to an end in spectacular fashion.

THIRTEEN

Down by the Riverside

The Call

One day in early 1977 the phone rang in Strafford, Vermont. From the New York City headquarters of the United Church of Christ, Valerie Russell was calling her old friend and mentor Bill Coffin. "I've been asked by the Black Christian Caucus at Riverside Church to talk to you." Coffin interrupted: "So how many of you are there? All four of you talking in one voice?" Her reply —"No, we make up 39 percent of the congregation"—got him thinking. Unruffled, she continued: "As you can imagine, our preference would have been for Andy Young, because he could have kept the whites. But seeing as Andy Young is at the U.N., we decided we'd like you to become minister, because you could keep the blacks." Suddenly Coffin had become a serious candidate for the pulpit of the flagship church of American mainline Protestantism.[1]

Across the street from Union Seminary in Morningside Heights on New York City's Upper West Side, Riverside Church has an unusual stature. An enormous cathedral modeled on European Gothic structures, especially Chartres, it towers massively and intricately, twenty-two stories high, over its Manhattan neighbors on the edge of Harlem. Because so many religious agencies and denominations have had their headquarters in the large building (known as the "God Box") across the street at 475 Riverside Drive, the congregation has included many staff from these groups, as well as faculty from Union, Columbia, Barnard, and other New York City educational institutions. Among its members (twenty-seven hundred in 1977), Riverside has counted some of the most eminent and influential people in one of the world's great cities.

Since its founding in 1841 in downtown Manhattan as the Stanton Street Baptist Church, the church had undergone physical moves as well as congregational transformations. But from the early teens, it had stood for theological liberalism against the fundamentalist tide that swept over much American Protestantism in the 1920s. Its best-known minister had been Harry Emerson Fosdick, a remarkable preacher who became deeply embroiled in the modernist-fundamentalist controversies of that decade. Forced to resign from the First Presbyterian Church in New York, Fosdick was hired as the preaching minister by the Park Avenue Baptist Church, Riverside's immediate predecessor. He set conditions: first, no doctrinal or denominational barriers could be placed in the way of potential members; second, the congregation had to commit to a new building.

With the generosity of its most eminent member, John D. Rockefeller Jr., the church built the Riverside cathedral and literally relocated the congregation "from a street symbolic of wealth to one of the world's greatest student centers, with Harlem at its doors. The move was to be made, not in an effort to get away from the city, but toward one of the city's most crowded areas." Begun in 1927, the new church opened for worship three years later.[2]

Over the next four and a half decades, Riverside became known as a great preacher's church, as well as a citadel of socially involved liberal Protestantism. From the Depression through the 1970s, under Fosdick and his successors Robert J. McCracken (1946–1967) and Ernest T. Campbell (1968–1976), the church and its preachers took on international, national, and New York City issues. Originally affiliated with the Northern Baptist Convention (as of 1973 the American Baptist Churches in the USA) and later with the United Church of Christ as well, Riverside had always seen itself as an inclusive and nonsectarian congregation.

Coffin had been a candidate for the post briefly when McCracken retired and recalled being visited by the head of the search committee in September 1967, weeks before the Boston draft-card turn-in: "And for a moment I wavered as to whether I should go ahead with turning in the draft cards, and then fortunately it didn't last more than about twenty seconds, and it hit me very clearly: you never do anything in your present job, or you never *not* do something in your present job simply because you want another one. That would be a total lack of integrity."[3]

During the summer of 1976, still jobless, Coffin had paid a visit to Bill and Helen Webber on the Maine coast and learned that Campbell had suddenly resigned. Webber, the same man who had talked Coffin into going to seminary more than twenty-five years earlier, who tried to get Coffin to be a "liberal Billy Graham," said, "Bill, that's the job you ought to have."[4]

The Riverside search committee began collecting names in November 1976. From an initial 250 candidates, members narrowed the list to 80, then to 20, and to 11. By February or March they were deciding which candidates to interview. At that point one member asked Sidney Lovett his opinion of Coffin's suitability for the position. When "Uncle" Sid raved about Coffin, Edith Lerrigo, the committee chair, called her old friend Lovett, indicating that Coffin was "one of a few leading candidates for the position." Lovett offered to act as intermediary to find out whether Coffin was interested and wrote him in Vermont. Coffin quickly called back, agreeing to an interview, and Lerrigo followed up.[5]

Coffin did not think much of his chances. "Well, that's very sweet of you," he had told Valerie Russell, "but I can't imagine a church taking a guy with my marital record, you know. Twice—pretty bad." Unfazed, she told him, "I don't think many churches could, but Riverside might." Lovett had warned him that several members of the committee "will be concerned with your marital track-record." But when Coffin got to the interview, he remembered the questions as "pretty damn dull"—mostly about administration—until one member asked him to describe "a situation where you had a religious crisis." Finally, "an interesting question," he thought. "So I figured I might as well talk about the divorce [from Eva]. They're not bringing it up, and obviously it's central to all this. And it was a religious crisis, so I talked about the divorce," arguing that divorce was a sin but not one that lay "beyond the pale of forgiveness." They wondered whether he could "be a minister with this kind of marital record." He maintained that people learned more from failure than from success.[6]

The search committee went to hear four candidates preach; Coffin's "neutral pulpit," as it was called, was at the First Congregational Church in Old Greenwich, Connecticut, where, he remembered, "you could tell when the Riverside selection committee came in because they were all the blacks." Afterwards they cut the list to two: Coffin and Methodist Bishop James Armstrong. Both candidates came to Riverside for a final round of interviews and met with the senior staff as well. The committee received an impressive range of unsolicited letters on Coffin's behalf from his friends and acquaintances around the country, including some of the most eminent men in the religious world. Robert McAfee Brown (who had moved back to Union from Stanford) called him "one of the great preachers of our time"; so, in very similar words, did Union President Donald Shriver, Yale Divinity School Dean Colin Williams, Episcopal Bishop of New York Paul Moore Jr., and J. Irwin Miller. Webber described him as "one of the most versatile and gifted human beings of our generation."[7]

On July 21, after nearly ten months of reading résumés and sermons, listening to preachers, and interviewing candidates, the nearly twenty-member search committee sat down and took its first straw poll to test the waters. Each member, it turned out, thought that he or she would be Coffin's only supporter. The unanimous result, therefore, stunned the committee. "It seemed a miracle to us that we were at last of one mind," Lerrigo reported to the deacons, "and we thanked God by singing the Doxology together."[8]

Committee members chose Coffin above all because of his preaching, which they loved for its biblical base and prophetic theology; for its Christian engagement with the "pressing issues of the day"; for its clarity, simplicity, and profundity; and for its ability to reach a very broad range of current and former members of the church. They thought Coffin would reach young sophisticates as well as "the poor and oppressed"; New York's governmental, business, and cultural leaders along with the church's academic and religious neighbors. They had lost nearly a thousand members since 1973—and they clearly hoped that putting Coffin in the pulpit would attract newcomers and bring some of the lapsed members back to church.[9]

But they also hired him because he could pastor individuals, because he could provide leadership to the church's staff and active laity, and because he loved the city. They worried about his divorces, about his administrative abilities, and about whether he would spend too much time on national and international issues and not enough on Riverside itself. Coffin convinced them, or they convinced themselves, that his marital failures had made him more attuned to his own and others' weaknesses; that if he could not administer the admittedly complex organization, he could at least provide good leadership to those who did; and that he was prepared to make Riverside his home.

The press would have paid attention no matter whom Riverside hired, but Coffin stirred up more than the usual notice. When the Board of Deacons nominated him unanimously on August 10, 1977 (for a congregational vote on Sunday, August 14), the *Times* considered it worth an article. That Sunday morning, the paper endorsed his election, on the grounds that "his color, verve, and calls to social action would enliven New York City." After an hour-long meeting with the congregation marked by some hard questions about divorce, some trademark Coffin witticisms, and two standing ovations, members elected him nearly unanimously.[10]

"Coffin's Church"

Coffin started officially on Monday, October 31, but early the previous day he drove down from Vermont and visited with the church's children and youth during the interim minister's farewell service. He preached his inaugural sermon November 6. The search committee had stressed administration because Riverside Church was an extremely complex organization. Unlike businesses, church operations rely on a combination of paid staff and volunteers. In churches, congregational members generally carry out more tasks, attend more meetings, and exercise more governance than their counterparts in other nonprofit organizations. Riverside Church was governed by a Board of Deacons responsible for programs and spiritual issues, and a Board of Trustees responsible for finances and church property. These two volunteer boards cooperated through a joint committee on certain key matters such as personnel and the church budget. Literally dozens of committees and task forces (organized into seven "councils"), from one overseeing the Sunday flowers to the Black Christian Caucus, filled out the organizational chart. But the church also had thirty-five full-time program and administrative staff members, along with another sixty-plus full-time people working on the building, from engineering to parking, security, and housekeeping.

Coffin found Riverside unwieldy, even chaotic. The Baptist distrust of hierarchy had led the church to multiply boards, councils, and committees to do the work without making clear lines of authority. There was, Coffin argued, "no clear understanding of what's staff and what's board" and "no very clear understanding of what kind of respect and authority is due an ordained person." While he had told the search committee that "for a year I'll put myself out to administer," the truth was that he had little interest in administration, had "no ego investment in it," and would much rather "inspire and have somebody else organize." He felt a number of key senior staff were fundamentally incompetent, yet because of the church's diffuse structure, and their personal constituencies, he found it impossible to fire them. As a result, Coffin felt "torn," knowing that he had to help develop personnel policies, for example, but resenting the fact that trustees were not willing to take charge of their own organization and make the hard personnel decisions. He talked so much to Randy Wilson about these frustrations that after just one month she asked, angrily, if it was "now to be my role that I must listen every waking hour to the same complaints, about the same dumb people who get in your way and slow you down and rob you of your energy." Eventually, forced by a budget crisis, Coffin got deeply involved in money matters, but he did not enjoy the experience.[11]

"I would say," one former parishioner recalled, that "Bill took over Riverside in a year or two," rather than the usual seven years. But Coffin led without controlling. He paid close attention to the Sunday service, for example, but "hardly ever" chose the hymns, leaving the choice to his minister of music. Rather than picking hymns to match the sermon, in other words, he enjoyed the challenge "to find something in every one of the hymns that maybe I could use in the sermon." His own musical background made him "want to defer to the musician," and his music ministers responded. At the same time, Coffin forged a bond with the choir by visiting their Sunday morning practices and singing with them sometimes. As one former parishioner put it to another, "Remember how people volunteered for that choir? . . . Suddenly all of the choir loft was full. It was just great, because they loved this minister who knew music also."[12]

He saw his role, he reflected later, as giving "permission" for things to happen at the church. In terms of the Sunday service, parishioners "needed permission to relax a bit. . . . I sensed right away . . . that the thing that's going to make this service really work is a combination of the severity of the architecture and the formal quality of the liturgy, [and] a lot of free-flowing stuff going through it. And this I think I learned a lot from the spirit of the Blacks around here. There's a lot of good Black Baptist spirit around here." So he made a few changes, such as inviting "the whole congregation [to] say Amen" and exchanging the "greeting of peace" because "they weren't ready for the kiss of peace, I could see that, or even the embrace of peace." Coffin enjoyed pointing out that after a while "everybody's hugging themselves."[13]

Coffin was able to communicate his feeling for the congregation through the liturgy, through the music, and through the pulpit. Seeing him regularly changed the views of those who worried that he would only be an activist: "It was actually a tremendous experience for all of us in the church to realize the ability and compassion and concern and the preaching [that] opened a whole new side of Bill to a great many people who had identified him only with social action." Coffin traveled a good deal, of course, but when he returned, "he would give the feeling that he just felt at home. . . . He was so glad to be back to the family." When he got back in town he walked around the offices, shaking hands, chatting with staff. After nearly two years out of the public eye, Coffin was delighted to be in the middle of a large community, and communicated the feeling to his colleagues and congregation.[14]

By his own admission Coffin had no vision for the church when he arrived. He knew it was a "progressive church that's interested certainly in such issues as peace and social justice," but he had no idea or plans for the form those interests should take. So as he had done at Yale, Coffin waited for people and issues to seek him out, knowing that, over time, "you get a feel of what you can do and who comes around offering what." "Because I was giving permission for things to happen," he explained, "people would make them happen." The church's pastoral counseling center, for example, began when Joan Kavanaugh came to see Coffin and persuaded him that it would be a good idea and that she was the right person to organize it.[15]

The Riverside Disarmament Program began in a similarly accidental fashion. In March 1978, Coffin's friend Richard Barnet of the Institute for

As senior minister for a decade at Riverside Church in New York City, Coffin made this flagship church of American liberal Protestantism into a central institution of American liberalism, even as the broader political spectrum shifted dramatically to the right. In this pulpit Coffin attained his greatest influence as a preacher. Courtesy of Randy Wilson Coffin.

Policy Studies came to town, and Coffin asked his old peace movement friend and colleague Cora Weiss, also a friend of Barnet, to join them. As Coffin put it later, "I was telling Cora that she ought to get back into the whole disarmament program now that the war in Vietnam was over." He had asked Barnet to help him "lean on Cora." As they made their case, he recalled, "Cora was obviously enjoying the attention of two men whose company she liked very much, and she said, 'I'll make you a deal. I will get back into the disarmament field if Riverside Church will hire me.'" They stopped. "I looked at Barnet and we looked at each other and we observed a moment of silence and respect for a great idea." Weiss offered to put on three national conferences for different constituencies. They fleshed out the idea a bit more and took it to the Board of Deacons as a proposal to launch a one-year pilot program to honor both the hundredth anniversary of the birth of Harry Emerson Fosdick, a committed pacifist, and the upcoming United Nations disarmament conference. "So we presented it to the Board of Deacons and there was a similar moment of silence, and then I'll never forget Marjorie Horton, who was then about 65, . . . said, 'I've been waiting twenty years for an idea like this.'" The deacons passed it unanimously.[16]

Their timing was perfect. Both the United States and the USSR had continued to expand their nuclear weapons arsenals, even as their negotiations for a successor to the first Strategic Arms Limitation Treaty dragged on. The Soviet buildup alarmed administration officials who had long counted on overwhelming American nuclear superiority. The administration of President Jimmy Carter had begun considering development and deployment of the MX, projected to be a newly accurate, mobile, intercontinental ballistic missile with multiple, independently retargetable nuclear warheads that many felt would dramatically destabilize existing arms control treaties. At the same time the American economy was mired in a combination of inflation and stagnation as the bill for the Vietnam War came due.

Coffin and Weiss discovered that the Disarmament Program's emphasis on reversing the arms race and refunding human needs struck a chord with many members of the church as well as with religious people all over the country. Their first convocation, in early December 1978, drew hundreds of clergy and laypeople to Riverside, where the speakers included Institute for Policy Studies staffers (such as Barnet and Michael Klare), arms control activists (like Randall Forsberg, soon to be author of the Nuclear Freeze, and David Cortright of SANE), academics (Robert McAfee Brown and the economist Seymour Melman), and politicians (Hartford mayor George Athanson and Congressman Ron Dellums).[17]

International tensions heightened in 1979, with the collapse of the U.S.-supported Somoza dictatorship in Nicaragua, the Iranian takeover of the American embassy in Tehran in November, and the Soviet invasion of Afghanistan in December. President Carter had already approved production of the MX missile in June, just ten days after hearing Coffin preach at Carter's home church in Washington and complimenting him on the sermon. Now Carter canceled grain exports to the USSR, ordered resumption of draft registration, suggested an American boycott of the upcoming Moscow Olympics, and began an arms buildup. Coming after a period of relative détente with the Soviet Union, and a new official U.S. concern for human rights, these measures, apparently reviving the Cold War, helped ignite a new peace movement in America. The near-meltdown at a nuclear reactor at Three Mile Island, Pennsylvania, helped fuel general antinuclear sentiment as well. From college campuses, where the draft once again became a hot topic, to churches and synagogues across the country, even to small towns in Vermont, Americans began questioning the wisdom of the nuclear arms race as never before.

But Coffin's and Weiss's insight about the possibility of organizing against the arms race predated most of these measures by a year. Nearly two months before the Soviet invasion of Afghanistan, the Disarmament Program sponsored a conference titled "How to Reverse the Arms Race" that drew roughly nine hundred people from thirty-five states. Weiss planned Riverside conferences to be training sessions for local organizers who would then hold their own conferences at home. Over the next two months, they received word of 156 "spinoff conferences" around the country.[18]

Coffin himself, along with two other American clergy, accepted an invitation from the Iranian government to celebrate Christmas with the hostages in Tehran in 1979. Braving a firestorm of criticism from the national media, who saw him as a simple-minded puppet of the Ayatollah Khomeini, Coffin never considered not bringing good news to the captives. Just as he had spearheaded an effort to provide medical supplies to the North Vietnamese on Christian principles, so he defied international power politics on behalf of basic Christianity. Since he never wasted an opportunity when the cameras were on him, he also criticized the Carter administration for its policies regarding Iran.[19]

It is hard to overstate the importance of the Riverside Church Disarmament Program in the revived peace movement of the 1980s. Weiss was an extremely shrewd organizer, with a keen sense of how to multiply the effects of her resources around the country. The program launched a Peace Sabbath/Peace Sunday program on March 31 and April 1, 1979, for example, encouraging synagogues and churches to feature sermons on peace in their services and sending out five thousand copies of sample Jewish and Christian sermons. The following year the Disarmament Program commissioned sample Catholic, Protestant, and Jewish sermons to be sent out in organizing packets; in 1980 two thousand congregations held Peace Sabbath or Peace Sunday observances in forty-six states.[20]

The Disarmament Program lay at the center of the loosely coordinated national antinuclear weapons movement organized around the Nuclear Freeze, the citizens' proposal to stop the nuclear arms race in its tracks. Activists from all over the United States, many of whose local peace organizations were based in churches and synagogues, relied on Riverside's information, ideas, materials, and leadership. The program hosted the meetings that organized the largest march and demonstration in American history on June 12, 1982, as a million people rallied against the arms race in Central Park to support the second U.N. Special Session on Disarmament.

Weiss knew how to use Riverside to raise the profile of the movement. Coffin contributed funds from his outside speaking engagements; the church offered some financial support; and Weiss herself raised "a lot of money," as Coffin put it later, from individuals and foundations. Riverside's stature and Coffin's reputation attracted public interest, publicity, funds, and internationally important figures. By Pearl Harbor Day of 1980, Riverside's "Evening for Peace" could draw thirty-five hundred people to hear, among others, Olaf Palme, former prime minister of Sweden, and Dom Helder Camara, a Brazilian archbishop prominently identified with liberation theology, nonviolence, and advocacy for the poor.

But Cora Weiss was a controversial figure at Riverside. A Jew heading a high-profile program at a leading Protestant church did more than raise eyebrows. Moreover, Coffin organized the Disarmament Program so that Weiss reported directly to him (and he reported to the deacons); other programs reported to the deacons. She gained "a lot of independence," Coffin recalled, but "the deacons felt that they didn't own this program and they got kind of surly about that." Finally, Weiss's style—she did not suffer fools gladly—and evident competence, particularly in a woman, unsettled those accustomed to slower, gentler, more bureaucratic ways of doing business. "As good a colleague as I ever had," he called her, Coffin loved Weiss's quickness, and competence, and was more than willing to run interference for her. She knew how to use him, and he appreciated being so well staffed: "I never had to suggest what she had to do; she always suggested what I had to do. And I almost always took her advice."[21]

By virtue of his position, more and different kinds of media sought Coffin out than ever before. Coffin needed fewer inspired publicity-driven schemes to reach a wide audience. Riverside's own communications staff distributed videos of his sermons and speeches, as well as of significant events at the church. Coffin's tenure coincided with the explosion in popularity of the video camera and the videocassette recorder, tools that advocacy groups soon used to multiply the effects of their most eloquent leaders. As a result, his image, his preaching, and his leadership spread across the mainline church landscape. Riverside sponsored a series of preaching convocations that drew hundreds of ministers from all over the country—five hundred or more at a time—to hear Coffin, as well as a range of well-known preachers and activists, and to attend workshops for a week. Ministers remembered these for decades.[22]

For a modest fee, the "Sermons from Riverside" series distributed forty sermons a year—most of them Coffin's—to more than a thousand subscribers, mostly clergy. Many of the recipients looked forward eagerly to their monthly packet; to this day some recall saving the little booklets, putting them aside until they could savor Coffin's take on the very biblical passages they had just engaged from their own pulpits. Many went further. An Episcopal bishop in California was caught delivering one of Coffin's sermons word for word.

Through much of the 1980s Coffin, Riverside Church, and liberal Protestantism were as alive and active as they had been since the mid-1960s in the flush of the successes of the civil rights movement and the optimism of the early anti–Vietnam War movement. At the same time, however, a huge conservative political and religious revival was putting political and religious liberalism on the defensive. The landslide victory of Ronald Reagan and the Republican party's senatorial and congressional candidates in 1980 brought the senate under Republican control for the first time since 1954. Liberal stalwarts George McGovern, Birch Bayh, and Frank Church lost their seats as new groups of fundamentalist Christians, such as the Rev. Jerry Falwell's Moral Majority, wielded sophisticated political clout. Stunned by the Republican electoral and public relations victory, the Democratic-controlled House of Representatives cooperated with the Reagan agenda, slashing taxes and human services budgets while embarking on the largest peacetime defense buildup in American history.

President Ronald Reagan reinvigorated the Cold War with the Soviet Union, increased aid to the right-wing dictatorship in El Salvador, invaded the Caribbean island of Grenada and overthrew its leftist government, and launched a covert war to oust the leftist Sandinista government in Nicaragua. Enjoying widespread domestic popularity, Reagan and his communications operation made militant anti-Communism a popular ideology once again. And in the face of this conservative, militaristic, often fundamentalist ascendancy, Riverside Church and William Sloane Coffin Jr. thrived. Church membership grew, as twenty-five- to forty-year-olds returned to the pews.

"The Most Divisive Issue Since Slavery"

Every development affecting liberal Protestantism in the 1980s also flowed through Riverside. The most divisive issues for Protestant churches in these years revolved around gender and sexuality: the advent of women clergy, the language of hymns and liturgy, abortion rights, and, above all, homosexuality. Each of these issues became battlegrounds in what commentators later called the "culture wars." In the world of the liberal church, homosexuality raised many questions: Was homosexuality—or were homosexual acts—a sin? If so, what kind? What did the Bible say? Could homosexuals be Christians? What rights could they have in the church? Could they be ordained? Could they be adoptive parents or Sunday school teachers or youth group leaders?

Coffin had begun making references to homosexuality early in his pastorate at Riverside, and when he gave the prestigious Beecher lectures at Yale during 1979–1980, he talked some about tolerance for homosexuals. But when he showed the lectures to his friend Richard Coram, a Dartmouth English professor (his "severest critic"), Coram accused him of waffling: "We should be tolerant? Big deal." In "thirty seconds, he crushed me, you know. I knew he was absolutely right." Then Randy Wilson chimed in, suggesting, "I don't think Bill's ready to take a stab at homosexuality. I think he's scared." But Coffin had already been at Riverside nearly four years, and at that point he decided, "I've really got to come to terms with this," and resolved to preach directly on the subject later that year.[23]

In preparation for the sermon Coffin did a lot of biblical and theological homework so that he could make the case to go beyond "tolerance" to a positive affirmation of homosexuals—and homosexual love. The subject had become "the most divisive issue since slavery split the Church," he began; he was preaching on it because "the once-unmentionable has become unavoidable."[24] Ministers were preaching the allegedly divine "judgment that gay men and women are not only different, but sinfully different." Gays were being "physically and psychologically abused," so "we have no choice but to bring up the issue. Straight and gay American citizens, and especially American Christians, can remain neither indifferent nor indecisive."

The biblical case rested on close analysis of the passages, principally in Leviticus, in which the term used to condemn homosexual acts is the same one used to condemn eating pork, misusing incense, and having sexual intercourse during menstruation. Moreover, "while homosexual *acts* are condemned, nowhere does Scripture address a homosexual *orientation*." Clearly, therefore, "it is not Scripture that creates hostility to homosexuality, but rather hostility to homosexuality that prompts certain Christians to retain a few passages from an otherwise discarded law code." After all, few Christians obeyed the injunctions "do not plant your fields with two kinds of seed," or "do not wear clothing woven of two kinds of material" (Lev. 19:19). The larger issue was "not reconciling homosexuality with Scriptural passages that appear to condemn it, but rather how to reconcile the rejection and punishment of homosexuals with the love of Christ. I don't think it can be done."

Coffin acknowledged that he had previously tended toward the position of "many sensitive straight Christians": that gay people deserved equal rights. "But they [himself included] can't picture a gay spouse in the parsonage; they're uncomfortable with public displays of gay affection. In their heart of hearts they feel that homosexuality is not really on a par with heterosexuality," in the way that many Christians believed, deep down, that Judaism was inferior to Christianity instead of "just different." "How," he asked, "can you champion equality while nourishing the theological roots that make for inequality?" Coffin himself had been persuaded by a certain logical similarity between the "black problem," which "turned out to be a problem of white racism, just as the 'woman problem' turned out to be a problem of male sexism," and the "'homosexual problem' is really the homophobia of so many of us heterosexuals." "So enough of these fixed certainties," he pleaded. "If what we think is right and wrong divides still further the human family, there must be something wrong with what we think is right."

Soon afterwards some of his gay members proposed "an all gay service," and Coffin, intrigued, handled the negotiations personally. Later, he knew "we should have done it the Riverside way," that is, through channels, "but I'm always impatient with those things." The gays wanted to change the Lord's Prayer to "Our Lover, who art in heaven." He insisted that they defend their position theologically, "and I realized that theologically they were correct." But Coffin had other agendas as well, as in "how well we're going to communicate this. And I want the folks who are visiting from Dubuque to go back to Dubuque and say, 'You'll never believe it, what we saw and heard at Riverside. It was terrific.' Now that's what we have to produce. And this is too strong. It won't go." He recognized that gays had "thought about it a lot more than I have," but, he pointed out, "I have to accept final responsibility for this. . . . It's too strong." The well-known lesbian theology professor Carter Heyward preached at the service, in which Coffin had also asked to participate because "it would be good to have one straight." He was pleased at the result: "it was accepted, you see."[25]

By 1985, four years after Coffin's first sermon on the subject and nearly eight years into his pastorate, Riverside Church was well along in the process in the United Church of Christ that could result in the church voting to become "Open and Affirming"—that is, open to homosexuals and affirming of them as Christians and as gays and lesbians. Given the composition of the church —a mixture of very liberal younger white New Yorkers, many new to the church, including many gays and lesbians, and the older, more socially conservative African-American Baptists—this process was bound to generate a certain amount of controversy. For while the gay and lesbian membership had been growing, so had opposition to gay visibility.

The simmering tensions boiled over on Sunday morning, May 5, 1985, a month before the "Open and Affirming" vote. Coffin was preaching out of town, and Associate Minister Channing Phillips was in the pulpit for the sermon. Near the end of a respected career, Phillips, as the only senior black minister at Riverside, was also the natural sounding board for the church's black members.

Without warning his colleagues, Phillips preached what Coffin called a "moral horror of a sermon," warning against deviating from gospel pronouncements on the evils of divorce, promiscuity, and the sanctity of heterosexual marriage. While Phillips did not himself explicitly condemn homosexuality and divorce, he did insist that "as far as the biblical understanding of human sexuality is concerned, any and all deviation from the parable given in Genesis [that male and female were at the foundation of human sexuality] and referenced by Jesus, whether within heterosexual or homosexual relationships, is sin, is contrary to the will of God. And no theological or exegetical *sleight of hand* can erase that 'word of the Lord.'"²⁶

To many in church that day, particularly those who felt Riverside was "going too far" toward homosexuality, this "word of the Lord" was balm to troubled spirits. To hundreds of others, it felt like a thundering fundamentalist condemnation, "the most God-awful sermon I have ever heard in my life," in the words of Phillips's colleague Patricia de Jong, not only "because he preached against gays and lesbians, but also there was a part of the sermon that divorced people in the congregation felt condemned [by]. I mean it was a very condemning sermon." At the end of the communion service a young graduate student at Union said to her, "'I'm going to protest the sermon at the close of worship. Will you join me?' I looked at him and said 'I'll try.'" He came to the front of the church and invited everyone who had disagreed with the sermon to "gather in love around the communion table during the singing of the final hymn."²⁷

Perhaps five hundred worshippers (out of thirteen hundred that day)—including counseling service director Joan Kavanaugh and much of the church leadership—left their seats, the choir loft, and the dais and gathered in the center of the church to sing in protest, many of them weeping. Coffin returned that evening to division and chaos, to anger and a feeling of betrayal. African Americans were as furious as the gays. Many "thought they had heard the word of God, then saw this demonstration as being racist," Coffin recalled, "because, as they said afterwards, 'You know, we don't agree with everything Bill says, but it would never occur to us to pull a demonstration on him. And here a young white fella pulls a demonstration against an older black man, that is racist!'"

Phillips refused to take responsibility for his sermon, maintaining that it represented an important position, even if it was not necessarily his own. At Coffin's insistence the Collegium (the senior ministers) met daily for the next week; they invited theologians to help them think through the issues, but remained at loggerheads. And the following Sunday was Mother's Day.

Many preachers dread Mother's Day—the single most sentimental Sunday in the calendar—for the exact reasons their congregations love it. Victorian sentimentality overwhelms the modern sensibility and parishioners take pleasure in an older, apparently less complicated era. Fictions abound. Special church breakfasts absolve Mom from making breakfast on "her day." Children, husbands, and fathers do their best to get dressed for church without Mother's help and anticipate gathering around a large family table.

Mother's Day arrived on May 12, and in the grand cathedral the air lay heavy with the fragrance of flowers; there were sprays of lilies and corsages for all the mothers. Expectancy jostled with fear, anxiety with anger, as Coffin ascended into the pulpit to read the New Testament Scripture lesson (Luke 2:41–

51) and face a church seriously divided over homosexuality. Under his leadership, the flagship congregation of American liberal Protestantism was heading toward public acceptance and affirmation of gays and lesbians. His own colleague had dissented from that direction the previous Sunday. And Coffin had to take up the issue on the most gender-conservative Sunday in the year.[28]

The biblical passage tells the story of the boy Jesus running away from his parents as they left Jerusalem and being found some three days later as a young prodigy with the scholars in the temple. Jesus explains to his mother that he "had to be in his Father's house." Mary, according to Luke, "kept these things in her heart."

It is hard to imagine a parable better suited to illuminate Coffin's life in the ministry. His career had followed that of the father he had barely known (active in war, at Yale, in the church) and the eminent uncle he had known well. The story could also describe any gifted child's assault on the world, but this day it gave Coffin additional psychic energy for his task.

Referring to "my beloved colleague's sermon" and the reaction it prompted, Coffin first acknowledged the "hurt and anger" of those offended by the sermon and then the "pain" of those offended by the demonstration, whom he exhorted to understand that the protest was called, "I believe genuinely, in the name of healing and love." He opened the doors to the ministers' studies, letting the worshippers know that they had "thought of and dealt with little else all week."

Then he went straight at the issue: "Dearly beloved in the Lord, we now have a sharply divided church." Riverside was hardly alone: "American churches are more divided over this issue than they have been over any issue since slavery." The hint of a smile played about his lips as Coffin sailed into battle on behalf of the gospel and the love of God. "What are we going to do? . . . We are going to behave as those who believe in the Lord Jesus Christ." After all, "What is at stake," he thundered, was not us, our thoughts, our sexual preferences, even our lives, but "nothing less than the Gospel." The issue was the nature of Christianity itself, the meaning of God's love.

"If we obey the simplest, most fundamental, and difficult injunction of Scripture, we will love one another, gay and straight. If we are of one heart, we can, as the Collegium has discovered this past week, be of two minds." (In fact, despite Coffin's efforts, Phillips was resisting his colleagues' efforts to "be of one heart.") Coffin offered no sociology, no psychology of gender orientation. As always, his inspiration came directly from the Bible, what Bill Webber called his "Biblical theology." Only the gospel, he declared, "can clear our thoughts and liberate our lives." And while St. Paul had called homosexual acts "unnatural," he also used the same word to describe men wearing long hair, and called women speaking in church "shameful." There was, in other words, plenty in the Bible that was "as foreign as can be to the minds of contemporary Bible readers." That was why he "read the Bible most, not for its ancient laws, but its ancient wisdom."

He recapped his own evolution from grudging acceptance to affirmation and rejected promiscuous sexuality of any orientation as unchristian. Finally, Coffin connected the love of mothers and parents for their children, even gay children, to the love of God for humankind.

The sermon and Coffin's actions during the entire episode displayed his gifts working at a very high level. Furious at Phillips, he was more upset by his colleague's attack on their common parishioners. He felt personally betrayed but turned that set of private feelings into a public response and called the entire church to engage its genuine differences. He disagreed politically with Phillips but insisted that the issue was above all religious.

Coffin relished his immersion into the most difficult issues, while most preachers would have tried to paper over the conflict, to offer platitudes about pluralism. Coffin, however, contended that the issues engaged by Phillips's sermon lay at the heart of the Christian understanding of God and the world. "Christianity has not been tried and found wanting," he told them in one of his favorite sayings (reworked from Chesterton), "it has been tried and found *difficult*." Utterly confident in Christianity's wisdom and power, he invited his parishioners into these inconvenient challenges with evident pleasure. He even modeled the point he made in the sermon in the very language he used: "beloved Riversiders, beloved colleague."

Here, Coffin displayed one of the keys to his ministry at Riverside. The external (non-Yale, non-Riverside) perception of Coffin's religiosity was that of an updated Old Testament prophet, calling his church and nation to account for its wickedness, exhorting it to righteousness and justice. In such a mode, Coffin could have simply insisted on the correctness of his position and flatly opposed his (subordinate) colleague. But Coffin believed in the gospel of love and preached a sermon he hoped would begin a process of reconciliation. The solution to Riverside's problems and to the "problem" of homosexuality or homophobia lay in the biblical injunction to love one another. The capacities and practices of human love could only be properly measured against God's insistence on unconditional love for all human beings.

Coffin must also have enjoyed the opportunity to think these thoughts and preach this sermon on Mother's Day. He had begun the sermon with a humorous Yiddish proverb: "God could not be everywhere, so God made mothers." For all of his mother's efforts to keep Bill on the right track, and her attentiveness to his choices, her criticism, her physical distance, and emotional reserve, Catherine Butterfield Coffin's powerful, enveloping love for her son had given him the experience he had been preaching about for decades. She had given him the feeling that he had enormous promise and that he was worthy of a woman's devotion. At no point in his young life had Coffin ever had reason to doubt that he was loved, and that belief carried over into his adult conviction, which he almost never doubted, that he was loved by God.

Mother's Day at Riverside accomplished most of what Coffin wanted it to. The Collegium continued to meet daily for the next few weeks and helped the opposing factions to clarify their positions. Some gays "wanted Channing run out of the church," while the mainly African-American Sunday school mothers who felt they were "protecting their children and their families" from homosexuals and from a promiscuous gay lifestyle wanted a different kind of assurance from their church. At last, just days before the special church meeting to vote on "Open and Affirming," Coffin recalled, "we finally brought them together," a representative group of proponents and opponents, and "we hammered out a statement." Coffin pushed for compromise wording, something that included "traditional Christian family," even though he knew "it's not Biblical." The key sentence read, "While reaffirming the traditional Christian family, we wish also to affirm all human relationships based on the Christian understanding of love and justice." After about three or four hours, "finally we got that sentence in there and both sides agreed to it . . . and at the end of it we were all weeping because it was a reconciliation. A genuine reconciliation. The church was being the church."[29]

During the special meeting, de Jong recalled, "Bill and I were sitting in the front." When the vote came in, 320 in favor to 80 opposed, "I almost jumped up in my seat, because I was so happy." But before she could, she "felt this strong arm coming across [me], saying to me 'Don't get too excited; remember those who are in pain.' And that, for me, is classic Coffin." In reality, it was an older and wiser Coffin, now more than sixty years old. "Let me tell you something about Coffin in 1959," John Maguire commented. "He would have been jumping up there, hootin' and hollerin' with the rest of them."[30]

Coffin acknowledged several years later that while scars remained from the battle, he also felt that there were limits to what could be reconciled. Finally, there were conflicts that could "only be decided by taking one side or another. And homophobia is like racism. You cannot reconcile that. You've got to come down on the right side. It's the only way it's going to be solved."[31]

The Collegium never recovered. When Channing Phillips fell sick the following year with his last illness, he sent word that he did not wish to be visited by Coffin. Although Coffin won the immediate battle, he lost the larger struggle to reunite Riverside. De Jong and others thought that Coffin's interests in programs rather than administration made it difficult for the church to articulate a coherent vision of itself: "There was no real direction in the congregation other than, let's do everything, and let's do it at once," she recalled. She offered an echo of Eva Rubinstein: "And let's be large people. And I think Bill is such a large person, he forgets sometimes that many people are wounded and many people are small spirited."

Coffin never had an overall strategy for the church. Tactically, he could be brilliant, as when he made people deal with each other and "act like a church." But an accumulation of tactics did not add up to strategy. Moreover, the church had stretched its members in many different ways. By 1985 Riverside had developed an internationally renowned Disarmament Program, had voted to become a "sanctuary church" (that is, it would harbor refugees from the civil wars in Central America in defiance of U.S. immigration law), had become "Open and Affirming," had changed the language of its hymns to be more "inclusive," had sponsored numerous national conferences and convocations, had brought more press attention to the church than ever before, and had grown substantially in numbers. Even de Jong, who supported Coffin almost unreservedly, saw that on top of having to "stretch and stretch and stretch," the Phillips episode was an "awful experience." Coffin himself admitted it was "too many things" and that it "made the deacons nervous."

The causes the church had taken on most aggressively during Coffin's tenure were focused on either the national or international (disarmament, Central America) or cultural (gays and lesbians, new liturgical language) arenas rather than focused on New York City and Riverside's own neighborhood. In practice, that meant that the church acted more in areas that its African-American members perceived as "white" and far less on the urban issues—housing and homelessness, criminal justice, and poverty—closer to their hearts. Later, Coffin regretted that he had "done very little more than just talk" on the city's problems.[32]

The church faced a budget crunch soon after the Phillips imbroglio, and the Collegium had to meet frequently and with other staff to pare down the budget—a task Coffin did not enjoy at all. As he explained in late 1987, he felt that he never really got a good administrative hold of the entire operation. Particularly in the last year and a half, there seemed to be more free-floating hostility, and things seemed to spin more out of control.

In July 1987 he announced his resignation at the end of the year to take up the presidency of SANE/Freeze, the nation's largest disarmament organization, formed when SANE merged with the Nuclear Freeze. On December 20, the fourth Sunday in Advent, Coffin preached his farewell sermon, a poetic tour de force on the subject of joy, the way it could unite with pain, the way it could overcome grief and sadness and loss and injustice and death: "It is there always, this joy, for those who believe that despite the iniquity in warfare, despite the absurd, despite the apathy, the world is still fraught with mystery, meaning, and mercy." The church had invited parishioners to write letters to Coffin, which it compiled into a loose-leaf notebook as part of its farewell gift. Among the more than one hundred letters from congregants and staff members were two from men who had known Coffin for a very long time. One short note said much: "For nearly thirty years, since that first memorable sermon at Battell in 1958, your witness has continued to inspire me to the Christian life more times and ways than you could possibly imagine." Another writer remembered first coming to see Coffin as a Yale freshman in 1963, worried that "sinners would be damned" to hell. Coffin had reassured him then and for most of the next quarter century, during "which you have been my pastor in one place or another, I have learned from you, from your words and your life, about the other side of God: about God's grace, about the joy that can come from living one's life in obedience to God."[33]

During his decade as senior minister at Riverside Church, Coffin did with this wealthy, storied, imposing church almost exactly what he had done with the Yale chaplaincy. He took one of the most visible pulpits in the country— the most renowned in northern mainline Protestantism in this case—and moved it to a qualitatively different level. By the time he left, he had substantially increased the size of the congregation; nearly 60 percent of the membership when he left had joined during his tenure. Coffin felt strongly that it was up to "flagship churches" to "cast a mantle of respectability over controversial issues," and he used Riverside's prestige to influence liturgy, preaching, the interpretation of the gospel, and the political and moral life of the nation. In so doing, Coffin became the outstanding voice of liberal Protestantism in America, one of the last thoroughly unabashed liberal voices in American public life during the ascendancy of Reagan Republicanism, the rise of right-wing fundamentalism, and the dramatic rightward shift of public policy and discourse. Both organizationally and personally, Coffin provided articulate and energetic leadership for the nuclear disarmament movement of the 1980s, for the movement opposing intervention in Central America, and for religiously affiliated people, lay and ordained, across the country on a broad range of social and religious issues. During his time at Riverside Church, Coffin made himself the preeminent voice of religious dissent in America, a worthy successor to Harry Emerson Fosdick.[34]

While it is impossible to measure the precise effect of such a voice, a number of conclusions seem clear. First, no matter how well Coffin articulated the values of liberal Protestantism, a commitment to peacemaking and opposition to militarism, compassion for the poor and the downtrodden, neither he nor his larger constituents could arrest the rightward movement of American politics and culture during the 1980s. Democratic presidential candidates received some of the worst trouncings of the twentieth century at the time of Coffin's greatest influence, and Republicans—one of them, George H. W. Bush, a nearly exact contemporary of Coffin at Andover and Yale (whom Coffin frequently called a "perfect example of skim milk rising to the top")—occupied the White House from early 1981 until 1993. The gap between America's rich and poor, narrowing since the Great Depression, abruptly began growing again in the early 1980s. Manhattan had become, Coffin observed in his farewell sermon, "a playground for the rich and a jungle for the rest. . . . In all my life, I have never seen Americans turn their backs on the poor the way they are doing today."

At the same time, this decade saw the growth of the largest peace movement in American history, a movement that depended utterly on liberal churches (including Catholic churches) and synagogues and other religious institutions for its membership base, meeting space, funding, and spiritual inspiration. The thoroughgoing secularist Cora Weiss saw the fundamental importance of organizing churches and synagogues on these issues. Far larger and more mainstream than the movement to end the Vietnam War, the disarmament movement built a moderate (as well as liberal) constituency for arms control that helped change the attitude of administration officials from their early pronouncements about the ease of surviving a nuclear exchange. Even such former Cold Warriors as Robert McNamara and William Colby came to support the Nuclear Freeze, for example. Coffin and Riverside Church remained at or near the center of this movement from 1978 until Coffin and Weiss left Riverside in 1987. As the most experienced, articulate, and best-known disarmament preacher in the country when he left Riverside, he was the natural choice to assume the presidency of SANE/Freeze.

Coffin was not alone in his advocacy in these matters. Liberals in many denominations organized to fight conservatives and American policies. Religious life in the 1980s, in other words, went through one of its many periods of increased political activity.[35] But because of his location in New York City, alongside Union, Jewish Theological Seminary, and the "God Box," there was no more influential figure in American religious practice during this time than Coffin.

How much Coffin and liberal religious activism helped pave the way for the presidency of Bill Clinton is not clear. The peace movement proved completely ineffective in its opposition to the Gulf War. President George H. W. Bush was undone more by domestic economic considerations—and the superb campaigning of candidate Bill Clinton—than by opposition to his successful war against Iraq. But Coffin and his colleagues in liberal Protestantism helped nourish liberal activists during their "dark time," an essential task for any group that looks to have a long-term effect on political and moral life.

Coffin himself, fed by the promises of the gospel, never lost hope that things could be better and continued to preach—cheerfully and joyfully—on behalf of ideals and values that had little sway at the level of national and state policies. He had a visceral understanding of the long term: "I always used to feel that it's very important that we put something into the mainstream of American history today that will nourish a generation of the future. . . . The main thing is, ultimately in this world, you've got to do what's right. Penultimately, what's effective." After all, he pointed out, "Nathan Hale didn't ask, 'Will I be effective?'" He had, he admitted, a "stock answer" to those in the peace movement who said, "I'm so disillusioned": "Who the hell gave you the right to have illusions in the first place?" he said with a laugh. "They're not Niebuhrian enough!"[36]

The Personal and the Political

Coffin's decade of public ministry at Riverside confirmed him as a national voice on some of the most important public issues of the late 1970s and 1980s. But a number of personal issues also put him in the public eye as rarely before. Coffin's own life during his Riverside years could have been a text for the slogan of 1970s feminism: "the personal is the political."

The first of these was his divorce from Harriet Coffin. Not long after Bill had left Harriet in 1976, they went to see a mediator, who informed them that if they went to court a judge would probably insist that Bill pay her compensation for what she had given up by marrying him. He named a sum—eleven thousand dollars, Coffin recalled; she recalled just five hundred—that Coffin offered to pay on the spot. Harriet wisely refused.

For his part, Coffin let the whole matter slide and remained puzzled by his own passivity with respect to getting a divorce. "Maybe in a way," he said later, "it sounds sick now, maybe I wanted the protection of not being divorced so I could just be not decisive."[37] Coffin's impatience applied only to religious or political issues; he had rarely, if ever, confronted difficult personal issues when he did not have to. As long as Harriet did nothing about their marital status, he was just as content to do nothing. And no matter how smitten he was with Randy Wilson, he also knew that while he remained simply separated from Harriet, he could avoid a decision about remarrying.

Living off investments (liquidating some), writing foundation proposals, and trying to find freelance writing work, Harriet had not been having an easy time. She apparently suffered physically and psychologically from the stress of the breakup and looking for work. As long as Coffin himself remained unemployed, she had little to gain by suing him for divorce or alimony. That changed when he went to Riverside, and in November 1978 she sued him for support.

The affidavits and depositions and legal filings went back and forth for the next two years. Harriet first demanded $450 per week and produced doctors' letters attesting to her high blood pressure and stress, including her psychiatrist's recommendation that she not work for at least two years. She had a somewhat inflated notion of Coffin's financial situation and threatened, if "necessary," to "prove incidents of misconduct on the part of the defendant very much more serious than anything now contained in my complaint."[38] Neither Coffin nor his lawyers appear to have taken her seriously.

The following year Harriet was willing to settle, and Coffin recalled the meeting with a lawyer who turned to him and said, "One hundred thousand dollars, and you're getting off real easy, Reverend." Flabbergasted, he had no idea how he would get such a large sum, which he thought had to be paid all at once. Coffin's lawyer thought the figure ridiculous and tried to settle for much less, advising Coffin "that it is unlikely that the court would award Harriet more than $7,500 a year and perhaps might limit that to a relatively short period of years."[39] He offered five thousand a year for five years, as an opener, indicating that he might be able to do better. Harriet's lawyer would not come down from a hundred thousand, and began moving toward a trial. Without realizing it, Coffin was compounding his biggest personal mistakes.

For three days in late September and early October 1980, *Coffin* v. *Coffin* came to trial, furnishing lip-smacking material for the city's tabloids. Coffin's inability to remember anything having to do with finances made him appear an often-ridiculous witness. Harriet's lawyers produced documents to contradict his recollections on more than one occasion. Far more important, Harriet made good on her threat to expose Bill's "misconduct." She had saved the X-rays and pictures from when she had gone to the hospital after Bill had hit her, and she produced them in court, surprising Coffin and his lawyer. Once the papers had the "peacenik reverend" beating his wife, Coffin was trapped. The only way to defend himself, he felt, would have been to put her in "the worst possible light: say that she was a complete drunk, she was violent as all get out, and how I hit her, why I hit her, it was the only way to end the argument, as I could see it, at 3:00 in the morning . . . it just felt gratuitous [to] . . . drag her and her name into an alcoholic sewer." After all, he wanted her to get a job, too. But he did respond to charges that he had abandoned his children, partly at the insistence of David (who attended the trial) and Alex. "I have not abandoned my children ever," the *New York Post* quoted Coffin. "I left my wife because I couldn't take the violence and the alcohol any more." Coffin had thrived for more than twenty years in the culture of celebrity. Now he learned that he could be its victim as well.[40]

The judge awarded Harriet $1,083.33 per month ($13,000 annually), about $5,000 a year less than what she wanted (and no attorney's fees) but much more than Coffin had offered, and put no time limit on the monthly payment. Neither appealed.[41]

Members of Riverside's Men's Class also attended the trial, taking copious notes. This small group—estimates ranged from ten to twenty members in Coffin's day—had declined substantially from its "glorious past" in Fosdick's time. In the 1960s and 1970s it had become "completely and utterly reactionary," in one former member's words. Its publication, *The Messenger,* regularly attacked Coffin and the church leaders for the Disarmament Program, for their naiveté regarding the power of international Communism, and for their allegedly un-democratic governance of the church.[42]

Longtime church member William Peck, who believed that Coffin and Cora Weiss were trying to lead the church and the country into the arms of Soviet Communism, served as the group's indefatigable researcher. He not only covered the last two days of the divorce trial in 1980, he later obtained the tran-scripts and evidence and supporting affidavits, which he used in an attempt to prove that Coffin was secretly on the payroll of the Soviet Union in 1976 and 1977 when he was living in Vermont. Peck wrote a series of pamphlets modeled on *The Messenger* titled "Let Riverside Be Riverside"—attacking Coffin and Weiss, whom he generally referred to as Cora Rubin Weiss (to em-phasize her Jewishness), for politicizing Riverside—which he distributed outside the church on Sundays. Finally, the group managed to get press coverage for its point of view, though the *Times* held off at first. Eventually, though, the *Times* published a front-page article about the Men's Class and its call for Coffin's resignation. The staff had gone up the Hudson River for a staff retreat and, as de Jong recalled, when they arrived, Coffin "took one look at the *Times* and said, 'Let's turn around, we're going back.' And just like that, he went back and faced that." Coffin considered them "awful," "slanderous," "paranoid," "evil," and anti-Semitic, but since no one could make them go away, he tried to consider them "a thorn in the flesh." They did not drive him to resign.[43]

But when they attacked the church, he felt strongly that the leadership should defend Riverside, both to the congregation and to the press and general public. Eventually, he persuaded his deacons to confront the group. They met with nine members of the Men's Class in December 1980 to hear their charges against Coffin and the Disarmament Program; in the words of Chairperson Al Wilson, "We had seen evil in the face." During the service the next Sunday Wilson declared the deacons' complete confidence in Coffin—and the congregation "jumped up and cheered." But the dissidents did not go away. As Coffin put it later, "They wouldn't die! They went on and on. Had heart attacks, went blind, nothing stopped them. I'll tell you: bitterness does more than cortisone. It keeps people going!"[44]

"Alex's Death"

A natural leader among his peers, Alexander Sloane Coffin had wit and charm, an infectious smile, athletic skill, and his parents' good looks. As a teenager in the 1960s he charmed his way into the football games and dorm rooms of Yale students, and into the hearts of nearly all those who knew him. During Alex's peripatetic academic career, his teachers and headmasters wrote many different versions of the same letter to him and to his parents. The Eaglebrook School headmaster, for instance, wrote at the end of ninth grade, "You know full well how much I have enjoyed your company and companionship this year." On the other hand, "There is the possibility that your immense talent and charming personality will be wasted by an equally strong desire for total independence and carelessness of manner."[45]

Alex Coffin lived and played hard and recklessly, and with little concern for consequences to himself. He liked to drink and to party from a young age and frequently brushed up against the law or school authorities. Neither he nor Amy had much close adult supervision in New Haven, between their parents' divorce, their father's work and travel, and the chaos of the big house on Trumbull Street that Bill and Harriet moved into in 1969. He and his father had always had a bond, partly because he appeared to be a younger version of Bill. Bill and Alex were "peas in a pod," according to Randy Wilson, the two best athletes in the family, and the ones who competed the most with each other, mainly at tennis. As Bill wrote friends when Alex was nearly thirteen, "As for friend Alex—he still shows all my worst qualities, but is beginning to demonstrate that he has also inherited some of my sterling ones."[46]

Alex worked and lived in Boston and spent time in and out of college into his twenties. He had entered Boston University in 1977 and was scheduled to graduate in May 1983 with a degree in sociology. He had been through several years of health problems especially frustrating for an athlete, from bone spurs on his feet to a year-long bout with mononucleosis to a long recovery from breaking both legs in a skiing accident in 1982. Doctors had removed pins from his legs around Christmas, and he was beginning to play tennis again—one of his great passions. On the evening of Monday, January 10, 1983, Alex had gone to a Boston tennis club, played all night, and then went to the bar.

In Strafford, Randy Wilson got the call from the hospital. Alex had died in the early morning of Tuesday, January 11, 1983, driving in a bad storm on a dangerous curve at the edge of South Boston Harbor. He had been in a celebratory mood that might have included a beer too many. His car had crashed through a low seawall into the water around midnight; his passenger escaped, but Alex drowned. For the next few hours Randy called Coffin's apartment in New York City "every five minutes," but he was not answering the phone. Finally, she called Cora Weiss and Al Wilson and told them what had happened and asked them to find Bill. That is how Coffin learned that the child who took after him the most—handsome, competitive, charming, athletically talented, a daredevil—had died.[47]

The stunned, devastated family gathered first in Boston, then in Vermont, where Samuel Slie, one of Coffin's associate chaplains, still at Yale, performed the funeral. It had already been a bad time for the Coffin family. Catherine had died a month before, in New Haven, at age ninety, and Arthur Rubinstein had died a little over a week later at age ninety-five.

"One of the things that was so remarkable and devastating about his dying," Randy recalled, "was that my relationship with him was just like everybody else's. Alex had it within him to make all these people who loved him feel they had something nobody else had." Coffin did not talk much about what he felt. After the service, Randy recalled, the snow was coming down hard, "and it was quite magical." Coffin sought her out amid the crush of people in her living room, saying, "I have to get out of here." They bundled up and tramped out in the snow and into a field, walking in silence in the snowfall. Suddenly Coffin slipped on invisible ice; his feet flew out from under him and he "crashed onto the ground." Then Randy fell, too, and as the two of them lay there he began to laugh, and she joined him and they "laughed and laughed and laughed until it was over," she remembered, "an amazing thing." Afterwards they were "in much better shape to embrace everybody who was here, to deal with everything."

She had hoped that Coffin would stay in Vermont for a while after people left on Sunday and Monday. But the "next thing I knew Bill 'had to get back to New York.' Because the church needed him." That was "bullshit," as she put it, but there was no point in trying to hold onto him. So the next morning they set out at five, in snow, for the little airport in Hanover, New Hampshire. Midway there, the car died. They sat for a bit, wondering what to do next, when Coffin, "without saying anything, just gets out of the car and trots, as best you can in knee deep snow, up to Route 5, two hundred yards away, looking up and down, looking up and down, and lo and behold, sees lights in the distance. Turns around, tear-asses back, grabs his suitcase, and says, 'G'bye, I gotta go,' turns around, and runs back up to Route 5, and flags down a truck, and gets on the truck and goes away. And there I am sitting in this car, which doesn't work, at six A.M. in a blizzard, and I started to laugh, I mean, what are you gonna do? I just go fuckin' A, you know, this is unbelievable." Coffin called Randy that night to find out how she had gotten home, and told her he was writing a sermon about Alex.

Friday, Randy was shopping in Hanover with her children and a friend, when she suddenly stopped and said, "I have to go to New York. I just have to go be with Bill." Randy borrowed money, asked her friend to keep her children for the weekend, went to the airport, and took the next plane to New York. When Coffin got back to his apartment Friday, "I was sitting in the living room and he was as mad as I've ever seen him. And he said, 'What the fuck are you doing here?'. . . He was livid that I would presume to come in on his pain."

Many, including his family and friends, have wondered how Coffin could have climbed into his own pulpit less than two weeks after his son's death to preach on that very subject in a sermon titled, simply, "Alex's Death." "The mystery to me," Randy admitted, "is how anyone at a time like that could choose to handle [it] in that way as opposed to privately, quietly." The fact was that Coffin knew no other way to grapple with his own deepest emotions. For nearly thirty years he had addressed the most important things in his life by talking about them from a pulpit in front of a congregation. He was not given to long personal conversations about somber subjects. He did not want to be left alone with his thoughts and a few people in Vermont. He did not even want to be with the woman who loved him the most, and who had helped him raise Alex for the previous six years. The only way that Coffin knew how to mourn his son—to engage Alex's death and give it meaning and shape in his own mind—was to preach about it. He asked Richard Sewall for appropriate lines from Emily Dickinson; many of the hundreds of people who wrote him included favorite passages on the subject of death. Coffin copied over quite a few of these and pondered them as he wrote.

He opened by evoking Alex the "day-brightener," who "enjoyed beating his old man at every game and in every race," who had now "beat his father to the grave."[48] He then gratefully acknowledged the Hemingway quotation he had received among the "healing flood of letters": "The world breaks everyone, then some become strong at the broken places." His "own broken heart" was beginning to heal, "largely thanks to so many of you, my dear parishioners." Throughout the sermon he expressed his gratitude to Riversiders, hundreds of whom had come to his "rescue" and given him "what God gives all of us—minimum protection, maximum support."

But Coffin needed someplace to put his anger, too, so he criticized those would-be friends, especially ministers, who sent him the worst letters, proving "they knew their Bibles better than the human condition." After all, "while the words of the Bible are true, grief renders them unreal." That is why people who made no demands but simply brought food and flowers and held his hand helped far more.

He saved his real wrath, though, for an old friend (unidentified as such) who had made the mistake of implying that Alex's death was God's will. This "should never be said," he told the congregation, as he described "swarming all over her," demanding to know if it was "the will of God that Alex never fixed that lousy windshield wiper of his, that he was probably driving too fast in such a storm, that he probably had had a couple of 'frosties' too many?" He confessed that "nothing so infuriates me as the incapacity of seemingly intelligent people to get it through their heads that God doesn't go around this world with his finger on triggers, his fist around knives, his hands on steering wheels." Quite the contrary: "My own consolation lies in knowing that it was *not* the will of God that Alex die; that when the waves closed over the sinking car, God's heart was the first of all our hearts to break." This argument accounts for why clergy have been using this sermon in grief counseling ever since.

But Coffin also talked of consolations: that because he and Alex "simply adored each other, the wound for me is deep, but clean"; and that there would be "learning—which better be good, given the price." He quoted Emily Dickinson's "By a departing light / we see acuter quite / than by a wick that stays," as well as a half-dozen biblical passages that were "beginning, once again, to take hold." He concluded by taking the advice (and the line) from a friend's letter, promising to seek consolation "in that love which never dies, and find peace in the dazzling grace that always is."[49]

"Alex's Death" quickly became the most widely reprinted of all Coffin's sermons and to this day remains the best known. Perhaps most surprising, Coffin claimed to be on the other side of his grieving by the time he gave the sermon. "Whereas the rest of us," Randy maintained, "did not go to bed at night or wake up in the morning without thinking about Alex—for up to two years or more." Even knowing that Coffin could mourn Alex only in the pulpit, many among his family and friends felt that by preaching he had both claimed Alex as his own while sharing the family grief too much with the world. David Coffin had wanted him "to just be the father now, just suffer as a father." Bill Coffin could not do that.

By giving Alex a public funeral, he also closed off discussion of the more complicated issues in his relationship with his son, such as the tragic consequences of their similarities. For Alex "worshipped his father," in Harriet's words, and tried to emulate his "derring-do." And Coffin's own recklessness, particularly in automobiles, was legendary. He loved to speed, to whiz through tollbooths as quickly as possible, and had his driver's license suspended at least three times. Bill Coffin pushed himself to the edge of his abilities and loved to tell tall tales from his swashbuckling past. "To me," John Maguire recalled, "a parable of our relationship is he would insist I would get on the back of the motorcycle and then of course he would show off . . . daredevil to the nth degree." David Coffin, furious at the way Alex had died, lamented that Alex had lived "life on the edge the way he did all the time, doing everything to the extreme." Heir to his father's charm and joie de vivre, recklessness and athletic skill, Alexander Coffin did not inherit his father's luck. His untimely death would "always be painful" for Bill Coffin, Randy asserted; it was "the tragedy of his life."[50]

Safe Harbor

Bill Coffin and Randy Wilson had been seeing each other for seven years when Alex died. Twice burned in marriage, Coffin remained officially uncommitted while he worked at Riverside, spending June and August in Vermont, otherwise visiting a half dozen times during a typical year. She visited him in New York from time to time and provided a home for the Coffin children when they were not at school. Coffin occasionally sent her money and counted on being able to come to Vermont whenever he wanted, but he also saw other women in New York. In her own words, Randy "hated" this about him, but when he refused to engage in any conversation about his behavior, she had to decide which was more important: the relationship she had with him, or the one she wanted—married, sexually and emotionally faithful—and could not have. "Do you want to get married," she asked herself, "or do you want the relationship?"

She chose the relationship, even though it could be very, very difficult. Her letters during these years alternated between confidence in their love for each other, loneliness at their time apart, and not infrequent anger at feeling taken for granted: what she called his "<u>lazy-minded</u> love." There was still much keeping them apart. Catherine Coffin lived, though bedridden at the end, until December 1982. Without realizing it, Coffin so internalized his mother's point of view that he had seen his wives—and potential wives—with her jaundiced eye. In one almost comic near-encounter, he schemed to avoid having to introduce his mother to Randy. And whether because of Coffin's lawyer's incompetence or his own, his divorce from Harriet became finalized only around New Year 1983. For Randy, Harriet had been a "humiliating" presence in their relationship; now that she was gone, she wrote, "I feel like a new kind of love is possible." She also knew that Coffin would be resistant to any pressure, so she refused to put any on him, despite the advice of some of their friends. "I'm certainly not going to tell you to marry me or else. . . . I'd rather be single, a divine old maid—than be tormented by a grudging marriage."[51]

If Catherine's death and the finalized divorce from Harriet cleared Coffin's emotional decks, so to speak, Alex's death cluttered them up again. But Randy Wilson's devotion outlasted Coffin's indecision and caution. Finally, in 1984, after several counseling sessions with the head of the Riverside Counseling Center, Coffin got up the nerve to ask her to marry him, and she assented. Had they lived together during that time, Randy reflected later, she doubted they would have lasted. "Being apart for all those years was critical for our relationship," she asserted, and "allowed me to grow up." They were married in August 1984. By the accounts of Coffin's family and friends, he had at last made a good marriage.[52] For the first time in nearly thirty years friends delighted in "how good" a woman was for Bill.

FOURTEEN

"Flunking Retirement"

Although much of the steam had gone out of the disarmament movement by the late 1980s, there were still battles to fight in Congress and plenty of the faithful who needed rallying all over the country. Coffin's role was to do the rallying and the speaking at SANE/Freeze while others administered the organization. It turned out not to be as happy a fit as he had hoped. Coffin felt understaffed and therefore far less effective than he could have been. More to the point, however, was that while Coffin often talked to religious groups, for the first time in three decades, he was not employed to give sermons and did not have a regular congregation. Without a text, without a congregation, Coffin did not speak as well; nor was he as creative. On the other hand, no one else in the peace movement spoke as well as he did on as many different subjects, and few spokespeople had his skill, self-confidence, linguistic skills for international work (he spoke French, Russian, German, and Spanish), and comfort in front of television cameras.

During the late 1980s world events accelerated in ways that made citizen-based nuclear disarmament advocacy appear all but irrelevant to the general public. The collapse of eastern European Communist regimes in 1989, followed by the implosion of the Soviet Union itself in 1990, ended the Cold War in dramatic, mostly nonviolent fashion. At once relieved that the most dangerous nuclear rivalry in the world had suddenly ended, and confounded by the U.S. claim that its hard-line military policies had "won" the Cold War by bankrupting the USSR, peace movement activists found it difficult to find targets. They were further demoralized by the hugely popular military response to Iraq after Saddam Hussein's invasion of Kuwait in August 1990. After nearly three years Coffin left SANE/Freeze and moved toward semi-retirement.

In 1994 Coffin turned seventy. During the years to come, he occupied many of his days with reading, writing, playing the piano, occasional political action and guest preaching, and enjoying his family. Grandchildren came for holidays and during the summers. He published little books every few years, each of which collected thoughts and sermons and was organized into sermon format. Sensing that he had a legacy, and encouraged by his family and friends, he cooperated cheerfully with his biographer, providing access to what appeared to be all of his correspondence and financial records, spending dozens of hours answering questions about his life, encouraging family and friends to cooperate with the project, the results of which he awaited with surprising patience.

Coffin still took on causes, though he chose them more carefully as he aged and his energies waned. Having fought hard for nuclear disarmament from the late 1970s, he never let go of the issue, even though some of his colleagues thought it silly to keep pushing on something he could do so little about. When Daniel Ellsberg called him in 1997 about undertaking a fast at the United Nations on behalf of nuclear nonproliferation, he decided to go along, not least, perhaps, because he would be staying with old friends (Cora and Peter Weiss) in the city in which he had been such a prominent figure, and he would be able to talk to reporters on a regular basis about an issue close to his heart and his theology. He thoroughly enjoyed the fast, which generated a modest amount of publicity but little else.

The larger truth was that Coffin could not really retire. Between his own restlessness and his monthly financial obligation to Harriet, he needed to keep working. Randy Coffin knew that a quiet life in Vermont with her would not satisfy a man who had been accustomed to performing in front of so many people for so many years. She had noticed how antsy Coffin became during Augusts, especially, and came up with a diagnosis for his condition: applause deprivation. To a reporter, Coffin confessed, "I've been flunking retirement."[1]

The fact was, too, that Coffin had become the grand old man of liberal religion, and there were still congregations, universities, high schools, and divinity schools that wanted to hear him preach or teach about preaching and a whole range of religious subjects—and were willing to pay for it. More invitations came his way. Pacific School of Religion invited him out to Berkeley for a visiting professorship one term, as did Vanderbilt Divinity School another year. Randy liked to live in new places and to travel (she and her friends had once covered their general store with travel posters so they could imagine vacations), and she and Coffin needed more income than his Yale pension provided. Visiting at the expense of others solved a number of problems at once: Coffin got a position, an office, sometimes a secretary, the respect of younger colleagues, the friendship of older ones, and, perhaps most important, audiences. He remained a favorite on the preacher's lecturing circuit, and he often received large honoraria for his sermons.

At the same time, Randy could take courses, experiment with some of her own talents (painting and sculpture), explore the area, visit friends, and worry less about finances and her husband's state of mind. Lawrence University in Appleton, Wisconsin, first conferred an honorary degree on him (Yale University itself would follow in 2002 when it awarded Coffin an honorary Doctor of Divinity degree) and then offered him a distinguished professorship for the 1997–1998 school year. (Lawrence's president, Richard Warch, had gotten his divinity degree and American Studies doctorate from Yale, where he had taught American history and been a friend of Coffin in the 1960s and 1970s.)

Tolerating the odor of the local paper mill with the help of a beautifully appointed house, a sizable salary, and lively students, the Coffins liked it so much that when they were invited to return the following year (even without the house) they accepted. But while driving back to Vermont in the spring of 1998, Coffin suffered a heart attack while Randy, fortunately, was at the wheel. As a medevac helicopter prepared to take him to the nearest hospital—in Grand Rapids, Michigan—he and Randy said their good-byes, fully expecting this to be their last time together.

Instead, most improbably, and only after working on him with a defibrillator for many minutes, doctors saved his life, and Coffin recovered. Diagnosed with congestive heart failure, a condition that generally can be controlled with a balance of medications, he and Randy decided to stay closer to home in Vermont. Coffin's physical health had been deteriorating for some time. He needed hearing aids increasingly; a neck tremor (resembling that caused by Parkinson's disease) had become more pronounced; and neuropathy (nerve damage) in his legs had slowed him a good deal. Doctors told him to drink much less, advice he followed, but the feeling did not come back in his legs. The once vigorous athlete often had trouble walking the equivalent of several blocks, and old friends who had not seen him for a year or two were shocked at the apparent suddenness of his decline.

Then, the summer after his heart attack, in 1999, Coffin suffered two strokes, within minutes of each other, again while with Randy—this time at a hotel breakfast table. These slowed him down even more, though they did not appear to threaten his life. After several months of physical therapy and exercises, he recovered from most of the resulting paralysis on his right side. Despite extensive speech therapy and extremely disciplined efforts to get all of his speech back to normal, Coffin's speech remained permanently slowed, and slurred. He walked more commonly with a cane, now, and not for any distance at all. He needed help climbing steep stairs, and at a demonstration in November 2000, he was much better off in a wheelchair. But while his athletic ability had left him, his hands and fingers could still play the piano, and he could still write longhand. (He had never learned to use a computer.)

He still did some guest preaching and speaking but picked his spots more carefully, and Randy always accompanied him. In early November 2000, for example, the couple spent a weekend in Miami where he gave a talk on Sunday afternoon and preached an installation sermon that evening. The speech, to perhaps forty people, rehearsed Coffin's ideas on a variety of subjects, from homosexuality to fundamentalism to the basics of Christianity. Even though he was at home in front of a crowd, even a small one, Coffin had just returned from lunch and appeared tired, his tone at times flat. That evening, however, robed and in a raised pulpit, speaking to a packed church, Coffin's energy was of an entirely different order. He cracked a prepared joke about his slurred speech, quoting Mark Twain on Wagner—"It's better than it sounds"—and then ad-libbed another joke about the appropriateness of his bright red robe (even though *r*'s were particularly difficult for him to pronounce). As he made paragraph-long points, he leaned into the sermon, elevating onto his toes for emphasis, as he had done at Riverside. Fed by the crowd and the music, by the fact that he was in a church service, that he had a text, that he was preaching rather than speaking, Coffin showed that he could still preach, even if not with the same vigor or sharpness as he had when he was younger and in better health.

The 2000 presidential campaign pushed Coffin briefly into the news, and onto the op-ed page of the *New York Times,* as three of the four candidates for president and vice-president had attended Yale, and two, Governor George W. Bush and Senator Joseph Lieberman, remembered him quite well. That Bush remembered him with resentment and Lieberman with admiration accidentally demonstrated Coffin's centrality to the Yale, and to many college students, of the sixties. Young George remembered receiving the back of Coffin's rhetorical hand when Coffin observed of his old classmate in the 1964 Texas senatorial election, "I knew your father, and [he] lost to a better man [Ralph Yarborough]." Lieberman's social conscience on civil rights was, if not sparked by Coffin, certainly fanned into flame by the chaplain in 1963. Many future national leaders passed through Yale while Coffin presided at Battell Chapel; with reason, Coffin argued that one could learn something about the candidates by paying attention to how they had responded to the social issues of their college years, and that two of them—George W. Bush and Dick Cheney—in effect flunked that test. After all, the two great issues during his tenure, civil rights and the war in Vietnam, absorbed the energies, money, concerns, and worries of thousands of Yale students at that time. Why not future presidents and vice-presidents?[2]

Bill and Randy Coffin in Chautauqua, New York, 2002. Coffin met Randy
Wilson in Strafford, Vermont, in 1976. She soon became passionately
committed to him and his work. They married in 1984. Courtesy of Randy
Wilson Coffin.

Approaching eighty, Coffin still receives invitations to speak at peace rallies, to preach at ministers' (and bishops') installations, preside at weddings
and funerals, deliver commencement addresses, write articles, and publish
books of sermons. He works on epigrams to puncture President Bush's policies.
His brief letter to the *New York Times* in November 2001 endorsing a William
Safire column pointed out that "dissent is not disloyal; subservience is." The
real "axis of evil," he proclaimed at the National Cathedral in Washington,
D.C., in June 2002, is not Iran, Iraq, and North Korea, but rather "environmental
degradation, pandemic poverty and a world awash with weapons." This phrase
was quickly picked up by others, including National Council of Churches
head Robert Edgar.[3] At conferences and large gatherings, he continues to draw
crowds to formal presentations and informal conversations. He enjoys the limelight and can still be the life of the party.

The Last Crusade: Homosexuality and the Church

The issue that most animated Coffin's preaching and activism during his
seventies displayed a side of him that none of his friends or colleagues could
have predicted two decades earlier. Of course, few Americans in the 1970s
could have foreseen the nationwide prominence—and divisiveness—of gay
rights issues in politics, culture, and religion in the last years of the twentieth

century and the first years of the twenty-first. Coffin, typically, waited to take leadership on the issue until pushed by circumstances at Riverside Church.

He had, on the other hand, been more accepting of homosexuality than many straight male Americans for a long time. He may have been positively influenced many years earlier by his mother's clear openness to gay intellectuals in her salon, including the literary critic Wallace Fowler and the playwright Thornton Wilder. In 1964, when a foundation was considering a grant to support the work of civil rights leader Bayard Rustin, one of the foundation trustees asked for Coffin's personal opinion of him. Coffin read between the lines of the request and assumed that the trustee was asking about Rustin's homosexuality: "It is generally assumed he is a homosexual, although how much a practicing one I have no idea. . . . If I may express my personal views, it would be an awful shame if his extraordinary qualifications to administer—qualifications rare in the civil rights field—were not supported because his personal qualities were questioned."[4]

During the early 1970s Coffin allowed the Gay Alliance at Yale to use his office as a meeting space and defended his action to a critic, arguing, "I trust you agree with me that all people deserve pastoral concern, and as a local pastor that has been my concern for the Gay Alliance." At the same time, he was still struggling with what he considered "the real question, which is whether a plurality of sexuality is really a gift of God just as the pluralism of religions is a gift of God." As he wrote a fellow Presbyterian minister, "I couldn't agree more on avoiding judgment, but I can't myself figure out the theological statement which would make being gay altogether as right and proper and not tragic as being straight. Can you help me?" When he finally emerged with a well-thought-out position at Riverside, it was thoroughly rooted in his reading of the Bible and his understanding of Christianity. He preached his conclusions far and wide and published a version of this sermon in his book *The Courage to Love* in 1982.[5]

While the arguments deepened and sharpened with practice, they remained the arguments he used in that first Riverside sermon and then reused in his 1985 Mother's Day response to Channing Phillips. The central message of the Bible and the Gospels was love; the so-called biblical strictures against homosexuality in the book of Leviticus had the same doctrinal force as dietary prohibitions that most Christians ignored entirely; God had less interest in whom people made love to than whether they did so in love. Coffin took these propositions to their quite logical conclusion: that any form of discrimination against people on the grounds of their homosexuality—whether in adopting children or marrying or serving in the military or being covered by a partner's health insurance or qualifying for the ministry—would violate fundamental biblical precepts. Just as slavery had divided the Protestant denominations before the Civil War, Coffin predicted, battles over how to deal with homosexuality—particularly gay marriage and the ordination of gays and lesbians—would severely test mainline churches in the twenty-first century.

Coffin spoke with more theological certainty on homosexuality than he had on Vietnam. After all, people who agreed on the fundamental message of the Bible could disagree about Vietnam depending on their reading of politics and history. No such disagreement about the source or "rightness" of homosexuality could negate the obvious humanity of homosexuals, and therefore their rights to be treated as full human beings, as full members of any church or secular community. In that sense gay rights resembled the civil rights movement for him, and he preached on it as though it were very similar, gladly making audiences uncomfortable, forcing them to confront the radical, uncompromising power of the biblical injunction to love thy neighbor as thyself. He included an updated version of his basic position in his 1999 book *The Heart Is a Little to the Left: Essays on Public Morality.*[6]

Coffin joined a number of elder statesmen of the mainline Protestant churches on this issue, men like his friends Paul Moore and Bill Webber and Donald Shriver. His voice, however, that of a vigorously physical "man's man" (at least before his health began to falter), made him unique among the religious community's pro-gay spokespeople. In November 2000 in Washington, D.C., Coffin joined a group of two hundred protesting the Roman Catholic Church's position on gay rights, and got arrested—while in a wheelchair—insisting that "the Catholic Bishops are steering the car by what they see in the rearview mirror."[7] During the 1990s and later, when most academic work on homosexuality resembled preaching to a postmodern choir, Coffin engaged opposition biblically, with easily grasped language, clearly articulated principles, and an interest in changing minds.

FIFTEEN

A Holy Impatience

Coffin and His Contemporaries

Between the early 1960s and the end of the twentieth century, William Sloane Coffin Jr. was, after Martin Luther King Jr., the most influential liberal Protestant in America. The qualifiers are important. Protestants constituted a majority of American Christians during this period, but only by combining liberal and conservative denominations. The conservative Billy Graham, for instance, had almost unbroken access to the White House during this entire period and preached to many millions in revivals and on television across the United States. A host of right-wing radio and television evangelists have also had large and regular audiences.

During this time, also, Martin Luther King Jr. dominated the liberal religious landscape for a dozen years by leading the greatest movement of his era and achieving unanticipated preeminence. Never rising to King's level of influence, Coffin's effect remained more varied and diffuse, and less momentous. He preached nothing comparable to King's "I Have a Dream" speech, for example. Neither, of course, did any other minister in the twentieth century.

But the sheer force of Coffin's personality, his deceptively simple condensations of Christianity, his invariably ebullient, often witty, example, were felt intensely by—depending on the occasion—dozens, hundreds, thousands, or (on TV) even millions of Americans. Neither a theologian nor a denominational executive, Coffin ought not to be compared with his fellow liberals John Bennett and Robert McAfee Brown, or Abraham Joshua Heschel, Methodist Bishop G. Bromley Oxnam, or the Presbyterian Eugene Carson Blake. His controversial public stands at Yale University and at Riverside Church, his television appearances, and his frequent national press attention from the early 1960s through the 1980s all made him a household word—indeed a religious celebrity—like none of these colleagues. The closest parallels to Coffin may be those other flamboyant religious figures of the period: Daniel and Philip Berrigan.[1]

The Berrigans were willing to follow their God down nearly any path, dramatically attacking the war machine and creating a mystique that fed the sixties' appetite for "authentic" action. As a result, they drew so much attention to their own personal "witness" that many, even in the antiwar movement, found their example off-putting. By surrounding themselves with other Catholics, and by speaking a relatively impermeable language, the Berrigans showed little interest in the ecumenical movement in American religion that sparked so much clergy involvement in civil rights and the antiwar movement. Finally, while they had many admirers, they had relatively few followers.

Coffin's similarity to the Berrigans lay in his eagerness to stake out risky political positions grounded in a clear extrapolation of Christian faith and in his willingness to make his own actions the subject of controversy. His effort to send medical supplies to North Vietnam, for example, appeared to be a publicity-seeking kick in the teeth to the families of American soldiers then facing danger in Vietnam. But Coffin used the occasion gladly to explain to critics the fundamental, unimpeachable Christian principles on which it was based. Similarly, in 1979 Coffin celebrated Christmas with the American hostages in Iran because observing Christmas with captives was a more important Christian act than worrying that the anti-American government of Iran might be using him. He sought situations that would force people to rethink their assumptions regarding war and human community. Coffin consistently used his position in the heart of the American establishment to raise questions that people could answer without feeling they had to go to jail. And if he could not lead others, Coffin had little interest in an issue. He never heard the call to martyrdom. As he saw it, the biblical prophets were called to name and seek redress for the sinfulness and affliction of their people—not wander in the wilderness: to speak the word of God, to risk censure but not martyrdom.

Moreover, while never abandoning his own Christianity, Coffin preached to Jews as well as gentiles at Yale and elsewhere. Profoundly influenced by the ecumenical spirit of American religious activism in the early 1960s, Coffin lived in an ecumenical world, relied on ecumenical audiences, and worked on political issues in an ecumenical manner. While it shocked some Riverside Church members when Coffin hired a Jew to run the Disarmament Program, he himself gave the question no thought at all. Deeply affected by Heschel (and later by the Rabbi Marshall Meyer), and drawn above all to the Old Testament prophets (and Paul in the New Testament), Coffin preached a more open theology than his Catholic counterparts. His language invited listeners into the world of his belief—it appeared not to pose tests that most mortals would fail. Jews, by and large, did not respond emotionally to the language of Catholic radicalism, with its emphasis on witness, its monastic flavor, its rituals steeped in blood. A surprising number could respond to the morally charged language of Niebuhrian prophetic Protestant liberalism, perhaps because Niebuhr himself preferred what he called the emotional Hebraic-prophetic roots of Christianity.

Like Martin Luther King Jr., Coffin did not remain fully in the postwar Niebuhrian tragic sensibility. He either followed or paralleled King's turn toward a modern Social Gospel, combining Niebuhr's skepticism about human goodness with Gandhi's insistence on the transforming power of love. Coffin used Niebuhr as critique—of sentimentality, of self-righteousness, of pride—but thought and felt more like King and St. Paul when it came to love. In practice, for Coffin, that meant he preached the glories of a large God whose power he celebrated and praised (as he said over and over, "*Thy* kingdom come, *thy* will be done"). The gap between this relatively distant God and suffering, sinful humanity could be bridged only by love. That was a version of Christianity to which Catholics and Jews could relate easily; many, Jews in particular, found Coffin's preaching and religious advocacy not only congenial, but also moving and powerful.[2]

Precisely because Coffin could represent his Christianity in such ecumenical terms, he was gradually able to claim the role—previously held by Henry Ward Beecher in the nineteenth century and Walter Rauschenbusch, Harry Emerson Fosdick, and Martin Luther King Jr. in the twentieth—not only of liberal Protestant preacher, but of liberal preacher to the nation. As such, Coffin was the liberal counterpart to Billy Graham and, from the 1970s on, the true successor to Martin Luther King Jr.

Son, Husband, Father

That Coffin was "to the manor born," in his own words, gave him the visceral self-confidence that upper-class parents can pass onto their children simply by living wealthy, consequential lives. Catherine Coffin's extraordinary involvement in the life of her younger son gave him an equally instinctive conviction that he had been loved from his earliest years, in such a powerful, unquestioned manner that he may very well have confused his mother's love with God's. During his adolescence, Catherine's overwhelming presence took up most of the emotional space in his psychic universe and delayed his search for independence. She lived so powerfully in his mind and heart that, finally facing the reality of his choice to return to the United States after the war, he left Paris without telling Manya Piskounoff he had gone.

Over the years Coffin repeated this pattern of abandoning or limiting intimate—as well as less intense—relationships. In the moment, he could be joyous, playful, enthusiastic, romantic, charming, the life of the party. He thrived among people, in public. If women thought he would commit to them for the long term, and many wished for it, they were bound to be disappointed.

When Coffin did decide to marry, choosing the young and insecure Eva Rubinstein, neither his male friendships nor the male institutions he inhabited nor his previous girlfriends had taught him anything about intimacy or marriage. Given his own childhood experiences, he did not even know what he was missing. With no domestic skills, three children born within twenty-six months, a career that quickly burst into the national limelight, and a nearly complete disinterest in private life, Coffin was a marital disaster. Eva, and then Harriet, faced life with a man who was emotionally sustained by his public roles—not his role as a husband, partner, or father.

Like most men of his era, Coffin knew nothing about raising children, beyond exercising occasional discipline. The Coffin children often felt on their own despite the housekeepers and graduate students who helped run the household. Amy, Alex, and David became terrorizers of baby-sitters, ingenious rule-breakers, and sharp manipulators of the emotional chaos surrounding them.

Even so, Coffin gave them resonant images of a father who worked hard and cared deeply about genuinely important matters like racial justice and an end to war. He gave them the example of a man who derived extraordinary joy from his belief and his work—whether through preaching, holding press conferences, writing sermons, or speaking at demonstrations. He also gave them the unquestioned feeling that their father loved them unconditionally. Amy audited—and loved—a class her father taught at Pacific School of Religion when she was nearly forty. David walked into his father's study in New York City and delighted in seeing him hard at work on a sermon—the same process that had dominated his New Haven homes from Wednesday nights through Sunday mornings.

Coffin feared for many years that his children would ultimately reject him as an incompetent or callous father too absent while they were growing up. David even referred to this fear in a videotaped birthday greeting at a seventy-fifth birthday celebration for Coffin in Chicago. "Here it is, Dad," he began, "the 'talk' you've dreaded for so long."[3] Instead, Coffin's youngest, by several accounts the most troubled as a teenager, delivered a deeply felt tribute to his father.

With Randy Wilson, Coffin finally found a relationship that has nurtured him happily into his old age. She took him mostly as he was and did not expect to make him a (much) more sensitive or egalitarian partner. In fact, Randy offered Bill unflappable acceptance rather than the devotion combined with criticism that Catherine always offered. Randy Coffin remains willing to put up with Coffin's domestic incompetence because she feels that his work—his interaction with the larger world—would not get done if he were doing more laundry or dishes or learning to cook. As a result, she chooses to do what she knows how to do, on behalf of Coffin doing what he does best.

Coffin's intimate life has possessed a striking consistency over many decades. The simplest way to put it is to say that he did not have much of one—despite three marriages, one long-carried torch, a large number of relationships with other women, three children, two step-children, two siblings, a demanding mother, and dozens, if not hundreds, of good friends.

Coffin never developed the knack of reflection and self-exploration. His focus on productive engagement with the exterior world absorbed nearly all of his emotional and physical energy. He loved pursuing women and the social whirl of life lived intensely but never knew what to do when the music stopped. Coffin still tells the story of being asked in a counseling session, by a woman torn between two suitors, whom she should marry. The first fellow was steady, loving, reliable in a crisis, a little dull. The second had flair and energy but was likely to be useless in a crisis. "I found myself asking, 'So how often do you expect to be in a crisis?'"[4]

In many respects, Coffin was a man of his time—so consumed by his vocation that he could admit very little else into his emotional universe. He was also exceptionally lucky, finding women willing to provide a home for his children when he had no idea how to be a caretaking parent. Few men of Coffin's generation even tried to juggle family responsibilities with a demanding vocational life. The notion that truly great leaders can combine practical devotion to family with a fully engaged public life remains a myth. As millions of working parents know all too well, the public and working worlds are particularly unforgiving regarding the demands of family life.

"A Real Preacher"

William Sloane Coffin Jr. grew up in a world in which the mainline church was consequential to public life and Protestant preaching was a vital part of public discourse on a range of issues: morality as well as politics, culture as well as ideas. The Presbyterian Church, in particular, figured significantly at Yale for most of the twentieth century, and Coffin's blood ran deeply Yale blue: third-generation Skull and Bones blue, with an uncle on the Corporation. Before his own career, two generations of Coffin men had invested substantial money and time in the church and its works and in Yale. Henry Sloane Coffin's example always loomed large in the family. So while young Bill Coffin did not plan on a career in the ministry, the church inevitably remained a potential vocational choice. Combined with Yale, the church eventually made an especially attractive combination.

Blessed with musical talent, a fine ear and voice, and an outstanding memory, Coffin also possessed a physical restlessness and energy that made it difficult for him to do little. First with Catherine's supervision and then on his own, Coffin learned to focus his energy and talent in the service of the piano, of languages, of athletics, of preaching. Bill Webber thought it the secret of his success: "Well, the thing about Coffin . . . is that it's always impressive for me when somebody that has an incredible diversity of gifts to such a high degree is also willing to undergo the discipline of going from excellent to superb."[5] As a writer, too, Coffin worked hard at language, writing multiple drafts of sermons and of his memoir. Although he frequently made only minor changes from one draft to the next, he was nevertheless concerned about making a text just a little bit better. For the entire decade at Riverside, he read his sermons over the telephone to his friend Richard Sewall on Sunday mornings, partly as rehearsal, and partly to get the advice of a first-rate critic. He worked on the aphorisms that became "Coffinisms" as well, trying out different versions, carving away excess words, then cutting them in intellectual stone.

Coffin could occasionally get lazy. When he did not prepare speeches or sermons, he ended up quoting himself or stringing quotations (for which he has a prodigious memory) together. But numerous informants painted a more characteristic picture of Coffin's sermon preparation: books and articles so strewn about the study floor that there was barely room to walk.

Unlike many clergy who took risks on civil rights or Vietnam, Coffin managed to hold on to his job through the sixties. He understood the advantage of a regular pulpit when it came time to preach the uncomfortable gospel and soon saw that his Yale perch gave him automatic access to audiences and the media. Once chaplain, Coffin never sneered at Yale connections—he used them. He also understood that his freedom to take on large issues could only be assured by making sure that the "day job" got done. That meant preaching well when he was in the pulpit, lining up excellent preachers when he was away, meeting regularly with student and faculty deacons, taking Yale ceremonies seriously, appearing at appropriate campus events, staying in touch with key Corporation members, counseling students, writing letters of recommendation, and in general making himself a large presence on campus. He pastored students, faculty, and staff. He married, baptized, and buried Yale students, alumni, faculty, administrators, and members of their families. And he always made sure to cultivate his most important single constituent—the University president.

His confidence in the church—writ large—enabled him to delight in infusing Christianity into every corner of university life. He prayed at banquets and groundbreaking ceremonies and insisted that all serious campus questions were also religious questions. He aggressively invited freshmen to Battell Chapel, and because he never doubted the church's relevance to everyday life, he never felt the need to *make* it relevant by doing folk music or rock and roll services, or by watering down liturgy. In the complex environment of a great university, Coffin breathed a joyful, vigorous energy into campus religious life. Given the demands on him first at Yale, and then nationwide by the mid-sixties, he covered an extraordinary number of bases.

From time to time Coffin felt guilty about his failure to take up ministry in the slums. As a result, he loved telling—and retelling—the story of his old East Harlem supervisor Don Benedict confirming that he really belonged at Yale. It is impossible to know whether Coffin could have turned his patrician upbringing and education to a ministry among the urban poor, where his talent and training may have been of little effect.

Instead, by tending to the institutions in the world he knew, and by inspiring his staff to pick up the administrative pieces he frequently dropped, Coffin brought many thousands of students and other parishioners into engagement with issues they would otherwise have ignored or scorned. Coffin could polarize his audiences, but his net effect was to make his point of view respectable at Yale and at Riverside—and in liberal Protestantism around the country.

Coffin even inspired a character in "Doonesbury," the nationally syndicated cartoon strip that Garry Trudeau began in the *Yale Daily News*. A combination of Trudeau's friend Scotty McLennan (now Dean of Religious Life at Stanford University) and Coffin, the "Reverend Scot Sloan" was the bearded, hippie-ish, self-described "fighting young priest who can talk to the young." A longtime friend and admirer of Coffin, Trudeau nevertheless poked gentle fun at Coffin's style and movement credentials.

Coffin had the self-confidence—which some called self-righteousness— to take risks, and, particularly with regard to the draft, he took risks with young men's lives. When he engaged an issue with political import (civil rights, Vietnam, hunger, disarmament, gay rights), he did so with confidence that he could lead others. He forced people to think seriously, and in religious terms, about an enormous range of subjects, from civil rights to sexuality, from the war in Vietnam to the Christmas spirit to the meaning of a career.

Coffin's fundamental psychological and spiritual security, backed by money and his elite upbringing, gave him the strength to take on powerful opponents, whether they were his university president, conservative alumni, angry parishioners, or the U.S. government. Admirers talked of his courage in the face of danger, but in Coffin's case "fearlessness" and "impatience" may be closer to

The Reverend Scot Sloan of the "Doonesbury" comic strip was partly based on Coffin. Doonesbury © 1972 G. B. Trudeau. Reprinted with permission of Universal Press Syndicate. All rights reserved.

the mark. While he acknowledged, and had a healthy respect for, the raw power of institutions—as well as their capacity to maintain unjust structures, to do real harm, and to cause human misery—he never felt any fear of them. Because they were powerful, he did see the need to think and act strategically; he often paused, impatiently awaiting the moment to act so as to maximize his own leverage.

His civil rights work taught Coffin that he had resources—prestige, clout, a constituency, access to money—to bring to any issue; in order to use them wisely, it made sense to look before leaping. Given his natural restlessness and lack of patience with careful procedures, this strategy required real self-discipline and could cause him retrospective unease. (However unconsciously, Coffin revised reality in his memoir, writing that he got involved with Vietnam a year earlier than he really did.) When Coffin did commit himself to any issue, however, he invested everything he had.

His intensity, leadership, and early fundraising created the peace and social justice organization that still lives as Clergy and Laity Concerned. And Coffin eventually used every ounce of his influence to bring pressure against the Johnson and Nixon administrations on behalf of ending the Vietnam War. By attracting federal indictment, and by effectively beating the government's case even though he had plainly and publicly broken the law, he helped to further undermine the credibility of the U.S. government's overall war effort. By making himself a lightning rod for controversy over Vietnam, Coffin forced members of the Yale community, as well as millions throughout the country, to take stands on such matters as draft resistance and the morality of the war. He had a visceral understanding of Martin Luther King Jr.'s insistence that only non-violent "troublemaking" could shake people out of their complacent accommodations to injustice. Responding to his dramatic example, thousands contributed to Coffin's defense fund, most of whom had never before helped an indicted defendant fight the United States government. By virtue of his age and position, Coffin made it impossible for the war's supporters to dismiss all opposition as radical, Communist, or a youthful fantasy. Similarly, his responsiveness at Riverside Church and his willingness to make himself the spokesperson for nuclear disarmament and for gay rights meant that both issues had powerful, confident leadership with nationwide reach and significance.

Coffin's stature and influence on his times have been intimately linked to the rise and fall of American political and religious liberalism. He first came to the national stage during the liberal resurgence of the early Kennedy years and the heady days of the civil rights movement. Inspired by John F. Kennedy and Martin Luther King Jr., Coffin brought together an activist, ecumenical Christianity with a New Frontiersman's faith that much in the world could be made better. As many clergy and laity began to challenge the comfortable sub-urbanization of 1950s religious life, Coffin became the preeminent white voice of the changing times in mainline Protestantism.

Political liberals first divided over the war in Vietnam and the growth of the Black Power movement. As the conflicts of the late 1960s accelerated and intensified, liberalism itself slipped into decline, battered by the war and the antiwar Left, by President Richard Nixon, and by a stagnant economy through much of the 1970s. At the same time the religious landscape was changing; the more liberal Protestant denominations suffered a serious membership decline, while evangelical and fundamentalist churches experienced a growth spurt. From 1965 to 1975, Episcopalians, Methodists, Presbyterians, and the United Church of Christ lost between 10 and 17 percent of their members, while Southern Baptist membership shot up 18 percent. Billy Graham became an ever more influential leader of a growing conservative Protestantism—as well as Richard Nixon's confidant.[6]

Commentators debate the cause of this decline in religious liberalism and the rise of fundamentalism and conservatism. Some argue that both phenomena were the result of the "excesses" of theological and cultural liberalism during the sixties, from which many churchgoers finally recoiled. Others point more persuasively to largely demographic factors: that the boom in churchgoing population in the first place during the 1950s and 1960s was traceable to a huge bulge in the number of families with young children, the typical time in their lives that adults "return" to church. When those baby boomers reached ado-lescence in the 1960s, churchgoing fell off quite naturally. Moreover, since the conservative and evangelical denominations tended to be concentrated in the Sunbelt regions of the country, the movement of the American population to the South and West depleted the older northern- and midwestern-based denominations, such as the United Church of Christ and the Episcopalians.

No one disputes that in the 1980 elections, during which politically active fundamentalism had its greatest victories since the 1920s, political liberalism received a drubbing from which it has not yet recovered. During the early 1980s the remaining liberal senators ran for cover, the traumatized House Democrats (led by their own speaker) collapsed under the conservative onslaught, and the very word "liberal" became "the L-word."

More resilient than its political counterpart, liberal Protestantism survived. Even with the lack of Supreme Court decisions to institutionalize its achievements (such as political liberalism had), the rise of conservative caucuses within each denomination, and the undeniable power of the new Christian Right, religious liberals continued to dominate the mainline Protestant churches. Coffin remained an attraction on the preaching circuit—guest preacher, commencement speaker, visiting professor—long after such liberal political stalwarts as George McGovern and former Vice-President Walter Mondale had lost their luster.

Coffin, along with denominational executives of the mainline churches, the National Council of Churches, the U.S. Conference of Catholic Bishops, and international religious figures such as South African Anglican Bishop Desmond Tutu, kept religious dissent—and liberal religious practice—alive and vigorous. When the Democratic Party came to power under the presidencies of Jimmy Carter and especially Bill Clinton, it did so by adopting managerial, centrist, "third way" rhetoric that ceded much of the Republican ideological victory. Coffin, however, never considered embracing religious centrism to retain his power or influence or popularity as a preacher. Instead, he transformed Riverside Church into a central institution of the Left, one that reached out to offer support, sustenance, and training to thousands of liberal clergy from all over the country.

Churches—actually, all houses of worship—have the capacity to nurture points of view that have lost (or never had) large-scale political favor. Relatively stable institutions holding the allegiance of tens of millions of Americans, they wield influence not as organized political forces, but rather through the fact that they sustain ways of looking at the world that rely more on transcendent values than on the latest polling data or economic indicators. That is why, during the 1980s, as the U.S. government embraced an accelerated nuclear arms race, armed and protected right-wing dictatorships in Latin America, and reorganized tax and spending priorities to favor the rich, the most important dissenting voices could be heard in church and synagogue pulpits.

Throughout the decades of Coffin's fame, many Americans delighted in a religious figure who articulated what they believed with skill and panache.

Coffin never appeared on a television talk show without receiving dozens of letters congratulating him for making religion seem understandable, attractive, and relevant. The nondenominational and nondoctrinal character of his Protestantism appealed powerfully to people who saw themselves as believers, as adherents of the "Judeo-Christian tradition." Coffin's Christianity resonated with so many people because it combined well-expressed common sense, secure masculinity, knowledge of the secular world and its ways, biblical literacy, an unabashed delight in the power of love, and extraordinary joy. It is worth taking these in turn to see how Coffin's espousal of such qualities distinguished him from most white representatives of Christianity (or Judaism, for that matter).

First, Americans have inordinate respect for common sense. Consequently, the widespread notion that clergy (like academics) have their "heads in the clouds" and are therefore unrealistic often confines them to the sidelines of society's "real action." Coffin's succinct aphorisms counteracted the image of clergy as long-winded and beside the point. Whether because of Catholic priests' celibacy, churches' mostly female membership, strictures against cursing and drinking, the emphasis on flowers and music, or the Victorian sentimentality of much church culture, male ministers suffer from the image of effeminacy. The hard-drinking athletic priests of many urban immigrant communities were exceptions to this picture. But in the Protestant world, Coffin stood out on this score. He was physically imposing, athletic, and trim into his fifties, a tough guy who could drink hard and face anyone down, and his powerful masculinity shone through whatever he did. At the moment he came to national attention in 1961, he resembled nothing so much as a Kennedy-esque New Frontiersman of the cloth. The very fact that such a "man's man" could talk seriously about God's love made him an attractive and persuasive exponent of Christianity.

At the same time he displayed no "other-worldliness": he knew about current movies and sports teams and novels and politics and current events. He had not, in other words, chosen the religious world because he was ignorant of the "real world." On the contrary, Coffin knew the real world, and out of that knowledge he made the case for transcending it. Believers responded to a man who appeared to understand their daily lives.

Many Americans sense, accurately and with no little guilt, that previous generations knew the Bible much better than they do. Coffin had what his friend Bill Webber called a "biblical theology," by which he meant that the Bible "really does illuminate for him the human situation in which he finds himself. And when he encounters serious issues that he doesn't understand, he finds insights coming from the scriptures."[7] While few outside the fundamentalist world enjoy nonstop Scripture quoting, the fact that Coffin knew the

Bible so well, and took it so seriously, made his Christianity compelling. That he could sing hundreds of different hymns also gave him access to people's childhood experience of religion.

Finally, for a variety of reasons, including low pay and frequent public disdain for their beliefs, their sexuality, and their relevance, many white clergy give the impression of not enjoying themselves very much. They can display a petulance, a defensive and weary resignation born of being ignored and disrespected. By contrast, Coffin always presented his Christianity as good news, and did so with exuberant joy. He was nasty at times; his masculinity sometimes shaded into a swagger; and he held an Ivy League disdain for fundamentalists. But he nearly always seemed to be enjoying himself, whether he was debating, praying, baptizing, or preaching sermons on the most difficult topics. The smile with which he waded into the Riverside controversy over homosexuality on Mother's Day 1985 revealed as much as the content of the sermon. Since "nothing less than the Gospel" was at stake, Coffin rose—joyfully—to defend a loving God.

Through Coffin's career it is possible to see cultural consistencies over decades that too often get sliced and separated for the sake of textbooks and television retrospectives. The ecumenical spirit that created widespread northern white religious support for the civil rights movement made possible a series of religious and political coalitions over the next four decades that most Americans, particularly those on the Left, take for granted but acknowledge only rarely. Religion and American politics did not discover each other in the New Right or the antiabortion movement of the 1970s and 1980s. Leaving aside America's rich, centuries-old history of religiously inspired political ideals and movements, Coffin's career demonstrates anew the intertwined nature of liberal politics and religion in the latter twentieth century. Religious faith and religious values provided an indispensable underpinning for much of the period's activism. Coffin made a key contribution to the ecumenical spirit and political coalitions of this time.

Like many older principals in the antiwar movement, Coffin had little feel for 1960s counterculture. He never advocated "free love"; he never adopted the reflexive anti-Americanism of many of the young people; and he never learned anything about rock music. What did engage Coffin from the 1960s was the culture of publicity and celebrity. Coffin understood, much more quickly than most and even before such media-savvy activist-performers as Abbie Hoffman and Jerry Rubin, how much of modern politics would take place in front of reporters and cameras. He watched carefully as Ralph Abernathy turned a hostile reporter's question upside down and created a quotable line. And for the next four decades he made sure he was prepared, with sharp quotes and succinct observations. At ease in the limelight, Coffin appealed to the even larger audience of the mass media. The friends who wanted to put him on the road as the "liberal Billy Graham" may have been right about the way to maximize his effect. Nothing galvanized him more than preaching. On the other hand, the institutional base of Riverside Church provided many of the same benefits, with a guaranteed constituency and access to the media capital of the world.

At Riverside Coffin became the nation's unquestioned preeminent liberal minister and an internationally significant leader in the peace movement. Under Coffin, Riverside Church became the single most important institution in the country for those who dissented from official American policies during the Carter and Reagan years. Without the Riverside Disarmament Program, the largest demonstration in American history—on June 12, 1982—would not have happened. And despite many failures during these years, American liberals scored some important foreign policy successes in the fields of arms control and Central America policy. During Coffin's decade as senior minister, Riverside provided a home, and an institutional base, for religious and political liberals during their weakest years in the postwar period.

Coffin's powerful preaching, public advocacy, and personal example reached beyond movements and politics. Coffin also changed the lives of thousands of individual young people and adults at Andover and Williams and Yale, and at prep schools and colleges and universities across the country. Some joined the Peace Corps; others turned in their draft cards; some joined churches; others went into the ministry; some decided to work in Africa with Operation Crossroads; others, such as Connecticut Senator Joseph Lieberman (Yale '64), went South to work on civil rights. No minister of his generation affected college students more strongly. For Howard Koh (Yale '73), for instance, Massachusetts commissioner of public health from 1997 to 2003, Coffin remained the inspiration for his vocation in public health, as opposed to private practice. Koh has retold one anecdote from a Coffin sermon "literally thousands of times."[8] Gordon Coburn heard Coffin speak on the New Haven Green in 1968 and turned in his draft card, changing his life.

Inspired by Coffin as a student during the 1960s, Doug Mitchell, Presbyterian minister and former president of Boston's City Mission Society, still found him an important "model of staying power, of consistency" thirty years later. From Coffin he got "a sense that the faithfulness of the struggle—that being there consistently for as long as it takes whether that ever eventuates in actual change—that essentially doing the right thing is a faithful act, regardless of whether it has absolute impact on the way the thing turns out." Helen Webber, longtime official with the United Church Board for Homeland Ministries, considered him "one of *the* great men of our generation." Rabbi Arnold Wolf considered him "the single most gifted person I have ever known." Wolf pointed out that "the usual image of Bill Coffin is a political radical of international importance and something of a phony Christian pastor." But since "the media doesn't know what to do with a real Christian," he argued, "both of those assessments are wrong. Politically I think he was . . . not particularly radical, courageous in a personal way, but not particularly vanguard or unusual and certainly not profound. But as a Christian pastor I always found him wonderful. He was a real preacher: he wasn't giving lectures, he wasn't giving political addresses, whatever people thought. He was giving classical Christian sermons based on the Bible, based on theology, based on piety, and that was his strength. He was authentic in that sense."[9]

Coffin's preaching remained relevant and inspiring to his audiences for forty years because, like the biblical prophets, he never allowed his enemies— racism, war, nuclear weapons, hunger, homophobia—as much power as he ascribed to the love of God. By taking his God seriously and preaching Christianity joyously, William Sloane Coffin Jr. helped create a "holy impatience" with injustice—among Christians and Jews, believers and nonbelievers—that will live long beyond his own life.

Epilogue

Though the sun warmed the ground, the little church felt chilly and damp in the Vermont spring. On the stage, intent at his mother's Steinway, oblivious to his surroundings, Coffin practiced a Beethoven sonata. He leaned into the music, making a sound between a hum and a light grunt. The thick fingers danced with surprising nimbleness over the keys. An error: he peered at the score, turned back the page, and started the section over. Unseen, a visitor eased down gently into a rear pew as the music ricocheted around him. He had seen Coffin perform: from the pulpit, from the stage, even at the piano; he had never seen him prepare. Now he saw concentration: intense focus, self-discipline, and then a little smile, as the rough patch got smoother. Coffin finished the movement and paused, and the visitor clapped slowly, the sound echoing in the chill air. Coffin started, then explained: his concert with the violinist from over the mountain was only a few months away, and he did not want to embarrass himself.

Coffin has written many places that the truths of music are "apprehended rather than comprehended." If the precise definitions differ little, the former carries the idea of sensing and feeling rather than rational understanding. Music has always had special power in Coffin's life. It has given him a language for his emotions and influence over others. Music took him to Paris and gave him entrée to Russian and to Manya's world. It served him as a lingua franca wherever he traveled. The author once observed Coffin give a late evening speech to several hundred people at the United Church of Christ biennial General Synod. Before beginning, he sat down at the piano on the stage, playing and singing Russian folk songs, and thoroughly entrancing the audience.

There can be no true epilogue to a biography if the subject still lives— only an end to the story so far. William Sloane Coffin Jr. does not have many years left. His doctors have told him that his various medical conditions are not going to improve. Randy Coffin describes her husband in his seventies as "an old man in a hurry": to finish his most recent book or article, to get as many of his ideas down on paper as possible before he dies or becomes incapacitated. But, watching him, it is difficult to escape the impression that for someone in a hurry, he is also very much at peace: with his family and his God, even though he remains permanently engaged in the lover's quarrel with his country that has defined his politics for a half century. He still reads widely, and angers easily at politicians and church folk on the "wrong" side of his issues. Before a concert with his violinist friend in Strafford one summer afternoon close to July 4, Coffin led the assemblage in a rendition of "America the Beautiful," while offering a sharp criticism of the verse suggesting that Americans merely had to march across the continent to take possession of it.

Persuaded by his own near-death experience, as well as his reading of the Bible, that death has no sting and the grave no victory, he seems unafraid of dying. "I had been fearful" back in the early sixties, he admitted, when he nearly succumbed to pleurisy. "I just think every day that I'm not dead is a kind of a gift of grace," he said in 1995. "Seventy-one years, that's enough. I think I've never been happier."[1] When he nearly died a few years later, and he waited for the helicopter with Randy holding his hand, he explained several weeks afterwards, "I was profoundly sad and deeply determined" to "stay with it." There was also "an awful sweetness" about death, even longing, that Bach and Schubert had written of, that he had recognized as he appeared to be dying. Not that he had any firm belief in heaven. "Uncle Henry used to say to me, 'one world at a time.' . . . I remember that made a real impression on me. And I think that's quite right. As long as you know who's there, you don't have to know what's there. Our lives go from God in God to God again. Hallelujah. That's all basically you have to know. You may want to know a lot more. Will I see my father? Will I see Alex? . . . We'll see; it'll be interesting."

On the other hand, he allowed, "I can think of all kinds of reasons that God would hardly get us as far as He gets us and then say, 'Now that's it. You're out and somebody else is coming in.' I can see that that doesn't make too much sense." Theologically, however, Coffin refused to speculate seriously about the hereafter. For him, heaven and hell "symbolize the presence and the absence of God. In that sense, heaven and hell I think start right now."

When his children came to visit him in the Grand Rapids hospital where doctors saved his life, he was "determined that they know how much" he loved them. Coffin's sadness had come not from the fact of his infirmities, nor from the resistance of the world and the country to the marrow and power of his preaching—but from the prospect of having to leave a world he loves and in which he takes immense daily joy. He laughs at good jokes, saves them up to tell friends, and despite his speech difficulties, loves getting off a good line. He began a speech at a peace rally in Montpelier, Vermont, in February 2003, with, "At my age, it's good to be anywhere." In 2001 he told a reporter, "Nature gets more interesting as you're about to join it." His jests are not always gentle; he will likely not lose the edge that occasionally enjoys putting a barb into a quip.[2]

Much of Coffin's life remains similar as he ages. Mornings in New Haven he read and studied. In Vermont, too, thirty years later, "the mornings are for mastering." But mastery meant something different: "somehow practicing, in order to then let go. I have to master. I mean, that last thing I played for you, it came off very nice. Now that took a lot of work for it to become very nice. But then, it's like Blake who backs off from a great painting and says, 'Not I. Not I.' Suddenly he has been used." Always, back to music. "A singer has to be sung," he continued. "God is singing you. You have to think about it that way. . . . I'm not sure if that isn't the same thing when you're preaching also. You've mastered it finally. You're up in the pulpit and you're not trying to be in charge any more. You know your stuff; now you want to be played like [a] piano. . . . In preaching, you work hard, but finally you give up a bit on the mastery."

As he grows older Coffin masters less and less; his God plays him more and more.

Sources

Manuscript Sources

The papers of John C. Bennett, Union Theological Seminary Archives, The Burke Library, Union Theological Seminary in the City of New York

The papers of Henry Sloane Coffin, Union Theological Seminary Archives, The Burke Library, Union Theological Seminary in the City of New York

Presidential Records, Kingman Brewster Jr., Manuscripts and Archives Division, Sterling Memorial Library, Yale University

Presidential Records, A. Whitney Griswold, Manuscripts and Archives Division, Sterling Memorial Library, Yale University

The papers of A. Sidney Lovett, Manuscripts and Archives Division, Sterling Memorial Library, Yale University

Coffin Family Papers, including the Coffin scrapbooks, Strafford, Vermont

Yale Chaplain's Office Papers, formerly in author's possession, now in the William Sloane Coffin Jr. Papers in the Manuscripts and Archives Division, Sterling Memorial Library, Yale University

Author's Interviews

George Bailey, April 24, 1996
Browne Barr, January 17, 1994
Donald Benedict, October 11, 1993
Robert McAfee and Sydney Brown, September 11, 1995
David Chavchavadze, December 19, 1995
Gordon Coburn, October 27, 2000
Amy Coffin and Margot Gibney, January 17, 1994
David Coffin, July 25, 1994
Edmund Sloane Coffin, August 4, 1993
Randy Wilson Coffin, July 24, 2000
William Sloane Coffin Jr.
    August 6, 1993

December 22, 1993
December 29, 1993
July 28, 1994
June 12, 1995
August 18, 1995
September 1, 1995
March 8, 1996
May 6–8, 1996
July 15, 1998
November 22, 2000
February 27, 2003
William Sloane Coffin Jr. and Randy Wilson Coffin, August 18, 1995
Margaret Crockett-Dickerman, August 11, 1993; July 19, 1999
Ronald and Janet Evans, November 29, 1997
Harriet Harvey, December 18, 1995
Miriam Horowitz, September 26, 1995
Patricia de Jong, July 10, 1993
Paul Jordan, December 8, 1998
Deborah Kaback, October 18, 1995
Serge Karpovich, February 9, 1996
Margot Coffin Lindsay, January 13, 1994
Ellen Logan, August 2, 1993
John Maguire, January 14, 1994; March 7, 1996
Roger Manners, August 9, 1995
Joshua and Phoebe Miner, October 6, 1995
Doug Mitchell, July 19, 1993
Paul Moore Jr., September 8, 1995
David Murphy, March 15, 1997
Davie and Joy Napier, January 14, 1994
Pilgrim Place, January 14, 1994 (a United Church of Christ retirement home in Claremont, California, where the author interviewed a group of former parishioners of Riverside Church, including former members of the Board of Deacons)
Eva Rubinstein, September 7, 1995
Alexander Rusanowsky, November 13, 1996
Richard Sewall, December 8, 1995
Gaddis Smith, September 26, 1995
Maria Stromberg, May 19, 1995
George Stroup, November 14, 2000
James Thomas, September 20, 1995
George W. Webber, July 18, 1993
Helen Webber, July 17, 1993
Cora Weiss, May 25, 2000
Arnold Wolf, December 4, 1993
Philip Zaeder, October 5, 1995

Notes

Prologue

Unless otherwise noted, all correspondence and memoirs are located in the Coffin Family Papers.

1. William Sloane Coffin Sr. (hereafter cited as WSC) to Euphemia Sloane Coffin, April 22, 1918. See also January 7, February 18, March 10, January 16 and 17, April 3, March 10, May 14, 1918; WSC to Edmund Coffin, April 9, 1918, and September 26, 1918 (containing the quotation in the subheading).

2. WSC to Euphemia Sloane Coffin, June 6, 1918; WSC to Edmund Coffin, April 16, 1918.

3. WSC to Euphemia Sloane Coffin, June 1, 1918.

4. WSC to Euphemia Sloane Coffin, April 30, 1918.

5. WSC to Edmund Coffin, October 1, 1918.

6. Widely misunderstood as a simple-minded idealism, Woodrow Wilson's crusading liberalism synthesized free trade, universal democracy, Protestantism, and American economic predominance.

7. Much of this information on Catherine's early life comes from her memoirs in the Coffin Family Papers. The suggestion that Catherine's mother died of tuberculosis is contained in Henry Sloane Coffin (hereafter cited as HSC) to Dorothy Eels Coffin, September 20, 1920, The Papers of Henry Sloane Coffin, Union Theological Seminary Archives, The Burke Library, Union Theological Seminary in the City of New York.

8. Quotations from Catherine Butterfield Coffin (hereafter cited as CBC), Memoir C, typescript (1974), 5–6. Catherine's diaries, alas, come in several forms. Apparently, she did not preserve the original but made a typescript copy (which I have called Memoir A), which she edited and then incorporated sections of into a later version, which I have called Memoir C, written for her family, mostly grandchildren, probably in 1974. I have tried to use Memoir A whenever possible. When there are additions to these entries that appear consistent and contemporary, but come from Memoir C or elsewhere, I have added them. Occasionally, dates differ from one to the next; when in doubt, I have used the text and dating of Memoir A. I have designated other memoirs as B, D, E, and F. Copies in author's possession. On prewar Greenwich Village, see Sandra Adickes, *To Be Young Was Very Heaven: Women in New York before the First World War* (New York: St. Martin's Griffin, 1997).

9. CBC, Memoir C, 8.

10. CBC, Memoir C, 9, 11. See also Memoir A.

11. This last entry coincides with the Second Battle of the Marne, July 16–August 6, 1918; CBC, Memoir A, 6–8; Memoir C, 21.

12. CBC, Memoir A, 3, 5.

13. CBC, Memoir C, 17, 20.

14. Ibid., 30–31.

15. CBC, Memoir A, 32, 37, 41, 46; Memoir F (typescript, tour of her house for Francophiles), n.d., 11.

16. CBC, Memoir A, 48–49.

17. CBC, Memoir D, typescript, n.d., "New York in the 1920s," 1. Ancient New Englanders, Coffins traced themselves back to a seventeenth-century Nantucket whaler, Tristram Coffin. The first member of the family to make his way to New York City was Edmund Coffin (grandfather of William Sloane Sr.), who, born in Saco, Maine, ended up in the metropolis around 1832. An evidently successful merchant, this Edmund had a son, Edmund, born in 1844. The American Sloanes began with William, born in Scotland, who emigrated from Edinburgh in 1834. In 1852 he brought his brother John into his successful carpet business, now known as W. & J. Sloane and Company. Before emigrating, William had married Euphemia Douglass; she followed him to New York where she bore five children: four boys and a girl, Euphemia Douglass Sloane.

18. CBC, Memoir B, typescript (January 15, 1935), Carmel, California, 7–9; Morgan Phelps Stokes, *Henry Sloane Coffin: The Man and His Ministry* (New York: Charles Scribner's Sons, 1964), 6–7. When the seminary relocated from Seventieth Street and Park Avenue, Edmund Coffin assembled the parcels for the new (and current) site, between 120th and 122nd Streets, and between Broadway and Claremont Avenue.

19. Peter Dobkin Hall, *The Organization of American Culture, 1700–1900: Private Institutions, Elites, and the Origins of American Nationality* (New York: New York University Press, 1984), 174–175, 179; Lawrence R. Veysey, *The Emergence of the American University* (Chicago: University of Chicago Press, 1965), 285.

20. George M. Marsden, *The Soul of the American University: From Protestant Establishment to Established Nonbelief* (New York: Oxford University Press, 1994), 17–21; Elliott Gorn and Warren Goldstein, *A Brief History of American Sports* (New York: Hill & Wang, 1993), 160.

21. CBC, Memoir B, 13.

22. See E. Digby Baltzell, *The Protestant Establishment: Aristocracy and Caste in America* (New York: Vintage Books, 1966), 138–139; Christopher Lasch, *The World of Nations: Reflections on American History, Politics, and Culture* (New York: Alfred A. Knopf, 1973), 88.

23. CBC, Memoir B, 30–38.

24. "A Minute on the Death of William Sloane Coffin," adopted by the Christ Church Memorial House Committee, January 25, 1934; CBC, Memoir B, 18.

25. Three surviving—and extremely affectionate and detailed—letters from 1930 indicate that Will and Catherine had pet names for each other. She called him Peter or Pierre or Dearest (he called himself Pierre) and signed her letters "Nuck ____" [illegible]. WSC to CBC, August 30, 1932; CBC to WSC, June 25, 1930, n.d. [summer 1930].

26. CBC, Memoir D, 11; Memoir B, 23.

Unless otherwise noted, all correspondence and memoirs are located in the Coffin Family Papers.

1. CBC, Memoir E, "Babu's Notes" (winter 1974), 10; William Sloane Coffin Jr. (hereafter cited as WSC Jr.), *Once to Every Man: A Memoir* (New York: Atheneum, 1977), 3 (hereafter cited as *OTEM*).

2. *OTEM*, 4–5.

3. Author's interview with WSC Jr., August 6, 1993; author's interview with Edmund Sloane Coffin (hereafter cited as ESC), August 4, 1993; CBC, Memoir E, 12.

4. WSC to WSC Jr., n.d. [August 1930].

5. Evelyn Adams, "Supplemental Report to Parents," The Buckley School, March 16, 1934. Report cards from 1931 to 1934 are in the Coffin Family Papers.

6. Robert Cantwell puts this quite well in *When We Were Good: The Folk Revival* (Cambridge: Harvard University Press, 1996): "Privilege does not guarantee that parents will bestow the unequivocal love from which spiritual freedom flows, . . . But it does confer a certain sense of immunity, warranted or not, from the specters of disgrace and indigence, and hence a certain independence of social convention—and this may better equip a child to compensate [for] early emotional deprivations. . . . The true child of privilege need not think or do as others do; on the widened field where he will squander, repudiate, or sublimate his advantages, he enjoys a feeling of indomitability" (p. 250).

7. CBC to WSC, June 15, 1930, and undated [late June 1930]; CBC, Memoir B, 34.

8. CBC, Memoir E, 9; author's interview with John Maguire, January 14, 1994.

9. CBC, Memoir B, 46; Memoir E, 17.

10. CBC, Memoir E, 17–18.

11. *New York Times,* December 17, 1933. See also December 18, 19, and 25, 1933.

12. *New York Times,* December 20, 1933; CBC, Memoir E, 9.

13. CBC, Memoir E, 19–20. Financial statements of the Henry William Company are in the HSC Papers.

14. CBC, Memoir E, 20.

15. Author's interview with WSC Jr., August 6, 1993. Quotations following from Edmund (Ned) Sloane Coffin and Margot Coffin Lindsay regarding the Carmel years are from the author's interviews.

16. *OTEM*, 9–11.

17. Author's interview with WSC Jr., August 6, 1993. Copies of the *Carmel Sunrise* and subscription correspondence are in the Coffin Family Papers.

18. *OTEM*, 12; author's interview with WSC Jr., August 6, 1993.

19. Author's interview with George Bailey, April 24, 1996; author's interview with WSC Jr., August 6, 1993.

20. CBC to WSC Jr., n.d. [probably June 1935], July 9 and 16, 1935; CBC to WSC Jr., n.d. [after July 16, 1935]. The quotation is from William Blake's "Auguries of Innocence."

21. CBC, Memoir E, 1–2.

22. WSC Jr. to CBC, June 15, 1936.

23. *OTEM*, 14.

24. Ibid., 13–16.

25. WSC Jr. to CBC, n.d. [November 1937].

26. WSC Jr. to CBC, November 16, 1937; author's interview with James Thomas, September 20, 1995.

27. WSC Jr. to CBC, n.d. [fall 1937].

28. The HSC Papers indicate that Coffin was in frequent contact with his broker, managed the Coffin children's investments and income taxes, explained his decisions to Catherine, and provided the boys with an accounting of their holdings while they were minors.

Chapter 2. Europe

Unless otherwise noted, all correspondence is located in the Coffin Family Papers.

1. Author's interviews with Margot Coffin Lindsay and ESC.

2. Author's interview with WSC Jr., August 6, 1993.

3. *OTEM,* 19.

4. Catherine did not join Bill as he explored the city, as the vigorous twenty-five-year-old who had "dashed" back and forth from Paris during wartime with such vibrancy had become frail and easily tired in her thirties and forties. Their notebook of programs and composers' biographies is preserved in the Coffin Family Papers.

5. This and following quotations are from CBC to HSC, July 4, 1939.

6. *OTEM,* 22.

7. CBC to Edmund Coffin, December 17, 1939; February 14, March 6, 1940.

8. CBC to Margaret Bacon, May 11, 1940.

9. *OTEM,* 23. A photograph in the Coffin Family Papers, which appears to be from his soccer coach, shows Bill wearing the goalie's kneepads. "My congratulations on your excellent work as goalie," the coach wrote, "and for your terrific sportsmanship [ton très chic esprit sportif]."

10. Ibid., 26–27.

11. Ibid., 28–29.

12. Claude M. Fuess to Mrs. William S. Coffin, December 23, 1940; Fuess to HSC, November 5, 1940, HSC Papers.

13. For Coffin's Andover days, I have relied on letters and school papers in the Coffin Family Papers, Coffin's own account in *OTEM,* and the recollections of his longtime friend David Chavchavadze (author's interview with Chavchavadze, December 19, 1995).

14. WSC Jr., "Open letter to Mr. Percy Grainger from a student of Phillips Academy, Andover, Mass.," n.d. [1940–1942].

15. Following quotations are from WSC Jr., "The Parade," n.d. [1941–1942]. Like millions of other young men of his generation, Coffin had been influenced by the late-nineteenth- and early-twentieth-century effort of upper-class men—led by Theodore Roosevelt—to reengage the less vigorous members of their class in the hard, messy business of political and economic leadership. The manly exercise of physical force played a key role in this process, which had ramifications from college football fields to the outward thrust of American military power from the Spanish-American War to World War I. See Christopher Lasch, "The Moral and Intellectual Rehabilitation of the Ruling Class," in Lasch, *The World of Nations,* 80–99.

16. CBC to WSC Jr., n.d. [winter 1940–1941].

17. CBC to WSC Jr., December 9, 1941.

18. CBC to WSC Jr., January 1941 [though dated 1941, the letter is clearly from 1942].

19. CBC to WSC Jr., December 9, 1941.

20. *OTEM,* 33–34; WSC Jr. to CBC, May 9–11, 1943.

21. WSC Jr. to CBC, September 7, 1943.

22. Author's interview with WSC Jr., December 29, 1993.

23. WSC Jr. to CBC, June 27, July 4, 1943.

24. WSC Jr. to CBC, July 16, August 8, 1943.

25. *OTEM,* 35; WSC Jr. to CBC, August 8, 1943.

26. CBC to WSC Jr., September 5 or 6, 1943; WSC Jr. to CBC, July 4, 1943.

27. WSC Jr. to CBC, September 5, 1943; CBC to WSC Jr., September 10 or 17, 1943; CBC to WSC Jr., n.d. [September 1943].

28. CBC to WSC Jr., n.d. [September 1943]; CBC to WSC Jr., n.d. [September 1943].

29. WSC Jr. to CBC, July 19, 1943; July 31–August 1, 1943.

30. WSC Jr. to CBC, undated fragment [probably July 1943]; August 8, August 22, September 5 and 7, 1943.

31. *OTEM,* 37; author's interview with WSC Jr., December 29, 1993.

32. WSC Jr. to CBC, September 19, 1943. This letter contained what may have been Coffin's first written aphorism: "Selfish indolence isn't so much better than barbaric cruelty."

33. WSC Jr. to CBC, October 5, 1943.

34. CBC to WSC Jr., January 23, 1944; n.d. [late 1943 or early 1944]; n.d. [December 1943]; n.d. [early 1944].

35. WSC Jr. to CBC, March 29, 1944.

36. WSC Jr. to CBC, April 2, 1944.

37. Author's interview with WSC Jr., December 29, 1993; *OTEM,* 37, 41.

38. WSC Jr. to CBC, n.d. [April or May 1944].

39. CBC to WSC Jr., May 13, March 1944; WSC Jr. to CBC, March 3, April 2, August 12 and 24, 1944.

40. WSC Jr. to CBC, n.d. [October 1944].

41. *OTEM,* 44.

42. Following quotations are from three letters from WSC Jr. to CBC in October 1944, two undated and one written October 29.

43. Literally, "la vie libre" means "the free life"; figuratively, it suggests free love.

44. WSC Jr. to CBC, May 20, 1944.

45. WSC Jr. to CBC, December 6 and 16, 1944.

46. WSC Jr. to CBC, December 24, 1944. See also *OTEM,* 45–46.

47. WSC Jr. to CBC, February 2, 1945; *OTEM,* 42.

48. WSC Jr. to CBC, January 6, 1945.

Chapter 3. Russians White and Red

Unless otherwise noted, all correspondence is located in the Coffin Family Papers.

1. *OTEM,* 52. Unless otherwise noted, following quotations from WSC Jr. are from *OTEM,* 49–54, where this episode is recounted, along with quotations from author's interviews with George Bailey and with WSC Jr., May 6, 1996. Guirey wrote eloquently about the plight of the displaced persons and refugees from the USSR. He later succumbed to the madness that all had seen latent in him and retreated to a cabin in the woods of Westchester County. See Chingis Guirey, *The Shadow of Power* (Indianapolis: Bobbs-Merrill, 1953), 30–31.

2. WSC Jr. to CBC, May 12, 1945.

3. Ibid., and May 17, 1945.

4. WSC Jr. to CBC, May 23, 1945.

5. This chronology of Coffin's and Manya's meeting attempts to reconcile contemporary evidence and later recollections and is based on *OTEM*, 54–61, as well as with the author's interview with Maria Stromberg (Manya Piskounoff), May 19, 1995, from which following quotations are taken unless otherwise noted.

6. WSC Jr. to CBC, June 4, 1945.

7. Author's interviews with George Bailey and with WSC Jr., May 6–8, 1996.

8. Mark Elliott covers how Soviet repatriation officers operated in France in *Pawns of Yalta: Soviet Refugees and America's Role in Their Repatriation* (Urbana: University of Illinois Press, 1980), 143; *OTEM*, 60.

9. WSC Jr. to CBC, June 11 and 25, 1945.

10. Manya Piskounoff to WSC Jr., December 30, 1945.

11. Manya Piskounoff to WSC Jr., April 5, 1946, official authorization for Coffin and Rusanowsky to take a seven-day leave to visit Paris. The trip may be followed in WSC Jr. to Family, May 22, 1946; June 10, 13, 14, 16, and 17, 1946.

12. Coffin's liaison work can be followed in *OTEM*, 62–65.

13. WSC Jr. to CBC, August 22, 1945.

14. Author's interview with George Bailey.

15. WSC Jr. to CBC, November 10, 1945.

16. CBC to WSC Jr., November 18, 1945; WSC Jr. to CBC, November 25, 1945.

17. WSC Jr. to CBC, January 7, 1946; *OTEM*, 69–71.

18. *OTEM*, 61.

19. WSC Jr. to CBC, December 12, 1945.

20. Author's interview with George Bailey; *OTEM*, 71; WSC Jr. to CBC, January 16, 1946.

21. Joseph Dasher, Lt. Colonel GSC, Foreign Liaison Officer, to Director of Intelligence, Office of Military Government for Germany (U.S.), February 1, 1946. DI 210–101 (IB). Service Record Jacket, William S. Coffin.

22. Elliott, *Pawns of Yalta*, 19, 85–86.

23. Their story may be traced in Elliott, *Pawns of Yalta;* Nicholas Bethell, *The Last Secret: The Delivery to Stalin of Over Two Million Russians by Britain and the United States* (New York: Basic Books, 1974); Nikolai Tolstoy, *The Secret Betrayal: 1944–1947* (New York: Scribner's, 1978); and Alexander Solzhenitsyn, *The Gulag Archipelago*, 3 vols. (New York: Harper and Row, 1973–1978).

24. Elliott, *Pawns of Yalta*, 90–92, 111.

25. Ibid., 92–93, 110–113.

26. The following account relies on *OTEM*, 72–78; Coffin's contemporary letters to his mother, January 16, February 5, February 12, February 19, March 3, March 8, 1946; and author's interview with Alexander Rusanowsky, November 13, 1996, from which quotations from Rusanowsky are taken.

27. Elliott, *Pawns of Yalta*, 95–96; *OTEM*, 77.

28. WSC Jr. to CBC, May 22, 1946.

29. Edward N. Fickett, Colonel, GSC AC of S, G-2, to Commanding General, Third United States Army, March 7, 1946. Service Record Jacket, William S. Coffin.

30. *Christianity and Crisis*, October 17, 1977, 225, 229–232; *OTEM*, 72.

31. Coffin and Rusanowsky very likely exaggerated the effect that they could have had in any event. Even supposing that the Vlasovites had taken Coffin's warning and tried to escape, many would have failed, and most would have been recaptured. As Coffin's CIA colleague David Murphy explained, not only were such camps guarded, they often had a clandestine Soviet infrastructure. The commandant, he suggested, could easily have been a Soviet informant.

32. Manya Piskounoff to WSC Jr., April 5, 1946.

33. WSC Jr. to CBC, April 6, 1946.

34. CBC to WSC Jr., n.d. [early April 1946]; WSC Jr. to CBC, April 3, 1946; CBC to WSC Jr., April 17, May 4, 1946; WSC Jr. to Family, April 22, 1946; WSC Jr. to CBC, May 22, 1946.

35. WSC Jr. to CBC, June 24, 1946.

36. CBC to WSC Jr., July 7, 1946; WSC Jr. to CBC, July 16, 1946.

37. CBC to WSC Jr., August 12, 1946. See also WSC Jr. to CBC, August 20, September 18, October 26, 1946.

38. WSC Jr. to CBC, September 15, 1946.

39. CBC to WSC Jr., October 18, 1946; WSC Jr. to CBC, October 28, 1946.

40. CBC to WSC Jr., November 12, 1946.

41. WSC Jr. to CBC, November 10, 1946.

42. CBC to WSC Jr., November 23, 1946.

43. WSC Jr. to CBC, October 7, 1946; CBC to WSC Jr., October 18, 1946; WSC Jr. to CBC, November 18 and 24, 1946.

44. Author's interview with WSC Jr., May 6, 1996.

45. WSC Jr. to CBC, January 8, 1947; WSC Jr. to CBC, October 26, 1946; author's interview with Alexander Rusanowsky.

46. CBC to WSC Jr., November 12, 1946; WSC Jr. to CBC, December 12, 1946; CBC to WSC Jr., January 27, 1947; ESC to WSC Jr., November 16, 1946.

47. *OTEM,* 80.

48. Manya Piskounoff to WSC Jr., June 13 and 26, 1946.

49. WSC Jr. to Family, May 22, September 4, 1946; George Bailey to WSC Jr. [January or February] 22, 1947.

50. WSC Jr. to CBC, October 12, December 12 and 19, 1946.

51. WSC Jr. to CBC, December 26, 1946, January 8, 1947; Manya Piskounoff to WSC Jr., January 27, 1947; WSC Jr. to CBC and Margot, March 9, 1947.

52. *OTEM,* 80.

53. Manya Piskounoff to WSC Jr., May 13, 1947. Author's interview with Maria Stromberg.

54. Author's interview with George Bailey.

Chapter 4. The Education of a Warrior-Priest

Unless otherwise noted, all correspondence is located in the Coffin Family Papers.

1. *OTEM,* 82; author's interview with WSC Jr., July 28, 1994.

2. WSC Jr., "Les Avantages Littéraires des Thèmes Réligieux sur les Thèmes Seculaires— Propositions de Paul Claudel" (The Literary Advantages of Religious over Secular Themes— Paul Claudel's Propositions), April 1948; author's interview with WSC Jr., July 28, 1994.

3. The following narrative and quotations concerning Coffin's early religious insights are from author's interview with WSC Jr., July 28, 1994, and *OTEM*, 82–83.

4. The following quotations are from WSC Jr., "Presentation of My Social Philosophy," n.d. [November 1948].

5. On the popularity of this interest in world government, see Paul Boyer, *By the Bomb's Early Light: American Thought and Culture at the Dawn of the Atomic Age* (Pantheon: New York, 1985), 33–45.

6. Author's interview with WSC Jr., December 29, 1993. On the Wallace campaign, see Richard J. Walton, *Henry Wallace, Harry Truman, and the Cold War* (New York: The Viking Press, 1976); *OTEM*, 84–88.

7. On official anti-Communism, see Christopher Lasch, *The Agony of the American Left* (New York: Vintage Books, 1967); Leo P. Ribuffo, *Right Center Left: Essays in American History* (New Brunswick, N.J.: Rutgers University Press, 1992); Ellen Schrecker, *Many Are the Crimes: McCarthyism in America* (Princeton, N.J.: Princeton University Press, 1999).

8. On this milieu, see Kai Bird, *The Chairman: John J. McCloy, The Making of the American Establishment* (New York: Simon and Schuster, 1992), and *The Color of Truth: McGeorge Bundy and William Bundy: Brothers in Arms, A Biography* (New York: Simon and Schuster, 1988), esp. 154–176.

9. WSC Jr., "A Student's Report," *Et Veritas* (February 22, 1949), 17–21.

10. Richard Wightman Fox, *Reinhold Niebuhr: A Biography* (New York: Pantheon, 1985), 217, 234; see also 224–248. For an early 1960s critique of this perspective, see Christopher Lasch, *The New Radicalism in America, 1889–1963: The Intellectual as a Social Type* (New York: Vintage, 1965), esp. Ch. 9, "The Anti-Intellectualism of the Intellectuals," 286–349.

11. Eugene V. Rostow to Dean Acheson, n.d.; *OTEM*, 152. On the Stratton Bill, see Howard Morley Sachar, *A History of the Jews in America* (New York: Vintage Books, 1993), 559–562.

12. WSC Jr. to CBC and ESC, July 14, August 4, August 10, August 17, August 29, September 10, 1948; see also Margot Coffin to Family, July 14 and 27, 1948; Margot Coffin to CBC, August 16, September 10 and 14, 1948; *OTEM*, 84–86. Coffin kept a journal, organized by the towns he visited, in an untitled, unidentified spiral notebook.

13. Author's interview with George W. Webber, July 18, 1993.

14. *OTEM*, 88; author's interview with WSC Jr., July 28, 1994.

15. Ibid.

16. WSC Jr., "Notes Towards a History of Bolshevik Trade Unionism," unpublished senior essay, Yale College, May 1949, i–iii; "A Sermon on Prayer," May 1949.

17. *OTEM*, 89; WSC Jr., "A Demonstration of Higher Criticism," January 1950.

18. The following quotations are from WSC Jr., "Eye Hath Not Seen . . . ," delivered October 2, 1949, *Et Veritas* (November 1949), 12–17.

19. Author's interviews with Donald Benedict, October 11, 1993; with WSC Jr., December 29, 1993; with George W. Webber; *OTEM*, 89–90.

20. Author's interview with WSC Jr., July 28, 1994; *OTEM*, 91.

21. This account relies on (and quotations are from) author's interviews with retired CIA officers David Murphy (former head of section in Berlin and director of Coffin's operation), March 15, 1997; David Chavchavadze; Serge Karpovich, February 9, 1996; and George Bailey (who recently published a book with Murphy); and *OTEM*, 90–113. On the early history of the CIA, see David Wise and Thomas Ross, *The Invisible Government* (New York: Vintage Books, 1974), 94–97.

22. Coffin received a call several years ago from the daughter of one of these men—who had been captured and executed. She was trying to rehabilitate her father's name and asked for Coffin's help. Author's interview with WSC Jr., July 28, 1994.

23. WSC Jr. to CBC, November 14, 1950; January ?, August 10, 1952.

24. WSC Jr. to CBC, November 14, 1950; n.d. [early November 1951].

25. WSC Jr. to CBC, February 7, 1951.

26. WSC Jr. to CBC, December 19, 1952; February 7, March 21, February 27, 1951. The prayer reads, "God, give us the serenity to accept what cannot be changed; / Give us the courage to change what should be changed; / Give us the wisdom to distinguish one from the other." Fox, *Reinhold Niebuhr*, 290.

27. WSC Jr. to CBC, November 18, 1951.

28. WSC Jr. to CBC, January 21 and 2, 1953.

29. WSC Jr. to CBC, November 2, 1951; September 14, 1952.

30. Author's interview with WSC Jr., July 28, 1994; WSC Jr. to CBC, November 1, November ?, 1951.

31. WSC Jr. to CBC, January 30, 1951.

32. WSC Jr. to CBC, February 2, 1951.

33. Author's interview with Maria Stromberg; Manya Piskounoff to WSC Jr., May 1, 1951.

34. WSC Jr. to CBC, October 19, 1952.

35. WSC Jr. to CBC, November 8, 1952; January 2, February 26, 1953; *OTEM*, 114–115.

36. WSC Jr. to CBC, January 2 and 21, 1953.

37. Author's interview with David Murphy.

38. WSC Jr. to CBC, January 2, 1953.

39. WSC Jr. to CBC, August 10, 1952. The CIA man kept to his position. During the height of the Vietnam War, when Coffin faced federal prison for his antidraft activity, CIA colleagues asked Karpovich whether he wanted Coffin to go to jail. His response was simple: "Of course not. He's my friend." Coffin was touched by this story, which he told in *OTEM*, 111. Author's interviews with Serge Karpovich and George Bailey.

40. "A most wonderful birthday present was the birth of my Russian godchild on June first." WSC Jr. to CBC, June 8, 1952; author's interview with Serge Karpovich.

41. Coffin's account of this trip featured his new BMW motorcycle and omits any mention of Paris. *OTEM*, 114; author's interviews with Serge Karpovich and Maria Stromberg.

42. When Karpovich beat Coffin on the voyage home, Coffin cried foul, claiming that they had agreed to "put on a good show" and Karpovich had "cheated" by playing a defensive game. "I remember when they gave me the trophy," Karpovich recalled. "He said, 'It will tarnish.'" Author's interview with Serge Karpovich.

Chapter 5. From Education to Vocation

Unless otherwise noted, all correspondence is located in the Coffin Family Papers.

1. Author's interview with John Maguire, January 14, 1994; Maguire quotations following are from this interview.

2. Author's interview with Browne Barr, January 17, 1994.

3. *OTEM*, 115; author's interview with WSC Jr., July 28, 1994.

4. *OTEM*, 115; Reinhold Niebuhr, *The Nature and Destiny of Man. Volume I. Human*

Nature (New York: Charles Scribner's Sons, 1941), 16; WSC Jr., "Statement of Faith," January 1956.

5. *OTEM*, 114–118, 83.

6. Mark Silk, *Spiritual Politics: Religion and America Since World War II* (New York: Simon and Schuster, 1988), 50.

7. *OTEM*, 117–118.

8. Coffin either invented or hinted at numerous false stories at this time. He never parachuted behind enemy lines, served as a paratrooper, or lived in a brothel.

9. Harvey Sachs, *Rubinstein: A Life* (New York: Grove Press, 1995), 307, 313–314, 305.

10. Author's interview with Eva Rubinstein, September 7, 1995; Rubinstein quotations that follow are from this interview. The account of the early relationship of WSC Jr. and Eva Rubinstein can be found in (and quotations are from) Sachs, *Rubinstein*, 306, and *OTEM*, 124–126.

11. Author's interviews with Harriet Harvey (formerly Harriet Gibney and Harriet Coffin), December 18, 1995, and Margot Coffin Lindsay.

12. Author's interviews with George W. Webber and John Maguire, January 14, 1994.

13. WSC Jr. to CBC, November 17, 1955.

14. Quoted in Sachs, *Rubinstein*, 14. The maestro clearly paid no attention to Coffin's denomination.

15. *OTEM*, 126. In Eva Rubinstein's version, "My father would see Oral Roberts on TV, or something," she recalled, "and say, 'Is this what you want?' I'd say, 'actually, no!' "

16. Sachs, *Rubinstein*, 312.

17. WSC Jr. to CBC, December 14, 1955.

18. Ibid., November 17, and December 21, 1955.

19. WSC Jr. to CBC, December 14, 1955; Sachs, *Rubinstein*, 306.

20. Author's interview with WSC Jr., June 12, 1995.

21. Author's interview with Browne Barr.

22. *OTEM*, 126–127.

23. WSC Jr. to CBC, December 21, 1955; WSC Jr., "Christian Understanding of Love," January, February, May 1954, Yale Chaplain's Office Papers (hereafter cited as YCOP).

24. "Sermon on the main theme of Barth's *Commentary on the Epistle to the Romans*, n.d. [December 1955]; quotations are from untitled Christmas sermon, "Yale '55" noted on the first page, on the text "Let us now go even unto Bethlehem and see this thing which has come to pass"; both in the YCOP.

25. On Henry Sloane Coffin, see Fox, *Reinhold Niebuhr*, 105–106, 117–118; *OTEM*, 120–123.

26. WSC Jr. to CBC, December 21, 1955.

27. On the Graham crusade and the liberal response, see Silk, *Spiritual Politics*, 101–107.

28. Jackson W. Carroll, Douglas W. Johnson, and Martin E. Marty, *Religion in America: 1950 to the Present* (New York: Harper and Row, 1979), 14, 38–39; Robert Wuthnow, *The Restructuring of American Religion: Society and Faith Since World War II* (Princeton, N.J.: Princeton University Press, 1988), 181; Gibson Winter, *The Suburban Captivity of the Churches: An Analysis of Protestant Responsibility in the Expanding Metropolis* (Garden City, N.Y.: Doubleday, 1961).

29. Stephen Whitney to WSC Jr., November 23, 1956; author's interview with Joshua and Phoebe Miner, October 6, 1995 (following quotations from the Miners come from this interview). Some of these sermons may be found in the YCOP.

30. Personal communication from Edward Benson, November 3, 2002, in author's possession.

31. Author's interview with WSC Jr., December 29, 1993.

32. WSC Jr. to Gray Baldwin [1956].

33. *OTEM*, 128.

34. Ibid., 129.

35. Author's interview with WSC Jr., December 29, 1993; *OTEM*, 130–131.

36. *The Williams Record*, September 28, 1957.

37. Author's interview with WSC Jr., December 22, 1993.

38. *Williams Alumni Review*, November 1957, 5–6.

39. *The Williams Record*, December 18, 1957.

40. Ibid., December 18, 1957.

41. Ibid., February 7 and 15; March 12, 1958; *OTEM*, 130.

42. *The Williams Record*, April 16, 1958.

43. Ibid., April 16, 18, 23; May 16, 1958; *OTEM*, 131.

Chapter 6. "Bus-Riding Chaplain"

All correspondence, sermons, prayers, and reports are in the Yale Chaplain's Office Papers unless otherwise indicated.

1. The first two were Herbert Gezork, president of Andover Newton Theological School, and Robert McCracken, pastor of Riverside Church in New York City. See the various correspondence during late 1957 and early 1958 among these men in Presidential Records, A. Whitney Griswold, Yale University (hereafter cited as PR-AWG).

2. Paul Weiss to A. Whitney Griswold, February 14, 1958; Richard B. Sewall to Griswold, February 21, 1958; Griswold to "Miss A," n.d. [late February or early March 1958]; see also Benjamin DeLoache, Yale School of Music, to Griswold, October 10, 1957, all PR-AWG; author's interview with Richard Sewall, December 8, 1995.

3. A. Sidney Lovett to A. Whitney Griswold, February 28, 1958, PR-AWG; author's interview with WSC Jr., July 28, 1994; WSC Jr., *OTEM*, 133.

4. Charles Seymour to WSC Jr., March 19, 1958; Norman Holmes Pearson to WSC Jr., March 18, 1958; Allen Dulles to WSC Jr., March 1958; Archie Foord to WSC Jr., March 17, 1958; Dick Steadman to WSC Jr., March 17, 1958; Gardner Day to WSC Jr., March 8, 1958.

5. Author's interview with WSC Jr., July 28, 1994; *OTEM*, 135.

6. Author's interview with WSC Jr., July 28, 1994.

7. WSC Jr., "Heirs to Disillusion," *The Nation* (May 16, 1959), 449–451.

8. "Protestant Christian Ministry at Yale," enclosed in WSC Jr. to Harold E. Fey, December 19, 1959. Quotations following are also from this source.

9. Wuthnow, *The Restructuring of American Religion*, 71–99.

10. WSC Jr. to Griswold, October 28, 1960. The numbers are in Arthur Howe Jr. to A. Whitney Griswold, October 17, 1960, PR-AWG; Griswold to WSC Jr., October 19, 1960.

11. Coffin's nine pages of notes are handwritten, in a folder marked "Jewish Students," for the 1961–1962 academic year.

12. *OTEM*, 137–138. See Dan A. Oren, *Joining the Club: A History of Jews at Yale* (New Haven, Conn.: Yale University Press, 1985), esp. Ch. 9, 173–214. Because Oren did not have

access to memoranda in the YCOP listing the number of Jewish students in each class, these figures differ some from his. For example, according to the chaplain's office, 153 Jewish freshmen entered Yale in 1962; Oren cites a figure of 172.

13. Author's interview with WSC Jr., September 1, 1995. Coffin preferred to act in a supporting role: "let the students always take the initiative."

14. On alternate exam dates, see Richard Israel to Reuben A. Holden, March 27, 1961; Dean Harold B. Whiteman Jr. to Dean William C. DeVane, April 6, 1962; WSC Jr. to Whiteman, April 11, 1962; Whiteman to Deans William C. DeVane, Richard C. Carroll, Samuel Graybill, Arthur Howe Jr., Rev. William Coffin, Rabbi Richard Israel, April 24, 1962.

15. Author's interview with WSC Jr., July 28, 1994.

16. Author's interview with WSC Jr., December 29, 1993.

17. Prayer, Freshman Sunday, September 20, 1959; Commencement Prayer, June 13, 1960.

18. John B. Klingenstein to WSC Jr., April 27, 1960. For Coffin's doubts and their resolution, see WSC Jr. to James Robinson, March 15, April 13, 1960; Robinson to WSC Jr., March 29, 1960. The episode may be followed in *OTEM*, 138–143, and in the author's interview with Eva Rubinstein (see Chapter 10).

19. WSC Jr., "Report on Operation Crossroads Africa (Guinea)," n.d., typescript in "Africa" folder, 1960–1961; *OTEM*, 143.

20. WSC Jr., "Report on Operation Crossroads Africa." Coffin's proposal to the Yale Corporation and related correspondence is also a two-page typescript, n.d., in "Africa" folder, 1960–1961.

21. WSC Jr. to Howard Gambrill Jr., November 1, 1960; J. W. Fulbright to WSC Jr. and James Barton Neff, November 2, 1960; WSC Jr. to James Robinson, September 25, 1963.

22. Alfred C. Payne to WSC Jr., January 20, 1960; WSC Jr. to Payne, January 22, 1960.

23. Mary Prescott Little to A. Whitney Griswold, March 14 and 27, 1960; Griswold to WSC Jr., March 17 and 21, 1960; WSC Jr. to Griswold, n.d. [March 20], 1960; Griswold to Mary P. Little, March 21, 1960; WSC Jr. to Donald F. Campbell, March 29, 1960. All in PR-AWG.

24. Quotations here and below are from this exchange: A. Cameron Mann to WSC Jr., November 23, 1960; WSC Jr. to Mann, November 29, 1960.

25. WSC Jr., Sermon, April 17, 1960.

26. Taylor Branch, *Parting the Waters: America in the King Years, 1954–63* (New York: Simon and Schuster, 1988), 276. On the sit-in movement, see Branch, *Parting the Waters*, 271–293, and David Garrow, *Bearing the Cross: Martin Luther King Jr. and the Southern Christian Leadership Conference* (New York: Vintage Books, 1988), 127–135. The following account relies on the author's interviews with John Maguire (January 14, 1994, and March 7, 1996) and WSC Jr. (July 28, 1994, and March 8, 1996); Branch, *Parting the Waters*, 412–482; *OTEM*, 144–162; Garrow, *Bearing the Cross*, 156–161; Richard Reeves, *President Kennedy: Profile of Power* (New York: Simon and Schuster, 1993), 122–134; and Harris Wofford, *Of Kennedys and Kings: Making Sense of the Sixties* (Pittsburgh: University of Pittsburgh Press, 1980), 151–158. John Maguire's recollections of the Freedom Ride are in George Plimpton, ed., *American Journey: The Times of Robert Kennedy, Interviews by Jean Stein* (New York: Harcourt Brace Jovanovich, 1970), 96–103. George B. Smith's account of the ride is included in an interview with the *Hartford Courant*, April 3, 1988. Nearly all of these accounts, partly because they rely heavily on participants' memories, conflict slightly with each other and contain minor errors.

27. On the rally, see *New Haven Register,* May 24, 1960; *New York Times,* May 25, 1961. Coffin purposely did not publicize his upcoming action (he said later) to make sure that his boss did not have to take responsibility for knowing about it in advance.

28. Local newspapers painted a very different picture. The May 25, 1961, Opelika (AL) *Daily News,* for example, ran its Thursday afternoon lead story under the headline "Freedom Riders Launch New Assault on Montgomery Café." My thanks to Tim Dodge of the Microforms and Documents Department of the Ralph Brown Draughon Library, Auburn University, who kindly sent me copies of articles from the Opelika *Daily News.*

29. *New York Times,* May 25, 1961.

30. Ibid., May 26 and 27, 1961; Branch, *Parting the Waters,* 476, 966.

31. Within the civil rights movement nationally, Abernathy, of Montgomery's First Baptist Church; Walker, executive director of the SCLC; and Shuttlesworth, the Birmingham civil rights leader, were all celebrities. The news story identified them in the last paragraph by name only. *New York Times,* May 26 and 27, 1961; *New York Post,* May 26, 1961.

32. *New York Times,* May 26, 1961.

33. Ibid., May 27, 1961.

34. *Life,* "Why Yale Chaplain Rode: Christians Can't Be Outside," June 2, 1961, 46–55.

35. Branch, *Parting the Waters,* 476–477. A month after their arrest, each member of the group received sentences of a month in jail. They appealed, and the Supreme Court eventually overturned the convictions in 1965.

36. Branch, *Parting the Waters,* 478; Plimpton, *American Journey,* 103.

37. *Time,* June 2, 1961, 14–18; *Newsweek,* June 5, 1961, 18–20.

38. H. Gordon Rowe to WSC Jr., n.d.; "Omega" to WSC Jr., October 9, 1961.

39. G. R. Fowler to WSC Jr., May 28, 1961; M. Shapiro to WSC Jr., May 27, 1961.

40. Henry Dutton to WSC Jr., October 9, 1961; W. R. Parker to WSC Jr., May 30, 1961.

41. "A solid segregationist" to WSC Jr., May 27, 1961.

42. E. H. Chapman to WSC Jr., May 30, 1961; WSC Jr. to Chapman, June 22, 1961.

43. Quotations here and below are from this exchange: John H. Doeringer to WSC Jr., May 26, 1961; WSC Jr. to Doeringer, June 13, 1961. See also Floyd W. Jefferson (Yale '02) to WSC Jr., June 23, 1961; WSC Jr. to Jefferson, July 17, 1961; Harry O. King to WSC Jr., June 2, 1961; WSC Jr. to King, June 22, 1961; John A. Luttrell to WSC Jr., June 1, 1961; WSC Jr. to Luttrell, June 21, 1961; F. D. Childs to WSC Jr., May 27, 1961; WSC Jr. to Childs, June 22, 1961.

44. *New Haven Journal Courier,* May 29, 1961; *New York Times,* May 29, 1961.

45. *OTEM,* 163; letter of A. Whitney Griswold, June 12, 1961.

46. Quotations are from this exchange: Norman S. Buck to WSC Jr., May 29, 1961; WSC Jr. to Buck, June 5, 1961.

47. WSC Jr. to A. Whitney Griswold, June 16, 1961, YCOP.

48. *Yale Alumni Magazine* (hereafter cited as *YAM*), July 1961, 1; October 1961, 1–7. The magazine's editors said they had published all the letters they had received on the subject to date.

49. Quotations are from this exchange: Elliott Dunlap Smith to WSC Jr., June 1, 1961; WSC Jr. to Smith, June 20, 1961.

50. Author's interviews with WSC Jr., July 28, 1994; May 6, 1996.

All citations are from the Yale Chaplain's Office Papers unless otherwise indicated.

1. *Life,* September 14, 1962, 4.

2. WSC Jr. to Pat Kennedy, November 10, 1961; Fred Lanoue to WSC Jr., October 30, 1961; Robert Sargent Shriver Jr. to WSC Jr., December 13, 1961; *OTEM,* 177–197.

3. Author's interview with WSC Jr., July 28, 1994. For the Battell Chapel preaching schedule and for Coffin's schedule, see the "Preachers" and "Schedule" folders for the given year.

4. Coffin's secretary Charlotte Horton kept typescript lists titled, for example, "Preaching Engagements, 1962."

5. The Yale University News Bureau released the text of the prayer June 12, 1962, No. 414, "in answer to many requests by those who were in attendance."

6. WSC Jr., "Invocation, Groundbreaking Exercises, The Kline Geology Laboratory, May 4, 1962"; "Prayer by the Rev. William Sloane Coffin Jr., Chaplain of the University," at the dedication of Ezra Stiles and Morse Colleges, December 7, 1962."

7. WSC Jr., "Vocation," January 6, 1963.

8. Author's interview with WSC Jr., July 28, 1994; untitled report of a vote by the Yale Corporation, April 6, 1963, setting Coffin's salary "as recommended by the President," PR-AWG.

9. *YAM,* January 1964, 6–8; William M. Fine, ed., *That Day with God* (New York: McGraw-Hill, 1964).

10. WSC Jr., "Prayer," October 13, 1963; Kingman Brewster Jr., letter from the Office of the Provost, June 18, 1963.

11. WSC Jr., "Invocation, Inauguration Luncheon," April 11, 1964.

12. WSC Jr., "Invocation, Senior Dinner," April 23, 1964.

13. *New York Times,* July 5, 1963; *Time,* July 12, 1963, 17–18. For an excellent description of the event, connecting it to larger trends in clergy activism on civil rights, see Michael B. Friedland, *Lift Up Your Voice Like a Trumpet: White Clergy and the Civil Rights and Antiwar Movements, 1954–1973* (Chapel Hill: University of North Carolina Press, 1998), 82–84.

14. Friedland, *Lift Up Your Voice,* 8; Mitchell Hall, *Because of Their Faith: CALCAV and Religious Opposition to the Vietnam War* (New York: Columbia University Press, 1990), 5–6.

15. Friedland, *Lift Up Your Voice,* 74–76.

16. John Helms III to Editor, *YAM,* July 1963, 4; John W. Lucas to Editor, *YAM,* October 1963, 7; *OTEM,* 170–176.

17. WSC Jr., "On Certain Statements of Certain Southern Clergymen," n.d. [spring 1963]; Kyle Haselden to WSC Jr., June 18, 1963.

18. WSC Jr., "Music Sunday, '63," n.d. [May 12, 1963].

19. "THE BOMB THAT SHOOK THE NATION," flyer, n.d. For more on this incident, see WSC Jr. to Rev. John Cross, September 25, 1963; Samuel O'Neal to WSC Jr., October 5, 1963; and "Treasurer" to "Rebuilding Fund Committee, Sixteenth Street Baptist Church," October 14, 1963.

20. The following relies heavily on Garrow, *Bearing the Cross,* 316–318, 324–338, and David G. Miller's excellent, reliable account, "Report of a Trip Made by Yale Students and Faculty to St. Augustine, Florida," typescript, April 7, 1964; *New York Times,* March 29, 31, 30, April 2 and 9, 1964.

21. Enoch O'D. Woodhouse II to WSC Jr., April 10, 1964; Lynette Christian to WSC Jr., April 10, 1964; Rabbi Charles A. Kroloff to WSC Jr., April 9, 1964.

22. WSC Jr. to Edward Litchfield, May 19 (?), 1964; WSC Jr. to Roger G. Kennedy, June 2, 1964.

23. "St. Augustine Legal Defense Fund," April 3, 1964. See also Charlotte E. Horton to John Pratt, June 12, 1964; Barbara Schomburg to Horton, July 6, 1964.

24. WSC Jr. to Pamela Thayer, March 18, 1964.

25. All following quotations are from "Yale Reports," No. 237, "The Church and Civil Rights," January 14, 1962.

26. The Chesterton quotation is, "Christianity has not been tried and found wanting; it has been found difficult and not tried." A number of Coffin's aphorisms took this same rhetorical form, known as a *chiasmus,* in which word order is reversed in two successive phrases. Most others used the rhetorical form of *antithesis,* as in "Property rights should reflect human rights, and not reject them."

27. All quotations are from WSC Jr., "Suburbia—No Hiding Place," December 5, 1963.

28. *The Civil Rights Bulletin,* Connecticut Commission on Civil Rights, Special Supplement, July 1964.

29. WSC Jr., "Civil Rights—One Minute to Midnight," *SCOPE,* newsletter of the Union Free School District Number 1, Scarsdale, New York, November 1964, 1–4.

30. Mary F. (Mrs. James L.) Doucette to WSC Jr., December 9, 1963; Marjorie C. Hall to WSC Jr., December 9, 1963.

31. Betty (Mrs. Robert F.) Schier to WSC Jr., December 5, 1963; WSC Jr. to Schier, January 6, 1964.

32. *Mademoiselle,* April 1965, 176–177; *Parents' Magazine and Better Homemaking,* December 1963, 49, 144; *Glamour,* August 1964.

33. Cited in Silk, *Spiritual Politics,* 116.

34. Ibid., 116–117.

Chapter 8. Wading into the Big Muddy

All citations are from the Yale Chaplain's Office Papers unless otherwise indicated.

1. David Levy, *The Debate over Vietnam* (Baltimore: The Johns Hopkins University Press, 1991), 28–39.

2. Robert R. Tomes, *Apocalypse Then: American Intellectuals and the Vietnam War, 1954–1975* (New York: New York University Press, 1998), 85–116.

3. Hall, *Because of Their Faith,* 7–8; Friedland, *Lift Up Your Voice,* 142; Marilyn Young, *The Vietnam Wars, 1945–1990* (New York: HarperCollins, 1991), 96; *New York Times,* June 21, September 15, 1963; Fredrik Logevall, *Choosing War: The Lost Chance for Peace and the Escalation of War in Vietnam* (Berkeley: University of California Press, 1999), 55–60.

4. Edward P. Morgan, *The Sixties Experience: Hard Lessons about Modern America* (Philadelphia: Temple University Press, 1991), 140.

5. Logevall, *Choosing War,* 282–283.

6. *OTEM,* 209–210.

7. WSC Jr., "Prayer," February 14, 1965.

8. Stephen Dresch, "To the Faculty of Yale University," March 12, 1965, including a letter to "Fellow members of the faculty." For the "Open Letter to the President of the United States," see *Yale Daily News,* April 7, 1965.

9. *Life,* April 30, 1965, 31; WSC Jr. to Russel K. Havighorst, May 10, 1965.

10. WSC Jr. to [S.] Douglass Cater, May 7, 1965.

11. *OTEM,* 211–212.

12. All Paul Jordan quotations are from the author's interview with Jordan, December 8, 1998.

13. Coffin preached twice at Battell that May, on May 2 and 16, and not at all in early June. I have been unable to locate either sermon. See "University Preachers: Battell Chapel. The Spring Term, 1965."

14. *OTEM,* 200. Coffin recalled, perhaps wishfully, that this encounter took place in 1964.

15. "Yale Chaplain to Talk Against Viet Policy Aug. 1," undated Hartford *Courant* clipping.

16. *OTEM,* 213; Staughton [Lynd] to WSC Jr., August 16 [1965]. Lowenstein kept popping up in Coffin's life and circle. When he ran the summer 1965 Encampment for Citizenship in Riverdale (in the Bronx), Lowenstein brought Coffin in to speak about ethical issues and used him as a pastoral counselor when a close friend was about to have a breakdown. By the time Coffin had the idea that became Americans for Reappraisal of Far Eastern Policy, he knew that Lowenstein could be the engine to make it go.

17. WSC Jr. to John C. Bennett, August 25 [1965], enclosing "A Proposal," 3 pages, n.d.; Bennett to WSC Jr., September 3, 1965, The Papers of John C. Bennett, Burke Library, Union Theological Seminary.

18. Author's interview with WSC Jr., September 1, 1995.

19. The incident received front-page coverage in the *New York Times.* On the increasing alienation of intellectuals from the Johnson policies on Vietnam, see Eric F. Goldman, *The Tragedy of Lyndon Johnson* (New York: Dell Publishing, 1969), 505–510; Allen J. Matusow, *The Unraveling of America: A History of Liberalism in the 1960s* (New York: Harper and Row, 1984), 386.

20. Cited in Morgan, *The Sixties Experience,* 144.

21. For King's evolving feelings and public position on Vietnam, see Garrow, *Bearing the Cross,* 394, 422, 425, 428, 429–430, passim. King first opposed the war publicly in a speech at Howard University on March 2, 1965.

22. Garrow, *Bearing the Cross,* 444–446. But King could only hang back for several months. On his way to a month-long working vacation in Jamaica in January 1967, he picked up an issue of *Ramparts* magazine and saw pictures of Vietnamese children wounded or killed by American napalm. His reaction was even swifter than Coffin's after Coffin had read Jordan's folder. According to Bernard Lee, quoted by Garrow, "Then Martin just pushed the plate of food away from him. I looked up and said, 'Doesn't it taste any good?,' and he answered, 'Nothing will ever taste any good for me until I do everything I can to end that war" (p. 543).

23. Arthur J. Goldberg to WSC Jr., September 3, 1965; Jonathan Moore to WSC Jr., September 9, 1965, and WSC Jr. to Moore, September 16, 1965, A. Sidney Lovett Papers, Sterling Memorial Library, Yale University; W. Averell Harriman to Richard Reiss and WSC Jr., October 15, 1965; "Harriman, W. Averell," in Spencer C. Tucker, ed., *The Encyclopedia of the Vietnam War: A Political, Social, and Military History* (New York: Oxford University Press, 1998), 162.

24. WSC Jr. to John Bennett, September 10, 1965, The Papers of John C. Bennett, Burke Library, Union Theological Seminary; George Kennan to WSC Jr., August 27, 1965; WSC Jr. to Kennan, September 10, 1965, Lovett Papers; ESC to WSC Jr., September 1, 1965; WSC Jr. to ESC, September 10, 1965; ESC to WSC Jr., September 29, 1965. Kennan's letter was

remarkable, not least for its self-pitying revisionism: "I feel, in general, that I have had my day in court. My views are known. They have never commended themselves to our governmental leaders nor to our opinion-forming establishment in general. . . . now that they have been stated, and overwhelmingly rejected by influential American opinion, I can do no more, it seems to me, than to fall silent." On Kennan's Vietnam positions, see Tucker, *The Encyclopedia of the Vietnam War*, 201. These sentiments came from a man whose "Mr. X" article advocating containment of the USSR in 1946 became the single most influential diplomatic position paper of the entire Cold War era. Few Americans have had so much influence while cultivating the conceit that they have been soundly rejected by their fellow citizens.

25. *OTEM*, 214; WSC Jr. to Norman Thomas, September 29, 1965; WSC Jr. to John C. Bennett, Karl Deutsch, William Doering, and Hugh Borton, president, Haverford College, all October 1, 1965. For the revised proposal, see the three-page, undated typescript form letter beginning "Dear _____," including the "Statement of Purpose" and "People invited to October 13th meeting."

26. "Notes from Preliminary Meeting of August 29, 1965," n.d., n.p. On Lowenstein's organizing style, see William Chafe, *Never Stop Running: Allard Lowenstein and the Struggle to Save American Liberalism* (Princeton: Princeton University Press, 1998).

27. *OTEM*, 214.

28. WSC Jr. to Mary C. Wright, October 6, 1965; Wright to WSC Jr., October 18, 1965; Gardiner M. Day to WSC Jr., October 5, 1965; Day to WSC Jr., October 7, 1965; Nita Cothern (secretary to Michael Harrington) to WSC Jr., October 13, 1965; Archibald MacLeish to WSC Jr., October 18, 1965. Declining Coffin's invitation to speak on the 24th, MacLeish did "want to use this occasion to tell you how much I, in common with a very great number of graduates of our University, admire what you have done and are doing."

29. These and following quotations are from the "24 October" ARFEP brochure.

30. WSC Jr., "On Civil Disobedience," October 17, 1965.

31. *New York Post, New York Times,* October 25, 1965; *The Nation,* November 1, 1965.

32. Hall, *Because of Their Faith,* 13–14; Friedland, *Lift Up Your Voice,* 158–159; Miller, *The Sixties,* 144–145.

33. WSC Jr. to Mary C. Wright, October 29, 1965. See also WSC Jr. to Charles Bakst, October 29, 1963; WSC Jr. to Lenore G. Marshall, October 26, 1965.

34. WSC Jr. to Staughton Lynd, September 20, 1965; John C. Bennett to WSC Jr., September 20, 1965; WSC Jr. to Lenore G. Marshall, October 26, 1965; Marshall to WSC Jr., November 2, 1965; WSC Jr. to Marshall, November 5, 1965.

35. *New York Times,* December 10, 1965; "Americans for Reappraisal of Far Eastern Policy," *Newsletter* (January 1966), 2. On Coffin's loan, see leaflet, "ARFEP DESPERATELY NEEDS MONEY," n.d. [December 1965 or January 1966].

36. On Lowenstein, see Chafe, *Never Stop Running,* 248–249, 243.

37. Harold K. Hochschild to WSC Jr., November 24, 1965; WSC Jr. to Hochschild, November 26, 1965.

38. The *New York Times,* November 29, 1965, for example, ran two articles describing Vietnam protests and a picture of an "Italian Communist" parade in Milan the previous day protesting the war in Vietnam.

39. Hall, *Because of Their Faith,* 10, 13–14; Friedland, *Lift Up Your Voice,* 158–159, 149–152.

40. Hall, *Because of Their Faith,* 15, and Friedland, *Lift Up Your Voice,* 161.

41. Hall, *Because of Their Faith,* 15; Friedland, *Lift Up Your Voice,* 163.

42. Richard John Neuhaus to WSC Jr., December 9, 1965; Hall, *Because of Their Faith*, 15–16; Friedland, *Lift Up Your Voice*, 164; *OTEM*, 216–217.

43. *OTEM*, 217.

44. John V. Chamberlain to WSC Jr., January 7, 1966; WSC Jr. to Chamberlain, January 17, 1966.

45. *New York Times*, January 19, 1966; "Connecticut Committee, National Emergency Committee of Clergy Concerned about Vietnam," January 17, 1966.

46. "Clergy Concerned About Vietnam," *Christian Century*, January 26, 1966, 99–100.

47. WSC Jr., "The Spirit of Lamech," January 9, 1966.

48. The St. Augustine quotation is from the *Confessions*, Book Seven: "through my own swelling was I separated from Thee; yea, my pride-swollen face closed up mine eyes."

49. George H. Williams to WSC Jr., January 10, 1966.

50. Norman Hile to WSC Jr., January 17, 1966; WSC Jr. to Hile, January 24, 1966; Tom Schmidt to WSC Jr., January 11, 1966; WSC Jr. to Schmidt, January 17, 1966.

51. WSC Jr., "Plea to the President," January 28, 1966.

52. *New York Times*, January 31, 1966; WSC Jr. to Peter Grothe, March 8, 1966.

53. "Statement from the Steering Committee of the National Emergency Committee of Clergy Concerned about Vietnam," February 1, 1966; *New York Times*, February 2 and 5, 1966.

54. Author's interview with Robert McAfee Brown and Sydney Brown, September 11, 1995.

55. *OTEM*, 220.

56. Fox, *Reinhold Niebuhr*, 292–293; Silk, *Spiritual Politics*, 48–49; WSC Jr., untitled sermon, Battell Chapel, February 6, 1966; WSC Jr., "The Gods of the Land in Which You Dwell," *McCormick Quarterly* 20 (November 1966), 9. Heschel and Niebuhr shared a good bit of theological ground. Heschel even eulogized Niebuhr using the identical passage from Job that Niebuhr had cited while eulogizing his own father in 1913.

57. Author's interview with Robert McAfee Brown and Sydney Brown.

58. Young, *The Vietnam Wars*, 205; Mary McCarthy, *Vietnam* (New York: Harcourt, Brace, and World, 1967), 92.

59. On the conference, see Friedland, *Lift Up Your Voice*, 167–169; John C. Bennett to WSC Jr., December 4, 1965; Kay Shannon to WSC Jr., March 9, 1965.

60. Hall, *Because of Their Faith*, 26–28; *OTEM*, 233.

61. WSC Jr. to W. H. Ferry, May 20, 1966; *OTEM*, 223.

62. Hall, *Because of Their Faith*, 28. See, as examples, "The Raleigh Committee of Clergymen Concerned with Vietnam," n.d. [late March or early April 1966], Lovett Papers; "Fairfield [CT] Clergy Concerned about Vietnam," untitled flyer, n.d. [late February or early March 1966].

63. For the growth of the antiwar movement, see Young, *The Vietnam Wars*, 192–197; Thomas Powers, *Vietnam: The War at Home. Vietnam and the American People, 1964–1968* (Boston: G. K. Hall, 1984), 164–228; Nancy Zaroulis and Gerald Sullivan, *Who Spoke Up? American Protest against the War in Vietnam, 1963–1975* (New York: Holt, Rinehart, and Winston, 1984), 33–148.

64. WSC Jr. to Harold Taylor, February 4, 1966; on McGeorge Bundy and a clergy meeting with Robert S. McNamara, see Tom Wells, "Seeds of a Movement," in Andrew J. Rotter, ed., *The Light at the End of the Tunnel: A Vietnam War Anthology*, rev. ed. (Wilmington, Del.:

Scholarly Resources, 1999), 388, 386; Richard J. Neuhaus, "The War, the Churches, and Civil Religion," *The Annals of the American Academy of Political and Social Sciences,* Vol. 387 (January 1970), 131.

65. WSC Jr. to Kingman Brewster Jr., February 20, 1964; Brewster to WSC Jr., February 24, 1964, Kingman Brewster Jr. Presidential Papers, Yale University (hereafter cited as Brewster Papers).

66. WSC Jr. to Kingman Brewster Jr., May 5, 1966; Brewster to WSC Jr., May 9, 1966; WSC Jr. to Brewster, May 17, 1966.

67. For an example of alumni protest and the Yale response, see William S. Stewart and Dana McCloy (co-chairs of the Fortieth Reunion Alumni Fund Committee of the Yale Class of 1926) to Carlos F. "Tot" Stoddard Jr., April 15, 1966; Stoddard to Stewart, May 17, 1966; both enclosed in Stoddard to WSC Jr., May 19, 1966; author's interview with Davie and Joy Napier, January 14, 1994.

68. Sanford Gottlieb to WSC Jr., January 7, 1966; WSC Jr. to Gottlieb, January 17, 1966; Gottlieb to WSC Jr., March 2 and 30, 1966; Norman Thomas to WSC Jr., March 4, 1966.

69. WSC Jr. to Browne Barr, April 7, 1966; Barr to WSC Jr., May 5, 1966; WSC Jr. to Barr, May 17, 1966.

70. "Yale News Banquet," May 2, 1966; "Baccalaureate Service, Yale University, Prayer," June 13, 1965; "Baccalaureate Prayer, Yale University," June 12, 1966.

71. Yale University News Bureau, Release No. 448, June 13, 1966.

72. "Wesleyan, Commencement," June 5, 1966, *YAM,* July 1966, 13.

73. WSC Jr. to William A. Turnage, May 10, 1966; *New York Times,* May 31, 1965.

74. WSC Jr. to Samuel Solomon, June 23, 1966.

75. WSC Jr. to John C. Bennett, June 30, 1966; WSC Jr. to Charles P. Price, June 7, 1966; WSC Jr. to Richard J. Neuhaus, June 30, 1966. Coffin knew he was leaving an operation that needed him. Despite Coffin's recollection that money fell off trees for CALCAV, Fernandez's reports made it clear that the group was in fairly constant financial straits. Coffin hoped that Bennett would "keep bucking up Dick Fernandez. It's tough to take on a job at the time when all the preachers go off on vacation."

76. WSC Jr. to William P. Bundy, June 30, 1966.

77. Author's interview with Eva Rubinstein.

78. This episode may be followed in *New York Times,* October 9, 1966; *Yale Daily News,* October 3, 1968; *New Haven Journal-Courier,* October 10 and 11, 1966; *New Haven Register,* October 7 and 16, 1966. Staughton Lynd to Ross Flannagan, September 20, 1966; WSC Jr. et al. to Stanley Somerfield, Bureau of Foreign Assets Control, Treasury Department, September 30, 1966; Margaret W. Schwartz, Director, Foreign Assets Control, to "Gentlemen," October 7, 1966; Robert N. Giaimo to John W. Abbott, November 1, 1966; WSC Jr. to Giaimo, November 11, 1966; Henry J. Fast to "Sirs of Yale University," October 13, 1966; Pfc. T. G. Dixon et al. to WSC Jr., October 13, 1966; Robin (Mrs. C. G.) Hunt to WSC Jr., n.d.; Mary Janss Turner, "An Open Letter to Yale University Religious Leaders," October 9, 1966; Leo Seidman to WSC Jr., n.d. [received October 12, 1966]; "a marine corporal and the other guys" to WSC Jr., October 13, 1966; D. W. Lawrence to WSC Jr., October 17, 1966; WSC Jr. to Lawrence, November 13, 1966.

79. *Yale Daily News,* October 3, 1967.

80. Marie Brennan to WSC Jr., October 27, 1966; WSC Jr. to Brennan, November 6 (?), 1966; Michael Burns to WSC Jr., October 13, 1966; WSC Jr. to Burns, October 21, 1966.

81. Roland H. Bainton, "To the Editor of the *New Haven Register*," n.d.; WSC Jr. to Susan E. Richards, December 21, 1966.

82. Nathanael M. Guptill to WSC Jr., October 27, 1966; Guptill to Ben M. Herbster, October 27, 1966; WSC Jr. to Guptill, November 2, 1966; Guptill to WSC Jr., November 9, 1966.

83. [Richard Fernandez], "Report from Executive Secretary for July and August," n.d. [1966]; Fernandez, "To the Executive Committee," September 21, 1966; Fernandez to WSC Jr., October 27, 1966; Avery D. Post to WSC Jr., October 28, 1966; WSC Jr. to Fernandez, November 3, 1966; [Richard Fernandez], "Seventeen Day Trip Taken by Mr. Fernandez (Oct. 31/Nov. 18), n.d. [1966]; [Richard Fernandez], "What's Been Happening," n.d. [1966]; Richard Fernandez and Bobbi Wells, "Memorandum to Executive Committee," December 7, 1966.

84. WSC Jr. to A. J. Muste, November 2, 1966; see also Hall, *Because of Their Faith,* 32.

85. Colin Eisler to WSC Jr., October 19, 1966; WSC Jr. to Robert Brustein, November 22, 1966.

86. *OTEM,* 225.

87. Ibid., 228–229.

88. Hall, *Because of Their Faith,* 41–42; Garrow, *Bearing the Cross,* 549–552, 711, n. 30; "Vincent Harding," in MARHO, the Radical Historians Organization, *Visions of History* (New York: Pantheon, 1983), 229. On Lowenstein's role, see Chafe, *Never Stop Running,* 263–264.

89. Widely reprinted, the speech may be found in Robert J. McMahon, ed., *Major Problems in the History of the Vietnam War,* 2d ed. (New York: D.C. Heath, 1995), 470–475.

90. WSC Jr. to A. J. Muste, November 2, 1966.

Chapter 9. Moments of Truth

All citations are from the Yale Chaplain's Office Papers unless otherwise identified.

1. Personal communication from Richard Flahavan of the Selective Service System, June 14, 2002. In the author's possession.

2. *OTEM,* 233–234.

3. Ibid., 231–232.

4. Following quotations are from this speech, "On Civil Disobedience: Lecture for the Washington Seminar, February 21, 1967," in Charles E. Whittaker and William Sloane Coffin Jr., *Law, Order, and Civil Disobedience* (Washington, D.C.: American Enterprise Institute for Public Policy Research, 1967); see also *OTEM,* 232.

5. Kingman Brewster Jr. to WSC Jr., February 24, 1967; WSC Jr. to Brewster, February 24, 1967, containing his corrected speech and his Letter to the Editor, *Yale Daily News,* February 24, 1967; see also draft, undated telegram, and Memorandum, Kingman Brewster Jr. to Corporation Members, March 1, 1967, including *Chicago Tribune* Press Service clipping, February 21, 1967; Brewster to Mr. and Mrs. Ellis H. Clarkson, February 28, 1967, Brewster Papers.

6. WSC Jr. to Kingman Brewster Jr., n.d. [late February or early March 1967], enclosing his draft letter to the *YAM,* Brewster Papers; *YAM,* March 1967, 3, 8–9.

7. Howard W. Maschmeier to Kingman Brewster Jr., February 28, 1967; Brewster to Maschmeier, March 8, 1967, Brewster Papers.

8. Kingman Brewster Jr. to Oliver R. Grace, April 28, 1964, Brewster Papers.

9. Kingman Brewster Jr. to Charles P. Stetson, April 14, 1967, Brewster Papers.

10. Quotations here and following are from WSC Jr., "On Learned Paralytics," March 5, 1967.

11. WSC Jr., "Vietnam," n.d. [spring 1967].

12. The following story is based on correspondence, Mrs. X to WSC Jr., n.d. (probably November 1966, since Coffin spoke at Oberlin in late October), WSC Jr. to Mrs. X, December 30, 1966; and author's interviews with the son, October 28, 2000, and with Mrs. X, October 29, 2000.

13. See [————————], two-page undated carbon typescript; "Statement by [————],
A1C [Airman First Class] USAF, 1971; "Hon. John F. Seiberling, Memorial Service for the Indochina War," *Congressional Record* 117, No. 70 (May 13, 1971); "Area Air Force Dove Fights Discharge," *The Evening Times* (Trenton, N.J.), September 29, 1971; "Air Force Reversal Revokes Discharge of Antiwar Sarge," *The Evening Times* (Trenton, N.J.), October 10, 1971. Copies in author's possession.

14. The following story is based on correspondence, Ralph G. Coburn to WSC Jr., November 20, 1968, WSC Jr. to Coburn, November 26, 1968; and the author's telephone interview with Gordon Coburn, October 27, 2000.

15. Michael Ferber and Staughton Lynd, *The Resistance* (Boston: Beacon Press, 1971), 88–91, 110; Maurice Isserman and Michael Kazin, *America Divided: The Civil War of the 1960s* (New York: Oxford University Press, 2000), 183. Ferber and Lynd date the origin of "the Resistance" by name to a meeting in Palo Alto, California.

16. Text in the YCOP.

17. On the evolution of the "Call to Resist Illegitimate Authority," see Ferber and Lynd, *The Resistance,* 116–125; *OTEM,* 340–341; Jessica Mitford, *The Trial of Dr. Spock, The Rev. William Sloane Coffin Jr., Michael Ferber, Mitchell Goodman, and Marcus Raskin* (New York: Vintage, 1970), 31–33, 49–50.

18. Mitford, *The Trial of Dr. Spock,* 30–34, 26–29; *OTEM,* 240–251; *Yale Daily News,* October 3, 1967; *New York Times,* September 27, October 3, 1967; *Yale Daily News,* September 28, 1967; *Newsweek,* October 16, 1967. In her very useful Appendix, Mitford reprints the "Call," Coffin's and Ferber's October 16 sermons, and Coffin's October 20 speech.

19. Author's interview with WSC Jr., November 22, 2000.

20. Kingman Brewster Jr. to WSC Jr., n.d. [clearly October 6–7, 1967], three drafts; Brewster to WSC Jr., October 7, 1967, Brewster Papers.

21. *OTEM,* 241; *New York Times,* October 13, 1967.

22. The following is based on and takes quotations from WSC Jr., "Speech in Boston on October 16, 1967"; *OTEM,* 243; and *Boston Globe,* October 17, 1967.

23. Norman Mailer, *The Armies of the Night: History as a Novel, The Novel as History* (New York: New American Library, 1968), 82–87.

24. Drafts of the speech may be found in the YCOP.

25. Mitford, *The Trial of Dr. Spock,* 40–44; *OTEM,* 248–251.

26. Mailer, *The Armies of the Night,* 95; *New Haven Register,* October 20, 1967.

27. Isserman and Kazin, *America Divided,* 184–185; Zaroulis and Sullivan, *Who Spoke Up?,* 136–142.

28. Author's interview with George Stroup, November 14, 2000.

29. *New Haven Register,* October 24 and 30, 1967; *Stamford Advocate,* October 25, 1967.

30. *New York Times,* October 26, 1967.

31. "Remarks of President Kingman Brewster Jr. of Yale University. Parents Day Assembly, Woolsey Hall, Saturday, October 28, 1967." The following story and quotations also rely on *OTEM,* 254–257; "Brewster Scores Yale's Chaplain: University's Chief Deplores Coffin's Antiwar Actions," *New York Times,* October 29, 1967; *Yale Daily News,* October 30, 1967; *YAM,* November 1967, 12–14; *New Haven Register,* October 29, 1967. Monday's *Yale Daily News* ran the speech and an editorial attacking Brewster's "vilification" of Coffin. The *YAM* devoted three pages to Coffin's antidraft activity and ran the full text of Brewster's speech. See also the withering attack on Brewster by two seniors, H. Neil Berkson and Michael E. Mandelbaum, "The Rhetoric of Morality," *Yale Daily News,* November 2, 1967. Many of Brewster's correspondents, even old friends and longtime donors, thought he had not gone far enough. Brewster thanked one for a letter "much more patient, temperate, and thoughtful than many which have flowed across my desk recently." Brewster admitted to being "torn about all this. . . . This draft resistance thing is only the most recent manifestation of the activist church, stemming back to the early civil rights freedom riding days of the earlier sixties. On the whole I think that the church cannot remain effective if it stays aloof from the most morally troublesome issues of the times, and these are almost bound to be screechingly political." William S. Beinecke to Kingman Brewster Jr., November 7, 1967; Brewster to J. William Stack Jr., November 14, 1967, Brewster Papers.

32. This account and quotations are from author's interview with WSC Jr., November 22, 2000; and WSC Jr., "On Martin Luther," November 5, 1967.

33. The story and quotations are from author's interview with George Stroup; Dave Bartlett to WSC Jr., November 9, 1967; *Yale Daily News,* December 5, 1967. See also 393 U.S. 233 (1968): *Oestereich* v. *Selective Service System Local Board No. 11, Cheyenne, Wyoming, et al.*

34. *Yale Daily News,* December 5, 1967. Having learned that the FBI would not accept cards in person, Coffin mailed the cards to the New Haven FBI office (certified mail, return receipt requested), quipping, "Herewith you will find some draft cards and other papers which I trust you will be able to accept through the mails." Coffin to Charles Weeks, December 13, 1967.

35. *New Haven Journal-Courier,* December 11, 1967.

36. *New York Times,* January 6, 1968; *Washington Post,* January 6, 1968; *New Haven Journal-Courier,* January 6, 1968. See also Mitford, *The Trial of Dr. Spock,* 251–269, for the indictment.

37. These quotations and the following are from *OTEM,* 260–262, and Fred C. Shapiro, "God and That Man at Yale," *New York Times Magazine,* March 3, 1968.

38. WSC Jr., "On Hope," January 7, 1968; *Yale Daily News,* January 8, 1968; *Los Angeles Times,* January 8, 1968.

39. *OTEM,* 268–269; Shapiro, "God and That Man at Yale."

40. *Yale Daily News,* January 17, 1968; "Statement by Yale Faculty Members Concerning the Indictment of William Sloane Coffin," January 13, 1968, Brewster Papers; press release dated January 25, 1968, in Coffin Scrapbooks; *Yale Daily News,* February 23, 1968.

41. Author's interview with WSC Jr., July 28, 1994.

42. Kingman Brewster Jr. to Richard H. Warren, January 16, 196[8], Brewster Papers; *Yale Daily News,* January 8, 1968.

43. See, for example, the letters from Hugh Davis Graham, '58, and James B. Rogers Jr., '64, in *YAM* (February 1968), 3, 5.

44. Mitford, *The Trial of Dr. Spock,* 82.

45. *Yale Daily News,* March 4, 1968; *The Westport* (CT) *News,* March 7, 1968. Both in Coffin Scrapbooks.

46. In an envelope postmarked March 30, 1968, in New Haven, Connecticut.

47. Harry Rudin to Kingman Brewster Jr., March 8, 1968, Brewster Papers.

48. Kingman Brewster Jr. to Richard H. Warren, January 16, 1967, Brewster Papers; Geoffrey Kabaservice, "The Birth of a New Institution," *YAM* (December 1999), 26–41.

49. Author's interview with Paul Moore Jr., September 8, 1995.

50. See Brewster to Douglas Ayer, January 22, 1968, Brewster Papers.

51. Kingman Brewster Jr., "Dear _____," April 25, 1968; Brewster to John Hay Whitney, April 25, 1968, Brewster Papers; author's interview with Paul Moore Jr.

52. Kabaservice, "The Birth of a New Institution," 26, 39. See also Geoffrey Mark Kabaservice, "Kingman Brewster and the Rise and Fall of the Progressive Establishment," unpublished Ph.D. dissertation, Yale University, 1999.

53. Kingman Brewster to John Jay Schieffelen, January 3, 1968, Brewster Papers.

54. "Excerpt from transcript of 'Yale Today' Panel—Alumni Reunion, June 15, 1968," Brewster Papers.

55. *OTEM,* 255; Kabaservice, "Kingman Brewster," 503.

56. Kabaservice, "Kingman Brewster," 57.

57. The following examples can be found in the Brewster Papers: Eugene F. Williams Jr. to Kingman Brewster Jr., May 22, 1968; Tracy Barnes to Sam Chauncey, June 4, 1968; Brewster to Williams, June 13, 1968. Letters to Brewster from Reginald L. Auchincloss Jr., May 15, 1968; John E. Bierwirth, May 1, 1968; William S. Beinecke, May 2, 1968; Henry P. Becton, May 3, 1968; Robert L. Popper, n.d. [received May 27, 1968]; and Elmer Alpert, April 30, 1968.

58. Letters to Kingman Brewster Jr. from Robert A. Raines, March 18, 1968; Alan Simpson, February 21, 1968; Paul W. Rahmeier, March 22, 1968; David S. King, March 27, 1968; and Robert F. Kaufman, May 14, 1968, Brewster Papers.

59. Mary R. Shepard [Mrs. Roger B. Shepard Jr.] to Kingman Brewster Jr., August 14, 1968; see also Carol J. [Mrs. C. M.] Simms to Brewster, March 29, 1968, Brewster Papers.

60. Mitford, *The Trial of Dr. Spock,* 55–56. Mitford's is the authoritative account. See also Dan Lang, "A Reporter at Large: The Trial of Dr. Spock," *The New Yorker,* September 7, 1968.

61. Mitford, *The Trial of Dr. Spock,* 77; WSC Jr., Draft "Statement at the Press Conference Following the Sentencing of the Boston Five," June 10, 1968, Coffin Scrapbooks.

62. *Los Angeles Times,* June 30, 1968.

63. *Boston Globe,* June 1, 1968.

64. Mitford, *The Trial of Dr. Spock,* 135–136, 116–117; author's conversation with Michael Ferber, 1995.

65. Zaroulis and Sullivan, *Who Spoke Up?,* 149.

66. On the verdicts, see, for instance, *New York Times,* June 15, July 11, 1968; *New Haven Register,* June 15, 1968; *Christianity and Crisis,* July 8, 1968.

67. C. M. O'Hearn to Robert E. Hunter Sr., July 9, 1968, Brewster Papers; *Parade,* July 14, 1968.

68. *OTEM,* 284; Jay H. Topkis to WSC Jr., July 23, October 3, December 8, 1969; Abraham S. Goldstein to WSC Jr., September 9, 1969; Charlotte E. Horton to Talmage G. Rogers Jr., September 3, 1968.

69. See the lists and letters in the YCOP. Coffin's mother sent $500, as did his Aunt Margaret. A wealthy Yale student gave $10,000. Yale faculty sent an appeal to their colleagues and the Yale Russian Chorus contributed $8,000 from a benefit concert. Robert Lowell, Elizabeth Hardwick, and Nat Hentoff hosted a fundraising party in New York City in early January, which garnered more than $11,000 in contributions and pledges from, among others, Pete Seeger, Helen Frankenthaler and Robert Motherwell, Robert Heilbroner, Arthur Miller, Lenore Marshall, Alexander Calder, Ursula and Reinhold Niebuhr, Balfour Brickner, Paul Moore Jr., Lillian Hellman, Norman Cousins, Stewart Mott, Barbara Silvers and Jason Epstein, Rose Styron, Ronald Dworkin, Richard Fernandez, and Cora and Peter Weiss. *OTEM,* 284; Jay H. Topkis to Elias Clark, December 8, 1969; WSC Jr. to Sidney Mathews, January 21, 1970; author's interview with Ronald and Janet Evans, November 29, 1997.

70. *New Haven Register,* July 11, 1969; *Boston Globe,* July 12, 1968. For substantial excerpts from the court decision, see Mitford, *The Trial of Dr. Spock,* 272–287.

71. WSC Jr. to Michael Ferber, September 11, 1969; James D. St. Clair to WSC Jr., March 6, 1969; WSC Jr. to St. Clair, March 18, 1970; St. Clair to WSC Jr., April 21, 1970, enclosing the U.S. attorney's filing of a *nolle prosequi,* April 15, 1969.

72. See the widely distributed Associated Press story in the Springfield (MO) *Daily News,* October 31, 1968, Coffin Scrapbooks.

73. *Christianity and Crisis,* July 8, 1968, 149.

74. Louis Polk to WSC Jr., June 26, 1968.

Chapter 10. Marriage and Family Life

Documents cited are located in the Yale Chaplain's Office Papers unless otherwise identified.

1. Author's interview with WSC Jr., June 12, 1995, and Eva Rubinstein; "Jo" to WSC Jr., January 8, 1969, Coffin Family Papers. Unless noted otherwise, following quotations from Eva Rubinstein are from the author's interview.

2. Eva Rubinstein Coffin to WSC Jr., July 15 and 30 [1960]; CBC to WSC Jr., n.d. [late July, early August, 1960]; John [Maguire] to WSC Jr., July 20 [1960].

3. Eva Coffin to WSC Jr., July 30 [1960].

4. Eva Coffin to WSC Jr., July 15 [1960].

5. Ibid.; WSC Jr. to Mike Woldenberg, February 1, 1962.

6. Eva Coffin to WSC Jr., July 30 [1960].

7. Author's interviews with George W. Webber and with John Maguire.

8. There is a very thinly disguised but quite similar version of these events in Gail Sheehy, *Passages: Predictable Crises of Adult Life* (New York: Dutton, 1976), 182–189.

9. Quotations are from this sermon, delivered May 6, 1962.

10. Quotations are from this sermon, delivered February 9, 1964.

11. James J. Finnegan, *Manchester Union Leader,* to WSC Jr., March 6, 1965; WSC Jr. to Finnegan, March 10, 1965.

12. Author's interviews with Margaret Crockett-Dickerman, August 11, 1993, and July 19, 1999.

13. Quotations are from this sermon, delivered March 1, 1964.

14. Quotations are from *Glamour,* August 1964.

15. Marilyn Mercer, Feature Editor, *Glamour,* to WSC Jr., August 3, 1964; Margaret Har-

grove to Editor, *Glamour,* September 23, 1964; WSC Jr. to Hargrove, September 30, 1964. For samples of the letters and Coffin's responses, see Sandra Toth to WSC Jr., February 15, 1965; WSC Jr. to Toth, March 31, 1965; Cappy Brown to WSC Jr., March 22, 1965; WSC Jr. to Brown, March 25, 1965; Diane Campbell to WSC Jr., February 19, 1965.

16. Elaine F. Richard to WSC Jr., September 19, 1964; WSC Jr. to Richard, September 22, 1964; Winke Self to WSC Jr., n.d.; WSC Jr. to Self, January 11, 1966.

17. For example, see WSC Jr. to Robert Moses, July 3, 1964.

18. *OTEM,* 203.

19. Ibid., 204–205, 208.

20. WSC Jr., Sermon, March 7, 1965.

21. Quotations are from this sermon, delivered April 10, 1966.

22. *OTEM,* 286.

23. Not entirely accurately, Gail Sheehy portrayed Eva as a feminist heroine who left Bill and the children and bravely struck out on her own.

24. *OTEM,* 287–288.

25. Author's interview with Browne Barr; *OTEM,* 286–292.

26. *OTEM,* 289; author's interviews with David Coffin, July 25, 1994, and Ron and Janet Evans. The following story and quotations are from the interview with the Evanses as well as with WSC Jr., August 18, 1995, and Amy Coffin and Margot Gibney, January 17, 1994.

27. The following story and quotations are from the author's interviews with Ron and Janet Evans; Harriet Harvey; WSC Jr., August 18, 1995; David Coffin; and Amy Coffin and Margot Gibney.

28. Author's interviews with Robert McAfee and Sydney Brown and George Bailey.

29. Author's interviews with Robert McAfee and Sydney Brown and with John Maguire, January 14, 1994.

30. *Vogue,* June 1971, 89–91, 151.

31. Author's interviews with John Maguire, January 14, 1994; Deborah Kaback, October 18, 1995; and Miriam Horowitz, September 26, 1995.

32. Author's interview with Arnold Wolf, December 4, 1993.

33. Harriet Harvey Coffin, "Themes on WSC Book," typescript, October 1974.

34. Author's interview with Arnold Wolf.

35. Author's interview with Miriam Horowitz.

Chapter 11. Activist Episodes

Documents cited are located in the Yale Chaplain's Office Papers unless otherwise indicated.

1. On the Moratorium and the New Mobilization, see Zaroulis and Sullivan, *Who Spoke Up?,* 265–273; Isserman and Kazin, *America Divided,* 268–269; William L. O'Neill, *Coming Apart: An Informal History of America in the 1960's* (Chicago: Quadrangle Books, 1971), 405; and Chafe, *Never Stop Running,* 328–334. The number of inductions, by month, is available on request from the Selective Service System.

2. *Providence Journal,* November 5, 1969.

3. Author's interview with WSC Jr., June 12, 1995; *OTEM,* 298–299.

4. WSC Jr., "The Whole Creation Will Be Set Free," September 22, 1968.

5. See WSC Jr., "Service of Remembrance," June 15, 1969; "Commencement Address,

Radcliffe College," June 11, 1969 (draft); "Resurrection may be a demand," *Radcliffe Quarterly* (August 1969), 5–7.

6. WSC Jr., Sermon, October 5, 1969.

7. On May Day, see John Taft, *May Day at Yale: A Case Study in Student Radicalism* (Boulder, Colo.: Westview Press, 1976); Kabaservice, "Kingman Brewster," 478–546. Taft's account of "the facts" is generally reliable; the same cannot be said of his frequent, gratuitous political judgments. For other accounts of May Day, see John Hersey, *Letter to the Alumni* (New York: Alfred A. Knopf, 1970); Nora Sayre, *Sixties Going on Seventies*, rev. ed. (New Brunswick, N.J.: Rutgers University Press, 1996); and James F. Ahern, *Police in Trouble: Our Frightening Crisis in Law Enforcement* (New York: Hawthorn Books, 1972), 31–72.

8. The untitled sermon was printed in the *Yale Daily News*, April 20, 1970.

9. Taft, *May Day at Yale*, 32–33; author's interview with WSC Jr., February 27, 2003.

10. Taft, *May Day at Yale*, 36.

11. Ibid., 55–71.

12. Author's interview with WSC Jr., September 1, 1995. See also *OTEM*, 301–302; Taft, *May Day at Yale*, 76–77; "Statement by Kingman Brewster Jr., April 19, 1970," *Documents* [relating to May Day], Brewster Papers.

13. Kabaservice, "Kingman Brewster," 522–523.

14. Ibid., 523–524.

15. Reuben A. Holden, University Secretary, to Yale alumni and parents, May 22, 1970. For copies of the faculty resolution, Brewster's subsequent directive, and Brewster's statements, see the packet titled *Documents,* one of three compiled by Holden during May and mailed to parents and alumni, Brewster Papers.

16. Taft, *May Day at Yale*, 108–109, 120–121.

17. *OTEM*, 303.

18. Author's interview with Richard Sewall. Different versions of what may be the same story appear in Taft, *May Day at Yale*, 143–144.

19. Taft, *May Day at Yale*, 159–161; *OTEM*, 306; *New York Times*, May 4, 1970.

20. Cited in Kabaservice, "Kingman Brewster," 538.

21. Kingman Brewster Jr. to Alfred Van Sinderen, June 1, 1970; Brewster to Fred Wacker, December 21, 1970; both cited in Kabaservice, "Kingman Brewster," 541–542.

22. George Herring, *America's Longest War: The United States and Vietnam, 1950–1975,* 4th ed. (New York: McGraw Hill, 2002), 310.

23. Coffin quotations here and following are from *OTEM*, 307–331. See also Coffin Scrapbook, "Hanoi Trip."

24. See, for instance, *St. Louis Post Dispatch*, September 18 and 23, 1972; *New Haven Register*, September 24 and 25, 1972; *New York Times*, September 24 and 26, 1972; *Washington Post*, September 25, 1972.

25. *Washington Post*, September 28, 1972.

26. Ibid.; *Long Island Press*, September 28, 1972.

27. *OTEM*, 331; *New Haven Register*, September 28, 1972; *Fresno (CA) Bee*, September 28, 1972.

28. *Long Beach (CA) Press Telegram*, September 29, 1972; *New York Times*, September 29 and 30, October 1, 1972.

29. *New Haven Register*, October 2, 1972; *Newsday*, n.d. [early October 1972], "Going in after the Bombers—Part 3." For the five syndicated articles, see *New Haven Register*, October 9, 10, 11, 12, 13, 1972.

30. WSC Jr., Sermon, October 15, 1972; "Amnesty: A Statement to the Religious Community of America, Interreligious Conference on Amnesty, Passover and Holy Week, 1972"; Sermon, April 16, 1972; WSC Jr. to Gloria Schaffer, Connecticut Secretary of State, July 14, 1972.

31. "Remarks by the Rev. William Sloane Coffin Jr.," National Conference on Amnesty, May 5, 1973.

32. A copy of the award citation, May 26, 1973, is in the Coffin Scrapbooks.

33. *Boston Globe*, June 15, 1973.

34. *New York Times*, June 19, 1973.

35. Jeb Stuart Magruder to WSC Jr., June 26, 1973; Jeb Stuart Magruder, *An American Life: One Man's Road to Watergate* (New York: Atheneum, 1974), 339.

36. Studs Terkel, "Reflections on a Course in Ethics: Jeb Stuart Magruder and a Question of Slippage," *Harper's Magazine* (October 1973), 59–62, 67–70; WSC Jr., "Personal Salvation," *Harper's Magazine* (August 1974), 94–95; Jeb Stuart Magruder to WSC Jr., December 2, 1974.

37. Kingman Brewster Jr., to WSC Jr., n.d. [probably November or December 1973].

Chapter 12. Interregnum

All citations are from material in the Yale Chaplain's Office Papers unless otherwise noted.

1. Personal communication with Donna Schaper, Associate Chaplain of Yale University from 1977 to 1980.

2. Author's interview with Deborah Kaback.

3. WSC Jr., "Sermon of September 15, 1974"; "Columbia Baccalaureate," May 1, 1975; *People Weekly*, May 5, 1975, 42–44.

4. WSC Jr., "Sermon of September 15, 1974."

5. WSC Jr., "Sermon of January 19, 1975."

6. WSC Jr., "Dear Members of the Corporation," February 7, 1975, published in the *Yale Daily News*, February 10, 1975.

7. *Yale Daily News*, February 10, 1975; *People*, n.d., clipping in Coffin Scrapbooks. For coverage of Coffin's decision, see, for example, *New York Times*, February 10, 1975; *New York Daily News*, February 10, 1975; North Adams (MA) *Transcript*, February 17, 1975; *Connecticut Daily Campus*, March 5, 1975; *Boston Globe*, February 11, March 2, 1975; *Baltimore Sun*, February 26, 1975; *Newsweek*, April 7, 1975.

8. Quotations are from this sermon, "Do Not Be Anxious about Your Life," delivered February 23, 1975.

9. Author's interview with Ellen Logan, August 2, 1993.

10. Kingman Brewster Jr., "Baccalaureate Address," reprinted in *YAM* (June 1975), 10, 13–16.

11. Author's interview with Harriet Harvey.

12. Author's interview with George W. Webber; "Draft Social Change–Evangelism Proposal," n.d. [probably May 1973]; Sidney Lovett to WSC Jr., October 15, 1974, and WSC Jr. to Lovett, October 22, 1974, asking for a copy: "I'd like to see it again. I'm open." This proposal appears to have been the handiwork of Clergy and Laity Concerned staffers Paul Kittlaus and Richard Fernandez. The later proposal, which Coffin drafted, envisioned two- to four-day preaching and teaching missions "in a variety of cities across the country, with

Coffin doing most of the inspiring and Fernandez doing most of the organizing." See untitled handwritten manuscript and corrected typescript, n.d. See also Bill Webber to WSC Jr., n.d., disavowing a desire "to be pushing you about a decision. All I can do is be sure you know that I can verify your gifts and the appropriateness of your using them as a resounding prophetic voice from the religious community."

13. WSC Jr., sermon of September 21, 1975; sermon of November 23, 1975.

14. *Yale Daily News,* December 17, 1976; Richard B. Sewall, "My Dear Hero," December 11, 1976.

15. *New Haven Register,* December 12, 1975; *Yale Daily News,* December 17, 1975.

16. *Christian Science Monitor,* January 23, 1976, 16.

17. Kingman Brewster Jr. to WSC Jr., December 31, 1975.

18. WSC Jr. to Bungalows Las Palmas, November 4, 1975; WSC Jr. to Don Alfonso Mejia, December 3, 1975, including a receipt for a fifty-dollar money order; *Christian Science Monitor,* January 23, 1976, 16.

19. *OTEM,* 343; author's interview with WSC Jr., August 18, 1995, and with Harriet Harvey. Since Harriet later claimed that the date he left was January 16, 1976, they were either leaving much earlier for their Mexican cottage or she remembered the dates closer together for dramatic effect. See *Harriet Harvey Coffin* v. *William Sloane Coffin,* "Order to Show Cause," November 17, 1978, Coffin Family Papers.

20. Author's interview with WSC Jr., August 18, 1995; *OTEM,* 343.

21. Amy Coffin to Alexander Coffin, [postmarked] January 19, 1976, February 13, April 11, 1976, Coffin Family Papers; author's interview with Harriet Harvey.

22. *Harriet Harvey Coffin* v. *William Sloane Coffin,* "Affidavit," December 13, 1978, 4, Coffin Family Papers.

23. Regarding the women in Coffin's life at this time, see, for example, "Lois" to Coffin, October 17, 1976, Coffin Family Papers; author's interview with Randy Wilson Coffin, July 24, 2000. The following quotations from Randy Wilson Coffin are from the author's interview.

24. Randy Wilson Coffin: "And I couldn't help but have the feeling that he was coming here because of me. He may tell you a different story, but that's what I thought." Coffin: "No, it's true. I did come because she was here." Author's interview with WSC Jr. and Randy Wilson Coffin, August 18, 1995.

25. WSC Jr. to Randy Wilson, November 18, 1976, Coffin Family Papers.

26. WSC Jr. to Randy Wilson, November 23, 1976, Coffin Family Papers.

27. Author's interview with David Coffin.

28. Author's interview with WSC Jr., August 18, 1995.

Chapter 13. Down by the Riverside

All documents, tapes, and videotapes are from the Coffin Family Papers unless otherwise noted.

1. Author's interviews with WSC Jr., August 18, 1995, and May 6, 1996.

2. "The Riverside Church: Its Structure and Organization" (New York: Riverside Church, May 24, 1967), 3, 4.

3. Interview with WSC Jr. conducted by George David Smith and Robert Handy, November 23, 1977, 8 (hereafter cited as Smith and Handy Interview).

4. Author's interview with George W. Webber.

5. Edith Lerrigo, "Search Committee Report to the Board of Deacons," July 28, 1977; A. Sidney Lovett to WSC Jr., March 15 and 21, 1977; Lerrigo to WSC Jr., March 27 and April 6, 1977.

6. Author's interviews with WSC Jr., August 18, 1995, and May 6, 1996; Smith and Handy Interview, 5; *New York Times,* August 15, 1977.

7. Smith and Handy Interview, 11; Lerrigo, "Search Committee Report."

8. Lerrigo, "Search Committee Report."

9. Memorandum, Central Records to Emily Deeter, "Corrected membership information data," March 28, 1977.

10. *New York Times,* August 11, 14, 15, 1977.

11. Smith and Handy Interview, 5–6, 16; Randy Wilson to WSC Jr., November 30, 1977.

12. Author's Pilgrim Place interview, January 14, 1994; author's interview with WSC Jr., May 6, 1996; Smith and Handy Interview, 131–132; Barbara Nelson to WSC Jr., December 1, 1987.

13. Smith and Handy Interview, 60.

14. Pilgrim Place interview, January 14, 1994.

15. Smith and Handy Interview, 68, 67.

16. Author's interview with WSC Jr., May 6, 1996; Smith and Handy Interview, 62–64; Cora Weiss, "Introduction," to Marjorie Keeler Horton, *The Disarmament Program of the Riverside Church: A History, 1978–1988,* n.p., n.d. [1990 or 1991], copy in possession of the author, courtesy of Cora Weiss (hereafter cited as Horton).

17. Horton, 23–24.

18. Ibid., 27, 30.

19. On this episode, see *New York Times,* December 24, 25, 26, 27, 28, 30, 31, 1979; WSC Jr., "Iran," sermon of December 2, 1979.

20. Horton, 27.

21. Author's interview with WSC Jr., May 6, 1996.

22. Author's interview with Roger Manners, August 9, 1995; flyer, Second Fosdick Convocation on Preaching, "Preaching in America: Speaking Truth to Power," October 18–21, 1982.

23. Author's interview with WSC Jr., May 6, 1996.

24. Quotations are from this sermon, "Homosexuality," delivered July 12, 1981.

25. Smith and Handy Interview, 38–39. For an account of the controversy over homosexuality, see also Smith and Handy Interview, 28–33, and James Nelson, *Body Theology and Human Sexuality* (Louisville, Ky.: Westminster/John Knox Press, 1992), 55–57.

26. Channing E. Phillips, "On Human Sexuality," May 5, 1985.

27. Author's interview with Patricia de Jong, July 10, 1993. All following de Jong quotations are from this interview.

28. Quotations are from this sermon, "The Fundamental Injunction: Love One Another," delivered May 12, 1985. The author had access to a videotape of the service.

29. Smith and Handy Interview, 32–33.

30. Author's interview with John Maguire, January 14, 1994.

31. Smith and Handy Interview, 35.

32. Author's interview with WSC Jr., May 6, 1996; Smith and Handy Interview, 76.

33. WSC Jr., "The Farewell Sermon as Senior Minister," December 20, 1987; Robert Grant Irving to WSC Jr., December 9, 1987; Michael Winger to WSC Jr., November 30, 1987.

34. Smith and Handy Interview, 104–105, 41–42.

35. For an interesting description and analysis of this phenomenon, see Wuthnow, *The Restructuring of American Religion*, 244–257, 297–322.

36. Author's interview with WSC Jr., May 6, 1996.

37. Author's interview with WSC Jr., August 18, 1995. Quotations following from WSC Jr. are from the author's interviews unless otherwise indicated.

38. *Harriet Harvey Coffin* v. *William Sloane Coffin*, Harriet Harvey Coffin, "Affidavit," October 19, 1978.

39. Roger Bryant Hunting to WSC Jr., November 5, 1979.

40. *New York Post*, October 2, 1980; author's interview with David Coffin.

41. *Harriet Harvey Coffin* v. *William Sloane Coffin*, "Judgment of Separation," December 29, 1980.

42. *The Messenger of the Men's Class of the Riverside Church* 50 (June and July 1981).

43. Author's interview with WSC Jr., May 6, 1996; Bob Collins to WSC Jr., December 2, 1987; William Peck to the author, June 2, 1996, with enclosures, in author's possession.

44. Author's interview with WSC Jr., August 6, 1996; Smith and Handy Interview, 87–88.

45. O. Stuart Chase to Alex Coffin, June 25, 1974. See also Harrison F. McCann, Director of the Northfield Mount Hermon Summer School, to WSC Jr., August 2, 1976: "I must admit he is the type of student that makes me nervous, for I like him very much and I fear that, at any moment, he is capable of doing a foolish act that both he and everyone else would regret. He has a great deal of energy and spark, and a great deal of leadership potential, and as long as it can be channeled in a constructive way, both he and anyone that he comes in contact with will benefit."

46. Author's interview with Randy Wilson Coffin; WSC Jr. to Kathy and Lou Pollak, November 13, 1971, YCOP.

47. Author's interviews with David Coffin and Randy Wilson Coffin, with Cora Weiss, May 25, 2000, and with WSC Jr., May 6, 1996. For coverage of the accident, see *The Berkshire Eagle*, January 12, 1983. Quotations following from Randy Wilson Coffin and David Coffin are from the author's interviews.

48. Quotations are from the sermon "Alex's Death," delivered January 23, 1983.

49. Barbara [_____] to WSC Jr., n.d.

50. Author's interviews with Harriet Harvey, John Maguire, and Ron and Janet Evans.

51. Randy Wilson to WSC Jr., October 9, 1982, and January 8, 1983.

52. Author's interview with Margot Coffin Lindsay. As she asked rhetorically, "Do you think it's any coincidence that Bill is only happily married after the death of his mother?"

Chapter 14. "Flunking Retirement"

1. *New York Times*, July 15, 2001.

2. WSC Jr., "Fortunate Years at Yale," *New York Times*, August 10, 2000; for the Bush story, see *Washington Post*, July 27, 1999. Coffin did not remember this exchange but wrote a letter of apology anyway when the story became public.

3. *New York Times*, November 18, 2001; WSC Jr., "The Good Samaritan," June 1, 2002; Robert Edgar, "The Real 'Axis of Evil': War with Iraq Not the Best Option," *Wisconsin Christian News*, February 2003. For other uses of Coffin's phrase, see National Council of Churches, *Poverty Update*, November 2002; Richard Warch, President of Lawrence University, "Re-

marks at the Launch of Wisconsin Campus Compact," October 22, 2002; Nancy Jo Kemper, "Executive Director's Oral Report," 55th Annual Assembly, Kentucky Council of Churches, October 17, 2002. A quick Internet search turned up dozens more examples.

4. WSC Jr. to Paul C. Sheeline, October 16, 1964. Also see Sheeline to Kingman Brewster Jr., September 30, 1964; Brewster to Sheeline, October 6, 1964, all in YCOP.

5. WSC Jr. to Carleton M. Sage, January 4, 1972; WSC Jr. to Robert E. Hamilton, November 20, 1974, both in YCOP; WSC Jr., *The Courage to Love* (New York: Harper & Row, 1982), 39–47.

6. WSC Jr., "Homophobia: The Last 'Respectable' Prejudice," in *The Heart Is a Little to the Left: Essays on Public Morality* (Dartmouth, N.H.: University Press of New England), 27–40.

7. *Miami Herald,* November 15, 2000.

Chapter 15. A Holy Impatience

1. In a 1971 study Ellis E. Long sought to identify the most prominent antiwar religious activists of the period. Combing the *New York Times Index* for mention of antiwar activity by clergy, Long found 123 names, only 5 of which were mentioned more than 20 times from 1965 to 1970: Coffin (59), Daniel Berrigan (48), Martin Luther King Jr. (38), Philip Berrigan (29), and A. J. Muste (24). Among the twenty-one different peace organizations mentioned in the articles, CALCAV far outstripped all others, by a factor of between three and five. Ellis Eugene Long, "Communication and Social Change: The Verbal and Nonverbal Protest of Selected Clerical Activists Opposed to the Vietnam War, 1965–1970," unpublished Ph.D. dissertation, Florida State University, 1971, Chapter II.

2. Author's interview with Arnold Wolf. See also Howard Greenstein, "A Proper Role for Religion in American Politics"; Rabbi Richard Davis, "In Search of Gratitude," Letter, *New York Times,* May 31, 1997.

3. C-SPAN, "William Sloane Coffin 75th Birthday Tribute," May 6, 2000.

4. Author's interview with WSC Jr., June 12, 1995.

5. Author's interview with George W. Webber.

6. See Isserman and Kazin, *America Divided,* 241–259.

7. Author's interview with George W. Webber.

8. Howard Koh, "My Memories of Bill Coffin," September 11, 1996, copy in author's possession.

9. Author's interviews with Doug Mitchell, July 19, 1993, Helen Webber, July 17, 1993, and Arnold Wolf.

Epilogue

1. Quotations are from author's interviews with WSC Jr., June 16, 1995, and July 15, 1998.

2. WSC Jr., "Speech," February 15, 2003, copy in author's possession; *New York Times,* July 15, 2001.

Index

Abernathy, Ralph, 114, 117, 118, 119, 120, 331
American Baptist Association, 160
Americans for Reappraisal of Far Eastern Policy (ARFEP), 152–160
American Summer Conservatory, 24
American Veterans Committee, 65
Amnesty, conference of, 266, 267
Andover (Phillips Academy), 28–31, 95, 96–100
Anti-Semitism, of Protestant elite, 9, 41, 100–101
Antiwar movement: Americans for Reappraisal of Far Eastern Policy (ARFEP), 152–160; amnesty conference, 266, 267; Berrigan brothers in, 321; Clergy and Laymen Concerned About Vietnam (CALCAV), 169–170, 179, 180–181, 202, 207; Clergy Concerned About Vietnam (CCAV), 160–164, 166–169; Coffin's contribution to, 327–328; Coffin's initial response to, 148–150; death march proposal, 179–180; Education-Action Mobilization, 180; humanitarian relief program, 176–178, 321; King's involvement in, 181–182; National Inter-Religious Conference on Peace, 169; origins of, 145–147; Pentagon vigil, 149; policy alternatives of, 174–175; political influence of antiwar clergy, 170–171; in POW release, 261–265; public sup-

port for president and, 160; rhetoric of prayers and sermons, 156, 164–166, 173–174; SANE campaign, 173; speak-out, 151; teach-ins, 148–149, 156–157; Washington Mobilization, 249–251. *See also* Draft resistance
Arendt, Hannah, 99, 188–189
ARFEP (Americans for Reappraisal of Far Eastern Policy), 152–160
Army life: in basic training, 32–36; commendation from superiors, 50; contact with African Americans and racism in, 35, 37; in England, 38–39; French interpreter post turned down by, 57–58; impact of, 32–33, 40–41; as liaison to Soviet Army, 47–50; moments of truth, 193–194; at Officer Candidate School (OCS), 36–37; in Plattling DP camp repatriation, 52–56; at Russian Liaison School, Le Vésinet, 42–47; in troop training job, 39–40

Bailey, George, 46, 49, 50, 60, 70, 83, 84, 85, 235, 242
Baldwin, Roger, 156, 173, 215
Barnet, Richard, 289–290, 291
Barr, Browne, 86, 94, 97, 173, 239
Benedict, Don and Anne, 275, 326
Bennett, John, 72, 146, 149, 180; ARFEP and, 152, 153, 154, 156, 157, 159; on Coffin's influence, 222

371